Ski Minnesota

Ski Minnesota

A Cross-Country Skier's Guide to Minnesota, Northern Wisconsin, and Michigan's Upper Peninsula

THIRD EDITION

by Elizabeth and Gary Noren

including

Tim Knopp's historical perspective on ski trails in Minnesota, and future directions.

Tim Kneeland's articles on winter camping and cold weather effects on the body.

Dyke Williams's popular work from the second edition of *Ski Minnesota,* "Making Winter Work For Kids."

NODIN PRESS
Minneapolis, Minnesota

We wish to express our grateful thanks to
Tim Knopp, Tim Kneeland, and Dyke Williams for their scholarly works

Paul Nordell, Recreation Research Specialist, Trails and Waterways Unit, Minnesota
Department of Natural Resources

Kevin Walton for producing the maps

Minnesota Office of Tourism for its booklet *Explore Minnesota This Winter*

Wisconsin Department of Development, Division of Tourism, for its booklet *Wisconsin
Winter Escape*

Minnesota Department of Natural Resources: Division of Parks and Recreation, Division of Forestry, and Trails and Waterways Unit

Wisconsin Department of Natural Resources

United States Forest Service, Department of Agriculture: Chippewa National Forest,
Superior National Forest, Chequamegon National Forest, and Nicolet National
Forest

National Park Service, Voyageurs National Park

And our special thanks to Anders for organizing the "boring" index, to Peter for pick-
ing and snapping the "boring" beans, and to Anna for napping (very little)

ISBN 0-931714-25-7

Nodin Press, a division of Micawber, Inc.
525 North Third Street
Minneapolis, MN 55401

DEDICATED to Anna, Peter, and Anders, our patient and helpful children. Without Anna's help, we would have finished in half the time. Winter, in our children's view, is for cross-country skiing. Here's to winter.

CONTENTS

PREFACE

MINNESOTA SKI TRAILS: PAST,
PRESENT, FUTURE *Tim Knopp* 11

EFFECTS OF COLD ON THE BODY
AND WINTER CAMPING:
THE COMFORTABLE WAY *Tim Kneeland* 21

MAKING WINTER WORK FOR KIDS *Dyke Williams* ... 27

MINNESOTA
    Introduction to Minnesota Regions 33
    Minnesota's Cross-Country Ski Licensing System
        for Public Trails 34
    Rules of Use for Winter Travel in the BWCA Wilderness . 35
    State Corridor Trails 37
        Region 1 Northwest Minnesota 41
        Region 2 Northeast Minnesota 77
        Region 3 Central Minnesota 193
        Region 4 Southwest Minnesota 239
        Region 5 Southeast Minnesota.................. 265
        Region 6 Twin Cities Metro Area 295

WISCONSIN
    Introduction to Northern Wisconsin 348
        Region 7 Indian Head Country 349
        Region 8 Northwoods Council 377

MICHIGAN
    Introduction to Michigan's Upper Peninsula 394
        Region 9 Upper Peninsula..................... 395

SKI TRAIL REFERRALS 415

INDEX 417

PREFACE

Ski touring never did fall into the category of passing fad, as some insisted it would. It is now a solid, integral, and permanent way of life for people during the winter months.

Nordic skiing suits people for many reasons. It is a sport in which one may recreate as well as compete. The overall demand that it places on the body improves a person's level of relaxation and health maintenance. The setting for such activity is usually conducive to the feeling of getting away from it all. And the nature of the sport enables people of all ages and abilities to be involved.

With the sport comes a basic responsibility that rests ultimately in the hands of the individual skier. He or she cannot expect land, either public or private, to be open to cross-country skiing if that land is not respected, if "No Trepassing" signs are ignored, and if littering is not made a personal concern. Land abuse leads to land loss. And land abuse contradicts many skiers' belief in the importance of having a low impact on the environment, a belief inherent in gliding quietly through the winter world by using only the unmechanized strength of your own body.

While this is primarily a trails guide, we realize that skiers' needs are as varied as the skiers and that, while some prefer skiing on groomed, tracked trails, others prefer the untracked wilderness. Large land areas for the nontrail oriented should not be forgotten as public and private land use is determined.

United by a common delight and joy in the sport, all cross-country skiers can work together to brighten the future of ski touring—whether it be by active involvement in trail construction and land use determination or by simply passing on the serenity and peace that come from a wonderful day of skiing.

MINNESOTA SKI TRAILS: PAST, PRESENT, FUTURE

Tim Knopp

The attractions of cross-country skiing endure. Along with its unique appeal, cross-country skiing is consistent with the megatrends prominent in our society. Americans are becoming more responsible for their health and fitness; many look for a lifestyle that has minimum impact on resources and on others who share the environment. High tech has created a need for a balance of simple, less dependent skills, and many Americans are gradually learning to spend less and enjoy it more—they are richer because of it.

THE ROOTS OF CROSS-COUNTRY SKIING

Where did it all begin? The origin of cross-country skiing has been traced back to a 4,000-year-old stone carving discovered near Tjøtta, Norway. The oldest known ski was preserved in a bog near Øviedo, Norway, for over 2,500 years. Viking sagas are filled with the exploits of skiers. The most famous is the legendary Heming. His magic skis carried him over the frozen wastes in pursuit of the white bear. He also skied to victory in a competition with King Harald—and quickly away from the scene lest he be punished for embarrassing royalty.

More recently, Fridtjof Nansen, a pioneer in arctic exploration, returned from his 1888 ski crossing of Greenland to tell the people of Norway: "Skiing is something which develops not only the body, but also the soul, and it is of greater importance to a nation than is generally supposed. Long may it continue! May skiing develop and flourish as long as there are men and women in Norwegian valleys!" Nansen's enthusiasm is generally believed to have been a major factor in the growth of the ski touring tradition in Scandinavia.

Scandinavian immigrants brought their skills and traditions with them to North America. A Canadian logging engineer, acquired the nickname Jackrabbit Johannsen in recognition of his prowess on skis. Jackrabbit actively promoted the sport, especially during the depression years when inexpensive pastimes were in demand. Aged 108 years, he is living testimony to the benefits of a vigorous outdoor life.

But, by and large, America was not the most receptive territory for this simple, inexpensive form of recreation. The prosperity following World War II carried Americans in other directions. Our love affair with the internal combustion engine and the affluence to indulge ourselves did not encourage forms of recreation that many construed as deliberate deprivation.

Attitudes change. The renaissance in cross-country skiing began in the late sixties. A small residual of cross-country skiers from the thirties saw that the time was ripe to share their knowledge and skills—Americans were ready. Slowly the word spread to those seeking a better way to enjoy the outdoors. Madison Avenue didn't have much to do with it; in fact, some saw cross-country skiing as a threat to more lucrative sports such as downhill skiing and snowmobiling. However, the word was out and there was no stopping it.

THE MINNESOTA CONNECTION

It's hard to imagine a more fertile site for the growth of cross-country skiing: Minnesota has the climate, the terrain, and a Scandinavian tradition. In 1965, the United States Ski Association set up a ski touring committee to promote the sport in the Upper Midwest. These individuals formed the nucleus of a small group that in 1967 established the North Star Ski Touring Club (NSSTC), destined to become the largest cross-country skiing organization in the nation. These pioneers had a mission—not only did they want to promote the activity, they also had to find places to ski. It wasn't easy. There weren't any designated ski touring trails, and much of the open country had been taken over by the explosive growth of snowmobiling.

One of the first real trails resulted from a cooperative agreement between the club and Jonathan Village, a newly established, planned community near Chaska. The only other trails were training loops designed for the few high school racing teams. Weekend trips to Cloquet, Ely, and Duluth gave club members the opportunity to try these challenging tracks.

Other weekend trips had the flavor of exploration as members used primitive facilities and discussed who was going to break trail each day. The club's first guide was published in 1971. A thin 24-page booklet, it listed 23 different areas in Minnesota and an additional 8 in Michigan, Wisconsin, and Canada. Few of these had real ski trails, and some were only temporarily available to organized groups.

The needs of cross-country skiers went mostly unrecognized by the public land management agencies. The unobstrusiveness and low impact of the sport were both a blessing and a curse; politicians and other decision makers simply didn't see what was happening. Cross-country skiing also suffered from a misunderstanding prevalent among many administrators: skiers could go anywhere there was snow—they didn't need trails. In reality, cross-country skiers had two discouraging choices; they could force their way through the bush, or they could compete with the snow machines.

A notable exception in attitude was evident in the newly established Hennepin County Park Reserve District (HCPRD). By 1971, the District had just completed a major part of its acquisition program and was in the process of developing management plans and facilities. A young, vigorous staff was very receptive to the needs of cross-country skiers. The North Star Ski Touring Club worked closely with this farsighted agency to create some of the best trails in the region. Soon large crowds of skiers gave ample testimony to the wisdom of this action. The example set by the HCPRD did much to bring cross-country skiing to the attention of other agencies.

For the most part, however, the politics of ski trails were far from favorable. The state of Minnesota embraced snowmobiling with enthusiasm—huge areas of public land were allocated to this use. Fait accompli is a powerful factor; the process of reclaiming territory was slow and arduous.

At the state level, one of the first areas to be developed for ski touring was William O'Brien State Park. A well-designed system, comparable to those in the HCPRD, opened in 1974. Other metro area parks were eventually added: Fort Snelling, Lake Maria, Afton, and a new park called St. Croix Wild River. Several outstate parks, notably Itasca and Jay Cooke, were also reclaimed.

A few areas in the State Forest system were set aside for cross-country skiing. The Remote Lake Solitude Area was developed largely through the efforts of the local manager and a few hardworking skiers.

The early 1970s also saw the establishment of a grant-in-aid program financed by state gas tax revenues. This program made funds available to clubs and local agencies to build trails where they felt they were needed.

In 1972, a group of skiers saw the need for a statewide organization and formed the Minnesota Federation of Ski Touring Clubs (Minntour). This organization served as a voice for cross-country skiers and attempted to express their needs to land management agencies. It also sponsored trail development seminars and workshops to encourage skiers to take an active role. Minntour was instrumental in the fight to reclaim the Boundary Waters Canoe Area and to maintain its wilderness character. During recent years Minntour's struggle has borne fruit as winter wilderness treks have become more and more popular among experienced and novice cross-country skiers.

By the late seventies, the resort industry began to respond to skiers' growing demand for accommodations and nearby trails. North central and northeast Minnesota have done the most. Comfortable accommodations, well-maintained trails, and an aggressive advertising campaign attracted customers. Again, dedicated skiers played an important role. Volunteer work parties spent many fall weekends clearing the trails.

In 1977, Governor Rudy Perpich vowed to make Minnesota the "Ski Touring Capital of the Nation." A flush of additional funding spurred a period of accelerated activity on the state level. A task force of cross-country skiers was appointed to tackle problems such as signing, trail standards, and new legislation. Unfortunately, with the election of a new governor, much momentum was lost, and the growth of ski trails fell back to a slow pace during the early eighties. Efforts to expand the ski trail system were often frustrated by encounters with established snowmobile routes. Some administrators felt there were enough ski trails. The Department of Natural Resource projections, based on very limiting assumptions, reinforced this attitude by claiming that participation would grow very little in the next 5–10 years. In reality, the number of skiers was increasing at a rate of at least 10–15 percent annually.

Cross-country skiers had always contributed a great deal to the actual construction of ski trails. Seminars and training workshops have already been mentioned. By the early eighties, volunteer work crews had become a formal part of the NSSTC's operation. Crews were dispatched to all parts of the state and even into nearby Wisconsin—wherever land managers or resort operators were receptive to the needs of cross-country skiers. A cooperative enterprise with the resort operators along the North Shore of Lake Superior proved especially rewarding. Volunteerism was becoming the way to get things done.

A crisis developed in 1982 when snowmobiling interests, despite declining numbers, succeeded in getting the legislature to dedicate all unrefunded gasoline tax money exclusively to snowmobile trails and programs. The small amount of grant money formerly available for cross-country ski trails was lost. Many skiers had long recognized the need for a substantial and dependable source of funding for the construction and maintenance of ski trails. They also realized that this source would probably have to originate with the skiers themselves. Largely because of the efforts of cross-country skiers and the cooperation of the state legislature, a ski trail permit fee was initiated during the 1983–1984 season. Unaware of the previous struggles, many newer skiers had taken the trails for granted. Some have reacted negatively to the new charge and need to be convinced of its importance to the future of cross-country skiing in Minnesota.

Ski trails and facilities were not alone in undergoing change and development. Skiers and the image of cross-country skiing were also evolving. The most obvious change was a growth in numbers. The first state wide survey in 1978 estimated 500,000 cross-country skiers in the state. Participation increased rapidly and by 1983, a conservative estimate of one million skiers were taking to the trails.

Many recent adherents entered the scene with quite a different perception than did the early pioneers. Groomed, often crowded, trails were more or less the standard. Competition, in the form of citizen races, became a focal point for many skiers. Racing stimulated the development of high-tech equipment and skintight, one-piece suits. Much of this better suited skiing the hard, well-groomed track than bushwacking through the forest.

But none of these developments excluded the original attraction. Skiers are continually rediscovering the simple pleasure of moving quietly and leisurely through the winter landscape. Alone with nature or in the company of friends, they seek out uncrowded, if less carefully manicured, trails. Others are looking for more challenging adventures and are drawn to longer treks in remote areas that require the experience and skills to deal with unforeseen obstacles and unpredictable weather.

The essence of cross-country skiing is variety. Cross-country skiers have a choice: the absolute solitude of a remote forest or the bedlam of joining 8,000 others at the American Birkebeiner, a well-set track or breaking trail through two feet of new powder, luxury accommodations or a night in a snow cave, heart-pounding workouts or a leisurely pace, $300 state-of-the-art racing skis or a complete outfit for $69.95. Fortunately, Minnesota has the trails and the terrain to satisfy a wide range of preferences.

TRAILS TODAY

Our ski trails didn't just happen—they were the result of hard work and perseverance. But, most cross-country skiers are more interested in the question, Where can I ski today? The primary function of this guide is, of course, to provide an answer. First, it may be useful to present an overall perspective.

In 1983, the Minnesota Department of Natural Resources (MDNR) completed a statewide inventory of trails with the following results:

Minnesota Department of Natural Resources Ski Trail Inventory
Effective July 1, 1983

Administrative Agency	State Total	DNR Region					
		NW	NE	Cent	SW	SE	Metro
City	279	9	74	32	14	13	137
County	506	61	146	92	26	38	143
State Parks	447	72	142	108	37	48	40
State Forests	154	0	79	46	0	29	0
State Corridor Trails	77	21	0	6	2	12	36
Fish and Wildlife	26	14	0	8	0.5	0	4
Forest Service	367	23	277	67	0	0	0
Park Service	24	0	24	0	0	0	0
	1880	200	742	359	79	140	360

A quick glance tells us how many miles of trail are found in various regions of the state and within the jurisdiction of the different management agencies. It is easy to understand the concentration of trails in the northeastern region where terrain and snow conditions are close to ideal. The Twin Cities metropolitan region is a distant second in trail miles; although lacking in large areas of public land, the abundance of skiers in this region justifies considerable trail development.

Turning to the administrative categories, we observe that a large portion of the trails are on state lands, although the counties are not far behind, and federal and city trails account for significant percentages. Some trails may have been missed by this inventory, e.g., trails on private land are not included and probably cover about 100 miles.

This summary tells us nothing about the condition of the trails. A good part of the trails are well laid out, carefully marked, and maintained. Many, particularly those near the metro area and in state parks, are machine groomed on a regular basis. At the other extreme are trails that are barely passable or difficult to follow. This is not meant as a criticism; there is no reason why all the ski trails should be designed to meet some arbitrary standard. However, it is important that a cross-country skier know what to expect—we hope that this guide will help to fill that need.

We may also consider cross-country skiing opportunities by examining the various areas or categories of available land. Public lands are especially important. At the same time, we should keep in mind that access may be difficult, if not impossible, without designated ski trails. Here is a list of jurisdictional categories:

Major Public Land Designations within the State of Minnesota
(Approximate Total Area or Linear Extent)

Agency of Designation	Acres or Miles
City (parks and open space)	40,000 acres
County Lands	2,900,000 acres
State Parks	160,000 acres
State Forests	3,000,000 acres
Other State Forest Lands[1]	1,900,000 acres
State Corridor Trails	525 miles
State Wildlife Areas[2]	457,000 acres
State Controlled Water Surface	3,000,000 acres
National Forests	3,058,000 acres
National Park Lands[3]	139,000 acres
Fish and Wildlife Service Lands[2]	569,000 acres
Road and Highway Right-of-Way	100,000 miles

[1]These are lands administered by the MDNR but lie outside State Forest boundaries.
[2]Much of this area is small wetlands surrounded by private land leased for the purpose of waterfowl production.
[3]Does not include water surface area.

These figures say more about potential future development than they do about existing opportunities. A careful examination and comparison of trails and areas reveals the pattern of trail development to date. The trails tend to be concentrated in a very small portion of the total land area. In the State Parks, for example, ski trails provide access to far less than half of the lands within the parks. This pattern is even more pronounced on State Forest lands where approximately a third of the trails are concentrated on 8,000 acres of solitude areas. The rest are on small, isolated tracts throughout the system. County lands have been similarly used. These tight, network trail systems effectively provide a wide range of opportunities within a small area, but they also inherently limit the future of ski trails in Minnesota, a topic we'll discuss later.

Now, we'll highlight some of the newest, most exciting additions to our cross-country skiing opportunities. All have been developed since the publication of the last Ski Guide in 1977.

Perhaps the most significant addition is the North Shore Mountain cross-country ski complex. A 203-kilometer system connects a number of resorts and parks. This is an entirely new concept to the region because it breaks the confines of the closed network pattern and allows skiers to plan extended ski trips. Similar, if somewhat smaller, systems are being created along the Gunflint Trail and in the Ely area.

Not far down the North Shore, a new State Park, Tettegouche, promises some challenging cross-country skiing. A series of lakes surrounded by towering bluffs present a mountain-like landscape. Initial development is taking place during the summer of 1984.

Northeastern Minnesota offers yet another new experience. Recent legislation called for a phaseout of snowmobiling in the Boundary Waters Canoe Area Wilderness. As of January 1, 1984, snowmobiles are limited to two short routes into Canada. The entire border route, from the Gunflint Trail to Ely, should be quiet and free from machines. This 40–50 mile route is relatively easy to follow and should become increasingly popular with cross-country skiers as they gain confidence and undertake new and challenging treks.

Central Minnesota has also developed additional trails. Of special significance is the opening of an approximately 44-mile section of the National North Country Trail in the Chippewa National Forest. Near Bemidji, a new ski race, the two-day 100-kilometer Minnesota Finlandia, has become a focal point for trail development in the region.

Looking toward the Metropolitan Region, it is obvious that the scarcity of public lands has restrained the development of ski trails. Nevertheless, demand is also obvious and progress is being made. Of special note is the creation of more trails in the eastern part of the region where skiing opportunities had been relatively scarce. Additional trails and facilities in Fort Snelling and Afton State Parks have helped. Washington County has also developed new trails, as has Dakota County to the south.

The Metro Region has embarked on the beginnings of a system of connecting trails. North Hennepin County Corridor Trail joins Elm Creek Park and Coon Rapids Dam Park. Even more significant is a one-mile section of trail between Minnehaha Park in Minneapolis and Fort Snelling State Park. This linking trail permits many Minneapolis residents to ski directly from their homes into the State Park, thus avoiding the necessity of loading the car and taking the roundabout freeway route. Although difficult to establish, these connecting trail links promise to contribute the most in bringing cross-country skiing closer to everyone.

To sum up, trails have grown in number—but at nowhere near the increasing rate of growth in number of skiers. One limitation has been the lack of an adequate, reasonably assured source of funding. The most significant, if somewhat controversial, new development is the state ski trail permit fee introduced during the 1983-1984 season. The $5.00 annual permit is required for all cross-country skiers, ages 16–64, using state funded ski trails. If skiers cooperate and if revenues are used effectively, we could begin an exciting new era in trail development.

THE FUTURE

Some individuals claim that we have enough ski trails; a few of them are skiers. It's not too difficult to understand. Many new skiers simply don't know the full range of experiences the sport can provide. They often accept as a standard the confined, closed network systems with well-groomed tracks—and the crowds of other skiers. This, however, is a minority opinion. Surveys show that additional ski trails are recognized as the most needed recreational development. The 1978 state survey revealed that 83 percent of skiers wanted more trails. In 1984, the vast majority still call for more trails.

Why should cross-country skiers want more trails? First, many existing trails are crowded, especially those that are reasonably accessible. There is also a need to provide trails closer to where people live. We shouldn't expect people to drive long distances to ski a few miles—this defeats the purpose of a ski outing that takes us away from the hassle and stress of our mechanized society. New trails also promise new experiences: new terrain to explore, new goals to achieve. And finally, an expanded trail system can provide cross-country skiers better access to their public lands. As we pointed out in the previous discussion, only a small portion of state and county lands contain ski trails.

Public land administrators are naturally reluctant or cautious about expanding too rapidly—or at all. They want to be certain of a "real" demand as well as sufficient funding to maintain the system. There may be other, less valid, reasons for their hesitancy to expand beyond the small, closed network systems. Many managers are more familiar with downhill skiing and thus see skiing as an up-and-down or round-and-round activity. Cross-country skiing, as the name implies, is a here-to-there experience for skiers who are often motivated by the desire to go somewhere, to reach an objective.

Closed trail systems are easier to manage, and it is easier to capture economic benefits because controlled access to a trail head and parking area enables the manager to conveniently extract a fee. An open system necessitates a more imaginative revenue generating device. The statewide trail use permit is one solution.

An expanded trail system also means more work—and why undertake work if the same revenues can be produced from existing trails? Skiers must demand more for their money. Earlier efforts to expand trails into new areas reveal another problem. It is difficult to expand without encountering conflicts with existing land use, whether it be officially sanctioned or simply de facto. The generous allocation of public lands to snowmobiling occurred before the demand for cross-country ski trails was obvious. Reallocation is never easy.

None of these obstacles or attitudes should be thought of as insurmountable. Skiers, by persistence and willingness to do their share, can make a difference. This guide provides a baseline—with a clear view of what is available, skiers can contribute meaningfully to the planning and construction of new ski trails.

Where do we want to go? How do we break out of the drive-and-park opportunity? Here are a few suggestions.

The North Shore Mountain complex has demonstrated, on a limited scale, the appeal of an open system of connecting trails. Imagine expanding the idea to include the entire North Shore from Duluth to the Pigeon River! We can refer to this type of development as the "ladder model." In essence, it consists of parallel trail and transportation routes connected at intervals by "rungs." The system provides an almost limitless range of choices in skiing distances and destinations.

The same principle could apply to the St. Croix River Corridor that is roughly paralleled by Interstate Highway 35. Because of proximity to the Metro Region, it may have even greater potential. Three state parks, three state forests, and lands administered by the National Park Service form a nearly continuous strip of public ownership. The Minnesota–Wisconsin Boundary Trail has already been authorized, although development to date has been primarily for snowmobiling. A newly acquired segment, a portion of the abandoned Soo Line Railroad, brings the trail to the edge of Ramsey County. Another eight-mile segment, if acquired, will bring the trail to within 2 miles of the Capitol. The possibilities are exciting! Just the idea of skiing from St. Paul to Duluth stirs the imagination. In 1978, a portion of the trail connecting Wild River State Park and St. Croix State Park was laid out and flagged, although no work was done to clear the route. Perhaps now is the time. It would be a good project for skiers from the Metro Region.

Another kind of experience could be modeled after hut-to-hut skiing that is very popular in Scandinavian countries. Northern Minnesota has an abundance of public lands of a predominantly natural character. A recently initiated state forest planning program could expedite the project. Huts, spaced at reasonable intervals, could vary in comfort from a simple lean-to to a hostel with a place to prepare a warm meal. The trails needn't be groomed as long as they are cleared and well marked. They can provide for those seeking a more remote, uncrowded experience. Again, building these facilities is an excellent project for ski club volunteers.

The hut-to-hut concept would not require the designation of vast blocks of land for non-motorized recreation if ski trails were protected. Some might argue that control of so much open range for snowmobiling would be impossible. Approximately three million dollars of dedicated snowmobile money is generated annually—enforcement is one authorized use.

Specific routes could be worked out with local cross-country ski clubs; these people are in the best position to approach private land owners when it is necessary to bridge gaps in public land. It may even be necessary to use road right-of-ways for short distances to maintain continuity.

The federally authorized North Country Trail could provide a starting point. The State of Minnesota has offered to incorporate its existing corridor trails, if snowmobiles are allowed to continue using the trails. Cross-country skiers may want to contribute the additional effort to create alternate routes on state lands.

A very different opportunity could result if a proposal to establish a Nordic training center at Giant's Ridge near Biwabik is implemented. It might be modeled after Suomen Urheiluopisto in Finland, commonly referred to as Vierumäki for the nearby town. This expansive Finnish Sports Institute, located in the lake country, features many miles of trails, a complex of elaborate facilities, and, of course, plenty of saunas. It is a yearround operation for sports of all kinds. Vierunmäki is unique because it is designed to accommodate everyone—world-class competitors as well as citizen atheletes. Modest, inexpensive cabins are available for families. No one need follow a structured routine, and coaching is optional. The atmosphere is quiet and unpretentious, reflecting an attitude prevalent in the Scandinavian culture—fitness is for everyone. Not a bad idea to import to the lake country of Minnesota.

The preceding discussion concentrated on new experiences, the possibilities that we are just beginning to recognize. There will always be a need to build additional trails for the simple purpose of bringing cross-country skiing closer to more people. Skier-generated funding, political pressure, and volunteer labor will play an essential part in any program to expand the trail system. It will take a major effort and a change in attitude on the part of skiers and public land administrators to break from the confines of the current approach. The ultimate goal should not be to simply have a lot of places to go to ski, but, rather, to be able to ski any place one wants to go.

Tim Knopp has worked to develop ski trails—on the local level as a North Star Ski Touring Club member and past president, on the state level as a member of the Governor's Trail Advisory Committee, and on the national level as a part of the United States Ski Association/United States Forest Service Committee on Ski Trail Development. At the University of Minnesota, he teaches courses on outdoor recreation policy, planning, and design. Tim is a general advocate of self-propelled, low-consumptive forms of outdoor recreation.

EFFECTS OF COLD ON THE BODY AND WINTER CAMPING: THE COMFORTABLE WAY

Tim Kneeland

EFFECTS OF COLD ON THE BODY

It is important to understand the result of excessive heat loss: frostbite and hypothermia. Both are fairly easy to detect and treat (at least in the initial stages) and are quite avoidable if the individual is aware of his or her body signals.

FROSTBITE — Frostbite is the actual formation of ice crystals (freezing) in body tissue. It most frequently occurs in body parts distant from the heart—fingers, toes, ears, nose, and facial cheeks. It is usually preceeded by a condition known as frostnip—the loss of sensation and feeling in the affected area. It is usually described as a numbness and may follow pain in the fingers and toes.

Generally, if one of these areas feels cold, it isn't frostbitten. However, if you lose the cold feeling, the area has either warmed up (feeling is present) or is frostnipped. This is the time for immediate action. Simply warm the area by covering lightly with a warm hand; going indoors; running warm water over it; or by placing it in your armpit, under your shirt, or against someone else's stomach.

If you don't react soon enough, the affected area may under extreme conditions become frostbitten within a few minutes. A frostbitten area will usually appear whitish (lack of circulation) and feel hard. Don't rub or massage it, and never apply snow. Treat by warming rapidly. Submersion in warm water, 102–104°F, is best. Monitor the water temperature closely. Avoid breaking any blisters that form and seek medical attention.

Be extremely careful around fuel. Spilled fuel evaporates very quickly and can cause instant frostbite. Always wear protective clothing to prevent a moist, bare hand from freezing to metal. If you should accidently become attached, use any water or warm fluid available (even urine) to separate yourself. If you panic and pull your hand away, you may leave some skin stuck to the metal surface.

HYPOTHERMIA — Hypothermia is an overall lowering of the body's inner core temperature. If we are exposed to cooler air temperature (55°F and below), rain or wet weather, and wind, we need protection. If we aren't adequately clothed and/or producing enough heat, we begin to cool. As we cool, our body gives off signals and our hands and feet become cold due to reduced circulation. We may feel colder all over. Goose bumps may appear. And finally, at about 96°, we begin to shiver. Shivering produces a great deal of heat (like chopping wood) and serves as a signal for us to do whatever we can to reduce this excessive heat loss. We can get out of the wind, change wet garments, put on more clothing, eat or drink something (non-alcoholic), work harder, or go into a warmer environment.

If we don't improve our condition, heat loss increases and our core temperature continues to drop. As it falls to the lower 90s, judgment is impaired. Our efficiency and ability to do work of any kind deteriorates considerably. In fact, the lower our temperature drops (usually occurring over a period of minutes if submersed in cold water or hours if simply exposed to the wind), the less capable we are of recognizing the problem and taking emergency action.

Hypothermia is a serious but avoidable problem in most cases. Simply listen to your body, watch for signs in others, and do what is necessary to avoid excessive heat loss.

WINTER CAMPING: THE COMFORTABLE WAY

Excitement, comfort, beauty, solitude, peace, and adventure are reasonable expectations of winter camping. If you have toyed with the idea of extending your summer camping or backpacking treks into winter, make this the year. Each year, hundreds of people are becoming involved in this unique and rewarding activity. Unfortunately, too many become cold, wet, and miserable and give it up without a fair chance.

Successful winter adventurers start by psyching themselves into a positive winter mental state. They investigate and obtain the clothing and equipment necessary to keep them comfortable during the most challenging conditions. They try to cultivate a common bond with the environment—one of learning to live with nature, not trying to fight or conquer it. Through experience, they understand what their bodies are saying about their comfort and react quickly to remain as comfortable as possible.

The following are some basic tips to help you get started. If you can stay warm and comfortable—you should be able to—then you are apt to enjoy winter camping and give it a fair chance.

DEVELOP A POSITIVE WINTER MENTAL ATTITUDE — People have a variety of reactions to winter. Some curse the cold and threaten "This is the last year I will live in such a cold and miserable place!" Some simply postpone any serious outdoor activities until spring. Others, however, realize that winter is going to be a yearly event and that it *can* be enjoyed. They anticipate its arrival and eagerly involve themselves in activities that only winter allows. Their secret is a positive winter mind-set. They are determined to enjoy what only winter offers: cool walks, brisk runs, ice-skating, snowshoeing, cross-country skiing, and, for some, winter camping.

GATHER THE NECESSARY CLOTHING AND EQUIPMENT — It is critical that you obtain the clothing and equipment that will provide the necessary protection and warmth for any winter camping activity. As you cool, so does your interest.

• *Clothing*: Obtain Army surplus wool pants (wool retains body heat when wet), wool shirt, woolen or polypropylene long underwear (cotton is warm but looses its ability to retain heat when wet), light to medium weight socks (wool, polypropylene, silk) to be worn inside heavy weight woolen outer socks, insulated boots (Sorel-type—rubber bottom, leather upper containing a felt liner—are widely used), gaiters to hold pants next to boots and to keep out the snow, a good down or fiberfill coat, raingear (in case it warms up too much), stocking cap, scarf, and heavy gloves or mittens. Wrap a change of socks and underwear in plastic zip lock bags, and your clothing is set.

• *Equipment considerations.* Most people will keep warm to 0°F with a well-constructed nylon tent with waterproof fly or a strong tarp for shelter, insulating ground pad (ensolite, blue foam, etc.), and a three to four-pound down or four to five-pound fiberfill sleeping bag (mummy-style preferred). Select a stove with a pump and plenty of fuel, cooking kit with utensils, plenty of food agreeable to your tastes, and at least one quart of water. Remember a small medical kit, pocket knife, sun cream (zinc oxide), sunglasses, map and compass, flashlight with extra alkaline batteries, and toilet articles such as toilet paper, tooth brush, toothpaste, mirror, and comb. Don't forget matches, candles, line, and plenty of plastic bags to keep everything dry. Find a sturdy framed (internal or external) backpack to carry all needed equipment. Load it so that the weight is high and against the back if you have an external frame pack. Load an internal frame a little lower with the weight still against the back. Spend the necessary time to adjust all of the pack's straps so the pack will carry snugly and comfortably against your back.

START SMALL — Your first winter camping trip shouldn't be in a remote wilderness area. Instead, start close to home—in your back yard. After you have gained confidence, go to the local park. Then, after you have learned to keep warm when working or sleeping, consider heading for remote backcountry.

CONSIDER YOUR TRANSPORT — Some people hike to their camping spot as long as the snow isn't too deep. Once you get more than a foot of snow, snowshoes or cross-country skis are helpful. Snowshoeing is generally easy to master and will get you around in difficult terrain. Select ones that are suitable for your total weight with gear, usually a trail or modified bear paw design, and learn to secure them to your boots without cutting off circulation in your feet.

Cross-country skiing with a pack is a little trickier. Gain skills and confidence by practicing with a day pack. Then, select a route that is fairly level, don your loaded pack, and take your time. If the terrain and distance are manageable, you will arrive at your destination in ample time to set up a snug camp.

CAMPSITE CONSIDERATIONS — Select a relatively protected area without dead trees and branches overhead. It should obviously be far away from any avalanche danger. Select a level site for your tent and vestibule, a tarp extended like a porch for additional protection and as a shelter for your stove.

Keep all minimum impact considerations in mind. Don't cut any living wood, carry out your food wastes in ziplock bags, bury all human wastes and carefully burn toilet paper. Use extra care not to lose any of your gear or litter in the powdery snow. Leave radios, tape decks, loud song fests, and noisy activities at home. Finally, keep your group small, no larger than ten, for less impact on the environment and other wilderness users.

KEEPING WARM — Try to remain warm in spite of changing conditions and activity levels. As soon as you arrive in camp, strip and put on dry underwear. Some people carry overboots or down/fiberfill booties for foot comfort in camp. Use your closed cell pad to stand or sit on until it is time to retire. Be sure to put additional clothing on as soon as you begin to cool. If you get cold, hike or ski. You will soon warm up and have from 30 minutes to 2 hours of heat accumulated. Also, eat plenty of hot food and drink.

SLEEPING WARM — Place one or two pads under your entire body with any extra under your upper body. Fluff your bag for two minutes or so to redistribute the insulating materials and to warm you up. Take off all damp clothing and place outside your bag between you and the tent wall. Put on dry underwear, socks, and possibly a stocking cap and slide inside your bag. If you cool as the night progresses, simply reach through the opening in your bag and haul in dry clothes. As you wrestle your clothes on in the confines of your sleeping bag, you will rewarm in no time at all.

WINTER HAZARDS AND CONCERNS — In order to insure your survival as a winter enthusiast, consider the following circumstances and learn all you can about understanding and dealing with them.

• *Avalanches:* Every year, people who think they can second-guess avalances become statistics. Use extreme caution in any mountain area, especially when it is snowing heavily, raining, strong winds are blowing, dramatic temperature changes occur, or evidence of unstable conditions exist. Even on more stable days, exercise a good deal of caution and never venture into a potential avalanche area. Select another route or return home instead.

• *Frostbite:* Frostbite is a problem at subfreezing temperatures. It is usually first detected by the loss of sensation in the fingers, toes, ears, cheeks, or nose. If an area becomes numb, check it out. Warm the affected area by careful contact with a warm surface or submersion in 102–108° F water. Don't rub with snow. Tune into your body's signals to recognize the first warning of frostbite—numbness—and react before it becomes serious.

• *Hypothermia:* Another problem in below freezing conditions and above freezing temperatures to 55° F is hypothermia. You simply lose body heat faster than you can generate it. After a drop of a couple of degrees of internal warmth, you usually begin to shiver. As shivering increases and your temperature decreases, you may become disoriented, incoherent, and irrational. Again, listen to your body. As soon as you cool off, do what you can to warm up. Put on more clothing, change wet clothes, get out of the wind, eat a warm meal, get into shelter. If you never let hypothermia go beyond the initial shivering stage, you have little to worry about. Be concerned about your companions, and expect their concern.

GETTING INFORMATION — Ask your local National Park Service, National Forest Service, Department of Natural Resources, county or city park system, college student union, outdoor or environmental club, local American Lung Association (often run wilderness treks), or community education directors for information on programs, materials, and resources that will help you enter into winter camping with a high potential for success. Don't forget your library for magazines, books, and movies on all aspects of the subject.

Good luck, although it takes more than luck. Prepare, psyche yourself up, and give it a try. The rewards are many and are directly tied to your preparation and conduct while exploring our most misunderstood season of the year.

Tim Kneeland first served as a United States Air Force Survival Instructor and then as director of the Institute for Survival Education in Seattle and Minneapolis. He writes, teaches, and consults on survival, outdoor recreation, safety, and wellness education through his recently expanded business, Tim Kneeland and Associates, 317 North East 58th Street, Seattle, WA 98105; 206-523-7364.

"Effects of Cold on the Body" is taken from Tim's 25-page booklet, Cold Weather Guide: Working Outdoors in Comfort. *This booklet is very informative, to the point, and well illustrated. Easy to tuck in a pack, pocket, or the glove compartment of your car, it is a must for anyone considering a trek into wilderness areas, and is available for a few dollars from Tim's business. Contact:*

Jon Ridge, Midwest Director, Tim Kneeland and Associates, 1931 Buchanan Street North East, Minneapolis, MN 55418. 612-789-0940, 612-871-7332

MAKING WINTER WORK FOR KIDS

Dyke Williams

Kids are great snow people. They seem to come with a built-in love of sliding, piling, throwing, and rolling. In Minnesota, land of winter, it makes sense to introduce children to winter in a friendly and successful way so that they grow up knowing how to enjoy the outdoors comfortably and safely even in severe conditions. Winter for them should become a lifetime sport.

In Minnesota you have a choice—you can do it to winter or winter will do it to you. In fairness to your children, there are three things you should try to provide: good clothing, good equipment, and good trip planning.

The first is the easiest—provide adequate clothing. Dress in layers. Turtleneck, shirt, sweater, extra sweater, and windshirt or insulated jacket on top. Long underwear, more long underwear, pants, and windpants or warmups on the bottom. Remove extra layers (into your daypack) when warm; replace when cold. One-piece suits make this body temperature control difficult, and many breathe poorly or are totally waterproof.

Materials that are waterproof or breathe poorly prevent perspiration from escaping. Most fabrics when damp or set lose heat up to 400 times faster than when dry. Don't overheat—take off a layer. Avoid nonbreathable outer materials that trap excess moisture.

Wool (of the woven fibers) and Polarguard (of the insulations) warm best even if wet—have as much of each as possible. Cotton denim and sweatshirts have some of the least warming value and take longest to dry.

Wool or Polarguard mittens are warmer than gloves. Use high wool content ragg socks—most good ones are 95 percent wool. Wool felt innersoles (changed and dried often) really help.

Wool hats prevent large heat loss, and the roll-down-over-the-face balaclava is preferred. All clothing and footwear should be large and loose enough to allow movement and circulation.

Proper equipment is also important. There are good cross-country ski packages available (skis, poles, and mounted cable bindings) for folks from two or three years on up. Use an inexpensive, properly snowproofed leather hiking boot, canoe boot, or wafflestomper in those bindings, and you get year-long use from such boots.

Keep trip planning to a minimum. Don't set a goal for your youthful companions measured in distance or time. The greater the effort put into planning, getting ready, and to the starting point, the less able you are to be flexible. If you are inflexible when your charges are tired, cold, thirsty, then the trip is likely to be a disappointing one for them. The cardinal rule—leave expectation out of expeditions.

Kids from about six to eight months can go on many sensible outdoor trips with you—on your back. Don't use the frame baby carriers sold for the purpose—the diaper sling seat cuts off much circulation to the legs through the femoral artery, and that is not a good thing in winter. Even for kids up to three years, try the following: buy or make a large rucksack or frame pack. Roll up a sleeping bag, blankets, or use a couple of pillows to make a seat in the lower rear of your pack. Dress your child for winter and put him/her in the pack on the seat, high enough for a normal sitting position and thus normal circulation. An insulated Polarguard or down jacket will wrap around the whole child, retaining warmth (the pack is already windproof) and providing enough extra on top to snuggle up around neck and head if needed. Stick extra kid gear in the pack and tie in the favorite blanket or animal on a two-foot line that can be thrown out and retrieved endlessly. A child can spend time comfortably chatting, singing, eating, and napping right there while you ski.

Start kids skiing early, for short periods only, in your yard and without your skis on. In the beginning, all you are aiming for is developing the mental set "I am a skier"—with the experiential awareness that the world does not end with falls and snow up one's sleeve.

There are three plays to use for your three to five year old skier. (1) Encourage your child to ski as far as is possible. (2) At that point, take a 15–20 foot piece of ¼ inch nylon line out of your daypack, tie one end around your waist, and make a tied loop in the other end. On reasonably flat terrain, you now become a ski tow, pulling your youngster along (it's fairly easy with the right wax), providing an ongoing chance to be on skis, to practice balance, and to keep warm by doing some work. (3) When that wears thin, the child rides in the plastic SnoBoat a friend has been pulling (6 foot bridle on the SnoBoat, 15 foot line to your waist). Prop the child up on the cushions and wrap him/her in the blankets you have in the SnoBoat. Put the abandoned skis and poles in the SnoBoat alongside, and start the journey home at this point because there aren't really any plays left except a hot tub and cocoa promised for the end.

Finally, somewhere between the ages of 5–7, kids can actually cover the trip distance themselves. Rushing them does not help—they are already taking 2 or 3 steps to each of yours.

Another rule: with kids, travel from diversion to diversion, with no more than 20–30 minutes between. For you, skiing is the end—exercise, being outdoors. For them, skiing is simply the means to get to the ends: making snow angels, snacks, following animal tracks, picnic lunches, handicap races (kids should win sometimes), and more. Diversions should stop the progress of the expedition and should often require removal of skis.

Finally, make sure each trip has several exit points along the way, so that you can stop as the situation dictates. Carry a large daypack with replacement clothing for what will obviously get wet (socks, mittens), extra sweaters, and jackets. Wool socks make good impromptu mittens and even overboots. Dehydration is common—carry lots of liquid, preferably hot when you started. Don't forget the usual—first aid kit, matches, map and compass, space blanket, line, and the rest.

It really can be done. However, winter provides little margin for error, so start carefully, take little bites, and get good at it slowly. Continue carefully. Listen to the complaints, and get to know the difference between passing the time and something potentially serious. Find out what hypothermia is—it's your biggest potential problem for kids and grownups alike, and it's subtle. Get to know what it is, how to prevent and treat it, and most especially, how to see its circumstances and symptoms coming on.

What return do you get on your investment? Hopefully, you have a good time and share adventures and challenges with kids who become your good friends. They really, not vicariously, experience how you can do it to winter. They have the mental set that they can do it themselves, eventually on their own. They know now that they can do some things really well, and they have some tolerance for frustration, stress, exertion and failure—and they also feel the satisfaction of achieving a goal by their own effort.

Dyke Williams is a parent and former Associate Director of the Minnesota Outward Bound School. He is founder and former president of Country Ways Kits. Dyke is currently coordinating volunteers and developing new programs for the Hennepin County Park Reserve District.

Minnesota

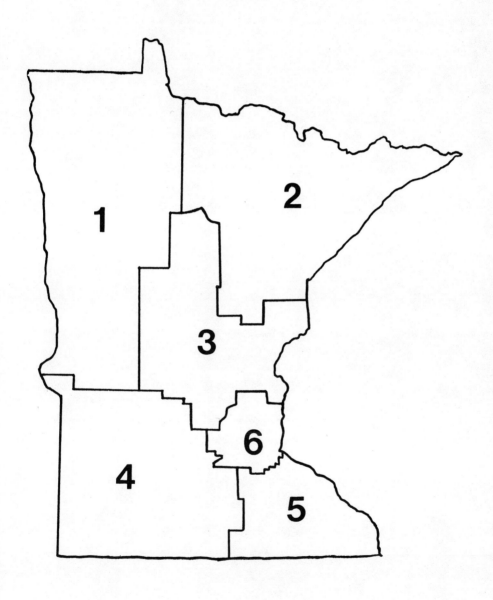

INTRODUCTION TO MINNESOTA REGIONS

We divided the State into six regions, following the boundaries of the six Minnesota Department of Natural Resources' Administrative Regions. These regions should *not* be confused with the Minnesota Office of Tourism's six regions that are similar but not the same. We also include the State Corridor Trails at the beginning of this chapter on Minnesota.

Each trail listing shows a map of Minnesota in the upper right-hand corner of the page. The DNR region for that trail is shaded on the map to provide a quick regional location reference, enabling readers to keep their bearings while reading through the information.

For an overall view of Minnesota's regions, as well as Wisconsin's and Michigan's, see the table of contents.

The addresses and telephone numbers for additional Minnesota cross country ski trail information are as follows:

Minnesota Department of Natural Resources, Trails and Waterways Unit, Box 52 Centennial Building, St. Paul, MN 55155. 612-296-6699

Minnesota Department of Natural Resources, Outdoor Recreation Information Center. 612-296-6699

Minnesota Department of Natural Resources, Division of Parks and Recreation, Box 39 Centennial Building, St. Paul, MN 55155. 612-296-4776

Forest Supervisor, Superior National Forest, P.O. Box 338, Duluth, MN 55801. 218-727-6692

Minnesota Department of Natural Resources, Division of Forestry, Box 44 Centennial Building, St. Paul, MN 55155. 612-296-4491

Forest Supervisor, Chippewa National Forest, Cass Lake, MN 56633. 218-335-2226

Minnesota Tourism Information Center, 240 Bremer Building, St. Paul, MN 55101. 612-296-5029.

MINNESOTA'S CROSS-COUNTRY SKI LICENSING SYSTEM FOR PUBLIC TRAILS

In response to revenue shortages for cross-country ski trails, a coalition of citizen ski touring interests formed to explore new ways to raise money for the acquisition, development, and maintenance of ski touring trails. The end result was legislation requiring skiers to buy a license to cross-country ski, as specified below. This legislation allows skiers an opportunity to help ensure a strong future for Minnesota's ski trail system. The licensing has been in effect since December 1, 1983.

A skier is required to have a license to ski on any nonfederal public trail that is designated and promoted (i.e., groomed, mapped, signed, or advertised) for cross-country skiing. There are approximately 1,400 miles of designated and promoted ski touring trails throughout the state. These include nearly 700 miles in DNR management trails (such as state parks and forests) and nearly 700 miles maintained for the public outside the DNR management units.

Any skier aged 16–64 who uses such public ski trails must buy a license to support the system. This license must be worn in a visible location on the skier's outer clothing. Usually this is the only fee that skiers will have to pay for trail use. However, at some recreational areas, an entrance fee and/or a parking fee will be charged.

The cost of an annual license valid from July 1 to June 30 is

$5.00 per skier

$7.50 per wife and husband.

A state ski permit for one-day use is

$1.00 per skier.

A license may be purchased in person at any of the following locations:

1) DNR License Bureau, 625 North Robert Street, St. Paul, Minnesota.

2) Any state park

3) Designated trail locations

4) Any county auditor or subagent (for example, participating sporting goods stores). An additional 50¢ issuing fee may be charged at these locations.

For further information, contact the Minnesota Department of Natural Resources in St. Paul or at any of the DNR regional offices. Addresses as follows:

Minnesota Department of Natural Resources, Trails and Waterways Unit, Box 52 Centennial Building, St. Paul, MN 55155. 612-296-6699

DNR Trails and Waterways, 2115 Birchmont Beach Rd. N.E., Bemidji, MN 56601. 218-755-2265

DNR Trails and Waterways, 424 Front St. Box 648, Brainerd, MN 56401. 218-828-2560

DNR Trails and Waterways, 1201 E. Highway 2, Grand Rapids, MN 55744. 218-327-1709

DNR Trails and Waterways, Box 756—Highway 15 South, New Ulm, MN 56073. 507-354-2196

DNR Trails and Waterways, 2300 Silver Creek Rd. N.E., Rochester, MN 55904. 507-285-7420

DNR Trails and Waterways, 1200 Warner Rd., St. Paul, MN 55106. 612-296-9115

RULES OF USE
FOR WINTER TRAVEL
IN THE BWCA WILDERNESS

Winter visitors to the Boundary Waters Canoe Area Wilderness Area are asked to cooperate with some rules to help preserve the primitive characteristics of this wilderness (in Region 2).

1. No motor or motorized equipment of any type is permitted within the BWCA except as specified below.

   Snowmobiles not exceeding 40 inches in width are permitted on the following routes:

   > The overland portage from the east bay of Crane Lake to Little Vermilion Lake in Canada.

   > The overland portage from Sea Gull River along the eastern portion of Saganaga Lake to Canada.

   With the exception of the above routes, snowmobiles are permitted only on that portion of periphery lakes lying *outside* the BWCA.

2. A visitor's permit must be obtained before entering the BWCA from May 1 through September 30. The U.S. Forest Service asks winter visitors to check in at the District Ranger Station to leave plans for their trip and to receive information about snow conditions and the advisability of winter camping.

3. Nonburnable, disposable food and beverage containers are not permitted. Returnable beverage bottles are not permitted even though a deposit is charged. All empty containers and other refuse must be burned or packed out.

4. It is unlawful to cut live trees, shrubs, or boughs. Only dead and down material should be used for firewood. Obtain firewood away from campsites and back from lakeshore.

5. No equipment, personal property, or supplies may be stored within the wilderness.

6. Use toilet facilities at existing campsites or dispose of human waste at least 100 feet from the waters' edge.

7. Obey all State and local laws and regulations. The use of National Forest land for hunting and fishing is permitted in accordance with regulations issued by the Minnesota Department of Natural Resources.

STATE CORRIDOR TRAILS

Douglas State Trail

20.8 km (13 mi) of trail

Douglas State Trail is a multiple-use trail developed on an abandoned railroad grade. It provides two separate treadways, each designed for different recreational activities. One treadway is surfaced with packed limestone screenings—it is to be used by bikers and hikers in the times without snow and by snowmobilers when there is snow cover. The parallel treadway is used by horseback riders during periods without snow and by skiers when there is snow.

The trail begins near Rochester (northwest of the city, on 55th Street, which is just off Highway 52), travels northwest through the small town of Douglas (for which the trail is named), and proceeds to its termination in the town of Pine Island. The trail possesses outstanding rural scenery and traverses some of Minnesota's richest agricultural land. The segment from Douglas to Pine Island is situated in the Dorer Memorial Hardwood State Forest. Both the south and middle branches of the Middle Fork Zumbro River are crossed en route.

Parking lots with rest facilities are provided at the three access points in Rochester, Douglas, and Pine Island.

For further information, contact

Regional Trails and Waterways Coordinator, DNR Headquarters, 2300 Silver Creek Rd. N.E., Rochester, MN 55904. 507-285-7176

Minnesota Department of Natural Resources, Trails and Waterways, Box 52 Centennial Building, St. Paul, MN 55155. 612-296-6699

State Corridor Trail
Heartland State Trail

43.2 km (27 mi) of a total length of 80 km (50 mi)

Heartland State Trail is an 80-km (50 mi) multiple-use trail being developed in two segments on an abandoned railroad grade. The first segment, which is 43.2 km (27 mi) long, begins at Highway 34 in Park Rapids and ends at Cass County Road 12 in Walker. This segment may be used for cross-country skiing. It moves through the towns of Dorset, Nevis, and Akeley and enters the southwest corner of the Chippewa National Forest, just south of Walker.

The second segment is 33.6 km (21 mi) long and runs from approximately one-half mile south of the Kabekona Bay Bridge to a point two miles south of Cass Lake. This portion is open to snowmobiling. It is planned that the two segments be joined eventually. Much of the trail moves through farmland, interspersed with lakes, ponds, and woods of aspen and jackpine. Parking lots and rest areas have been established along the route in Dorset, Nevis, Akeley, and Kabekona Bay.

For further information and the trail map, contact

Arden Belcher, Department of Natural Resources, 2115 Birchmont Beach Rd. N.E., Bemidji, MN 56601. 218-775-2265

Minnesota Department of Natural Resources, Trails and Waterways, Box 52 Centennial Building, St. Paul, MN 55155. 612-296-6699

Chambers of Commerce of the cities of Park Rapids, Walker, and Cass Lake

---

State Corridor Trail
Luce Line State Trail

Please refer to Region 6, page 328 for information on the Luce Line State Trail.

State Corridor Trail
Minnesota-Wisconsin Boundary State Trail

320 km (200 mi) of trails

Minnesota-Wisconsin Boundary State Trail is a multiple-use trail being developed from Arden Hills to Duluth. It provides a snowmobile trail with portions open to hiking, ski touring, and horseback riding.

The trail currently runs from the northern boundary of Wild River State Park (see page 231), through Chengwatana State Forest (see page 202), St. Croix State Park (see page 224), St. Croix State Forest, and Nemadji State Forest to the town of Nickerson. When completed, it will traverse six counties and provide access to four state parks and three state forests.

The trail passes through the scenic St. Croix River Valley and northern hardwood forests. It provides access to some of Minnesota's most picturesque scenery.

Many parking and rest areas have been provided enroute. Several take advantage of scenic vistas.

For further information, contact

Department of Natural Resources, Trails and Waterways, Box 52 Centennial Building, St. Paul, MN 55155. 612-296-6699

State Corridor Trail
North Shore State Trail

244.8 km (153 mi) of trail

North Shore State Trail is a multiple-use trail that has been developed between Duluth and Grand Marais. It winds behind the bluffs that overlook Lake Superior and provides access to some of the most rugged and beautiful scenery in Minnesota.

The trail traverses St. Louis, Lake, and Cook Counties and provides access to Cloquet Valley State Forest, Gooseberry Falls State Park (see page 103), Superior National Forest (see page 179), Finland State Forest (see page 97), George H. Crosby-Manitou State Park (see page 89), Temperance River State Park/Cross River Wayside (see page 151).

It provides a wilderness experience for the user by crossing over sixty rivers and creeks, passing next to several lakes, and including many spectacular vistas.

The trail is groomed weekly for snowmobile use, although it is intended for multiple-use throughout most of its length.

For further information, contact

DNR Trails and Waterways, 1201 E. Highway 2, Grand Rapids, MN 55744. 218-327-1709

Minnesota Department of Natural Resources, Trails and Waterways, Box 52 Centennial Building, St. Paul, MN 55155. 612-296-6699

State Corridor Trail
Sakatah Singing Hills State Trail

62.4 km (39 mi) of trail

Sakatah Singing Hills State Trail is a multiple-use trail developed on an abandoned railroad grade. It begins on the northeast side of the city of Mankato and travels eastward through the small towns of Madison Lake and Elysian to the town of Waterville. Here, the first segment ends. The second begins at the east side of Waterville, passes through Sakatah Lake State Park, crosses the Cannon River at Morristown,and continues past the town of Warsaw and around Cannon Lake to the city of Faribault.

The trail has two treadways: a limestone hard-surfaced route for bicyclists, hikers, and snowmobilers and a parallel treadway for equestrians and skiers. Wayside rests, picnic areas, and parking lots will be encountered enroute.

For further information, contact

DNR Trails and Waterways, Box 756—Highway 15 South, New Ulm, MN 56073. 507-354-2196

Minnesota Department of Natural Resources, Trails and Waterways, Box 52 Centennial Building, St. Paul, MN 55155. 612-296-6699

State Corridor Trail
Taconite State Trail

264 km (165 mi) of trail

Taconite State Trail is a multiple-use trail that stretches from Grand Rapids to Ely. It is designed for both winter and summer use and accommodates snowmobilers, skiers, and hikers. It provides a route through some of the most picturesque and historically significant areas in the state.

The trail traverses six counties, ties together five major population centers, and either enters or provides access to nine state parks, thirteen state forest recreational areas, two national forest areas, and one national park. Development is still progressing on the trail, with the addition of rustic wayside rests and picnic areas taking place now and in the future. Many of these facilities take advantage of scenic vistas.

For further information, contact

DNR Trails and Waterways, 1201 E. Highway 2, Grand Rapids, MN 55744. 218-327-1709

Minnesota Department of Natural Resources, Trails and Waterways, Box 52 Centennial Building, St. Paul, MN 55155. 612-296-6699

REGION 1
NORTHWEST MINNESOTA

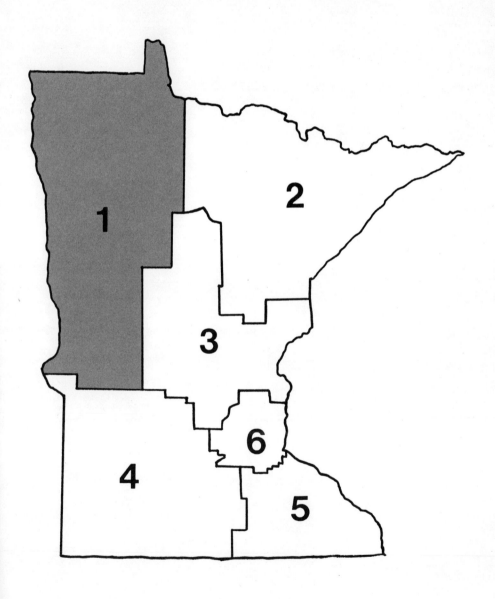

Andes Tower Trails
Alexandria, Minnesota

8.8–9.6 km (5.5–6 mi) of trails
beginner, intermediate, advanced

Andes Tower Hill Ski Area is located 15 miles west of Alexandria, in Douglas County, just off Highway 27. The trails are groomed regularly and double-tracked. All are marked, with maps available. They are situated on a variety of terrain, offering a wide range of opportunities for all skiers. Picnic areas with benches are located along the trails. Thousands of dollars have been spent on newly formed trails within the last year, and expansion is likely for the 1984–85 season.

In the past, Andes Tower Hill was only a downhill facility; as a consequence, there is the additional bonus of the adjacent downhill runs. The cross-country trails are located above the downhill area.

The chalet offers rental equipment, maps, hot food, shelter, and parking. Lodging is available at nearby Alexandria.

Daily trail fees are: children 11 and under, $1.50; over 11 and adults, $2.00; family, $6.00. A season pass is $10.00.

For further information, contact

Tom Anderson, Andes Tower Hill, Route 3 Box 258, Alexandria, MN 56308. 612-886-5420

See also Douglas County, Trollskogen Ski Area, Kensington Runestone County Park, page 52.

Radisson Arrowwood Inn and Resort
Alexandria, Minnesota

8 km (5 mi) of trails
beginner, intermediate, advanced

Radisson Arrowwood is a 450-acre, all-season resort located on the shores of Lake Darling, 4 miles northwest of Alexandria in Douglas County on Highway 22.

The trails are marked and are groomed regularly. Although snowmobiling is allowed at the resort,the cross-country trails are marked and posted against use by snowmobiles. The terrain ranges from level to very hilly and is well-suited to all skiers.

The Inn has 170 guest sleeping rooms, most with patios with a wide view of the landscape leading to the lake. Several rooms have special features. The Viking Room, also overlooking the lake, offers three meals a day. There is a cocktail lounge with fireplace and, in winter, live entertainment. For after-skiing there is a pool, whirlpool, and sauna. In addition, the Inn offers conference facilities for groups of 15-700.

The resort charges no fee for trail use. Equipment may be rented by the hour, day, or entire weekend, and charges vary between midweek and weekend periods.

For further information, contact

Radisson Arrowwood Inn and Resort, R.R. Box 639, Alexandria, MN 56308. 612-762-1124, 800-892-7006 (toll free Minnesota), 800-228-9822 (toll free elsewhere)

See also Lake Carlos State Park, page 62.

Becker County
Detroit Lakes, Minnesota

Becker County maintains three different ski trails in the south end of the county: Detroit Lakes Community Ski Touring Trails, Dunton Locks Ski Trails, and East Frazee Ski Trails. All are close to each other.

DETROIT LAKES COMMUNITY SKI TOURING TRAILS
10 km (6.25 mi) of trails

beginner, intermediate, advanced

This trail begins at the Industrial Park in town, approximately 0.75 mile north of Big Detroit Lake. From Randolph Road go north on Highland Drive to Mountain Meadow Road, and turn east to the Industrial Park.

The trail begins in a meadowland and moves into a forested area. Its entire length is marked. There are four loops; the outermost circles the Detroit Mountain Downhill Ski Area. Food service and restrooms are available here. You may park at the Industrial Park or Detroit Mountain.

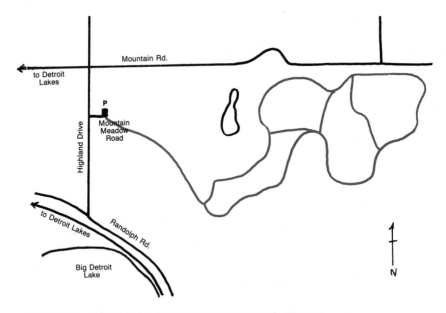

DETROIT LAKES COMMUNITY SKI TOURING TRAILS

DUNTON LOCKS SKI TRAILS
4.8 km (3 mi) of trails

Dunton Locks Ski Trails are located approximately 2 miles southwest of Detroit Lakes on Highway 59. They are situated on land on both sides of the channel between Lake Sallie and Muskrat Lake.

The seven loops, marked and groomed, meander through a forested area primarily. Toilets and parking are available.

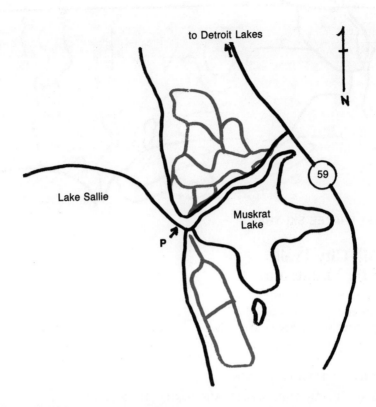

to Detroit Lakes

N

Lake Sallie

59

Muskrat
Lake

P

DUNTON LOCKS SKI TRAIL

EAST FRAZEE SKI TRAILS
16 km (10 mi) of trails

East Frazee Ski Trails are located approximately 1 mile east of the town of Frazee, which is 8 miles southeast of Detroit Lakes. Take Highway 87 northeast of Frazee, and turn east on Highway 150.

You may enter the trails at two locations on Highway 150. The trails are marked and groomed and include several loops through a variety of terrain, including meadows, lowlands, and woods. Four lakes dot the system. Additional trails direct to Frazee are planned for the future. Parking and toilets are available at the entrances on Highway 150.

For further information, contact

Floyd Svenby, Becker County Zoning Administrator, Becker County Courthouse, Detroit Lakes, MN 56501. 218-847-3938

Detroit Lakes Regional Chamber of Commerce, 700 Washington, Detroit Lakes, MN 56501. 218-847-9202

See also Maplelag, page 63 and Tamarac National Wildlife Refuge, page 70.

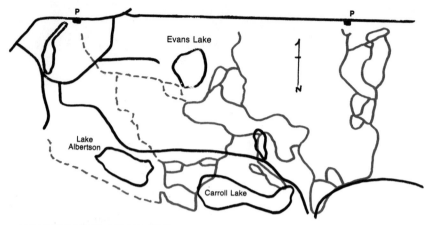

EAST FRAZEE SKI TRAILS

Bemidji City Trail
Bemidji, Minnesota

4 km (2.5 mi) of trails
beginner

Bemidji City Trail begins at the city arena, located at Ash Avenue and 23rd Street. It is marked, groomed, and tracked. Maps, water, and toilets are available. Park at the arena.

For further information, contact

Dan Haluptzok, City Hall, Bemidji, MN 56601. 218-751-5610.

See also Lake Bemidji State Park, page 60 and Wolf Lake Resort, page 73.

Blackduck Ranger District, Chippewa National Forest
Blackduck, Minnesota

Within the Blackduck Ranger District are three trails designated as ski-touring areas. They are well-marked but are not groomed or tracked. The trails are situated on lands of mixed hardwood and conifer forest. The terrain is gentle, and the trails are well-suited to the beginner. No fee is required. In addition, unplowed roads may be used for skiing, snowshoeing, and other non-motorized uses. Some forest roads, however, are open to snowmobiles and other motor vehicles. The District Ranger can provide a list of the designation of all roads in the Forest. Skiers are cautioned that parking may be difficult at times due to the lack of plowed access approaches to ski areas. National Forest campgrounds are not plowed or maintained in the winter, but camping is permitted in most other places on National Forest land. Water, shelter, and toilets are not available on site. Food and lodging is available in Blackduck or Bemidji. Ski rentals may be procurred in Bemidji. Maps of the ski trails may be obtained from the District Ranger.

CARTER LAKE TRAIL
TENSTRIKE, MINNESOTA
5.4 km (3.4 mi) of trails
beginner, intermediate

Carter Lake Trail is located approximately 2 miles south of the town of Tenstrike, on Forest Road 2419. Tenstrike is 8 miles southwest of Blackduck on Highway 71. Go east from Tenstrike on Forest Road 2418 for 1 mile, then turn south on Forest Road 2419, and travel 0.75 mile to the access point.

The trail meanders through aspen and hard timber. There is one loop in the system that is 2 km (1.25 mi) long.

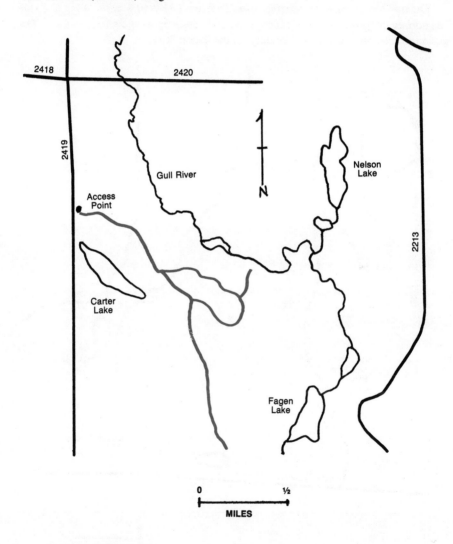

CARTER LAKE TRAIL

MEADOW LAKE TRAIL
TENSTRIKE, MINNESOTA
15 km (9.4 mi) of trails

beginner, intermediate

Meadow Lake Trail is located south of Tenstrike on Forest Road 2393. Access is achieved in a rather roundabout manner. From Tenstrike, go south on County Road 307 for approximately 6 miles, then turn southwest on County Road 27 for approximately 4 miles. Turn east on County Road 20 for 3 miles, to the junction with Forest Road 2393. There are eight access points along Forest Road 2393, and parking is available at two locations.

The trail has seven loops ranging in length from 0.8 km (0.5 mi) to 4 km (2.5 mi). The northernmost loop skirts Meadow Lake and passes by an old homestead site. One section of trail ends at a canoe landing on the Turtle River.

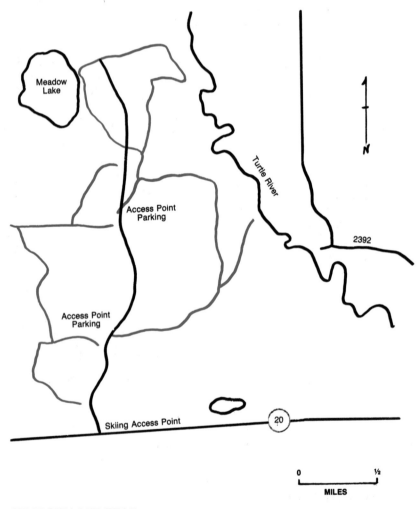

MEADOW LAKE TRAIL

WEBSTER LAKE TRAILS
BLACKDUCK, MINNESOTA
3.4 km (2.1 mi) of trails

beginner, intermediate

Webster Lake Trail is located about 10 miles south-southeast of Blackduck. Take Highway 39 (the "Scenic Highway") for approximately 7 miles to Forest Road 2236. Turn east on Forest Road 2236, and travel in a southeasterly direction for nearly 3 miles to the Webster Lake Campground.

The skiing access point starts at the old water pump in the picnic area. The trail moves in a leisurely fashion around Webster Lake. There are lake overlooks on the trail, and sites of beaver activity may be observed. Four miles of low standard road in the vicinity are open to snowmobiling.

For further information, contact

Robert W. Paddock, District Ranger, Blackduck Ranger District, Blackduck, MN 56630. 218-835-4291

Forest Supervisor, Chippewa National Forest, Cass Lake, MN 56633. 218-335-2226

See also Bemidji City Trail, page 46; Lake Bemidji State Park, page 60; Wolf Lake Resort, page 73; Deer River Ranger District in Region 2, page 91; Marcell Ranger District in Region 2, page 143; Cass Lake Ranger District in Region 3, page 202; and Walker Ranger District in Region 3, page 229.

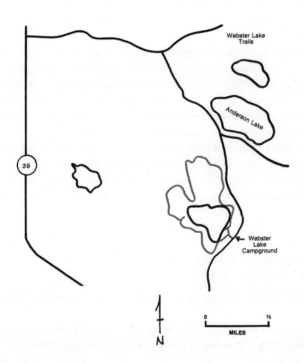

WEBSTER LAKE TRAIL

Buffalo River State Park
Glyndon, Minnesota

16 km (10 mi) of trails

beginner, intermediate

Buffalo River State Park is located in Clay County, 4.5 miles east of Glyndon, which is 13 miles east of Moorhead. The park entrance is on Highway 10. It is a prairie park, preserving a remnant of the landscape first seen by explorers in the Red River Valley—a sea of grass stretching as far as the eye could see, its hypnotic continuity broken only by the meandering river-bottom forests. This prairie within the park and its adjoining Scientific and Natural Area (operated by the Minnesota Department of Natural Resources and the Nature Conservancy) are judged to be one of the finest and largest remaining undisturbed virgin prairies in Minnesota.

Eight to ten thousand years ago, Glacial Lake Agassiz covered the Red River Valley, in which the park is located. The ancient lake's rise and fall, until its final retreat to the north, formed the dominant landscape features of this park. As the lake slowly retreated, it left prominent gravel ridges or beach lines still visible in many locations in Minnesota. The park is located at the point where the most conspicuous of these beaches crosses the Buffalo River. Called Campbell Beach, it most likely formed the western shore of Lake Agassiz for nearly 2,000 years. It may be seen on the eastern edge of the park.

The Minnesota Historical Society has scheduled an archaeological survey of an area including the ancient beach ridges used as travel routes for prehistoric Indians and the ford across the Buffalo River.

Of equal interest is the Red River Oxcart Trail that was established before settlement to transport furs, hides, tallow, and other supplies and tradegoods between St. Paul and Pembina, North Dakota, where a major trading post of the Montreal-based North West Fur Company was located (*see also* Old Mill State Park, page 67). The oxcarts used were all wood and the volume of sound produced by the creaking and groaning of the ungreased axles could be heard for miles.

The Buffalo River enters the park on its eastern border and leaves at its northwest corner. It is a tributary of the Red River of the North. The banks of the River are bordered by a deciduous river-bottom forest of elm, ash, cottonwood, oak, and basswood. Nearly all the ski trails follow the river and cross it at three different points along its course. A portion of the trail, the Ponderosa Trail, leaves the park on its eastern border and returns in a loop. The trails are marked. A warming house, toilets, and parking are located together at the trailhead. A map is available at the park headquarters. Food and lodging are at hand in Glyndon.

For further information, contact

Park Manager, Buffalo River State Park, Box 118 Route 2, Glyndon, MN 56547. 218-498-2124

Minnesota Department of Natural Resources, Division of Parks and Recreation, Box 39 Centennial Office Building, St. Paul, MN 55155. 612-296-4776

See also Ulen Park Trail, page 72.

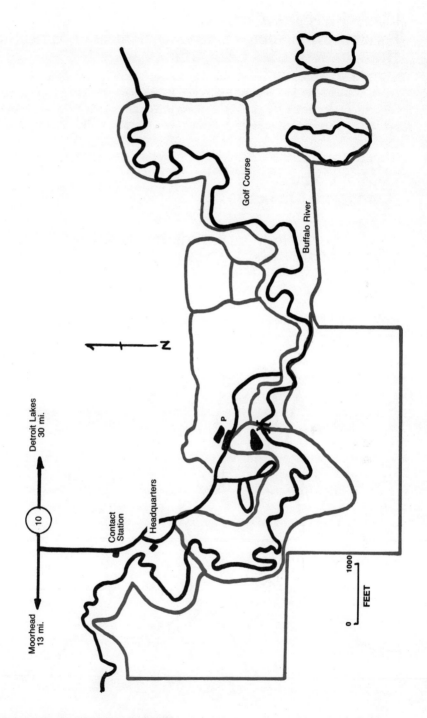

BUFFALO RIVER STATE PARK

Chippewa National Forest
Forest Service, United States Department of Agriculture
Headquarters: Cass Lake, Minnesota

The headquarters for one of the five Ranger Districts of the Chippewa National Forest is located in this region, Blackduck Ranger District. The office of the Forest Supervisor is located in the city of Cass Lake in Region 3. Deer River and Marcell Ranger Districts are located in Region 2, and Cass Lake and Walker Ranger Districts are located in Region 3.

Douglas County
Kensington, Minnesota

TROLLSKOGEN SKI AREA
KENSINGTON RUNESTONE COUNTY PARK
12 km (7.5 mi) of trails
beginner, intermediate, advanced

To reach Kensington Runestone County Park, go 14 miles southwest of Alexandria on Highway 27, then south on County Road 103 for 1 mile. The park is named in recognition of the 1898 claimed discovery of the Kensington Runestone by a pioneer farmer on what is now park land.

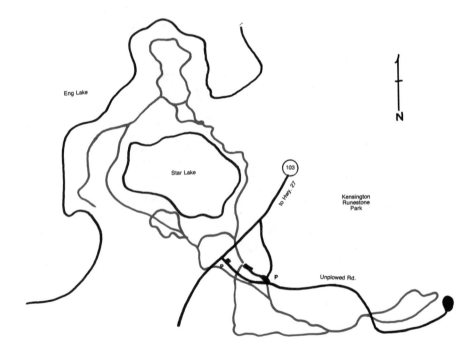

TROLLSKOGEN CROSS-COUNTRY SKI AREA

The trails are primarily intermediate in difficulty and are situated on rolling terrain in a heavily wooded area. They are groomed, double-tracked, and extensively signed. There are resting areas at various locations on the trails. One outhouse is also located on the system.

At the parking area is a heated, remodelled barn where water, vending machines, shelter, and toilets are available. You may pick up a trail map at the barn also. A state trail user permit is required at the park. No pets are allowed on the trails. A park caretaker resides on the premises.

The small town of Kensington is 3 miles south of the park, and food, liquor, and gas are available there. Alexandria provides all types of tourist accommodations.

Spruce Hill County Park of Douglas County is in the developmental stages at this time. It may not open until 1985–86 to cross-country skiing.

For further information, contact

Donald A. Lieffort, Superintendent, Douglas County Park Department, Route 1 Box 3A, Kensington, MN 56343. 612-965-2365

See also Andes Tower Trails, page 43.

Glacial Lakes State Park
Starbuck, Minnesota

8 km (5 mi) of trails

beginner, intermediate, advanced

Glacial Lakes State Park is located in Pope County, approximately 5 miles south of the town of Starbuck. Take Highway 29 south from Starbuck to County Road 41. Turn east on 41, and proceed to the park entrance.

The park's near-1,400 acres were shaped by glacial action about 10,000 years ago. The facility is situated on glacial moraines that run from east to west. Known as the Blue Mounds, these moraines represent the outermost point of the glacial lobe that pushed through this part of Minnesota. Cradled in the glacial basins are some of west central Minnesota's prettiest lakes. The largest lake in the park, Mountain Lake, lies in a deep valley surrounded by high hills that offer a rare scenic panorama. This spring-fed lake is known for its outstanding clarity and purity and is quite unusual because its entire watershed is within the park. The park contains several lakes, ponds, and marshes. The wetlands in the southeastern part of the park are located in gently rolling prairie. Some of these grasslands are virgin prairie. The park is on the eastern zone of the prairie where the oak savanna and forest lands of the eastern part of the state begin. Such areas support a large and diverse wildlife population and are especially fine for birdwatching.

The trails for ski touring are located on the hiking trails in the northern part of the park. They are marked and groomed. The only road that is plowed in the park is its main thoroughfare, County Road 41. Parking is available at three locations: just off 41 at the junction of the campground and service court roads, on 41 at its junction with the road to the boat ramp and beach, and on 41 at its junction with the road into the southeastern picnic area. Visitors may ski the short distances from any of these three locations to the trails.

The trail circling the campground is rated as a beginner route; the trail around Mountain Lake and the two loops by the southeastern picnic area are intermediate in difficulty; the trail that runs into the walk-in campsites and to the park's highest elevation (1,352 feet) is for advanced skiers.

Snowmobiling is allowed in the park, but these trails are located in the southern end of the park and are entirely separate from ski trails.

Winter camping is permitted. However, visitors must pack in to the campsites because some secondary park roads are not plowed in the winter. There are privies located throughout the park. Water is available at the park office.

Food, lodging, and supplies are available in Starbuck, Glenwood, and Benson.

For further information, contact

Glacial Lakes State Park, Park Manager, Route 2, Starbuck, MN 56381. 612-239-2860
Minnesota Department of Natural Resources, Division of Parks and Recreation, Box
   39 Centennial Building, St. Paul, MN 55155. 612-296-4776

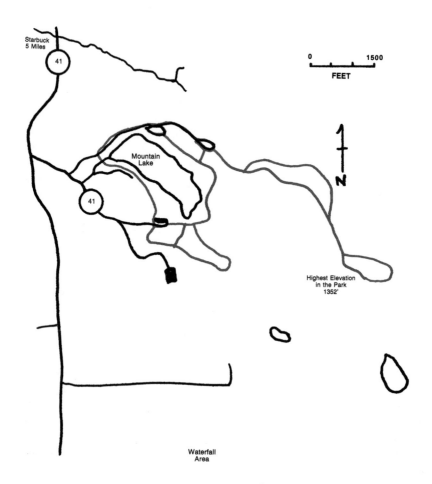

GLACIAL LAKES STATE PARK

Hayes Lake State Park
Roseau, Minnesota

9.6 km (6 mi) of trails

beginner

To reach Hayes Lake State Park, take Highway 89 south from Roseau approximately 14 miles, then turn east on County Road 4, and travel about 8 miles to the entrance. The park is located in Roseau County within the Beltrami Island State Forest.

The North Fork of the Roseau River flows through the park, and to provide a site for water-related recreation, Hayes Lake was created by damming the river. The ski trails skirt a great deal of the lake. They are marked, groomed, and contain two loops. Snowmobiling is allowed in the park, but the trails do not cross the ski trails and are restricted in large part to land across the lake. Parking, pit toilets, camping facilities, and maps are at hand in the park. Lodging, food, and other tourist accommodations are available in Roseau.

For further information, contact

Park Manager, Hayes Lake State Park, Route 4, Roseau, MN 56751. 218-425-7504.

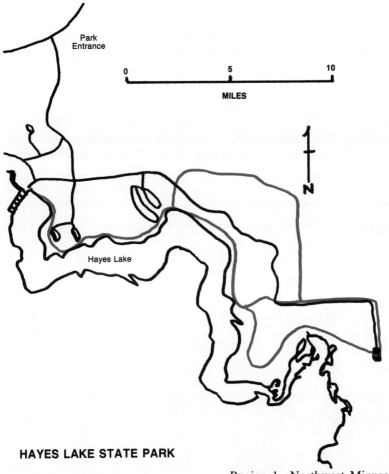

HAYES LAKE STATE PARK

Hubbard County
Park Rapids, Minnesota

Three trails, administered by Hubbard County, have been built by and are maintained by the Itascatur Ski Club. The Itascatur Trails are located to the north of Park Rapids and contain a 15.5-km advanced trail and an adjacent 5-km Family Trail. The third trail, just southeast of Park Rapids, is called Long Pine Trail. It is 13 km long and is for beginners and intermediates.

ITASCATUR SKI TRAIL—ADVANCED
15.5 km (9.7 mi) of trails
advanced

To reach the trails, take Highway 71 north from Park Rapids for 14 miles, a distance calculated from the junction of Highways 34 and 71 in Park Rapids. Turn west, and travel 1 mile and then south a short distance to the trail parking area.

The advanced trail is very hilly, and skiers *must* exercise caution and observe the strict one-way traffic rule. Those who do not will be asked to leave. The fastest hills are marked as such. On nearly all loops are exits to the return trail to the parking area. The trail is marked, groomed, and tracked. Maps, a three-sided shelter, and an outhouse are available at the parking area. Pets are not allowed on the trail.

Many resorts and eating places are close by. Additional tourist accommodations are available in Park Rapids. Rental of ski equipment is possible at both Pier 34 and Delaney's in Park Rapids.

ITASCATUR SKI TRAIL—FAMILY TRAIL
5 km (3.1 mi) of trails
beginner

The Itascatur Family Trail is located just across the road from the advanced trail. It is also a one-way trail with no full loops in the system. A toilet is available on site.

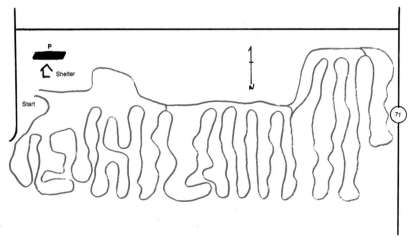

ITASCATUR SKI TRAILS

LONG PINE SKI TRAIL
13 km (8.1 mi) of trails
beginner, intermediate

To reach Long Pine Trail, go east on Highway 34 for 1 mile from the junction of 34 and 71 in Park Rapids (at the traffic lights). Turn south on County Road 6, travel south for 2 miles. Turn east, and go 0.5 mile to the parking lot at the trailhead.

The trail is a large one-way loop, arranged in such a convoluted manner that it is nearly a loop within a loop. There are nine crossovers in the loop. The trail traverses a rolling landscape heavily forested with pines. It is a well-marked and groomed trail. Much of its maintenance is supported by donations. Maps, donation envelopes, and a toilet are located at the trailhead. A snowmobile trail runs around the perimeter of the trail, crossing it at a few points.

Food, lodging, and supplies are available in Park Rapids.

For further information, contact

Itascatur Ski Club, c/o Kare Lid, Itasca Star Route, Park Rapids, MN 56470. 218-732-9680

Chamber of Commerce, Box 249M, Park Rapids, MN 56470. 218-732-4111.

See also Wilderness Bay Resort and Campground, page 72 and Itasca State Park, page 58.

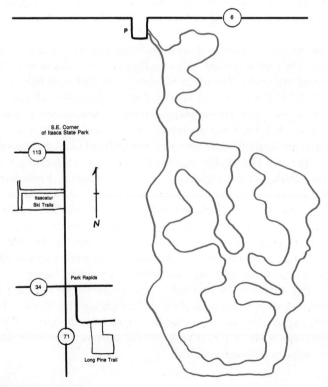

LONG PINE SKI TRAIL

Itasca State Park
Lake Itasca, Minnesota

43.2 km (27 mi) of trails

beginner, intermediate, advanced

There are three entrances to Itasca State Park. The North Entrance is located on Highway 200, 25 miles southwest of Bagley; the East Entrance is at the junction of Highways 200 and 71, 7 miles west of Lake George; the South Entrance is located on Highway 71, 18 miles north-northwest of Park Rapids.

Itasca, the oldest, best-known, and nearly the largest state park in Minnesota (32,000 acres), is of enormous historic significance to Minnesotans. The most well-known site in the park is the headwaters of the Mississippi River, first described in the summer of 1832 by the explorer, Henry Rowe Schoolcraft. He fabricated the word Itasca from the Latin *veritas caput*, meaning "truth head."

Archaeologists have excavated evidence of the presence of people in Itasca dating back 8,000 years. These migrant people traveled in small groups of a few families; hunted bison, deer, and moose; and possessed flint and bone tools as well as the knowledge of meat drying, hide dressing, and sewing. They fished, used edible plants as a diet staple, and kept pet dogs. There are also burial mounds at least 500 years old, adjacent to the headwaters. They are of the more advanced Woodland Indians who maintained permanent villages and hunted with bow and arrow, used pottery for cooking, made birch bark canoes and snowshoes, harvested wild rice, and tapped maple trees for syrup. These are all skills and traditions maintained and observed by Ojibwe people today.

Some of the state's finest trails exist in Itasca and are a real treat to the cross-country skier. The park is situated within the Pine Moraine (glacier-made hills) Region of north central Minnesota. The Itasca Moraine is a belt of steep hills, some of which approach 1,700 feet above sea level. The marked and groomed trails take excellent advantage of these geological circumstances, offering a wide variety of experiences for the skier. Many small lakes and impressive vistas please the visitor.

There are nine ski trails; eight intertwine in a series of loops in the southeast corner of the park. They are **Ozawindib** (named after Schoolcraft's Indian guide), **Okerson Heights, Deer Park, Aiton Heights** (ends at a lookout tower), **Eagle Scout, DeSoto, Nicollet** (the archaeological digs are located on this trail), and **Crossover**. By itself in the north end of the park is the **Schoolcraft Trail**. It skirts the northwest shore of Lake Itasca and involves the Mississippi Headwaters. Snowmobiling is allowed on the far north and east perimeters of the park and does not disrupt the ski trails.

The Forest Inn, a beautiful, massive Civilian Conservation Corps building, is open year around. It houses a souvenir shop and serves as a warming facility for skiers. Food and other tourist needs may be obtained locally outside the park at Lake Itasca, Lake George, or Park Rapids. Camping is allowed at designated sites. Firewood is to be purchased at the registration station and not scavenged from the forest. The park offers many opportunities to its visitors. Check with the administrators about scheduled programs. Use maps to facilitate your visit.

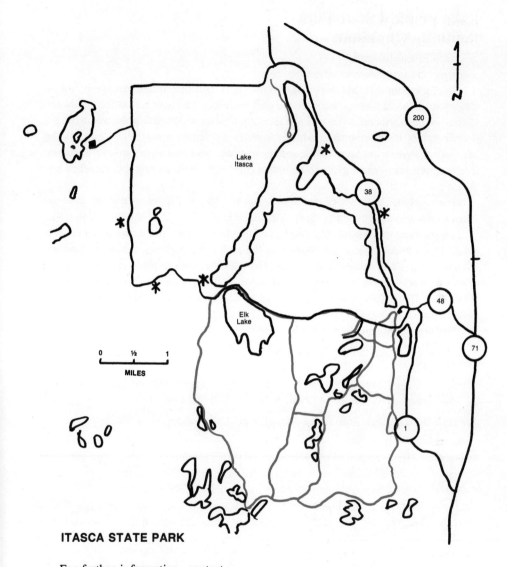

ITASCA STATE PARK

For further information, contact

Park Manager, Itasca State Park, Lake Itasca, MN 56460. 218-266-3654

Minnesota Department of Natural Resources, Division of Parks and Recreation, Box 39 Centennial Building, St. Paul, MN 55155. 612-296-4776

See also Itascatur Ski Trails, page 56 and Wilderness Bay Resort and Campground, page 72.

Lake Bemidji State Park
Bemidji, Minnesota

8 km (5 mi) of trails

beginner, intermediate, advanced

To reach Bemidji State Park, take Highway 71 north from Bemidji. Turn east on County Road 20, and go 1.7 miles to the park entrance. The park is located in Beltrami County on the northeast shore of Lake Bemidji. The name Bemidji is derived from the Ojibwe name, Pemidjigumaug, which translates as "cross water" and describes the Mississippi River's entrance on the south end of the lake and its departure on the east side. Bemidji was a name given to an Indian chief in the area by neighboring white settlers.

The combined energies of the Department of Natural Resources and the local ski touring club maintain the trails. Skiers of all levels of skill will be satisfied. The trails, well-marked and groomed, are situated on rolling terrain and offer a peaceful ski experience, as snowmobiling is not allowed in the park. The park welcomes snowshoers, hikers, birders, and those who ice fish. The park's efforts in planning a pleasurable winter recreation experience are commendable. Winter camping is permitted in designated areas. Toilets and a warming room are available. Food and lodging facilities may be obtained in Bemidji.

For further information, contact

Park Manager, Lake Bemidji State Park, Route 5 Box 44, Bemidji, MN 56601. 218-751-1472

Minnesota Department of Natural Resources, Division of Parks and Recreation, Box 39 Centennial Building, St. Paul, MN 55155. 612-296-4776

See also Bemidji City Trail, page 46 and Wolf Lake Resort, page 73.

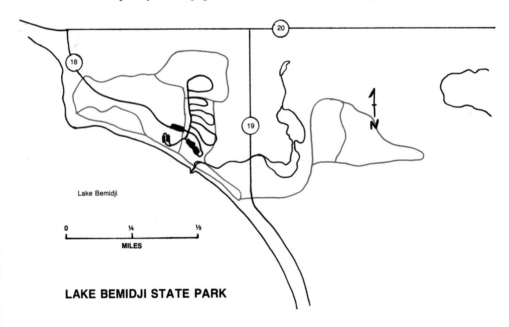

LAKE BEMIDJI STATE PARK

Lake Bronson State Park
Lake Bronson, Minnesota

4 km (2.5 mi) of trails
beginner

To reach the park entrance, take County Road 28 east from the town of Lake Bronson (located on Highway 59) for 1 mile. Lake Bronson State Park is situated in Kittson County on the boundary between two of Minnesota's major geographic zones. To the west is the former prairie land of the flat Red River Valley, and to the east is aspen parkland—rolling hills covered with aspen and prairie. Consequently, the visitor can see a tremendous variety of wildlife, the most notable being the moose. The park naturalist provides information on the latest wildlife sightings in the park.

The South Branch Two River runs through the park and was formerly used by the North West Fur Company to move furs and trading supplies in and out of the Pembina Trading Post in Pembina, North Dakota. Due to extremely dry conditions in the 1930s, the towns of Bronson and Hallock dammed up a portion of the river for a water supply and created a lake that is the focal point of the park. The ski trails are located on the north side of the west end of the lake by the dam. Marked and groomed, they move through varying landscape. Snowmobiling is allowed in the park, but the trails do not conflict with the ski trails, as they lead to the opposite end of the lake and the park.

Toilets, parking, and maps are available at the park. Food and lodging may be obtained in Lake Bronson.

For further information, contact

Lake Bronson State Park, Box 218, Lake Bronson, MN 56734. 218-754-2200

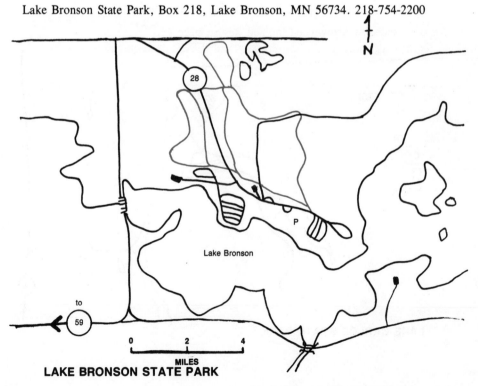

LAKE BRONSON STATE PARK

Lake Carlos State Park
Carlos, Minnesota

8 km (5 mi) of trails

beginner, intermediate

Lake Carlos State Park is located in Douglas County, 10 miles north of Alexandria on Highway 29. It is located within Minnesota's Leaf Hill Region of moraines (glacier-produced hills). These moraines cradle the woodland ponds, marshes, meadows, and lakes that provide such a scenic setting for the skier. The steeply rolling hills are forested primarily with deciduous species such as maples, basswood, aspen, and oak.

The park boasts that you can ski in minutes from a tamarack bog to a maple and basswood stand or from open grassland to forested ridges overlooking lakes. Each trail, well-marked and groomed, consists of three loops. The northeast loop is for the novice skier, and the west and southwest loops, which skirt small lakes, are for intermediate skiers.

The picnic shelter on the shores of Lake Carlos serves as a warming house. Toilets and parking are available adjacent to the trails. Snowmobiling is allowed, but trails do not cross the ski trails. Food and lodging are available within a short distance of the park.

For further information, contact

Park Manager, Lake Carlos State Park, Route 2 Box 34, Carlos, MN 56319. 612-852-7200

Minnesota Department of Natural Resources, Division of Parks and Recreation, Box 39 Centennial Building, St. Paul, MN 55155. 612-296-4776

See also Radisson-Arrowwood Inn and Resort, page 43.

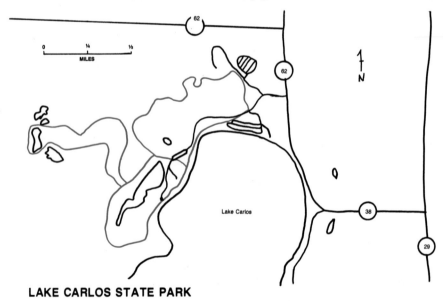

LAKE CARLOS STATE PARK

Maplelag
Callaway, Minnesota

30 km (18.75 mi) of trails

beginner, intermediate, advanced

Maplelag is approximately 20 miles northeast of Detroit Lakes in Becker County. Take County Road 21 north from Detroit Lakes for 12 miles to Richwood, then turn east-northeast on County Road 34 and go 6 miles to County Road 110. Turn west on 110 and travel 1.25 miles to the Maplelag driveway, which is 1 mile long. Exert caution on turns and curves.

Jim and Mary Richards have put forth great effort and used tremendous imagination in developing Maplelag. Maplelag is unique and special, completely different. It's far away from the typical urban forms of entertainment that too often are transplanted into the beautiful isolated settings of Minnesota.

The trails, marked and groomed, wind through 350 acres of woods, small clearings, and lakes. They challenge all skiers. Beginning skiing instruction is available, but ski rentals are not. A trail fee is required of nonguests. A 12-km family ski race, the Lotvola Cup, is held each year the Sunday before Presidents' Weekend at one o'clock.

The Richards offer the American plan with home cooking served family style and prepared with as many natural ingredients as possible, featuring their own maple syrup (Maplelag is one of the largest maple syrup operations in Minnesota). Friends who are regular Maplelagers say the food is always simply outstanding. Oranges, cookies, coffee, tea, and hot chocolate are always available at the Main Lodge.

There are four bunkhouses, which range in capacity from 10–14, and ten cabins, which house smaller numbers. The Sugarhouse can handle 18 people. Four of the cabins are old immmigrant log structures, moved to Maplelag and restored. All are wood-heated.

There are also two saunas and three outdoor wood-heated hot tubs on the deck of one sauna. Guests bring their own sleeping bags, towels, and swimsuits. Absolutely no pets are allowed.

For further information, contact

Jim or Mary Richards, Maplelag, Route 1, Callaway, MN 56521. 218-375-4466, 218-375-2986

See also Becker County Trails, page 44 and Tamarac National Wildlife Refuge, Pine Lake Ski Trail, page 70.

Maplewood State Park
Pelican Rapids, Minnesota

20 km (12.5 mi) of trails

beginner, intermediate, advanced

Maplewood State Park is located in Ottertail County, 7 miles east of Pelican Rapids on Highway 108. It skirts the east side of the South Arm of Lake Lida.

The park is situated within a series of rough, steep hills that are part of the Alexander Moraine Complex. The tree-covered hills cradle several lakes and wetlands in their deep valleys. This area is in Minnesota's transition zone between prairie land to the west and coniferous forests to the east. A deciduous region, it is well-known for

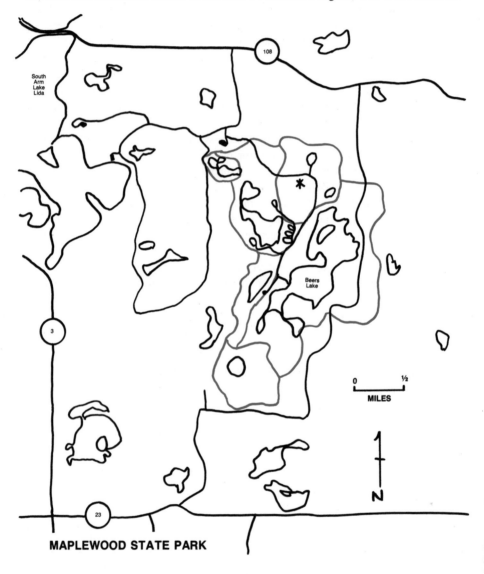

MAPLEWOOD STATE PARK

large hardwoods, including the State's largest ironwood tree. The park is characterized by beautiful sugar maples, basswood, American elm, and aspen. Archaeological surveys in the area have revealed the presence of people in the region dating back at least 6,000 years.

The ski trails are marked and regularly groomed. They wind around the many small ponds and lakes, the largest being Grass Lake and Beers Lake. The trails are designed for skiers of every ability. Steep hills will thrill the advanced skier and are located on separate loops to the south end of the system. Snowmobiling is permitted in the park, but the trails do not intersect ski trails and are located in the vicinity of the lake.

Water, toilets, parking, and maps are available at the park. Food and lodging may be obtained in Pelican Rapids.

For further information, contact

Park Manager, Maplewood State Park, Route 3 Box 281, Pelican Rapids, MN 56572. 218-863-8383

Minnesota Department of Natural Resources, Division of Parks and Recreation, Box 39 Centennial Building, St. Paul, MN 55155. 612-296-4776

See also Pomme de Terre Trails, page 68 and Spidahl's Ski Gård, page 69.

Movil Maze Trail
Bemidji, Minnesota

11 km (6.9 mi) of trails

Movil Maze Trail is located in Beltrami County, north-northeast of the city of Bemidji, on the east side of Lake Movil, which is north of Lake Bemidji. Take Highway 71 northeast from Bemidji to County Road 305; turn north on 305 to the first gravel pit, which is the parking lot at the trailhead.

The trail is a redeveloped section of the old route of the Minnesota Finlandia, a 100-km race run the first weekend in March each year. Although no longer a part of the race route, it is still marked and groomed for public use. The system has three loops: two are 3 km long each; the third is 5 km long. A snowmobile trail crosses the ski trail.

For further information on the trail or the Finlandia, contact

Duane Payne, President, Minnesota Finlandia, Security Bank, Bemidji, MN 55601. 218-751-1510

See also Bemidji City Trail, page 46; Lake Bemidji State Park, page 60; Wolf Lake Resort, page 73.

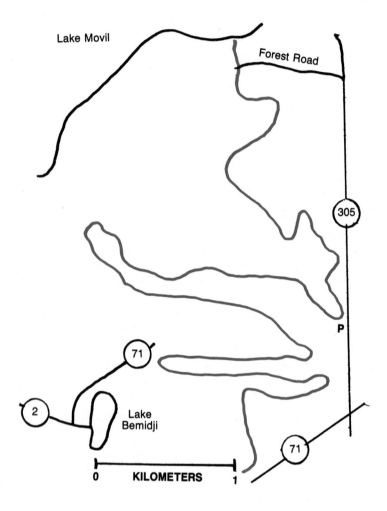

Lake Movil

Forest Road

305

P

71

2

Lake
Bemidji

71

0   KILOMETERS   1

MOVIL MAZE TRAIL

Old Mill State Park
Argyle, Minnesota
4.8 km (3 mi) of trails
beginner, intermediate

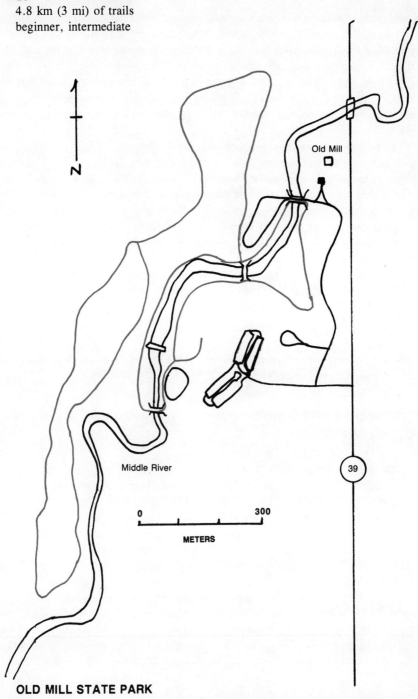

N

Old Mill

Middle River

0   300

METERS

39

OLD MILL STATE PARK

Old Mill State Park is located 13 miles east of Argyle and 11 miles west of New-folden on County Road 4 in Marshall County. It is the site of a grist mill that was built in 1889 by John Larson of native materials. It was operated by the Larson family for several years and then sold to the Skoglund brothers who ran the mill until 1937 when they sold it to the state. The rebuilt mill is now the focal point of the park, as is the restored log cabin adjacent to the mill. Since the early settler period of the Red River Valley, the mill has played an important part in the development of the area. Wheat and rye flour were ground in the mill, and a major oxcart route passed through the area that is now the park. These oxcart trains were notorious for the tremendous sound that they produced. Made entirely of wood, with ungreased axles, they could be heard for miles.

The park is surrounded entirely by developed cropland and is a primitive oasis, typical of the wild grasslands and deciduous woods seen by the first settlers in the area. The rolling terrain is located on the Middle River where an ancient beach ridge has been left by Glacial Lake Agassiz, which at one time covered the entire area. Ski trails cross the river at three points. They are adjacent to the snowmobile trails in the north end of the park and are intersected by these trails at two points. The remainder of the trails are situated in an isolated setting to the south of the park. All ski trails are intercon-nected and are marked and groomed.

Maps, parking, a picnic shelter,and toilets are in the park. There is also a sliding hill. Food and lodging are available in Argyle or Newfolden.

For further information, contact

Park Manager, Old Mill State Park, Route 1 Box 42, Argyle, MN 56713. 218-437-8174

Minnesota Department of Natural Resources, Division of Parks and Recreation, Box 39 Centennial Building, St. Paul, MN 55155. 612-296-4776

Pomme de Terre Trails
Dalton, Minnesota

9 km (5.6 mi) of trails

intermediate, advanced

Pomme de Terre Trails are located in Ottertail County, approximately 12 miles southeast of Fergus Falls, near the town of Dalton. From Fergus Falls, take Highway 210 east to County Road 33, turn south, and proceed on 33 past the Swan Lake Church. Continue southward on the Township Road. Turn east and south again to the trails. From Dalton go northwest on the Township Road approximately 2.25 miles. The trail-head is located just past the point where the road crosses the Pomme de Terre River. Ample parking is available.

The trails are marked and kept clean, but are not mechanically tracked and groomed. They are situated on a rough, hilly terrain and, consequently, are not suited to the novice. The trails all start at the warming house and go across the river and are arranged in four one-way loops. Skiers are asked to carefully observe the directional signs. The facility is open on Fridays, Saturdays, and Sundays; a $1.50 fee is charged of skiers. A warming house, Stugen Pä Kullen, is open when the trails are. Maps, water, and toilets are provided, although no ski rentals are available.

Food is available in Dalton or Fergus Falls; food, lodging, and rentals are available in Fergus Falls or Alexandria.

For further information, contact

Richard A. Fihn, Pomme de Terre Trails, Route 1 Box 314, Dalton, MN 56324. 218-589-8106

See also Maplewood State Park, page 64 and Spidahl's Ski Gård, page 69.

Red Lake Falls Club Ski Touring Trail
Red Lake Falls, Minnesota

32 km (20 mi) of trails
beginner, intermediate, advanced
You may enter the trail at either of two locations. The east end is situated at the Sportsman Park in Red Lake Falls; the west end is 4 miles northwest of Red Lake Falls on County Road 13.

Rated from beginner to advanced, the trail is marked, groomed, and partially tracked. It is located on rolling terrain adjacent to the river and involves long runs down the hills to flat land on the river bottoms.

Toilets and shelter are available; one may park either at the Sportsman Park or on the township road south of County Road 13. Food, lodging, and camping are avilable in Red Lake Falls.

For further information, contact

John B. Thibert, Red Lake Falls Ski Club, Box 176, Red Lake Falls, MN 56750. 218-253-2171

Spidahl's Ski Gård
Erhard, Minnesota

22.6 km (14 mi) of trails
beginner, intermediate, advanced
To reach Spidahl's, take County Road 1 northeast from Fergus Falls for 10 miles to the junction of County Road 43. Turn north on 43, go 4 miles to County Road 22, and turn east on 22. The entrance to the Ski Gård is immediately to the right on 22.

The Spidahls have developed seven different trails that wind through both hilly terrain forested with deciduous hardwoods and open rolling meadowland. All trails are clearly marked as to the degree of difficulty and are strictly one-way. They serve skiers of all abilities. The trails are groomed with a gyro-groomer and track-set with a National Track Setter. Approximately one-third of the trails are doubled-tracked. The system is entirely interconnected.

Beginner instruction is available, as are ski rentals for people of all ages and sizes. Rental fees are $6.75 per day or $4.75 for two hours. There is a trail fee of $2.00 per day. A large parking lot is close, and a warming room is located in the walk-out basement adjacent to the lot. This is also the location to check into the facility. The Ski Gård has a snack bar where light foods, hot cider, and cold pop are available. There are also toilets, waxing room, and retail ski shop that are open daily, 9:00 a.m. to dusk. It is an ideal setting for day group excursions and families.

For further information, contact

Liz and Walt Spidahl, Spidahl's Ski Gård, Route 1, Erhard, MN 56534. 218-763-5097

See also Maplewood State Park, page 64 and Pomme de Terre Trails, page 68.

Tamarac National Wildlife Refuge
Rochert, Minnesota

12.8 km (8 mi) of trails
beginner

PINE LAKE SKI TRAIL

Tamarac National Wildlife Refuge is 18 miles northeast of Detroit Lakes in Becker County. Drive east of Detroit Lakes on Highway 34 approximately 8 miles; then turn north on County Road 29; go through the town of Rochert to the Refuge. The entrance to the ski trail is located on County Road 29, just north of the junction with County Road 126.

Tamarac encompasses nearly 43,000 acres. Even in prehistoric times, it was an important life-sustaining area. The Refuge rice beds, which still exist, and the abundant fish and game that continue to thrive have been highly valued by people of all time periods. The stands of large red and white pine were logged by both lumber companies and homesteaders until little remained. Fires and agriculture and the companionate livestock grazing further disrupted the rich habitat. To reverse this trend, the Refuge was established by Executive Order in 1938. Duck stamp sales financed the purchase of the land, and efforts made by the Civilian Conservation Corps in the late 1930s produced the Refuge roads, trails, water control structures, and buildings. In the late 1960s, the Job Corps Conservation Center contributed greatly to Refuge development. Both winter and summer recreation are allowed if they do not adversely affect wildlife sanctuary and growth. Therefore, snowmobiles, all-terrain vehicles, and even camping are not permitted.

A terrain of alternating ridges and lakes formed by glacial ice make up the Refuge land. It is just west of a major continental divide, separating the Gulf of Mexico and Hudson Bay watersheds. Tamarac's waters run north to Hudson Bay through the Red River of the North via the Ottertail, Buffalo, and Egg Rivers.

Pine Lake Ski Trail is marked and has two loops; one circles Pine Lake. The Refuge staff groom it periodically. Situated on fairly level terrain, it nicely suits the novice skier. Various pine plantations and a scenic vista occur en route. There are toilets and a rest area on the trail, but no water is available. A parking area is located at the trailhead. No fees or permits are required of skiers. A map is available at Refuge Headquarters. Lodging, food, rentals, and camping are at hand in Detroit Lakes.

For further information, contact

Refuge Manager, Tamarac National Wildlife Refuge, Rochert, MN 56578. 218-847-2641

See also Becker County Trails, page 44 and Maplelag, page 63.

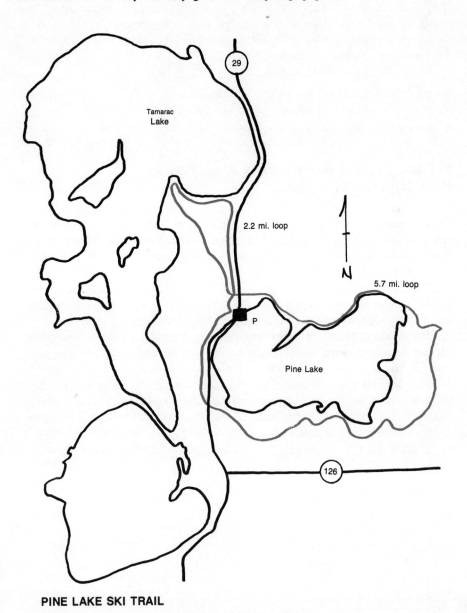

PINE LAKE SKI TRAIL

Ulen Park Trail
Ulen, Minnesota

4 km (2.5 mi) of trails

Ulen Park Trail is located in Clay County, 0.5 mile north of Ulen on Highway 32. Ulen is 16 miles north of Hawley, which is on Highway 10, east of Moorhead. The trail is marked but not groomed. There are pit toilets, shelter, and ample parking in the park. Camping is allowed. No fee is charged. Food is available in Ulen; both food and lodging are available in Hawley.

For further information, contact

Joseph Rikhus, Sr., Ulen, MN 56585. 218-596-8351

Marlys Burda, Secretary-Treasurer, Ulen, MN 56585. 218-596-8849

See also Buffalo River State Park, page 50.

Wilderness Bay Resort and Campground
Park Rapids, Minnesota

6.4 km (4 mi) of trails

To reach Wilderness Bay, go 14.8 miles north from Park Rapids on Highway 71, turn west on Boot Lake Drive, and go 1 mile to the first crossroads. Turn north and go 0.5 mile. The resort is located on Little Mantrap Lake, reputed by some to be the source of the Mississippi River.

The trails are located in a secluded, hilly, rolling terrain that is almost completely wooded. Guests and day visitors ski free. Snowmobiling is allowed, but the trails do not mix. The main lodge serves as a warming facility for skiers.

The resort can handle 44 guests. The American Plan is available by reservation. All cabins have hot and cold running water, modern toilet facilities, completely equipped kitchens (bring your own towels), and gas or oil heat. Showers are either in the cabins or in two central shower buildings. All bath and bed linens are furnished. Meals are served to groups by advance planning only. Babysitting and group rates are available. Pets are allowed if kept under control. Camping with hookups is available.

For further information, contact

Terry or Val Richardson, Wilderness Bay Resort and Campground, Itasca Star Route, Park Rapids, MN 56470. 218-732-4865

See also Itascatur Trails, page 56 and Itasca State Park, page 58.

Wolf Lake Resort
Bemidji, Minnesota

16 km (10 mi) of trails

beginner, intermediate, advanced

To reach Wolf Lake Resort from Bemidji, go 9 miles east on Highway 2, and take West Big Wolf Lake Road 2 miles north to the resort. From Cass Lake, go 5 miles west on Highway 2, and take West Big Wolf Lake Road 2 miles north to the resort.

Wolf Lake Resort is situated on the shores of Big Wolf Lake, one of the many lakes that are part of the Mississippi River system. The land in this area is extremely picturesque and affords the skier an opportunity to experience the great feeling of getting away from it all while still having modern comforts at the end of the day.

Ski trails wind through 400 beautiful acres of birch and pine in an area that is closed to snowmobiles, although snowmobiling takes place on the North Country Snowmobile Trail close by. Trails begin at the cottage doors and are marked, groomed, and track-set. They are set up in a loop system and will satisfy skiers of all abilities. Efforts have been made to encourage the presence of wildlife in the area. A complete line of quality rental equipment is available for people of all ages and sizes. The rental fee is $5.00 per person per day. Several other good cross-country trails are within a short driving distance from Wolf Lake Resort.

The Bjerkes have owned and operated the resort for several years. They have made great efforts to improve the establishment and cultivate its reputation as one of the cleanest, best-managed family resorts in the entire area. There are 16 winterized vacation cottages, complete with modern kitchens and bathrooms. The cottages are furnished with dishes, cooking equipment, a toaster, range, and refrigerator. Bed linens and blankets are furnished. Bath and dish towels are not included—they ask that guests bring their own. Cottage prices include the use of the whirlpool and sauna in the main lodge where there is a fireplace, jukebox, and indoor games. They sell snacks, pop, beer, ice, groceries, and lunches in the lodge also. No pets are allowed.

For further information, contact

Kermit or Mary Bjerke, Wolf Lake Resort, Route 3, Box 702-C, Bemidji, MN 56601. 218-751-5749

See also Bemidji City Trail, page 46 and Lake Bemidji State Park, page 60.

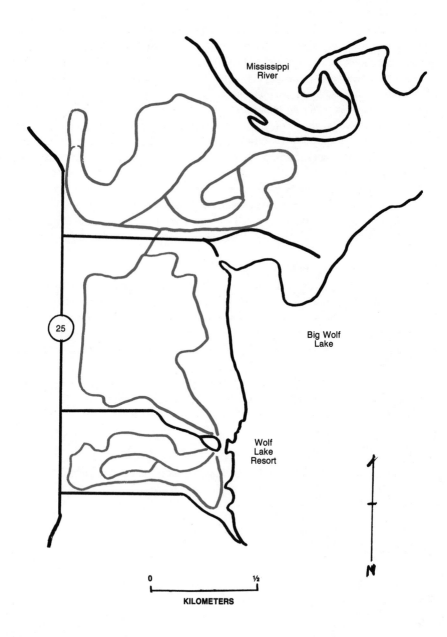

Mississippi River

25

Big Wolf Lake

Wolf Lake Resort

0   ½

KILOMETERS

N

WOLF LAKE RESORT

Zippel Bay State Park
Williams, Minnesota

1.6 km (1 mi) of trails
beginner

Zippel Bay State Park is located 10 miles northeast of Williams in Lake of the Woods County. On County Road 2 drive 5 miles north from Williams, then turn east on County Road 8, and travel another 5 miles to the park. The town of Williams is approximately 90 miles west of International Falls on Highway 11.

The park is situated on the south shore of Lake of the Woods, an important and conspicuous geographical feature of our state, comprising over 950,000 acres of water. It is of immense historical significance as well for, as early as 1700, voyageurs traveled this great lake, transporting supplies and articles of trade.

At one time it was believed that Lake of the Woods was actually two lakes. The enormous lower open area to the south, which is in Minnesota, was thought to be one lake and was called Sand Hill Lake—now it is named Traverse Bay. The northern part

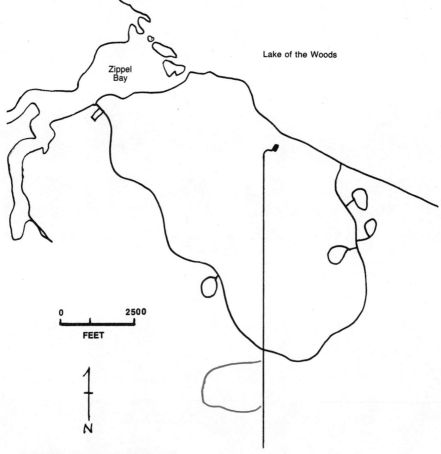

ZIPPEL BAY STATE PARK

of the lake, which is in Canada, is filled with a complicated network of over 14,000 islands. Naturally enough, the English name was Lake of the Islands. Eventually, the size of the lake became known, and it was renamed Lake of the Woods.

Zippel Bay leads into the lake and is named after a transplanted Canadian named William Zippel who ran a commercial fishing business on the bay in the late nineteenth century. His name achieved importance in the area and was chosen as the name for this state park.

The ski trail is a short novice trail. It is a marked loop and begins at the entry station to the park. A map is available. Snowshoeing is encouraged in the park. Snowmobiling is allowed, but only in a designated area away from the ski trail. Winter camping at primitive campsites is permitted. Toilets and parking are at hand for the visitor.

For further information, contact

Park Manager, Zippel Bay State Park, Williams, MN 56686. 218-783-6252, 218-783-4255

Minnesota Department of Natural Resources, Division of Parks and Recreation, Box 39 Centennial Building, St. Paul, MN 55155. 612-296-4776

REGION 2
NORTHEAST MINNESOTA

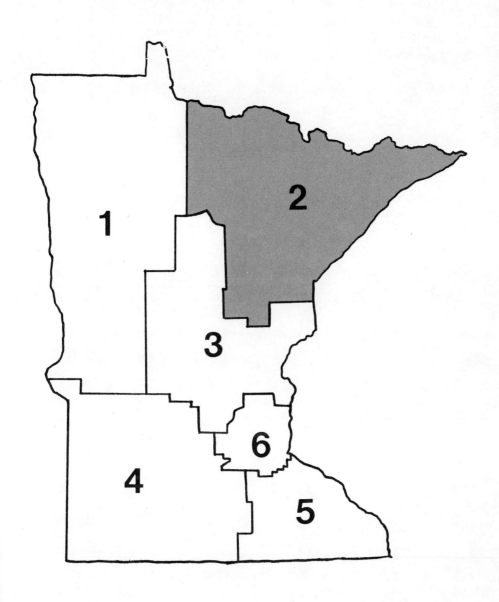

Aitkin County
Aitkin, Minnesota

There are three cross-country trails maintained by the Aitkin County Parks Commission.

BROWN LAKE SKI TOURING TRAIL
9.25 km (5.8 mi) of trails
intermediate

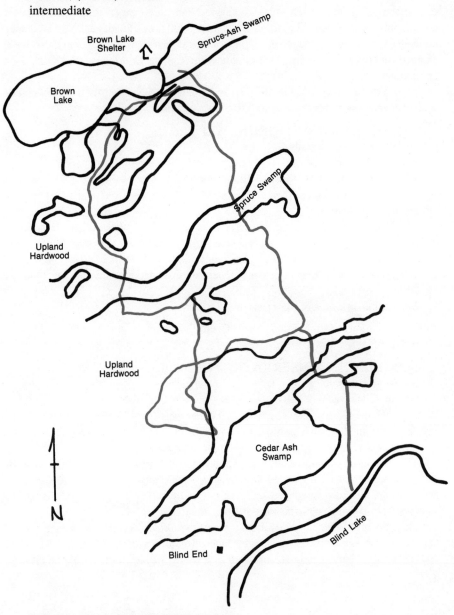

BROWN LAKE SKI TOURING TRAIL

Brown Lake Trail is located 11 miles north of Aitkin, a city that is 14 miles north of Mille Lacs Lake on Highway 169. To reach the trail, take County Road 1 north from town for 3 miles, then County Road 22 for 4 miles, then County Road 24 for another 4 miles to the trailhead, located on the north side of Blind Lake.

The trail is marked, groomed, and tracked. It winds through upland hardwood forests that skirt cedar-ash, spruce, and tamarack-spruce swamps, ending at Brown Lake. The trail consists of two loops, one large and one quite small. There is a shelter at trail's end where coffee and hot chocolate are served and toilets are available. This shelter is open only on weekends (Saturday, 10:00 a.m.–4:00 p.m.; Sunday, 1:00–4:00 p.m.), but may be open during the week by previous arrangement with the county. No fee is charged for trail use. The map is available at the County Courthouse in Aitkin. Food and lodging are at hand in Aitkin.

Snowmobiling is allowed in the area, and although the ski touring and snowmobile trails run in separate areas, they do cross at a few points.

NO ACHEN BICENTENNIAL SKI TRAIL
15 km (9.4 mil) of trails

intermediate, advanced

No Achen Trail, located just south of Aitkin, is reached by going 1.5 miles west of town from the stoplights, then turning south on Cemetery Road and traveling 0.75 mile to the trailhead.

The trails are marked and groomed and are set up in a pattern of two large loops and four small loops. They skirt several small lakes. Trail access is courtesy of several adjacent property owners, and skiers are requested to respect their privacy and property. A map is available at the County Courthouse in Aitkin. Lodging and food are available in town also.

For further information, contact

Aitkin County Parks Commission, Aitkin County Courthouse, Aitkin, MN 56431. 218-927-2102 ext. 33

LONG LAKE CONSERVATION CENTER
9.6 (6 mi) of trails

beginner, intermediate, advanced

To reach the Center, take Highway 210 either west from McGregor for 8 miles or east from the junction of Highways 169 and 210 for 7 miles to County Road 5. Turn north, and travel approximately 3 miles to the entrance.

This facility is a unique, full-time environmental learning center with a full staff and resource personnel interested in educating people in the conservation ethic. The programs are designed to educate children and adults alike. Thousands of elementary students have completed workshops at Long Lake.

Ski trails are situated on the hiking trails of the Center. They have been groomed, but are not marked or tracked. They meander through a variety of forest land, bogs, and meadows. There is a small track-set loop by the headquarters of the facility.

The Center offers food and lodging to groups only (minimum of 20 people) and can accommodate over 100 people. There is a dining-kitchen complex, and a modern lodge with private showers and baths. They offer instruction in ski touring as well as snowshoeing, igloo construction, wilderness cooking, natural shelter building, wild food collecting, orienteering, and many other fields.

The Center has a large variety of ski rental. A map is available. A snowmobile trail crosses over the ski trail at two points.

For further information, contact

Robert Schwaderer, Camp Director, Long Lake Conservation Center, Palisade, MN 56469. 218-768-4653

See also Savanna State Forest, Remote Lake Solitude Area, page 173 and Savanna Portage State Park, page 171.

Aurora Ranger District/Superior National Forest
Aurora, Minnesota

One trail is designated as a cross-country ski trail in the Aurora District of the Superior National Forest.

BIRD LAKE SKI TRAIL
28.8 km (18 mi) of trails
beginner, intermediate, advanced
Bird Lake Ski Trail runs from the east end of the city of Hoyt Lakes on County Road 565 in a southeasterly direction to Bird Lake, located on County Road 569, a road which intersects 565. Both roads are plowed regularly during the winter. The trail crosses other roadways that may be skied, but none is groomed or plowed unless winter logging operations are taking place in the area.

The trail winds through a characteristically beautiful Minnesota northwoods setting. It traverses both upland and lowland, passes through dense stands of aspen and birch, and crosses flat open bogs. The Bird Lake loop offers a challenge to more experienced skiers. The St. Louis River loop provides a flat course that is perfect for beginners or racers. Birch Run is a particularly pretty stretch of the trail. The Hush Lake portion is the only section that crosses a body of water. Motorized vehicles of any kind are prohibited on the trail, except Forest Service grooming vehicles. One outhouse is available on the trail. Shelters on both Lake Lillian and Bird Lake are to be built in the near future. Visitors may park at the trailhead in Hoyt Lakes or at the picnic ground on Bird Lake.

The staff at the Aurora Station encourage visitors to stop in to procure a map and to leave word of their plans to be out on the trail. There is no fee for trail use. Staff welcome comments and ideas concerning the trail so that they may better serve the public.

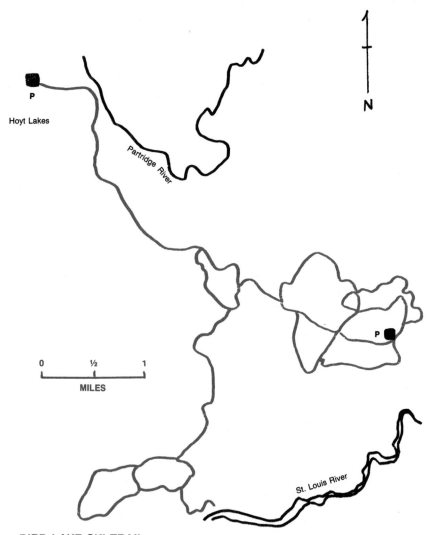

BIRD LAKE SKI TRAIL

For further information, contact

Aurora Ranger District, Superior National Forest, District Ranger, Box 391, Aurora, MN 55705. 218-229-3371

Forest Supervisor, Superior National Forest, P.O. Box 338, Duluth, MN 55801. 218-727-6692

See also Giant's Ridge, page 100.

Bearhead Lake State Park
Ely, Minnesota

13.6 km (8.5 mi) of trails

beginner, intermediate, advanced

Bearhead Lake State Park is located in St. Louis County, east of the city of Tower and southwest of the city of Ely. From Tower, take Highways 1 and 169 northeast for 9 miles, then turn south on County Road 128, and travel 6 miles to the park entrance. Or, from Ely, go southwest on Highways 1 and 169 for approximately 14 miles, then turn south on County Road 128, and travel 6 miles to the park entrance.

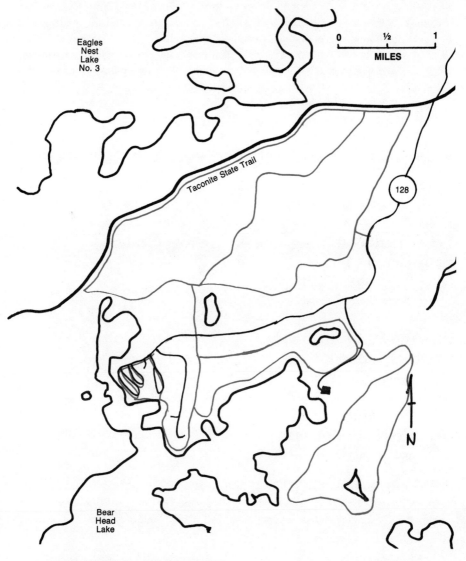

Eagles
Nest
Lake
No. 3

0   ½   1

MILES

Taconite State Trail

128

Bear
Head
Lake

N

BEARHEAD LAKE STATE PARK

The park's acreage surrounds Bearhead Lake and sits on the south shore of Eagles Nest Lake No. 3. Both lakes were formed by glacial action as were the rolling hills that fill the park. The bedrock of the park consists of ancient ely greenstone and giants range granite. Throughout the park, visitors will see this glacial debris of all shapes and sizes.

Around the turn of the century, this area was the site of much logging activity, but it was discontinued by 1911. Within the next two years, several fires swept the area, consuming the forest. Many of the old charred pine stumps can still be seen along the trails.

There are challenges for every skier at Bearhead Lake. Novices have 3.2 km (2 mi) of loops at the campgrounds. Those of intermediate ability may ski the Norberg Lake loop, which is 4.8 km (3 mi) long or ski up to the Taconite State Trail to either the Highline (6.4 km, 4 mi) or to the Cub Lake Trail (9.6 km, 6 mi). For the expert skier, the Becky Lake loop will provide a demanding course. It is 5.6 km (3.5 mi) long. Ski trails are shared in part with snowmobiles. Taconite State Trail crosses the north end of the park and intersects the ski trails at three points. From the picnic grounds to the Taconite Trail, skiers and snowmobilers have a common trail.

Maps, toilets, and parking are available at the park. Winter camping is allowed. Full tourist accommodations are available in either Ely or Tower.

For further information, contact

Park Manager, Bearhead Lake State Park, Star Route 2 Box 5700, Ely, MN 55731. 218-364-4253

Minnesota Department of Natural Resources, Division of Parks and Recreation, Box 39 Centennial Building, St. Paul, MN 55155. 612-296-4776

Bear Track Outfitting and Ski Touring Center
Bally Creek Camp
Grand Marais, Minnesota

See North Shore Mountains Ski Trail, page 167.

Best Western Cliff Dweller
Lutsen, Minnesota

See North Shore Mountains Ski Trail, page 158.

Blueberry Hills Ski Trail
Deer River, Minnesota

20 km (12.5 mi) of trails
intermediate, advanced

Blueberry Hills Ski Trail is located in Itasca County, 5 miles northeast of Deer River on County Road 144. To reach the trailhead, go 2 miles north from Deer River on Highway 6, 2 miles east on County Road 142, then 1 mile south on County Road 144.

The trail is rated half-intermediate, half-expert. Beginners are strongly discouraged from using it. It is designed for racing and is a network of interlocking loops. The trail is machine-groomed and track-set and is maintained by volunteer labor. A map is available at the trailhead.

For further information, contact

Rick Petrich, Route 1 Box 363A, Deer River, MN 56636. 218-246-2321 (evenings only)

See also Itasca County, Amen Lakes Trails, page 127 and Marcell Ranger District/Chippewa National Forest, Suomi Hills Recreation Area, page 143.

Bluefin Bay
Tofte, Minnesota

See North Shore Mountains Ski Trail, page 154.

Camp Mishawaka
Grand Rapids, Minnesota

14 km (8.75 mi) of trails

beginner, intermediate, advanced

To reach Camp Mishawaka, take Highway 169 south of Grand Rapids for 4 miles. Turn west at the camp sign, and drive 0.75 mile to the camp, following the signs.

The camp is a yearround facility, catering primarily to groups. Trails are fully signed and groomed. They suit skiers of all abilities and begin right at the camp. Maps are available. No fee is charged of guests; nonguests must pay $2.50 per person per day or $6.00 per family per day. Parking for nonguests is at the camp entrance.

In the summer, Mishawaka enlarges as a children's camp. In all other seasons, it can handle 50–55 people in its sleeping accommodations; the fully-winterized kitchen and dining room, with a stone fireplace, can supply meals to groups of 30–55 by prearrangement.

The Lodge sleeps 13 and is fully equipped with fireplace, dining room for 30, piano, fully equipped modern kitchen, two washrooms, shower, and heated waxing room also used to dry wet clothing. Three cabins each sleep 14 and have the same facilities as the Lodge, with the exception of dining room capacity, piano, and waxing room. Bed linens and towels are not provided, but they will rent blankets and pillows. Guests are encouraged to bring their own bedding. In addition, there are meeting areas at the camp.

Camp Mishawaka provides maps and trail information for many other groomed and tracked ski trails in the Grand Rapids area.

For further information, contact

Camp Mishawaka, c/o Nick Larsen, P.O. Box 368W, Grand Rapids, MN 55744. 218-326-5667

Nick and Sonia Larsen, 919-6th Avenue S.W., Grand Rapids, MN 55744. 218-326-5667

See also Golden Anniversary State Forest, page 101 and Sugar Hills Winter Resort, page 179.

Camp Northland (YMCA)
Ely, Minnesota

40 km (25 mi) of trails

intermediate, advanced

Camp Northland is located 15 miles northwest of Ely, just off the Echo Trail (County Road 116). From Highway 169 in Ely, turn north on County Road 88, travel a short distance to the Echo Trail, turn north on the Echo Trail, and travel to County Road 644 (the North Arm Road). Turn southwest on 644, and follow the road to the camp entrance.

The trails are in the Kawishiwi Ranger District of Superior National Forest; some portions are in the Boundary Waters Canoe Area Wilderness. Please refer to the Coxey Pond Trail description under Kawishiwi Ranger District in this region. Trails are maintained wilderness trails, but are not groomed specifically for ski touring. They involve traveling through forests and across lakes and are on challenging terrain. It is *not* novice skiing.

The camp offers food served family style in the dining room of the lodge where there is a fireplace. They can accommodate up to 80 people (6 cabins and 2 bunkhouses). They cater primarily to groups and families. There are modern toilets and showers as well as a sauna.

Nonguests may park at the trailhead at Northland. No parking or trail fee is charged of visitors.

For further information, contact

Director, YMCA Camp Northland, 1761 University Avenue, St. Paul, MN 55104. 612-645-2136

A very short distance away from Camp Northland are two other YMCA camps, Camp Du Nord and Camp Widjiwagan. Information may be obtained from their directors at the above address.

Cascade Lodge, Restaurant, and Ski Touring Center
Lutsen, Minnesota

See North Shore Mountains Ski Trail, page 163.

Cascade River State Park
Lutsen, Minnesota

See North Shore Mountains Ski Trail, page 165.

Chateau Leveaux, Condominium Motor Inn
Tofte, Minnesota

See North Shore Mountains Ski Trail, page 157.

Chippewa National Forest
Forest Service, United States Department of Agriculture
Headquarters, Cass Lake, Minnesota

Headquarters for two of the five Ranger Districts of the Chippewa National Forest are located in this region. They are Deer River Ranger District and Marcell Ranger District. The office of the Forest Supervisor is located at Cass Lake in Region 3. Please refer to the separate headings for both Deer River Ranger District and Marcell Ranger District.

Cobblestone Cabins and Ski Touring Center
Tofte, Minnesota

See North Shore Mountains Ski Trail, page 157.

Jay Cooke State Park
Carlton, Minnesota

44.8 km (28 mi) of trails

beginner, intermediate, advanced

Jay Cooke State Park is located in Carlton County, 3 miles east of the town of Carlton on Highway 210. It is approximately 10 miles southwest of Duluth. The park is traversed by the beautiful and impressive St. Louis River, a main focal point for visitors. The river has cut a spectacular gorge called the Dalles of the St. Louis. The river valley is wide and heavily forested. The St. Louis follows a tortuous course through steep gorges, creating numerous waterfalls framed by strange rock formations.

The near-9,000 acres of the state park are made up of a combination of slate, a dark-colored sedimentary rock called graywacke, and red clay. Throughout the ages, the slate and graywacke have been folded, fractured, and moved about by underground changes and pressures. After this initial deformation took place, molten lava was extruded through the fissures in the rock bed, and the resulting formations may still be seen in the river. In the park's midsection, the rock beds end abruptly and the river widens to form a gorge that is banked with red clay, deposited by ancient Glacial Lake Duluth that once covered the St. Louis River Valley.

Even as early as our country's colonial period, French fur trade thrived in the area of the park. The French and the Dakota Indians traded for many years. Eventually, the Ojibwe drove out the Dakota because of the ever-advancing westward settlement by the United States. Not long after this, the British and French began to clash over the trapping rights. Ultimately, the fur trade faded, and many towns built upon the trade died. The advent of the railroad brought large numbers of new settlers to the area, particularly those who wished to farm. But because of the rough, rocky terrain that comprises the area that is now the park, this land was never cleared. Initial acreage for the park was donated by the St. Louis Power Company in 1915.

The trails are marked and groomed for skiing. A map is available at park headquarters. Although there is novice skiing close to the headquarters and parking area, all of the trails are primarily intermediate to advanced in difficulty. The terrain is rugged and demanding. There are many sharp turns on the trails, and skiers should exercise caution and should not overestimate their abilities. However, with such geography comes rewards. The beauty of the setting is astounding. There are seven overlooks; enough cannot be said of the effect that the wildness of the river can have on the visitor. Although snowmobiling is allowed, the trails conflict only at the trailhead and at one point to the south of the park.

Winter camping is allowed. There are modern toilets, two heated shelters with fireplaces, and ample parking available. Supplies and lodging are at hand in Carlton.

For further information, contact

Park Manager, Jay Cooke State Park, Carlton, MN 55718. 218-384-4610
Minnesota Department of Natural Resources, Division of Parks and Recreation, Box 39 Centennial Building, St. Paul, MN 55155. 612-296-4776

See also Spirit Mountain, page 176; Duluth City Trails, page 93; Fond Du Lac State Forest, page 99.

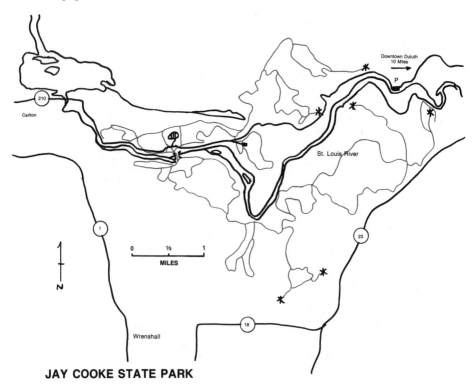

JAY COOKE STATE PARK

George H. Crosby-Manitou State Park
Finland, Minnesota

17.6 km (11 mi) of trails
advanced

George H. Crosby-Manitou State Park is on Highway 61, northeast of Duluth in Lake County. To reach the park, take Highway 1 northwest from Illgen City (approximately 60 miles from Duluth on 61) to the junction with County Road 7; take 7 northeast for 8 miles to the park entrance.

The rough, wild landscape of the park is its key feature. It has been produced by the rugged river basin of the Manitou River that rushes through the park on its way to Lake Superior. The North Shore Highlands were formed by the cooling of lava that volcanoes forced through fissures in the bedrock. At waterfalls and through the river gorge, visitors can see how thick the flows were. They are known as the Keweenawan Lava Flows. In a subsequent period, Glacial Lake Duluth covered the area and pushed and pulled at the rock formations. In retreat, the glacier left piles of rock and soil and lake that forms the watershed of the Manitou River.

Settlement of the land and the timber industry had their effect on wildlife found in the park today. Heavy logging and deliberate burning of forests to open the land for agriculture destroyed the habitat of the once abundant Woodland Caribou. It is now eliminated from the region. But these sudden environmental changes did provide an excellent habitat for deer that thrive on the new vegetative growth. With the deer came timber wolves. However, the relatively recent decline of the timber wolf has meant an ultimate decline in deer. Moose and black bears are common in the park. Visitors are urged not to approach them and to take intelligent precautions with storage and use of edible provisions.

The trails are rugged and demanding and should be attempted *only* by experienced skiers who are in excellent condition. The system is set up with two large and two small loops; the large loops are outermost in the network. One small loop skirts Bensen Lake where there are primitive toilets and a picnic area. There are campsites on the trail. Motorized vehicles are not allowed in the park.

Food and lodging are available in Silver Bay.

For further information, contact

Park Manager, George H. Crosby-Manitou State Park, Box 482, Finland, MN 55603. (no telephone)

Minnesota Department of Natural Resources, Division of Parks and Recreation, Box 39 Centennial Building, St. Paul, MN 55155. 612-296-4776

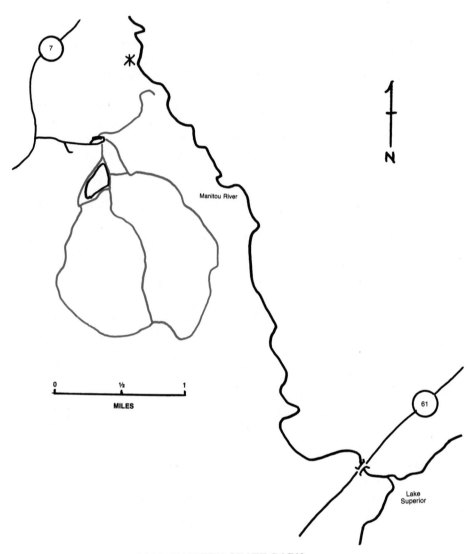

Manitou River

7

61

N

0   ½   1
MILES

Lake
Superior

GEORGE H. CROSBY-MANITOU STATE PARK

Deer River Ranger District/Chippewa National Forest
Deer River, Minnesota

There are two trails in the Deer River Ranger District that are suitable for cross-country skiing. Both are located in the Cut Foot Sioux Area, 18 miles northeast of Deer River.

CUT FOOT SIOUX TRAIL
35.2 km (22 mi) of trails

beginner, intermediate, advanced

To reach the trail, take Highway 46 northwest from Deer River for 18 miles to the Cut Foot Sioux Interpretive Center, located at the junction of Highway 46 and County Road 35. The trailhead is at this point. Another access point is farther northeast on Highway 46 at the Continental Divide Wayside.

The trails are marked, but are not groomed and tracked especially for ski touring as they are primarily designed for hiking. They are situated approximately on the route used by early fur traders and Indians as an overland portage between the Hudson Bay watersheds and all the watersheds that contribute to the Mississippi River. The terrain has great variety, and many lakes are involved in the layout of the trail. The northern part of the trail sits on the Subcontinental Divide. A short distance up the trail, parallel to County Road 35, is a small trail (0.4 km) to the Turtle Mound, made by prehistoric Woodland Indians. The mound cannot be distinguished easily in the winter, however. There are also carvings made by Indians in the 1860s at this location.

There are backcountry campsites, each with a tent pad, fire ring, and pit toilet. In the vicinity of the trail are five campgrounds, three resorts, and Cut Foot Sioux Interpretive Center.

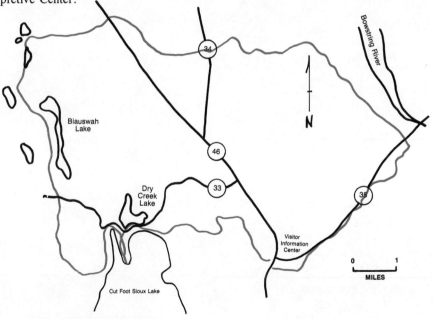

CUT FOOT SIOUX TRAIL

SIMPSON CREEK TRAIL

20.2 km (12.5 mi) of trails

beginner, intermediate

Directions to Simpson Creek Trail are the same as those to Cut Foot Sioux Trail. Access is at three main points, with several others on County Road 33, which joins Highway 46 just beyond the junction of 46 and County Road 35.

Simpson Creek Trail is intertwined with the southern part of Cut Foot Sioux Trail and is signed and groomed for skiing. The area is closed to motorized vehicles. The land on which the trails are located is surrounded on three sides by the Big and Little Cut Foot Lakes.

One backcountry campsite with a tent pad, fire ring, and pit toilet is located out on the trail. There are three campgrounds, two resorts, and Cut Foot Sioux Interpretive Center nearby.

For further information, contact

District Ranger, Chippewa National Forest, U.S. Forest Service, Deer River, MN 56636. 218-246-2123

Forest Supervisor, Chippewa National Forest, Cass Lake, MN 56633. 218-335-2226

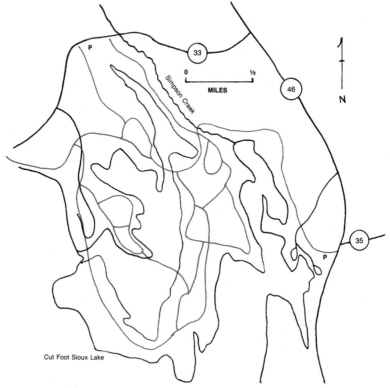

SIMPSON CREEK TRAIL

City of Duluth
Minnesota

There are six excellent cross-country trails maintained by the city of Duluth, the county seat of St. Louis County. They offer many opportunities for skiers of all abilities. All trails begin and end within Duluth city limits and are marked, groomed, and tracked. A state trail user permit is required to ski the trails. Maps are available. There are an unlimited variety of tourist accommodations in the Duluth area.

CHESTER BOWL
3 km (1.9 mi) of trails
advanced

The park is located off Skyline Parkway adjacent to the College of St. Scholastica. The trail is designed in a one-way loop for the racer, with demanding hills and turns. There is an overlook of Lake Superior. This is also an alpine facility with two ski jumps. A chalet is available.

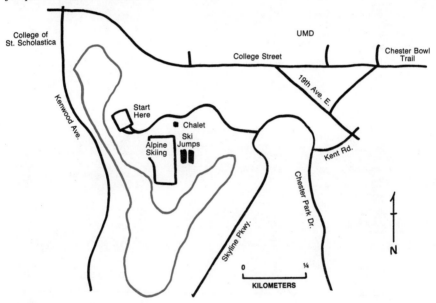

CHESTER BOWL TRAIL

HARTLEY
5 km (3.1 mi) of trails
beginner, intermediate

The Hartley system has two trailheads: at the end of Fairmont Street off Woodland Avenue and at the end of Hartley Road off Arrowhead Road. In the system are basically two main loops that are situated on a gentle, rambling landscape. The north-south routes on the outer loop offer more hills. Skiers should be advised that skiing early or late in the season may be dangerous here because the trail needs snow at least a foot deep for a safety cushion. It is a single-tracked trail. A snowmobile trail passes to the west end but does not conflict with the ski trails.

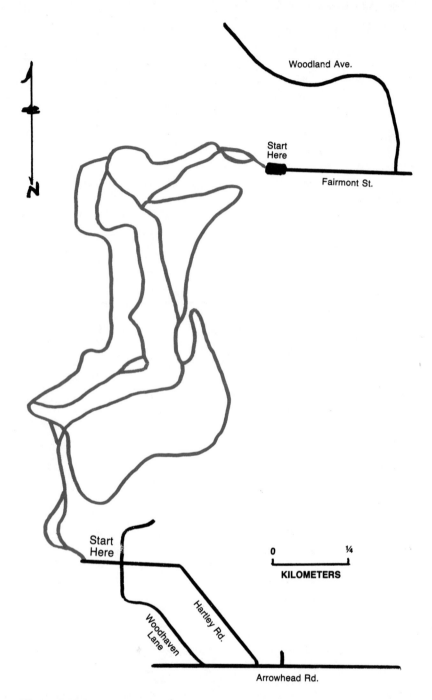

Woodland Ave.

Start
Here

Fairmont St.

Start
Here

0   ¼
KILOMETERS

Hartley Rd.

Woodhaven
Lane

Arrowhead Rd.

HARTLEY TRAIL

LESTER-AMITY

15 km (9.4 mi) of trails

beginner, intermediate, advanced

The trailhead of Lester-Amity is located at the junction of East Superior Street and Lester River Road at the Lester Park Pavillion. Only a small portion of the system is for beginners, and it basically involves the initial loop. There is a scenic overlook on this segment. Most trails are intermediate and advanced. There are many shortcuts in the loops. The hilly terrain is situated in forests of aspen, birch, and pine. A snowmobile trail crosses the trails at many points.

Lester Park Golf Course Trail is connected to Lester-Amity Trails.

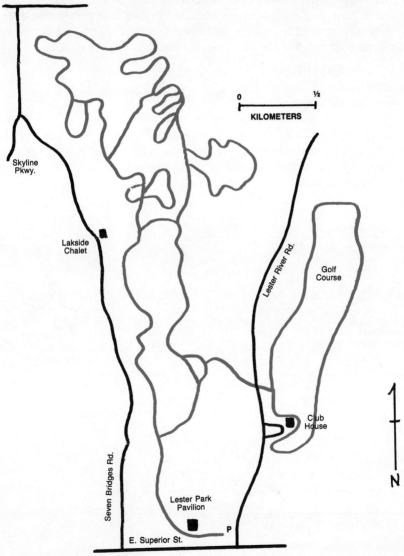

LESTER-AMITY TRAIL

LESTER PARK GOLF COURSE
4 km (2.5 mi) of trails

beginner

The trail is located across Lester River Road from Lester-Amity Trails. The two systems are interconnected. Parking is available at the clubhouse. Please refer to the Lester-Amity map.

PIEDMONT
4 km (2.5 mi) of trails

beginner, intermediate

The trailhead of Piedmont is located at the intersection of Adirondack Street and Hutchinson Road. It is a one-way loop, intersected by two short passes. One of the three rest stops on the trail has a scenic overlook. A snowmobile trail crosses the ski trail just at the trailhead, but otherwise does not interfere with the skiing.

MAGNEY-SNIVELY
10 km (6.25 mi) of trails

intermediate, advanced

The trailhead is located off Boundary Avenue near Spirit Mountain. It is a demanding trail, situated on rugged terrain, and beginners should not attempt it. There are large hills involved in the system. The area is covered with a deciduous hardwood forest. The trail is set up in a clockwise loop with a shortcut. A snowmobile trail crosses the ski trail at the trailhead and at a point adjacent to the cutoff.

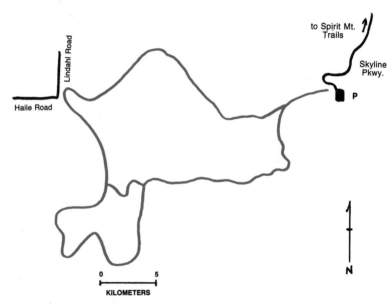

MAGNEY-SNIVELY TRAIL

For further information, contact

Tim Howard, Duluth Parks and Recreation Department, Room 208 City Hall, Duluth, MN 55808. 218-723-3337

See also Spirit Mountain, page 176 and Jay Cooke State Park, page 87.

City of Ely
Minnesota

HIDDEN VALLEY SKI AREA
10.4 km (6.5 mi) of trails

This city-owned and maintained trail is machine-groomed and tracked. It is located 1 mile east of Ely on Highway 169. Ski instruction is available. This is also a downhill facility and has a 60-meter olympic caliber ski jump.

For further information, contact

Ely Ski Club, P.O. Box 475, Ely, MN 55731. 218-365-5543
Hidden Valley, Ely, MN 55731. 218-365-3097

See also Bearhead Lake State Park, page 83; Camp Northland (YMCA), page 86; Kawishiwi Ranger District, page 130.

Fenstad's Resort
Little Marais, Minnesota

See North Shore Mountains Ski Trail, page 151.

Finland State Forest
Two Harbors, Minnesota

WOODLAND CARIBOU SKI TRAIL
32 km (20 mi) of trails
intermediate

Finland State Forest is located in south central Lake County and southwestern Cook County. It overlaps the southeastern corner of the Superior National Forest. It is accessible from Highway 61 on the North Shore of Lake Superior by traveling on either County Road 2 north from Two Harbors or on Highway 1 northwest from Illgen City. The preferable route to the Woodland Caribou Ski Trail is County Road 2. The trailhead is 38 miles north of Two Harbors.

The Forest was established in 1933 for timber production and harvesting of related forest products, to provide an area for recreation, to protect watersheds, and to preserve and assure continued growth of distinctive and often rare species of plant and animal life. The area is managed by state, federal, and county agencies to provide ongoing production of forest resources and to maintain and improve wildlife habitat. The area surrounding the trail was the site of the last stronghold of Woodland Caribou in Minnesota, before they were eliminated in the northwoods around the turn of the century. The Laurentian Divide, a major Minnesota watershed, meanders through the trail.

The ski trail consists of two loops with two spurs. It is marked and regularly maintained. Although the terrain is quite level, the trail is fairly difficult because of its length. There is a scenic overlook on the trail section between Bonga and Lobo Lakes. A shelter is situated on the outer limits of the larger loop. An outdoor toilet and parking are available at the access point.

For further information, contact

Finland State Forest, Woodland Caribou Cross-Country Ski Trail, City Hall, Two Harbors, MN 56616. 218-723-4669

Minnesota Department of Natural Resources, Division of Forestry, Box 44 Centennial Building, St. Paul, MN 55155. 612-296-4491

See also Isabella Ranger District, page 123 and National Forest Lodge, page 148.

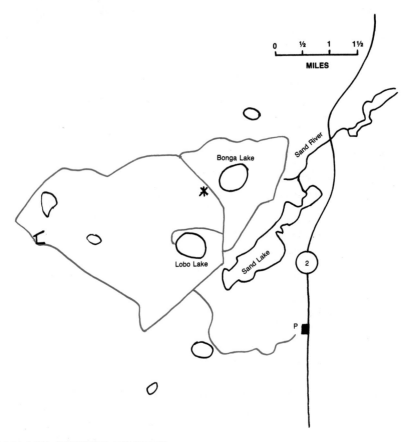

WOODLAND CARIBOU SKI TRAIL

Fond Du Lac State Forest
Cromwell, Minnesota

17.6 km (11 mi) of trails

beginner, intermediate, advanced

Fond Du Lac State Forest is located to the northeast, east, and southeast of the town of Cromwell, in north central Carlton County and south central St. Louis County. Cromwell is on Highway 210, 20 miles west of the Carlton exit on Interstate 35. The Ranger Station is just north of Cromwell on Highway 23.

The access point to the ski trails is approximately 5 miles east and north on County Road 120, a short distance north of the Lookout Tower. The trails have an even mix of levels of difficulty and are marked and groomed. The terrain is flat to rolling. The lowlands are peat bogs and are covered with tamarack, cedar, and spruce. The uplands are forested with maple, aspen, birch, and red, white, and jack pine. There is a shelter on the seven-loop trail that is located by a small lake. Parking is available at the trailhead.

A snowmobile trail system converges and passes through the middle, also the largest, loop. However, snowmobilers have a separate access point located at the Lookout Tower.

For further information, contact

DNR District Forester, Fond Du Lac State Forest, Cromwell, MN 55767. 218-644-3664

Minnesota Department of Natural Resources, Division of Forestry, Box 44 Centennial Building, St. Paul, MN 55155. 612-296-4491

See also Jay Cooke State Park, page 87 and Moose Lake Recreation Area, page 147.

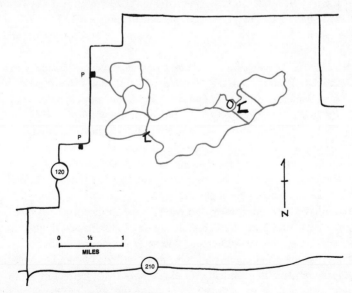

FOND DU LAC STATE FOREST

Gateway Hungry Jack Lodge
Grand Marais, Minnesota

34 km (21.2 mi) of trails

beginner, intermediate, advanced

During the skiing season of 1984–85, Hungry Jack will be closed. But it will re-open the following year to cross-country skiers. It deserves mention because of its fine facilities and the availability of all types of marked and groomed trails. Ski rentals, instruction, and maps are available. Other activities such as snowshoeing and ice fishing are encouraged. There are housekeeping cabins, a lounge, and a dining room at the Lodge.

The facility is located 29 miles up the Gunflint Trail (County Road 12) from Grand Marais. Turn on Hungry Jack Road (County Road 65), and travel 2.5 miles to the Lodge.

For further information, contact

Gateway Hungry Jack Lodge, GTHJ Box 39, Grand Marais, MN 55604. 218-388-2265

See also Golden Eagle Lodge, page 102; Gunflint Area Cross-Country Ski-Thru Program, page 115; Nor' Wester Lodge, page 170.

Giant's Ridge
Biwabik, Minnesota

45 km (28.1 mi) of trails

beginner, intermediate, advanced

Giant's Ridge Ski Area is located in St. Louis County, approximately 5 miles northeast of the town of Biwabik, on County Road 416. Take Highway 135 east and northeast from Virginia to Biwabik. Continue through Biwabik on 135 for 1.5 miles until you see the Giant's Ridge sign. Turn left at the sign (County Road 416), and proceed to the facility.

The Iron Range Resources and Rehabilitation Board (IRRRB) has purchased the Giant's Ridge Ski Facility and will develop downhill and cross-country ski trails. Things are in both planning and developmental stages, but work is proceeding at a swift pace, and the facility will be open by the winter of 1984–85.

Of the 45 km of trails, 25 km (15.6 mi) will be designed for competition. These will be double-tracked and situated on variable terrain. The remaining 20 km (12.5 mi) are for general recreation and will be situated on variable terrain, ranging in difficulty from novice to expert. They will also be groomed and double-tracked. A portion of trail (2.5 km) will be illuminated for night use.

The trails have been designed by Al Merrill, the former head ski coach at Dartmouth College, who designed the trail system at the Lake Placid Olympic Course and is presently designing the 1988 Olympic Course at Calgary, Canada.

In addition to the cross-country system, there will also be an Olympic Biathalon Course. There are plans to eventually develop a speed-skating facility of first-quality specifications. This will be the ultimate training site for skiers of Olympic caliber and, in the future, for the country's best speed skaters. It will be an important feather in Minnesota's cap.

Food, ski rentals, and parking are available at the Giant's Ridge chalet. Lodging and ski packages are available at area motels in the towns of Aurora, Biwabik, Eveleth, and Virginia.

For further information, contact

Giant's Ridge Ski Area, P.O. Box 190, Biwabik, MN 55708. 218-865-4620

Iron Range Resources and Rehabilitation Board, c/o Mike Gentile, P.O. Box 441, Eveleth, MN 55734. 218-744-2993

Please note: For summer use of the trails, roller skis are available for rent at Saransen's in Aurora (218-741-7920, c/o John Jeffrey).

See also Virginia Ranger District, Wynne Creek Ski Trail, page 184.

Golden Anniversary State Forest
Grand Rapids, Minnesota

Golden Anniversary State Forest is located in Itasca County, about 8 miles southeast of Grand Rapids. From Grand Rapids, follow County Road 3 (Great River Road). If coming from the south, take Highway 200 to County Road 3, and travel northwest to the Forest. It was established in 1961 to commemorate the golden anniversary of the Division of Forestry. Its terrain is gently rolling and is wooded with aspen, cedar, northern hardwoods, Norway and white pine, and spruce-fir, providing a perfect habitat for a variety of wildlife. It has a total acreage of approximately 6,800 acres, managed by the Division of Forestry of the Department of Natural Resources and by Itasca County. State forests exist to provide regulated production and harvest of timber and related crops, sites for outdoor recreation, to protect watersheds, and to preserve and maintain species of plants and animals that are distinctive and often rare.

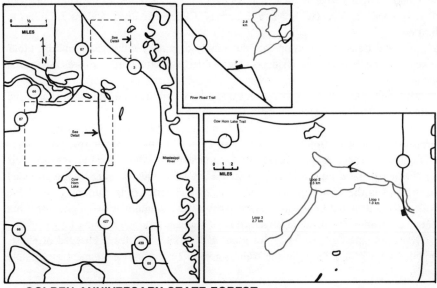

GOLDEN ANNIVERSARY STATE FOREST

COWHORN LAKE TRAIL
7.5 km (4.7 mi) of trails

beginner, intermediate

To reach the trailhead, take County Road 3 southeast of Grand Rapids approximately 5 miles, then turn south on County Road 67. Travel 2 miles to County Road 427. Turn southeast on 427, and go nearly 2 miles to the access point. Parking is available at this location. The trail is comprised of three loops. There is a shelter at the middle loop. A large winter deer yarding area is being maintained near Cowhorn Lake.

RIVER ROAD TRAIL
2.8 km (1.75 mi) of trails

beginner, intermediate

The trailhead is located approximately 1 mile southeast of the junction of County Roads 3 and 67 on County Road 3. Parking is available at this location. The trail is a meandering loop. It crosses a plank bridge and passes by McKinley Lake.

For further information, contact

Golden Anniversary State Forest, 1201 East Highway 2, Grand Rapids, MN 55744. 218-327-1734

Minnesota Department of Natural Resources, Division of Forestry, Box 44 Centennial Building, St. Paul, MN 55155. 612-296-4491

See also Camp Mishawaka, page 85 and Sugar Hills Winter Resort, page 179.

Golden Eagle Lodge
Grand Marais, Minnesota
50 km (31.3 mi) of trails

beginner, intermediate, advanced

Golden Eagle Lodge is located in Cook County, 28 miles up the Gunflint Trail (County Road 12) from Grand Marais. Turn on Clearwater Road, and go 3.5 miles to the Lodge.

John and Irene Baumann operate this family-oriented facility yearround on Flour Lake where they are the only residents. This wilderness setting provides welcome peace and solitude.

The trails are entirely groomed and tracked. All are marked and start right at the cabin doors. The terrain ranges from flat to hilly.

There are two and three bedroom modern housekeeping cabins that are completely furnished, some with fireplace stoves. Two cabins are fully barrier free. All cabins have refrigerator and range. Dishes, cooking utensils, bedding, and one set of towels per person per week are furnished. A sauna is available. Outside plug-ins are provided for vehicles in the winter (please bring your own electric cord). Parking is available by the cabins or in the Lodge lot. Guests must stay a minimum of two nights for cabin rental. Baumanns can make arrangements for suppers at a neighboring lodge.

Nonguests are charged $3.50 for maps and parking. No fee is charged of guests or those staying at a lodge in the trail system. Rental of ski equipment is possible nearby.

For further information, contact

Golden Eagle Lodge, John or Irene Baumann, Box 27, Grand Marais, MN 55604. 218-388-2203

See also Gateway Hungry Jack Lodge, page 100; Nor' Wester Lodge, page 170; Gunflint Area Ski-Thru Program, page 115.

Gooseberry Falls State Park
Two Harbors, Minnesota

22 km (13.8 mi) of trails

beginner, intermediate, advanced

Gooseberry Falls State Park is located in Lake County along the North Shore. It is 12 miles northeast from Two Harbors on Highway 61. The Gooseberry River plunges to Lake Superior through the park, from its northwest boundary to its southeast perimeter, the rugged shoreline of the lake. On its trip, the river encounters five waterfalls. Four of them are below the bridge on Highway 61, where the water drops a total of 170 feet.

The present landscape of the park began to form over 700 million years ago when volcanoes erupted, spewing lava over existing rock to form new bedrock. This hardened lava may be seen at the Upper and Lower Falls and along the lake shoreline south of the river.

The volcanic period was followed by a period in which glaciers repeatedly pushed and pulled on the area, exerting tremendous force on the land forms. When the final retreat occurred, melted ice formed the ancient Glacial Lake Duluth. As this lake receded, it deposited sediment and soil that fostered new plant life on the rocky terrain.

Gooseberry River appeared on maps as early as 1670 and was probably named after the French explorer Shur des Groseillers. It developed into a commercial and sport fishing area by the 1870s, and, by the 1890s it was an important logging area for the growing timber industry. There were two railroad lines in the park at this time to carry the pine to the lake where it was rafted to sawmills. When lumbering began in the area nearly 100 years ago, the land was covered with gigantic white pines. The people of the day thought that the trees were endlessly available, and they logged with such intense pressure that this type of pine disappeared by the early 1920s. Stumps of the trees may still be seen on the trails, where the present forest is comprised of other conifers, aspen, and birch.

The park was established in 1933, and in the following year the Civilian Conservation Corps began to develop the facility. Crews built the park's handsome stone buildings and laid out the campground, picnic ground, and trails.

There are five main trails at the park: Gitchi Gummi, Voyageur, Upper Falls, and Upper and Lower Rim Trails. They are all marked and groomed and offer ascents and descents through the spectacular North Shore highland setting. There are nine overlooks on the trails, one with a shelter. Detailed maps on the trails are available at park headquarters. The trails on the lakeside of Highway 61 are for the novice; the trails on the opposite side are rated as entirely intermediate and advanced. A snowmobile trail passes through the park, with minimal interference to the ski trails.

Winter camping is allowed. Parking, toilets, and water are available within the park. Food and lodging are at hand in Two Harbors.

For further information, contact

Park Manager, Gooseberry Falls State Park, East Star Route, Two Harbors, MN 55616. 218-834-3855

Minnesota Department of Natural Resources, Division of Parks and Recreation, Box 39 Centennial Building, St. Paul, MN 55155. 612-296-4776

See also Split Rock Lighthouse State Park, page 177 and Two Harbors City Trail, page 183.

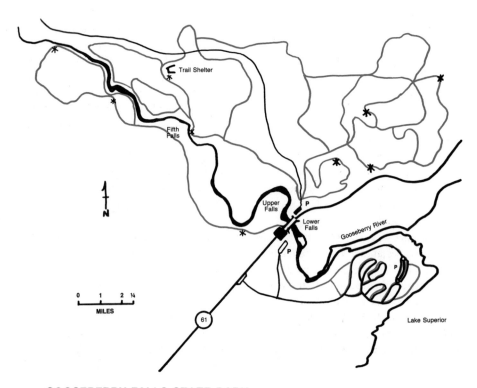

GOOSEBERRY FALLS STATE PARK

Grand Mound Center
International Falls, Minnesota

4 km (2.5 mi) of trails

intermediate

Grand Mound Center is located 17 miles west of International Falls on Highway 11. This facility is administered by the Minnesota Historical Society and includes an interpretive center.

In 1857, a group of Canadian explorers on its way to the Red River stopped by the second rapids of the Rainy River to record the presence of "two immense mounds." These Indian burial mounds, which seemed so unusual to the Canadians were only two of at least 10,000 mounds that existed in Minnesota alone before white settlers began changing the landscape. They were once a common sight in the river valleys of the Midwest. Some mounds were not striking in appearance, but many were impressive earthen abstractions of serpents and animals. A few were as enormous and magnificent as Egyptian pyramids.

Explorers and early settlers recklessly excavated the mounds and ransacked them for treasures. Steamboats from Fort Frances, Ontario used to make special stops at the Grand Mound so that passengers could indulge in recreational digging. As expected, they created romantic myths of lost civilizations in connection with the Mounds. But in 1894, the Smithsonian Institution's Bureau of Ethnology published conclusive proof that not only put to rest all the fanciful legends, but also confirmed that the Mound Builders were ancestors of the American Indian.

Painstaking archaeological study over the following years has revealed, as the Historical Society states, that these were "peoples whose hands not only moved mountains of earth but created art of enduring beauty; peoples who contrived elaborate funeral rituals and a complex spiritual life from the mysteries of nature; and peoples, like the Laurel, the builders of Grand Mound, who adapted, innovated, and endured in the harsh latitudes of the northern lake-forest environment."

Artifacts of the Laurel Culture (500 B.C.–800 A.D.) and the later Blackduck Culture (800–1400 A.D.), such as tools, pottery, and weapons, are on display at the Interpretive Center.

The nature trail at the Center doubles as a ski trail in the winter. It is situated on mostly level terrain, with some short steep hills, and is groomed and tracked for touring. The trail bypasses five mounds, including the Grand Mound. A one-way trail with loops; it meanders primarily through a wooded landscape that is located on a point of land at the confluence of the Rainy and Big Fork Rivers.

Maps, toilets, and water are available at the Center, open Saturdays and Sundays 10 a.m.–4 p.m. The parking lot is located at the Center also. There is no admission fee for the Interpretive Center or use of the trails. Food, lodging, and ski rentals are available in International Falls.

For further information, contact

Michael K. Budak, Manager, Grand Mound Center, Route 7 Box 453, International Falls, MN 56649. 218-279-3332

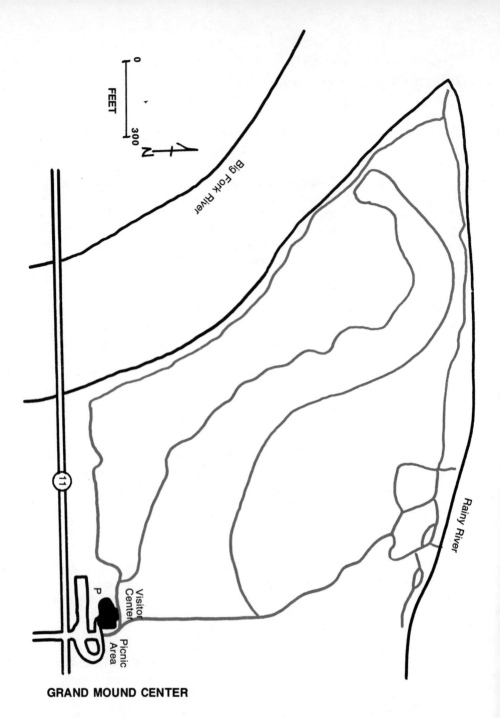

GRAND MOUND CENTER

See also Kabetogama State Forest, Ash River Falls Ski Trail, page 128 and Voyageurs National Park, Black Bay Ski Trail, page 186.

Grand Portage Lodge and Conference Center
Grand Portage, Minnesota

120 km (75 mi) of trails

beginner, intermediate, advanced

Grand Portage is 150 miles northeast of Duluth and 40 miles southwest of Thunder Bay, Canada, on Highway 61. The town is at the very tip of northeastern Minnesota. The landscape is rugged and beautiful, a sharp contrast to the empty open vistas of Lake Superior.

There are thirteen trails at Grand Portage Lodge. In addition, there is Grand Portage Trail, which is not maintained by the Lodge. Its trailhead is at the Grand Portage National Monument. The Lodge's trail system is maintained regularly with state-of-the-art mechanical grooming and track-setting equipment. All trails are clearly marked. Some portions of the trails are two-way. Skiers are asked to observe directional and caution signs and to sign out and in at the Trail Register in the lobby of the Lodge.

Equipment rentals and guide service are available for skiers. No trail fee is charged of Lodge guests. The Lodge has sauna, swimming pool, restaurant, and ample parking. All accommodations are top-notch.

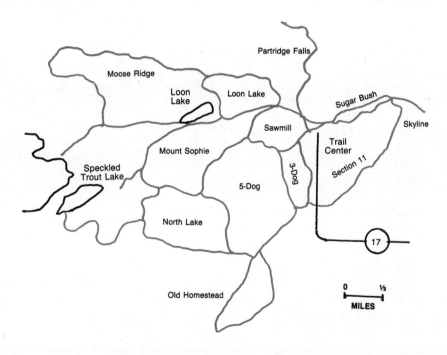

GRAND PORTAGE TRAIL SYSTEM

PORTAGE VALLEY SKI TRAIL

7.2 km (4.5 mi) of trails

beginner, intermediate

This trail begins at the front door of the Grand Portage Lodge and gives access to the entire trail system via the Skyline Trail. Portage Valley Trail is a loop that moves over flat to gently rolling terrain. At the halfway point of this trail, advanced skiers can take the Skyline Trail Cutoff to the Trail Center trailhead, 5 miles west of the Lodge.

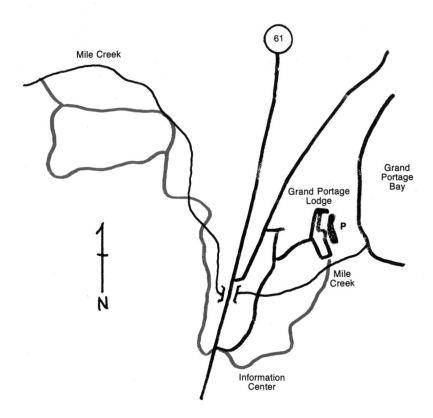

PORTAGE VALLEY SKI TRAIL

SKYLINE TRAIL

9.75 km (6.5 mi) of trails

advanced

This trail is rated for advanced skiers because of many steep climbs and fast downhill runs. The trail's distance is measured from the Lodge to the Trail Center. Portions of this trail follow the old route that the Ojibwe people once used to travel to maple sugaring camps near Swamp Lake. This is a very scenic trail as well as a very challenging one. It is a two-way trail; when climbing the hills, yield to skiers coming downhill!

The next trails begin and end at the main trailhead (Trail Center). To reach Trail Center, go south on Highway 61 to the County Road 17 turnoff, turn right, and continue 5 miles to the parking area at Trail Center.

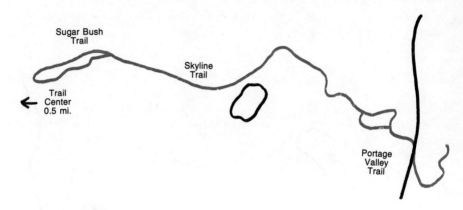

SKYLINE TRAIL

SUGAR BUSH SKI TRAIL
4 km (2.5 mi) of trails
beginner

The halfway point of this loop trail is a clearing where Sugar Bush Trail turns sharply to the left and Skyline Trail goes straight ahead. The forest canopy along this trail is sugar maple, the same tree that produces the sap for pure maple syrup and maple sugar candy.

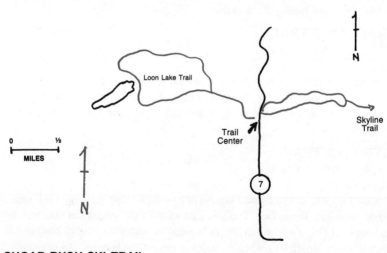

SUGAR BUSH SKI TRAIL

LOON LAKE SKI TRAIL
8 km (5 mi) of trails
intermediate
While on this loop trail, the skier is following a section of the legendary Sugar Bush or Skyline Trails. This is maple country where for centuries Ojibwe people have come to collect sap for boiling into maple syrup.

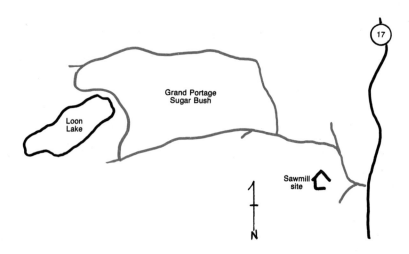

LOON LAKE SKI TRAIL

SAWMILL TRAIL
4 km (2.5 mi) of trails
beginner
This pleasant loop is well-suited for a quick warmup trip for the distance skier or a leisurely afternoon outing for a family.

THREE DOG TRAIL
6.7 km (4.2 mi) of trails
beginner
This very scenic trail is set up in a loop and, for over half of its length, meanders through a young forest of pure spruce and pine. Be sure to have someone take your picture next to the upturned tangle of weathered cedar roots that marks the halfway point.

FIVE DOG TRAIL
9.6 km (6 mi) of trails
intermediate
This trail is rated intermediate because of its length. One weekend each year, Five Dog Trail, with the Three Dog Trail, is part of the race course for the now famous Rendezvous Sled Dog Race, when the trails are alive with the sound of hissing dog sled runners and eager Siberian purebreds straining against the harness. As one of the most

beautiful ski trails in the Grand Portage system, its rolling terrain and gentle downhill runs are well-suited to ski touring.

SECTION 11 SKI TRAIL
10.4 km (6.5 mi) of trails
intermediate

This loop trail follows Loon Lake, Sawmill, and Three Dog Trails before heading east at the Hollow Rock Creek crossing. After crossing County Road 17, it winds through a mixed forest of aspen, spruce, birch, and maple before joining Sugar Bush Trail. Skiers pass several beaver ponds along this stretch, good places for pictures.

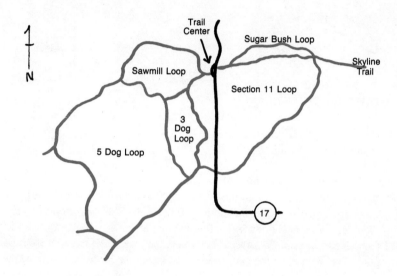

SAWMILL, THREE DOG, FIVE DOG, AND SECTION 11 TRAILS

MOOSE RIDGE TRAIL
16 km (10 mi) of trails
intermediate, advanced

This loop trail receives its advanced rating due to its length. It passes through some of the wildest country in the state; the primeval cedar swamps near the middle are a favorite winter haunt of the majestic moose. The terrain along the trail alternates between flat and gently rolling. This route combines the exciting downhill runs and breathtaking views of Loon Lake Trail with the solitude and more challenging distance of Moose Ridge Trail.

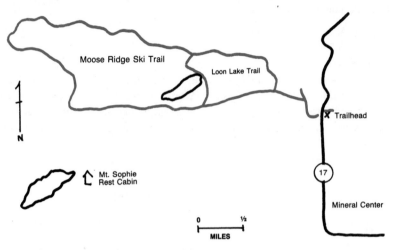

MOOSE RIDGE TRAIL

MOUNT SOPHIE SKI TRAIL
11.2 km (7 mi) of trails

intermediate

One of the most scenic in all of Minnesota, this trail is arranged in a loop. The terrain is gently rolling over most of the trail except for the one steep hill marked on the map; skiers are urged to use extra caution on this run. The main point of interest is Mount Sophie, the highest point of land on the Grand Portage Indian Reservation (el. 1,814 feet). Near the summit a rest cabin greets the skier, and from its front porch a spectacular view of some of the most rugged country in the Midwest is offered the visitor.

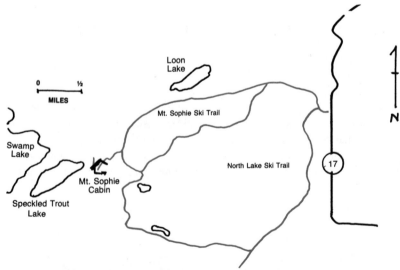

MOUNT SOPHIE AND NORTH LAKE SKI TRAILS

NORTH LAKE SKI TRAIL
14.4 km (9 mi) of trails
intermediate
The terrain of this loop trail is gently rolling. If you are feeling adventurous, take a side trip off this trail to Trout Lake or Taylor Lake. You may have to break trail here as this is not a regular part of the groomed trail system.

OLD HOMESTEAD SKI TRAIL
13.6 km (8.5 mi) of trails
intermediate
This loop trail is graced by two beautiful overlooks, the second providing a fine view of Lake Superior from amidst a young red pine plantation.

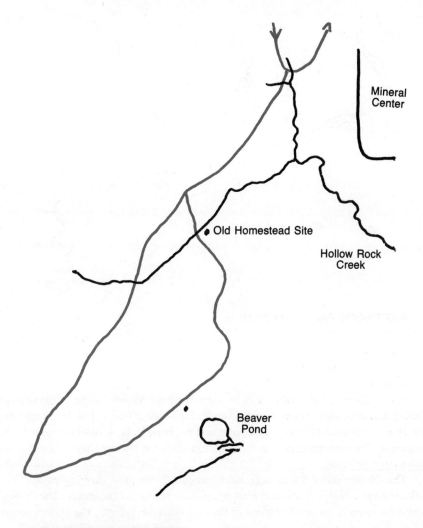

OLD HOMESTEAD SKI TRAIL

PARTRIDGE FALLS SKI TRAIL

19.2 km (12 mi) of trails

intermediate

The round trip on this two-way trail is 19.2 km (12 mi). It cuts off Loon Lake Trail 0.4 km (0.25 mi) from Trail Center. This trail is for well-conditioned skiers, due to its length. At the halfway point (the turnaround), the Pigeon River forms the boundary between the United States and Canada. Use extreme caution when approaching the gorge at Partridge Falls; the edge is very slippery and the drop is forty feet.

For further information, contact

Grand Portage Lodge and Conference Center, Grand Portage, MN 55615. 800-232-1384 (toll free Minnesota), 218-475-2401 (toll free elsewhere)

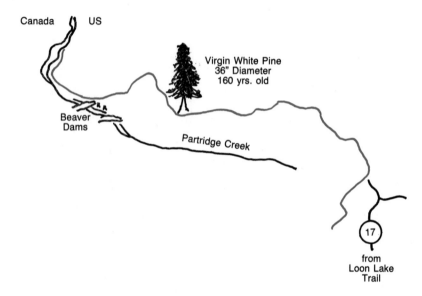

PARTRIDGE FALLS SKI TRAIL

GRAND PORTAGE TRAIL

28.8 km (18 mi) of trails

advanced

Pigeon River, a link in the chain of water from the Atlantic Ocean to the heart of the North American continent, is not navigable for its last 20 miles. Before it joins Lake Superior in northern Minnesota, cascades and the High Falls, a 104-foot drop, choke its course. There are other falls as well. Thus, a land crossing or portage of nearly nine miles must be made.

The Ojibwe called the portage Kitchi-onigum, "the great carrying place." For unknown ages, Native Americans used this path for travel and commerce. The French, seeking a route to the west, learned of the trail from the Indians. The French named it Le Grand Portage. For a hundred years it was the heart of the fur trading empire between the Indians and the European nations.

Today, Grand Portage Trail remains an important link—not in navigation or fur trading, but to the past. Grand Portage is a reminder of how time and place give importance to a small trail in the middle of the wilderness that once was the crossroads of a continent.

The trail begins at the site of the reconstructed North West Fur Company stockade on Lake Superior and runs to the former site of Fort Charlotte on the Pigeon River. No camping is permitted on the trail, but there is a primitive campsite at Fort Charlotte. Firegrates are at the campsite, but backpacking stoves are recommended. Water is not available.

To ski the Grand Portage takes an entire day. Exercise extreme caution on the downhill runs; some have sharp turns at the bottom. *Remember, this is a primitive wilderness trail, and it was not designed for ski touring.* To the conscientious and well-conditioned skier, it can open up some beautiful winter landscapes. This trail is not maintained by Grand Portage Lodge.

For further information, contact

Superintendent, Grand Portage National Monument, Box 666, Grand Marais, MN 55604. 218-387-2788

Gull Harbor Condominiums
Tofte, Minnesota

See North Shore Mountains Ski Trail, page 158.

Gunflint Area Cross-Country Ski-Thru Program
Grand Marais, Minnesota

180 km (112.5 mi) of trails

beginner, intermediate, advanced

There are four lodges on the Gunflint Trail (County Road 12) that are owned by the originators of the first midwest ski-through program. Skiers start at one lodge, ski its trails, and then move out to the main artery trail and ski-through to the next lodge. Their luggage and car will be moved on ahead to the next participating lodge. This gives guests the opportunity to ski many more trails of the Gunflint community and to enjoy the hospitality of a number of small country lodges that cater to skiers. Hosts can go over maps with skiers and help plan trips that will match their abilities and aspirations. This program is full American Plan (with meals) and includes a minimum stay of two nights at at least two of the four lodges—Bearskin Lodge Ski Touring Center, Young's Dog Sledding, Gunflint Lodge, and Borderland Lodge.

Approximately 48 km (30 mi) of trails, called the Central Gunflint Area Trails, are located at Bearskin Lodge. These trails connect with the Banadad Artery Trail (called the Tucker Lake Ski-Through Trail by the Forest Service) that moves deeper into the Gunflint Region to Young's Dog Sledding, located on Young's Island on Poplar Lake.

From this point the Banadad Artery Trail proceeds to Gunflint Lodge and farther on to Borderland Lodge, both located on Gunflint Lake. These two lodges jointly maintain over 130 km (81.25 mi) of trails; this area is collectively known as the Gunflint Lake Area Trails.

Nearly the entire system lies within the Boundary Waters Canoe Area Wilderness and meanders through the heavy forest of the Laurentian Highlands. The trails vary tremendously in their level of difficulty, length, and the type of terrain involved. No fee for trail use, maps, or parking is charged of guests registered at participating lodges; otherwise, one pays $5.00.

For further information, call

218-388-2296, 800-323-3325 (toll free Minnesota)

BEARSKIN LODGE SKI TOURING CENTER
48 km (30 mi) of trails

beginner, intermediate, advanced

Dave and Barb Tuttle's Bearskin Lodge Ski Touring Center is located 26 miles northwest of Grand Marais, just off the Gunflint Trail (County Road 12) on East Bearskin Lake. Because the facility is the only resort on the lake, the setting is secluded and peaceful. It is immediately adjacent to the Boundary Waters Canoe Area Wilderness.

All trails begin right at Bearskin Lodge; therefore, no driving or shuttling is involved. There are over 48 km (30 mi) in the wilderness trail network, ranging in difficulty from novice to rough and challenging for the well-conditioned, experienced skier. The trails vary in length also. Visitors have their pick of trails for a quick ski or a daylong excursion. All trails are marked and are groomed and tracked daily. They meander through the scenic northwoods forest, in and about the BWCA. The trails that are maintained by Bearskin Lodge are collectively known as the Central Gunflint Area Trails and include the following:

BEAVER DAM TRAIL — 8 km (5 mi); beginner, intermediate. Offers several scenic overlooks while circling Rudy and Ruby Lakes; moves through several majestic spruce swamps. Watch for active beaver engineering on the west end of Rudy Lake.

EAST BEARSKIN CAMPGROUND TRAIL — 1.6 km (1 mi); beginner.

MOOSE RIDGE TRAIL — 2 km (1.25 mi); intermediate, advanced.

NORTH-SOUTH LINK — 2.4 km (1.5 mi); intermediate. This multi-use trail is a shortcut back to the Lodge.

OLD LOGGING CAMP TRAIL — 14.4 km (9 mi); intermediate, advanced. Circles by Flour Lake, following a series of old logging railroad grades to an old logging campsite. It is a combination of relatively flat land and several difficult hills. There are scenic overlooks on Wampus and Flour Lakes. Note the massive virgin white pine en route.

OXCART TRAIL — 4 km (2.5 mi); beginner, intermediate. This popular short loop follows an old oxcart trail used in the early 1900s, traversing lowland beaver ponds, aspen swamps, and ridges of highland pine forests.

POPLAR CREEK TRAIL — 11.3 km (7 mi); beginner, intermediate. Leads to a large gravel pit that is perfect for practicing downhill skills. This trail connects the Bearskin system to Banadad Artery Trail, enabling ski-through.

UNPLOWED SUMMER HOME ROAD — 11.2 km (7 mi); beginner. A good starter or warm-up trail, offering rolling hills and wide spaces.

BANADAD ARTERY SKI-THRU TRAIL — 40.2 km (25.1 mi); intermediate, advanced. This main thoroughfare between participating establishments is jointly maintained. The ski-through trail leads to Young's, then to Gunflint Lodge, and on to Borderland Lodge.

The resort caters only to skiers and snowshoers. Expert ski instruction may be obtained. There is a new waxing and ski storage room; a full line of ski and snowshoe equipment is available for rent. A very popular event at Bearskin Lodge is the 2.5-km evening tour; the trail is illuminated with kerosene lamps. There are no trail fees for guests. Nonguests are charged $5.00 for maps and parking.

In the new Main Lodge, the Tuttles serve hot, spiced wine in a fireside lounge. In addition, there is a Gift and Ski Shop. Dairy goods and groceries are available. Family-style meals are served in the dining room, with beer and wine if desired.

A variety of lodging options exists. There are four 1–3-bedroom Housekeeping Lodges, each with fireplace and private deck with a great winter view. The completely modern 2–3-bedroom Housekeeping Cabins are a second option, some with fireplaces and woodstoves. They are more secluded than the lodges and have a beautiful view of the lake. The third choice is the Ski Hus, a two-story vacation home; the two bedrooms with skylights are upstairs. This most secluded accommodation is fully carpeted and has a fireplace. All lodgings have fully equipped kitchens; bedding is included. Firewood is always on hand. Bearskin Lodge has its own private sauna and a new Hot Tub Spa Hus for after-ski relaxation, free for guests. Monday through Thursday a midweek special is available, 20% off regular rates. Children under three are always free. No pets—no exceptions.

For further information, contact

Dave and Barb Tuttle, Bearskin Lodge Ski Touring Center, Box GT-S 10, Grand Marais, MN 55604. 218-388-2292, 800-622-3583 (toll free Minnesota), 800-328-3325 (toll free elsewhere)

YOUNG'S DOG SLEDDING

Ted and Barbara Young's Dog Sled Service is located on Young's Island on Poplar Lake, a midway point on the Banadad Artery Trail between Bearskin Lodge's Central Gunflint Area Trails and Gunflint and Borderland Lodges' Gunflint Lake Area Trails. Ted can go on day trips with two people on his handmade sled, with its team of fifteen huskies. This exciting opportunity to enjoy a dog sled ride can be arranged for any day of your stay—perhaps as a day trip between participating lodges, as a day trip while staying at a participating lodge, or as an overnight at the Youngs' remote island cabin. Ted has had years of wilderness experience and is a congenial host. When out on a run on the trail, he prepares trappers' stew for lunch. Their cabin is a fifty-year-old log structure; guests have a private room, meals, and the use of the wood-fired sauna while staying with the Youngs. A new addition this year is the introduction of their use of an Asian Yurt, an exotic domelike tent that can sleep six. Arrangements can be made for its use in a secluded, remote setting.

Youngs can also take larger groups out for shorter dog sled rides. Advance reservations are suggested. Remember, warm clothes are a *must* while dog sledding.

For further information, contact

Ted and Barbara Young, Young's Dog Sledding, Box GT-S 67-1, Grand Marais, MN 55604. 218-388-4487

GUNFLINT LODGE
130 km (81.3 mi) of trails, in cooperation with Borderland Lodge
beginner, intermediate, advanced

Bruce and Sue Kerfoot's Gunflint Lodge is approximately 42 miles up the Gunflint Trail (County Road 12), northwest of Grand Marais. It is situated on the southwest side of Gunflint Lake, right on the historic route of the voyageurs. The north shore of the lake is Canada; about 1 mile to the south, you enter the Boundary Waters Canoe Area Wilderness. This wilderness area of Minnesota is deep within Superior National Forest, located in the Laurentian Highlands, and is heavily forested with pine, spruce, birch, and poplar. The amount of active winter wildlife far exceeds the number of visitors that come to recreate in the snowy, northwoods setting. Referring to the peace and solitude of their area, the Kerfoots have said, "Often the loudest noise heard while skiing is the call of the birds or the wind rustling through the snow-laden trees."

The Gunflint Area Trail System is now perhaps the largest privately developed network in Minnesota. Although the land is primarily National Forest land, Gunflint Lodge and their close neighbors to the northwest at Borderland Lodge have marked, groomed, and track-set the trails entirely on their own and are doing a remarkable job. The trails offer something for every skier; they vary tremendously in length and degree of difficulty. All are well-signed, and good maps are provided to all guests. Otherwise, you pay $5.00 for maps and parking. Kerfoots, like the other participants in the Ski-Thru Program, will be able to offer a great deal of advice and assistance in planning a ski tour to suit the skier's ability and ambition.

There are easily enough trails in the Gunflint Area for a week's skiing. Warming huts and shelters are scattered throughout the system for lunch stops or a rest break. The trails wind through heavy forest, into valleys that are perfect beaver habitat, up and down the rolling hillsides, and at times follow old tote roads and trappers' trails. Many combinations and options are possible.

The main trails are the following:

BIG PINE TRAIL — 9.7 km (6 mi); intermediate. This main trail ultimately connects with the Banadad Ski-Thru Artery.

KINGS ROAD-WARRENS ROAD TRAIL — 11.3 km (7 mi); beginner, intermediate. Another trail connects to the Banadad Artery.

EAST END TRAIL — 12.9 km (8 mi); beginner. Located on the Canadian shore of the lake.

WEST END TRAIL — 8 km (5 mi); advanced. Connects to the Banadad Artery.

MAGNETIC ROCK TRAIL — 8 km (5 mi); advanced. Named for the enormous monolith on the trail that is magnetic. Bring along a compass and see what happens.

CUT ACROSS TRAIL — 3.2 km (2 mi); beginner. This trail leads directly to Border-land Lodge.

LOWER CLIFF TRAIL — 5 km (3.1 mi); beginner.

OVERLOOK TRAIL — 1.6 km (1 mi); beginner. Connects to the Banadad Artery.

ASPEN ALLEY AND RIVER TRAIL — 3.2 km (2 mi); beginner. Connects to the Banadad Artery.

BANADAD ARTERY TRAIL — 40.2 km (25.1 mi); intermediate, advanced. The main thoroughfare between participating establishments is maintained by all.

There are a variety of accommodations available at Gunflint Lodge. The Main Lodge has a comfortable living room with fireplace, recreation room with pool table, and dining room where evening meals are served family style by reservation. The Bungalow Building has two suites on the ground floor with one or two bedrooms, bath, living room, and well-equipped kitchen. Upstairs there are private rooms, accommodating two to four people each, with adjacent communal kitchen facilities. Each room has its private toilet and sink. Bathing facilities are just down the hall. There are also new chalets at Gunflint Lodge. They are earth-sheltered in the hillside by the lake and have up to four bedrooms; each has two baths, full living room with a fireplace, and kitchen. A sauna is available free for guests.

Open to both Minnesota and Canadian lake trout fishing is a system of fishhouses set up by the Kerfoots on Gunflint, North, and South Lakes. Arrangements can be made for fishing. They also have ski rentals by reservation and snowshoe rentals for both adults and children. They offer excellent, well-seasoned guide service.

For further information, contact

Bruce and Sue Kerfoot, Gunflint Lodge, Box GT-S100, Grand Marais, MN 55604. 218-388-2294, 800-328-3362 (toll Free Minnesota), 800-328-3325 (toll free elsewhere)

BORDERLAND LODGE
130 km (81.3 mi) of trails, in cooperation with Gunflint Lodge
beginner, intermediate, advanced

Jim and Nancy Thompson's Borderland Lodge is located approximately 45 miles up the Gunflint Trail (County Road 12), northwest of Grand Marais. It is situated on the west side of Gunflint Lake, just adjacent to the Minnesota-Canadian border, south of Magnetic Lake.

Borderland is a complete, yearround facility, offering fully modern amenities in a rugged wilderness setting. The 130 km of trails are marked, groomed,and tracked in joint effort with Gunflint Lodge. They offer nearly everything that makes up a wonderful skiing experience—varying trail lengths, all degrees of difficulty, outstanding and often spectacular wilderness scenery that abounds with wildlife. Please refer to Gunflint Lodge for more complete trail description. The special bonus of the Ski-Thru Program makes it possible for skiers to make the most of their recreation time.

The Main Lodge has a comfortable lounge with a sunken conservation area around a large fireplace. Hot coffee is always in the lounge for returned skiers. There is also a giftshop and little grocery store for basic food needs (except meat). Beer is sold on the premises. In the Voyageur View Dining Room, meals are served to guests on the American Plan, as well as to housekeeping guests who occasionally want to skip fixing their own fare. Accommodations include: one- or two-bedroom villas over the Main Lodge, with decks overlooking the lake; cabins, spaced along the shoreline, provide seclusion and privacy; and deluxe cabins called Cedar Hus that have two to four bedrooms, airtight woodstoves that convert to fireplaces, and decks overlooking the lake. All accommodations are designed and equipped for full housekeeping, have private baths, and are carpeted.

For further information, contact

Jim and Nancy Thompson, Borderland Lodge, Box GT-S 102, Grand Marais, MN 55604. 218-338-2233

Please note: There are several other lodges in the area of the Gunflint Ski-Thru Trail that are not participants. Nevertheless, they provide immediate access to the BWCA trails and have their own trail systems. They are Golden Eagle Lodge (close to Bearskin Lodge), Gateway Hungry Jack Lodge, Nor' Wester Lodge (close to Young's), and Heston's Country Store and Cabins (close to Gunflint Lodge)—all are described in this region.

Gunflint Ranger District/Superior National Forest
Grand Marais, Minnesota

PINCUSHION MOUNTAIN SKI TRAIL
14.1 km (8.8 mi) of trails
beginner, intermediate, advanced

To reach Pincushion Mountain Ski Trail, take the Gunflint Trail (County Road 12) north for 2 miles from Grand Marais. Turn right on the Sawtooth Mountain Scenic Overlook access road. Travel 0.25 mile to the parking lot where the trailhead is located.

This trail is claimed by many to be among the finest trails in the area for cross-country skiing. It offers a variety of ingredients that, combined, make a wonderful skiing experience. The trail is marked and groomed regularly. There is a short uphill climb at the trailhead (located by the overlook), then a descent to the junction of the beginner, intermediate, and advanced loops. The beginner loop is only 0.5 km (0.3 mi) long and begins and ends at the junction. The intermediate loop is 7.6 km (4.75 mi) long and offers the best scenery. The first part of the loop leads to Devil's Track Canyon where there is an imposing view of the canyon, with Devil's Track River running 200 feet below the trail. On this length of the trail, the skier can gently glide downhill for nearly a mile before reaching Pincushion Mountain. You may remove your skis and hike 300 feet to the summit (el. 1,160 feet). Across Devil's Track canyon is a spectacular panorama of Lake Superior and its rugged shoreline. The trail then resumes with a caution hill and proceeds to level out. The final stretch is a gradual climb to the trailhead.

The advanced trails are a combination of hills, dips, and corners that have inspired the Forest Service to bestow descriptive names such as Pulse Pounder and Free Fall. The combined length of these trails is 6 km (3.75 mi). Nearly all the advanced trails are *strictly* one-way.

There is ample parking at the trailhead. Maps are available from either the District Ranger or local outfitters in Grand Marais. Tourist accommodations are at hand in Grand Marais.

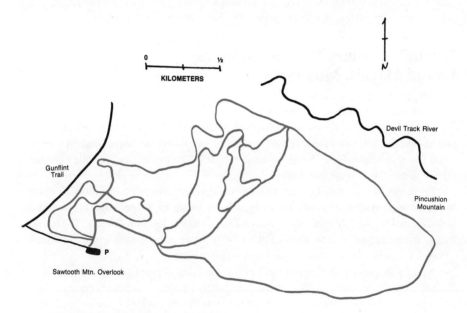

PINCUSHION MOUNTAIN SKI TRAIL

GEORGE WASHINGTON MEMORIAL PINE PLANTATION SKI TRAIL
1.2 km (0.75 mi) of trails
beginner

To reach the trail, take the Gunflint Trail (County Road 12), and travel six miles north from the Ranger Station in Grand Marais. The trail is on the west side of the road and is marked by a Forest Service sign.

This trail is excellent for beginners and first-time skiers or for senior citizens who wish to stay on a very level terrain. The trail is quite short. Although this is not a groomed trail, it is well-used and nearly always has tracks on it. It is very easy to follow, despite the fact that it is not marked. The trail runs through a beautiful deep wood pine plantation that was planted by fifteen Grand Marais boy scouts five years after a major fire on the Gunflint Trail in 1927. It moves through the plantation to Elbow Creek. The skier must turn around at this point and either ski back on the same route or bushwhack back through the adjacent landscape.

For further information, contact

District Ranger, Gunflint Ranger District, Superior National Forest, Grand Marais, MN 55604. 218-387-1750

Forest Supervisor, Superior National Forest, P.O. Box 338, Duluth, MN 55801. 218-727-6692

See also Gateway Hungry Jack Lodge, page 100; Golden Eagle Lodge, page 102; Gunflint Area Ski-Thru Program, page 115; Heston's Country Store and Cabins, page 122; North Shore Mountains Ski Trail, page 148; Nor' Wester Lodge, page 170.

Heston's Country Store and Cabins
Grand Marais, Minnesota

120 km (75 mi) of trails

beginner, intermediate, advanced

Heston's is located off the Gunflint Trail (County Road 12), 50 miles northwest of Grand Marais, 160 miles from Duluth. From the Gunflint Trail, travel east on County Road for approximately 0.75 mile to Heston's. It is situated on the Canadian border, on the south side of Gunflint Lake.

From this facility, the skier has access to enormous recreation possibilities. It opens the door to a system of trails, maintained by a group of lodges, that are marked, groomed and tracked. Lengths vary from 3.2 km (2 mi) to 19.2 km (12 mi). The terrain ranges the entire gamut, from nearly flat for the beginner to mountainous for the expert. These are among the most beautiful trails in Minnesota.

No trail or parking fees are charged of those staying at participating lodges. Meals are not served at Heston's, but cabins are completely equipped for housekeeping. There is a small grocery store for supplies. Arrangements can be made to rent ski equipment. Parking is available. Rates are reasonable.

For further information, contact

Heston's Country Store and Cabins, Sharlene and Chuck Gecas, SG 50, Grand Marais, MN 55604. 218-388-2243

See also Gunflint Area Cross-Country Ski-Thru Program, page 115.

Isabella Ranger District/Superior National Forest
Isabella, Minnesota

Three ski trails are maintained by the U.S. Forest Service in the Isabella Ranger District, Superior National Forest.

FLATHORN-GEGOKA CROSS-COUNTRY SKI TRAIL
24 km (15 mi) of trails
beginner, intermediate, advanced

Flathorn-Gegoka Cross-Country Ski Trail is located on Highway 1, approximately 35 miles southeast of Ely, 8 miles west of Isabella, or 30 miles northwest of Highway 61 (Illgen City). The trailhead is at the Lake Gegoka Public Boat Access just off Highway 1.

The trail consists of groomed, double-tracked and single-tracked trails that are marked with orange or blue plastic diamonds. All intersections are marked with numbered posts and maps. The trails suit skiers of all abilities. They begin with a short run across Lake Gegoka. Early and late in the season (December and March), the lake surface may be slushy. The beginner section of the trail (also the most popular) is double-tracked. It can be skied by a beginner or intermediate skier in about one and one-half hours. The single-track trails, which go to the right, head north of Flathorn Lake along Little Isabella River. The loops in this section are long and have hilly stretches best-suited to the intermediate or advanced skier. The single-track trails, which go to the left, head northwest of Lake Gegoka through spruce bogs. There are some hills involved, but it still is a segment suited to the beginner. Farther northwest, the trails go through stands of large Norway pine and contain hills with steep grades and corners. This area is designed for the advanced skier. Visitors traveling to the outer limits of the trails should plan on at least a three-hour trip and are encouraged to take a day pack with water, snacks, and extra clothing. Shelters will soon be built on the trails.

There is a resort located at the trailhead called the National Forest Lodge where full tourist accommodations are available. There are also two yearround resorts in the Isabella area and a small cafe and tavern with food in the town of Isabella.

See also National Forest Lodge, page 148 and Finland State Forest/Woodland Caribou Ski Trail, page 97.

The other two trails maintained by the U.S. Forest Service in the Isabella Ranger District are designed as hiking trails and are not groomed especially for ski touring. They are not marked for winter use. No shelters or water are available. The trails, particularly the Pow Wow Trail, are absolutely REMOTE wilderness trails and should be attempted only by skiers with both *expert ability* and *plenty of experience* in a winter survival setting. Visitors must GO PREPARED. Please stop at the Ranger Station in Isabella and inform the District Ranger that you intend to use these trails. Check back in with them when your tour is complete, if possible. They will be able to provide good maps and perhaps vital information on the condition of the trails.

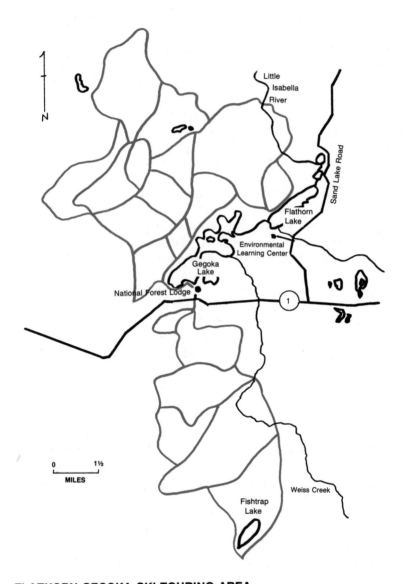

Little
Isabella
River

Sand Lake Road

Flathorn
Lake

Environmental
Learning Center

Gegoka
Lake

National Forest Lodge

1

0   1½
MILES

Weiss Creek

Fishtrap
Lake

FLATHORN-GEGOKA SKI-TOURING AREA

HOGBACK TRAIL
8 km (5 mi) of trails

very advanced

To reach the trail, take Highway 1 northwest from Illgen City (located on Highway 61) to Finland. Then take County Road 7 north-northwest to the trailheads. This is the only reasonable way to the trail as Forest Road 172, east of Isabella, is unplowed during the winter. Two access points are on County Road 7, and another is farther up the road at the Hogback Picnic Ground.

It must be emphasized that this is a trail designed for hiking use, not skiing use, and may be extremely difficult at times due to the very hilly terrain.

The unique scenery in this area is produced by the ridges or hogbacks that run through the landscape. Hogbacks are long, sharply crested uplands composed of steeply inclined layers of rock that are very resistant to erosion. The trail on the hogback between Scarp and Hogback Lakes offers a spectacular view of the lakes in the region— the trail system involves seven lakes. The Laurentian Divide, the great point of division between the Hudson Bay watershed (northern water systems) and the Lake Superior and Mississippi River watersheds (southern water systems), meanders through this area. At the narrows between Hogback and Canal Lakes is an abandoned railroad trestle used during logging in the 1930s.

Five primitive campsites lie along the trail route. Each has a small clearing, firegrate and latrine. Do not camp at the picnic ground. Before using water from the lakes, boil it for five minutes. All garbage must be packed out. No fee is charged for trail use.

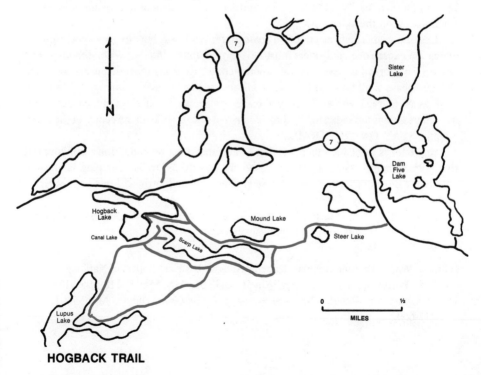

HOGBACK TRAIL

POW WOW TRAIL
88 km (55 mi) of trails
advanced

Access to the Pow Wow Trail is off Highway 1, approximately 15 miles east-north-east of the junction of Highway 1 and Forest Road 173. This junction is about 25 miles southeast of Ely and 30 miles northwest of Illgen City. Take 173 east to Forest Road 377, and proceed to the trailheads at Isabella Lake. There are two trailheads that can be used by skiers; they are both located on the extreme end of Forest Road 377. This is a primitive stretch of the road, unplowed in the winter. Typically, you cannot drive the last 8 miles to the trailheads, unless timber harvesting is taking place nearby and the road is clear. Please check with the District Ranger in Isabella before making plans.

The parking area at the trailhead is the site of a once-bustling townsite of 250 people. It was called Forest Center and, for fifteen years, was Logging Camp #3 for the Tomahawk Timber Company. There was a store, post office, church, school, and restaurant. Individual dwellings, barracks, and a mess hall provided shelter and meals for the lumberjacks. A sawmill processed the timber, and a railroad moved the lumber from the area. It was not uncommon to have 100,000 cords of wood stockpiled at the tracks at one time. Many of the trails in the system are old logging roads.

The trails move through a variety of landscape types including stands of both virgin timber and young seedlings, boggy lowlands, rolling hills, and rock ledges overlooking lakes. The western third of the system is classified as very difficult because it is hilly and rocky and very demanding. The remainder of the trails are flat to gently rolling and can be skied easily. However, the trail length is enormous and requires excellent conditioning on the skier's part.

Use of this area demands that *you come prepared*. It was built to provide a primitive recreation experience, and skiers must have *expert* ability, *top-notch* conditioning, and *extensive* winter wilderness survival experience. When skiing the trails, use a good map and a compass at all times to keep yourself oriented and to avoid confusion. Most trail sections are marked with an occasional blaze—an axcut on both sides of the tree. Major trail intersections are indicated by a rock cairn—a pile of rocks in the center of the intersection. STAY ON THE TRAIL.

No water is available other than lake water that must be boiled for a minimum of five minutes before using it. There are no shelters on the trails. Camping is allowed only at the developed campsites with steel firegrates and latrines. Fires are restricted to the firegrates only. Otherwise, use a cookstove.

This trail is located in the Boundary Waters Canoe Area Wilderness, and skiers must follow the regulations that apply to this area.

For further information, contact

John R. Ward, District Ranger, Isabella Ranger District, Superior National Forest, U.S. Forest Service, 2759 Highway 1, Isabella, MN 55607. 218-365-6185

Forest Supervisor, Superior National Forest, P.O. Box 338, Duluth, MN 55801. 218-727-6692

Itasca County
Grand Rapids, Minnesota

The Itasca County Land Department administers three cross-country ski trails: Amen Lake Ski Trails, Big Ridge Cross-Country Ski and Hiking Trail, and Wabana Trails and Wildlife Sanctuary. Amen Lake Trails and Wabana Trails are approximately 6–7 miles apart. At all trail systems, parking is available at the trailhead. Maps may be obtained at the Itasca County Courthouse in Grand Rapids. No toilets or water are available on site. Lodging and supplies are at hand in Grand Rapids.

AMEN LAKE TRAILS
6.4 km (4 mi) of trails
intermediate, advanced

The trailhead for the Amen Lake Ski Trails is reached by traveling 12 miles north-northwest from Grand Rapids on Highway 38 to the junction with County Road 19. Turn west, and travel 1.75 miles to County Road 246. Turn north, and go 0.25 mile to the access point.

Trails are marked and contain five loops. They interconnect with the Suomi Hills Recreation Area of the Marcell Ranger District of the Chippewa National Forest, a 29-km (18.1-mi) advanced system.

See also Marcell Ranger District/Suomi Hills Recreation Area, page 143 and Blueberry Hills Ski Trail, page 84.

BIG RIDGE CROSS-COUNTRY SKI AND HIKING TRAIL
10 km (6.25 mi) of trails
beginner, intermediate, advanced

The trail is located 4.5 miles north of Goodland. Go northwest of Goodland on Highway 65 for 4 miles to the junction with County Road 560. Turn northwest on 560, and travel 0.5 mile to the trailhead.

The trails are marked and are all two-way. They are set up in a system of three large loops and one small loop. The outermost loop is strictly for advanced skiers.

Food and lodging are available in Goodland, Pengilly, and Grand Rapids.

WABANA TRAILS AND WILDFLOWER SANCTUARY
9.6 km (6 mi) of trails
intermediate

Wabana Trails and Wildflower Sanctuary is located 15.8 miles north of Grand Rapids. It may be reached by taking Highway 38 north from Grand Rapids to County Road 49. Stay on 49 until it meets County Road 59. Continue east on 59 for 0.4 mile to the entrance of the Sanctuary on the south side of the road.

This 480-acre tract of land is being developed and maintained by the Itasca County Land Department, in cooperation with the DNR and the Izaak Walton League of Grand Rapids. The trails are situated on a diversified terrain. They are marked, but are not groomed especially for ski touring. Although the seven interpretive markers proceed counterclockwise on the main trail, it is recommended that skiers move clockwise for the most enjoyable tour.

Motorized vehicles are prohibited in the area. To prevent defacement, snowshoers are asked to stay off the ski trails.

Itasca Trails
Coleraine, Minnesota

4.6 km (2.9 mi) of trails

intermediate, advanced

From Grand Rapids, take Highway 38 north for approximately 2 miles to the junction with County Road 61. Turn east, and proceed for nearly 4 miles to the trails. Or, from Coleraine, go 0.5 mile west of town on County Road 61.

Itasca Trails are marked and groomed, but are not track-set. They are situated on a hilly terrain that is forested with hardwoods. No water is available on site. A chalet is sometimes open at the trailhead where light snacks may be obtained and toilets are located. Parking is available at the access point. The gate to the trails closes at dusk. A state trail license is required for trail use. Lodging, rentals, and food are at hand in Grand Rapids.

For further information, contact

Cavour Johnson, Itasca Ski and Outing Club, Box J, Coleraine, MN 55722. 218-245-1250

See also Blueberry Hills Ski Trail, page 84; Camp Mishawaka, page 85; Golden Anniversary State Forest, page 101; Itasca County, page 127; Sugar Hills, page 179.

Kabetogama State Forest
Orr, Minnesota

ASH RIVER FALLS SKI TRAIL

20.1 km (12.6 mi) of trails

intermediate, advanced

Kabetogama State Forest is located in the northwestern corner of St. Louis County, south of Voyageurs National Park and northwest of Lake Vermilion. The Forest can be reached by traveling north from Virginia on Highway 53. The Ash River Falls Ski Trail is in the north central portion of the park, very close to the border with Voyageurs National Park. To reach the trail, take Highway 53 northwest from Orr for 26 miles, turn east on County Road 129, and travel 5 miles to the trailhead.

Due to the intensive logging of the Backus and Brooks Company and the Virginia and Rainy Company, the Forest was completely cut over from 1910–1930. The slash, most nonsalable forest species, and cull trees were burned, leaving an enormous wasteland of burned snags, stumps, and bare rock. This assault was followed by other uncontrolled fires in the area until fire control and forest protection programs were instituted in the 1930s. Kabetogama State Forest was established in 1933. Today it is still in the reproductive stages, and the former vast stands of cedar, spruce, and white pine have been replaced with aspen and other northern hardwoods, mixed with cedar, spruce, pine, balsam, and tamarack.

As with other state forests, Kabetogama was established to produce timber and other forest crops, to provide a site for outdoor recreation, to protect watersheds, and to perpetuate and protect rare and distinctive animal and plant life.

The topography of the area of the Ash River Falls Ski Trail is generally rolling to hilly, with rock ridges interspersed with small lakes and low wet areas. The trails are marked and divided into two basic loops. Loop A wanders through a variety of forest types, and a portion follows the course of the Ash River. Loop B is approximately 11 km (6.9 mi) long and provides more challenging terrain. It follows ridgelines and ravines and offers some spectacular scenery.

Parking is available at the trailhead and at a cutoff from Loop B. A map is available from the Area Forest Supervisor in Orr. Tourist needs may be obtained in Orr or in Cook.

For further information, contact

Department of Natural Resources, Area Forest Supervisor, Kabetogama State Forest, Orr, MN 55771. 218-757-3274

Minnesota Department of Natural Resources, Division of Forestry, Box 44 Centennial Building, St. Paul, MN 55155. 612-296-4491

See also Voyageurs National Park, Black Bay Ski Trail, page 188.

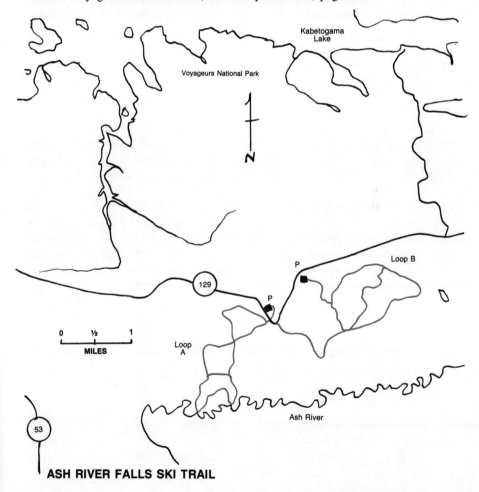

ASH RIVER FALLS SKI TRAIL

Kawishiwi Ranger District/Superior National Forest
Ely, Minnesota

The Kawishiwi Ranger District is rich in opportunities for the skier and winter camper. More than 300 km (187.5 mi) of mapped cross-country ski trails wind through the forests in the Ely area. Some are groomed and tracked, while others are wild and remote. For further information, please refer to Superior National Forest.

ANGLEWORM LAKE-SPRING CREEK TRAIL
32 km (20 mi) of trails
advanced

To reach the trailhead, travel 17.5 miles north of Ely on County Road 116 (Echo Trail). From the Chamber of Commerce building on the east edge of Ely, at the junction of Highways 169 and 1, continue toward Winton on 169 for 1 mile. Turn left on County Road 88, and go 2.3 miles. Turn right on County Road 116, and continue on 116 for 13.8 miles to the Angleworm parking lot on the right side of the road.

This is a beautiful Natural Environment Wilderness Trail. Land trails can be difficult, and care should be exercised. Lake travel is easy unless conditions involve slush. You should set aside an entire day for the trip if the circle route is to be skied. This is probably the most beautiful day trip in the District. The trail is usually tracked into Angleworm Lake, but not beyond this point.

The Angleworm Trail follows gentle terrain before dropping down a steep hill to Spring Creek. After Spring Creek, the trail climbs a ridge and crosses several lesser ridges before encountering the junction of three trails. The south trail leads to Trease and Hegman Lakes. The middle trail goes to the east side of Angleworm, but is only skiable for a short distance. The left or North Trail is the most direct route to Angleworm Lake. Upon reaching Angleworm, the only feasible ski route is up the lake itself. As the lake narrows, you come closer to the steep, rocky, pine-covered shorelines.

From this point, you can return the way that you came or continue on to Home, Gull, Thunder, and Beartrap Lakes before heading west on the Beartrap River to Spring Creek. (Please note: There is a shorter route that follows beaver ponds north from Home to Beartrap Lakes, but it involves some bushwhacking.) Upon reaching Spring Creek, do *not* follow the winding creek, but instead follow the old road along the west edge of the marsh. Spring Creek draw is particularly beautiful during the sunny days of late winter skiing. Continue back down to the intersection with Angleworm Trail and follow it back to your starting point. Carry a good map and a compass because you are on your own in the wilderness. Use U.S.G.S. map: Quadrangles-Angleworm, Fourtown, and Iron Lakes.

See also Kawishiwi Ranger District/Superior National Forest, Hegman Lake Trail, page 134.

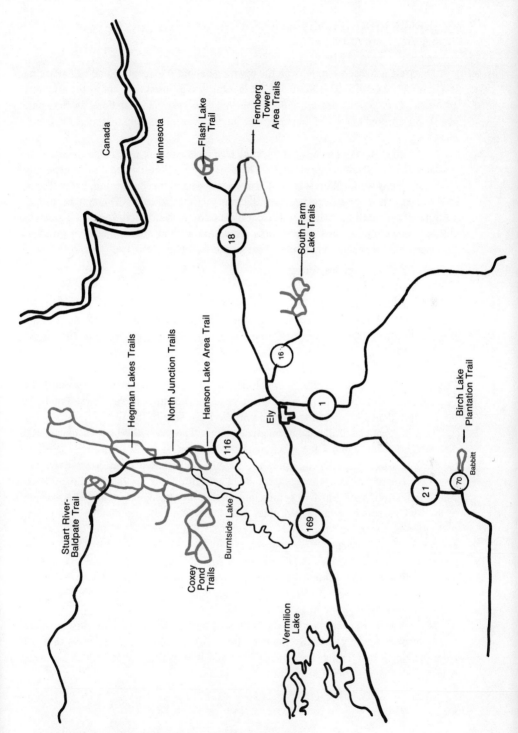

KAWISHIWI RANGER DISTRICT AREA TRAILS

BIRCH LAKE PLANTATION TRAIL

6.4 km (4 mi) of trails

beginner, intermediate

This trail is located 1 mile from the town of Babbitt on County Road 623. Parking is along 623, east of Forest Road 131. It is a fairly well-used trail and is occasionally groomed. This system lies partially within the Superior National Forest's first pine plantation, planted in 1915. Skiers may see on the trees white paint that marks research plots.

This trail system is a maze of connecting trails with you-are-here maps at each junction and blue markers along the way. The area east of Forest Road 131 is generally quite flat. Areas west of Forest Road 131 are somewhat more challenging, but still relatively easy. All trails are marked as to their degree of difficulty. The system utilizes portions of the multi-use pathway that parallels 623; consequently, you may occasionally see snowmobiles. Most of the trails are within a stand of red pines that provides a pleasant ski. If the sun is shining through the tall pines, it is truly inspiring.

COXEY POND TRAILS

19.7 km (12.3 mi) of trails

intermediate, advanced

Coxey Pond Trail is located 17 miles north of Ely on the North Arm Road (County Road 644). From the Chamber of Commerce building on the east edge of Ely, at the junction of Highways 169 and 1, continue towards Winton on 169 for 1 mile. Turn left on County Road 88, and go 2.3 miles. Turn right on County Road 116 (Echo Trail). Continue on 116 for 9.4 miles to the North Arm Road, 1 mile past the Fenske Lake Campground. Continue on the North Arm Road for 3.5 miles to the Coxey Pond and Slim Lakes Trail sign. Parking space is on the right side of the road.

This is a popular trail for intermediate skiers. The Ole Lake Loop is considered difficult, however. Follow the recommended direction of travel to insure a safe and pleasurable winter experience. Trails are usually well-tracked from use, but are not groomed. Near the parking area, Coxey Pond and Slim Lake Trails split. Coxey Pond Trail gradually climbs 200 feet before intersecting an old logging road. This portion of the trail passes some large, old pines called the Sentinels, a reminder of the past. Just past these trees, the trail splits. Coxey Pond Trail continues to the left where it crosses the Troll's Bridge before connecting with the old Coxey Pond Road. From the junction of the trail to Coxey Pond, you are on an old logging road that travels through stands of pine that were thinned in previous years. This trail also intersects with Ole Lake Trail, which is more difficult but beautiful. Plan on coming out via the south road and then back North Arm Road to your vehicle.

North Star Trail heads north at the Sentinels, traversing some minor hills and open stands of pine before eventually joining Coxey Pond road. Two other trails take off from the North Star Trails, Lost Lakes Trail and Barren Ridge Trail, which connects with the Slim and Keneu Lakes Trails.

Slim Lake Trail begins near the parking lot on the North Arm Road. The beginning mile is through the forest. The terrain is generally level with interesting small rises and falls. High bluffs are visible as you near Slim Lake. Take time to enjoy the scenery along the way. Stop and sun yourself on these rocky bluffs. When you reach Slim Lake, it is less than 0.5 mile to a land bridge between these lakes; you then proceed downhill to a swamp as you enter the south end of Keneu. A junction with the Barren Ridge Trail leads back to the North Star Trail. The trail between Slim and Keneu Lakes passes by a group of large druid pines that stand as reminders of the past. The rest of the loop crosses lakes and portages before rejoining itself near the south end of Slim Lake.

Use U.S.G.S. map: Quadrangles Angleworm and Crab Lakes. Carry a compass and know how to use it.

See also Camp Northland (YMCA), page 86.

FERNBERG TOWER AREA TRAIL
9.6 km (6 mi) of trails
beginner, intermediate

To reach the trailhead, take Highway 169 and County Road 18 (Fernberg Road) 20 miles east of Ely. The road dead-ends at a parking lot at Lake One landing.

The trail involves a series of forest roads winding through woods and provides a variety of experiences. The trail may be tracked from use, but it is not groomed. It is unmarked except at junctions. It is easy to ski; unbroken snow will be the most challenging thing encountered.

Looking back toward Ely from the parking lot, you see a trail off to the left, leading west and connecting with Forest Road 1544 (Old Fernberg Road). The trail then cuts cross-country on old logging roads, crossing swamps and pine plantations. This is generally a good wildlife area—be alert and you may see something. The hillside to the north once held the Fernberg Lookout Tower. The fire tower is now gone, replaced by a radio tower. The trail eventually joins Forest Road 439. From here you can cross 439 and continue on, or you can follow 439 to the north, intersecting Forest Road 1544. Follow 1544 to the right (east), keep to the right at the first intersection, and then left at the second one as you climb steadily higher. Eventually, there are two long hills that provide an exciting run on a fast snow day and take you back to the parking lot. The alternate way to go on Forest Road 439 is called the River Route. From the parking lot you can venture down the Kawishiwi River, but use caution in those areas marked on the map because rapids cause poor ice and open water. It's advisable to go on the river with someone that knows the area. Upon reaching Triangle Portage, follow it to Triangle and Ojibway Lakes, going to the far east end of Ojibway, where a trail will lead back eastward to Forest Road 439. This is a beautiful route that provides a challenging experience to those wanting to explore new areas.

Use U.S.G.S. map: Quadrangles Forest Center and Gabbro.

FLASH LAKE TRAIL
CHARLES L. SOMMERS NATIONAL HIGH ADVENTURE BASE
BOY SCOUTS OF AMERICA
beginner, intermediate, advanced

To reach the trailhead, go east on 169 from the Chamber of Commerce building in Ely. This highway later becomes County Road 18 (Fernberg Road) for 17.7 miles. Turn left on Forest Road 438 (Moose Lake Road), and travel for 2.5 miles to the canoe base, just east of the public landing at Moose Lake.

There are all classes of trails involved in the system. Consult the map, and inquire at the office at Sommers when you check in. All trails are groomed, and some are track-set. Refer to the map. The degree of difficulty is marked on the map and at trail junctions.

These trails are all used quite heavily on the weekends. During the week you encounter few people on the system. It is a maze of trails, particularly near Blackstone Lake. Most of these are signed. The loops make the length of the outing variable. The trails generally go through the Forest and across or along ridges. Occasionally a marsh or lake gives a longer vista. Logging roads are used whenever possible as they provide a good, smooth trail. Again, check at the Sommers administration building for more specific details. Trail maps, water, toilets, and parking are available at this location.

HANSON LAKE AREA TRAIL
beginner, intermediate

From the Chamber of Commerce building in Ely, at the junction of Highways 169 and 1, continue towards Winton on 169 for 1 mile. Turn left on County Road 88, and go 2.3 miles. Turn right on County Road 116 (Echo Trail). Continue on 116 for 7.4 miles to the Everett Lake Portage, or continue on to Fenske Lake Campground, 1 mile north.

If you start skiing at the Everett Lake Portage, travel to Everett Lake and across to Twin Lake. Approximately ⅓ mile down the west shore of Twin Lake is a trail that leads off to the northwest, eventually joining an old logging road. At this point is a short spur into Hanson Lake. As you continue north on the road, which has many hills, you eventually come to County Road 116, near Fenske Lake Campground. From this point you can ski down Fenske Lake to the Everett Lake Portage and then back overland to your vehicle. The alternative route would be to walk down 116 from Fenske Lake back to your vehicle.

Use U.S.G.S. map: Quadrangle Shagawa Lake.

HEGMAN LAKES TRAILS
6.4 km (4 mi) of trails
intermediate, advanced

From the Chamber of Commerce building in Ely, at the junction of Highways 169 and 1, continue towards Winton on 169 for 1 mile. Turn left on County Road 88 and go 2.3 miles. Turn right on County Road 116 (Echo Trail), and go 11.4 miles to the Hegman Lake parking area.

This trail is moderately difficult to North Hegman Lake. The trail to Angleworm Lake is more difficult. It is for experienced, well-conditioned skiers only! These are Natural Environment Wilderness Trails. They are normally tracked from use, but are not machine-groomed.

From the parking area on the Echo Trail, there is a quarter mile downhill run through a stand of pines that had its origin from a fire in 1840. Take a few moments to enjoy these magnificent trees. This downhill run can be difficult for those not used to well-packed, steeper trails. If you must walk down the hill, please walk off to the side so that your footprints don't make the trail hazardous for other skiers.

As the trail nears the lake, there is a junction. The main trail drops down a short, steep hill to the lake. *Be careful!* There is a trail to the left, just before this steep portion, that leads to North Hegman. This alternate route provides a change of scenery and leads to North Hegman and the Indian pictographs. This side trail is usually more difficult than the lake travel.

For those wanting a longer ski, the route into Little Bass Lake is a great side-trip. Also, a circle tour can be made by going from Trease to Angleworm and then back to the Echo Trail, via the Angleworm Trail or Spring Creek.

The area, entirely within the Boundary Waters Canoe Area, is known for the Indian pictographs on the west side of North Hegman, just before the narrows leading into Trease Lake. They are excellent pictographs within easy viewing for photographing. The general landscape is typical of the north country. The pines etched against the snow-covered rocks are thrilling to see as you travel across the frozen lake.

Use U.S.G.S. map: Quadrangle Angleworm Lake. There are no signs except at the trailhead. Carry a good map and compass. Know how to use them.

See also Kawishiwi Ranger District/Superior National Forest, Angleworm Lake-Spring Creek Trail, page 130.

NORTH JUNCTION TRAILS
12.8 km (8 mi) of trails
beginner, intermediate, advanced

This trail system is located 13 miles north of Ely on County Road 116 (Echo Trail). From the Chamber of Commerce building in Ely, at the junction of Highways 169 and 1, continue on 169 for 1 mile. Turn left on County Road 88, and go 2.3 miles. Turn right on 116, and proceed 9.4 miles to County Road 644 (North Arm Road), located 1 mile past the Fenske Lake Campground. Parking space is provided on the left side of the road.

This popular trail is generally for skiers of intermediate ability, although it does contain some novice portions. Follow the recommended direction of travel to ensure a safe and pleasurable tour. Some of this area has been harvested for timber products. Much of the trail system exists as the result of logging. The completed timber sale roads can be utilized for skiing purposes and should provide good trails through pine stands. Occasional openings provide good wildlife habitats that should also add to the enjoyment of the trails.

Three trails diverge from the trailhead at the junction of Echo Trail and North Arm Road. South (Spruce Road) Trail is an intermediate trail with a wide variety of terrain and forest species. The trail goes through a spruce swamp and across beaver ponds, eventually tying in with Beaver Meadows Trail. This last trail, a beginner to intermediate trail, goes the length of a long beaver meadow. The third loop, Pine Hills Trail, follows old logging roads through young plantations. There are some long downhill runs that will challenge intermediate to advanced skiers. This loop is on the north side of the North Arm Road.

At the west end of the Beaver Meadow Trail, intermediate Widji Trail leads to Camp Widjiwagan and then back up Hunch Creek to Hunch Lake or to the east and Pine Hill Loop. Hunch Creek Trail opens up into a long swamp meadow with high hills on both sides. While on the road through Widjiwagan, respect their private property. Where trails cross the lakes, use caution. Be alert for water holes and weak ice.

See also Camp Northland (YMCA), page 86 and Kawishiwi Ranger District/Superior National Forest, Coxey Pond Trails and Hanson Lake Area Trail, pages 132 and 134.

SOUTH FARM LAKE TRAILS
beginner, intermediate

The trailhead is located 7.5 miles east of Ely on County Road 16. from the Chamber of Commerce building in Ely, at the junction of Highways 169 and 1, continue toward Winton for 1.5 miles. Turn right on St. Louis County Road 58, which becomes Lake County Road 16 after 1 mile. From the previous right turn, it is 3 miles to the Silver Rapids Bridge and then another 3 miles to the parking lot at Superior Forest Lodge.

From the parking area, the trail either crosses Farm and South Farm Lakes or follows the multi-use trail to the bridge at the sound end of South Farm Lake. Taking the bridge route, the trail splits a few yards later. The multi-use trail goes to the right and south. The ski trail goes to the left and north. Follow the north trail over gently rolling terrain until you come to a junction. At this point, you can go down a long hill to the lake and back to your starting point on Farm Lake. Or, head east to the circle route known as Spruce-Muskeg Trail. This trail follows old roads recently cleared by a group of volunteers, Iron Range Resource and Rehabilitation Board workers, and the U.S. Forest Service. Gentle trails provide a pleasant ski tour. The muskeg swamp especially gives the visitor a feeling of the far north. The trails are wide and the hills relatively easy. Bridge Run and Spruce-Muskeg Trail are groomed and tracked. The others will be groomed as conditions permit. Be alert for water holes and, in early and late season, weak ice.

Use U.S.G.S. map: Quadrangle Farm Lake. Carry a compass, and know how to use it.

STUART RIVER-BALDPATE TRAILS
16 km (10 mi) of trails
beginner, intermediate, advanced

The trailhead is located 20 miles north of Ely on County Road 116 (Echo Trail). From the Chamber of Commerce Building in Ely, at the junction of Highways 169 and

1, continue toward Winton on 169 for 1 mile. Turn left on County Road 88, and 2.3 miles, and turn right on County Road 116. Continue on 116 for 17.3 miles to the Stuart River parking lot on the right side of the road. You may also park at the resort on Big Lake or alongside the road. A parking area will be built in the future.

These trails accommodate skiers of all abilities. The junctions are marked, and the trails receive occasional grooming. The system is arranged in a series of interconnecting loops. Portions of the trail follow old winter logging roads through the swamps that are considered easy skiing and still provide a sense of the deep woods. Ridge Trail follows a logging road from Baldpate Lake back to Echo Trail. Watch for moose in this area. Pine/Meadows Trail flows through deep stands of pine and spruce interspersed with open marsh meadows. This portion of the trail starts at Baldpate Lake and joins Stuart River Portage. From Stuart River Portage, you return to Echo Trail over gentle hills (except for a steep hill marked on the map) and pass an old sentinel pine, a good place to stop and take in the wilderness surroundings.

Use U.S.G.S. map: Quadrangle Angleworm. Carry a good map and compass. Know how to use them.

For further information, contact

Kawishiwi Ranger District, District Ranger, Superior National Forest, U.S. Forest Service, Ely, MN 55731. 218-365-6185

Forest Supervisor, Superior National Forest, P.O. Box 338, Duluth, MN 55801. 218-727-6692

La Croix Ranger District/Superior National Forest
Cook, Minnesota

There are six trails designated for cross-country skiing in the La Croix Ranger District. No fees are charged for trail use. The trails are not marked as to their degree of difficulty, but all the trailheads are signed. They generally are not groomed or machine-tracked, although usage may keep them groomed, with a track available from previous skiers. Water and shelter are not available on the trails. Tourist accommodations and supplies are at hand in Cook, Crane Lake, and Ely. Please refer to Superior National Forest for further information.

ASTRID LAKE TRAILS
9.6 km (6 mi) of trails
intermediate
Astrid Lake Trails are located approximately 50 miles northeast of Cook, and approximately 38 miles northwest of Ely. There are two access points.

Access 1 is at the Lake Jeanette Campground, off County Road 116 (Echo Trail), approximately 14 miles east from County Road 24. Parking is available, but the campground road and parking area are not plowed in the winter. Snowpack may inhibit accessibility. The trailhead, 150 feet south of the boat landing, is signed.

Access 2 is at the Astrid Lake Portage, off Forest Road 200, approximately 2.5 miles south of County Road 116 (Echo Trail). Limited parking is available along the

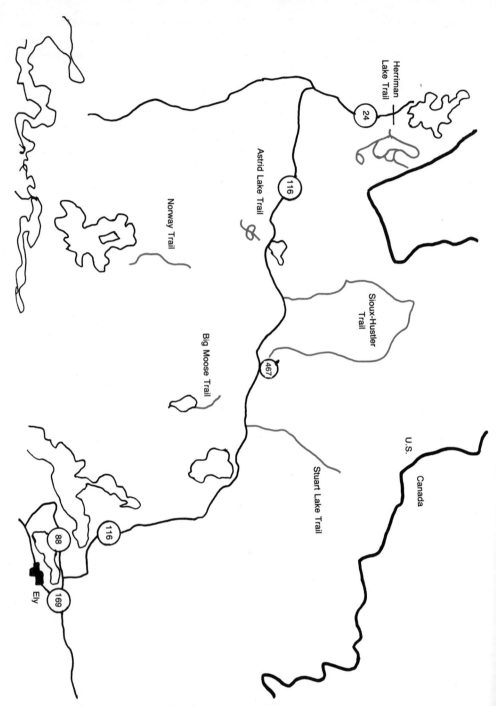

LA CROIX RANGER DISTRICT AREA TRAILS

west side of the road. Check with the La Croix Ranger Station for snow conditions and plowing reports on the Forest Road. The trailhead is signed.

There are over six miles of trails in the Astrid Lake Trail system. Visitors may ski a variety of loops for a day tour or choose a winter camping experience. Permits are not required for use of this trail system since it is outside the Boundary Waters Canoe Area. There are wilderness campsites, with firegrates and box latrines, on the lakes along the trail. They are generally located on short spur trails off the main trail. These spur trails are not signed. Remember to leave no trace of your visit and to pack out all burnable trash. Opportunities for solitude are excellent during the winter season.

Less than a half mile from the trailhead at Lake Jeanette, skiers approach County Road 116 (Echo Trail). Use extreme caution when crossing this road, as motorists who use it are generally unprepared for meeting pedestrians. Once across, the trail meets the portage from Lake Jeanette to Nigh Lake. This is a rare chance to experience a spruce bog while keeping your feet dry.

Almost at Nigh Lake, the trail heads south from the portage, and skiers get a glimpse of some imposing bluffs. The point nearest Nigh Lake on the southeast is a scenic overlook of the lake and area vistas. Either route from this area traverses ledge-rock, with jackpine, maple, birch, and oaks. Watch for rock cairns that mark the trail.

The trail loop between Pauline and Nigh Lakes is unique because you will see some of the largest exposed boulders known anywhere in this area, as well as some old growth giant red and white pines. The section of trail around Astrid Lake is of more gentle terrain, with views of the lake from all around the south side. The trail then meets the portage that takes skiers to Forest Road 200.

Safety is an important consideration in winter travel, when weather conditions may compound any minor difficulty. Follow your map carefully. Carry a spare ski tip, extra clothes, high energy food, and matches. Ski so that you are always in control. Use caution on the hills. Watch for wind-fallen trees and branches which may obstruct the trail. Check with the La Croix District Office for trail conditions.

BIG MOOSE TRAIL
3.2 km (2 mi) of trails
beginner, intermediate

Big Moose Trial is located about halfway between Ely and Crane Lake, just south of the Echo Trail (County Road 116). The trailhead is off Forest Road 464 (Moose Loop Road), approximately 1.5 miles from its eastern junction with the Echo Trail. It is signed; pull-off vehicle parking is available across the road. Moose Loop Road may not be plowed in the winter, however, and snowpack may inhibit vehicle accessibility.

This trail is easy skiing in rolling red pine and jackpine country. The trail enters the Boundary Waters Canoe Area Widlerness near Big Moose Lake and continues on to a campsite on the lake's rocky shoreline. A travel permit is not required for winter BWCA use, but all other wilderness regulations remain in effect. Within a half mile from the trailhead, the trail crosses two old winter roads. Continue across both roads, veering slightly to the left. The rock cairns marking the way in this area may be snow-covered. Just before you arrive at the lake, you pass a grassy pond where standing dead snags make good nesting and roosting sites for wildlife. The trail continues through a stand of white pines to a BWCA campsite on the shoreline of Big Moose Lake. This trail makes a pleasant day trip.

See also Kawishiwi Ranger District, Coxey Pond Trail, page 132.

HERRIMAN LAKE TRAIL
22.4 km (14 mi) of trails
beginner, intermediate, advanced

Herriman Lake Trails are located about 43 miles northeast of Cook, near Crane Lake. The trailhead is located off County Road 424, about 2 miles east of County Road 24. It is on the east side of the road and is signed. A plowed parking area is on the west side of the road.

Approximately 14 miles of hiking and ski touring trails in the Herriman Lake system are now completed. Loops of different lengths and difficulty offer a wide variety of skiing adventures for novices to experts. About half of the completed distance lies within the Boundary Waters Canoe Area Wilderness. BWCA travel permits are not required in the winter, but all other wilderness regulations remain in effect. Signing is minimal (there are a few caution signs); no trail signs are used within the Wilderness.

Echo River picnic site is located at the rapids, 0.4 mile from the trailhead. This is a day-use area only. There are three BWCA campsites on the trail system, reached by spur trails off the main route. Primitive box latrines are available at the Echo River picnic site and at the campsites.

Shortly after you cross the bridge over the Echo River, your choices of trail routes begin. You can continue eastward on the main trail past Knute Lake to the shores of Little Vermilion Lake. This route includes some challenging hills and corners, particularly east of Knute Lake. One loop east of Knute Lake begins and ends at the main trail. Another trail switchbacks to the south side of Herriman Lake for some bird's-eye views, and then drops to join the trail along the Echo River. This section of trail is recommended for hiking only, but can be skied by experts.

The southern route along Echo River, from the picnic area to the Herriman Lake junction, is the easiest section. This gently rolling trail becomes more difficult as it climbs to the ridgetop south of Baylis Lake. Vistas of oxbows along the river and views of the surrounding miles of forest are worth the climb, as is the wild race down to the Echo River picnic site.

The Dovre Lake loop is the most recent addition to this system. On its 4-mile length, it crosses a number of ledgerock outcroppings and provides good viewpoints of Dovre Lake, beaver ponds, and surrounding forest.

See also Voyageurs National Park, Mukooda Ski Trail, page 188.

NORWAY TRAIL
4 km (2.5 mi) of trails
intermediate

Norway Trail is located approximately 53 miles northeast of Cook and approximately 38 miles northwest of Ely. The trailhead is at the end of the Nigh Creek Road

(Forest Road 471), about 5 miles south of the Echo Trail (County Road 116). Road side parking is available at the trailhead. The Nigh Creek Road is not plowed in the winter, however, and snowpacking may inhibit vehicle accessibility.

Norway Trail is named for its stands of Norway or red pines. It was originally used as an administrative trail to a fire watchtower. The last 0.5 mile of the trail, adjoining Trout Lake, lies within the Boundary Waters Canoe Area Wilderness. A travel permit is not required for winter BWCA use, but all other wilderness regulations remain in effect. No BWCA campsite exists at the trail's end, but there are BWCA campsites elsewhere on Trout Lake.

The trail begins south of Norway Creek, with its grassy meadows, and climbs a sidehill to a spruce and jackpine blowdown area. Take plenty of time in this area; identify the trail by the windfallen trees that have been cut away.

Beyond the blowdown area is a stand of magnificent old Norway pines that once sheltered a ranger cabin. Still evident is the trail up the rocky edge to the fire lookout tower site. Telephone wire and insulators can still be found in the area. The trail crosses a beaver drainage before finally emerging on the shoreline of the North Arm of Trout Lake.

This trail had previously been maintained for 8 miles, until the Nigh Creek Road was extended southward. The trail now makes a good day trip.

SIOUX-HUSTLER TRAIL
DEVIL'S CASCADE
41.6 km (26 mi) of trails
intermediate, advanced

Sioux-Hustler Trail is located approximately 55 miles northeast of Cook and approximately 45 miles northwest of Ely. This horseshoe-shaped trail has two access points off Echo Trail (County Road 116) and crosses five portage trails within the Boundary Waters Canoe Area Wilderness.

Access 1 is off Echo Trail, approximately 16 miles east of County Road 24. Parking is available; however, the parking area is not plowed in the winter. The trailhead is signed.

Access 2 is at Meander Lake Picnic Site, off Forest Road 467 (Meander Lake Road), about 1.25 miles north of the Echo Trail. The trailhead is signed at the picnic site. Parking is available; however, Meander Lake Road and the parking area are not plowed in the winter, and snowpack may inhibit vehicle accessibility.

Most of this 41.6-km (26-mi) trail lies within the BWCA. A travel permit is not required for winter BWCA use, but all other wilderness regulations remain in effect. The trail is intersected by five portage trails within the BWCA: Elm Creek Portage, Lower Pauness Lake/Shell Lake Portage, Devil's Cascade Portage, Loon Lake/Heritage Creek Portage, and the Hustler Lake/Oyster Lake Portage.

Only very experienced winter ski-campers should venture farther than a day's trek on the Sioux-Hustler Trail. Winter weather compounds any minor difficulty you might encounter, and during this season, such remoteness might be undesirable. This trail was designed primarily for hiking, so it is not cleared as wide as most ski trails. There may be windfallen trees with which to contend, and difficulty in locating the trail in open aras is increased when the trail is under snow.

From the trailhead adjacent to the Echo Trail the skier descends toward Little Indian Sioux River. The trail intersects Elm Creek Portage and then crosses the river. The lack of a bridge invites some ingenuity in the crossing. The trail rises from the river bottom to the high point at Devil's Cascade Portage.

The route to Pageant Lake follows a ridgeline before dropping to beaver flowages where the beaver dams are used as part of the trail. Pageant is one of the more isolated lakes in the BWCA, as it is one of the few not accessible by a water route. There is a path from the Sioux-Hustler Trail to the only developed campsite on the lake. Rangeline Lake is 2 miles from Pageant Lake.

From Rangeline Lake to Emerald Lake, the trail rises to the ridgetop, intersects the Hustler-to-Oyster Portage, and continues past the junction of a spur trail that leads to the campsite on Emerald Lake. Beyond Emerald Lake, the skier enters the burned area of the 1971 Little Indian Sioux Fire. Close to 15,000 acres were burned in that fire. Across two beaver flowages and through tall marsh grasses, the trail is sometimes obscure. Take plenty of time; look for windfalls that have been cut from the trail and for blaze marks. A short distance from the trail's Meander Lake end, there is an excellent vista where the skier can get some idea of the size and result of the Little Indian Sioux Fire.

Once you have completed the trail, the challenge remains to return to your starting point. Remember, it is 11.2 km (7 mi) between trailheads.

Day tours are possible on this trail. It is approximately 4 km (2.5 mi) from Echo Trail access to the waterfalls on Elm Creek Portage. From this point, it is another 4 km (2.5 mi) to Devil's Cascade. This 8-km (5-mi) stretch from Echo Trail to Devil's Cascade can make a challenging day trip. The view from the high point at Devil's Cascade Portage, overlooking the gorge, is ample reward for a good morning on skis. After lunch and a rest, there should still be enough time for you to return before dark. From Meander Lake trailhead to Emerald Lake is approximately 11.2 km (7 mi), a distance that could also make a day trip or a good place to stop for a rest on a longer tour. The entire length of the Sioux-Hustler Trail, with its adjacent lakes and campsites, allows for a variety of skiing adventures.

For those who wish to camp, there are five BWCA campsites on lakes and the Indian Sioux River that are accessible from the Sioux-Hustler Trail. They are at Devil's Cascade, Pageant Lake, Rangeline Lake, Hustler Lake, and Emerald Lake. Check the trail map for the campsite locations.

STUART LAKE TRAIL
(formerly, LA CROIX TRAIL)
12.8 km (8 mi) of trails
intermediate, advanced

Stuart Lake Trail is located about halfway between Ely and Crane Lake, on the north side of the Echo Trail (County Road 116). The trailhead is on Echo Trail, approximately 1.5 miles east of the eastern end of Forest Road 464 (Moose Loop Road).

The trailhead is signed, and offroad parking is available. However, the parking area is not plowed in winter.

Stuart Lake Trail ends at a BWCA campsite on the shoreline of Stuart Lake. All but the first 0.4 km (0.25 mi) of the trail lies in the BWCA. A travel permit is not required for winter BWCA use, but all other wilderness regulations remain in effect.

Safety is an important consideration in winter travel. Only the skier who is well-conditioned and experienced in winter survival should venture more than a partial length of this trail. An old gravel pit/heliport that marks the beginning of the trail is now maintained as a grassy wildlife opening. The trail intersects two portages from Stuart Lake, one around the falls where the Stuart River enters the lake and one on the way to Nibin Lake.

Stuart Lake Trail, formerly called La Croix Trail, was once an administrative trail to the Forest Service cabin on Lac La Croix. Telephone wires and insulators can still be found in places along the route.

For further information, contact

La Croix Ranger District, District Ranger, Superior National Forest, U.S. Forest Service, P.O. Box 1085, Cook, MN 55723. 218-666-5251

Forest Supervisor, Superior National Forest, P.O. Box 338, Duluth, MN 55801. 218-727-6692

Lutsen Resort and Ski Touring Center
Village at Lutsen Mountain
Lutsen, Minnesota

See North Shore Mountains Ski Trail, page 159.

Lutsen Sea Villas
Lutsen, Minnesota

See North Shore Mountains Ski Trail, page 158.

Marcell Ranger District/Chippewa National Forest
Marcell, Minnesota

Marcell Ranger District has one trail, Suomi Hills, that is suitable for cross-country skiing.

SUOMI HILLS RECREATION AREA
29 km (18.1 mi) of trails
advanced

Suomi Hills is located 19 miles north-northwest of Grand Rapids (milepost 19) on Highway 38. A parking lot is located at the trailhead. The southern trailhead at milepost 14.5 is not yet developed, but there are plans for this in the future. The management plan for this area specifies non-motorized recreational use. Timber harvesting does take place in the area, however.

This area consists of 5,000 acres of very hilly, very heavily wooded terrain, dotted with many small lakes. Only brief distances at the very beginning of the trail are suitable for novice skiers. And although there are occasional intermediate stretches on the trail, due to the terrain and the distances involved, it must be rated as an advanced system, designed for the expert skier. The trail is marked and groomed. Future plans exist for the layout of a 4-km (2.5-mi) beginner loop and for track-setting the entire trail system.

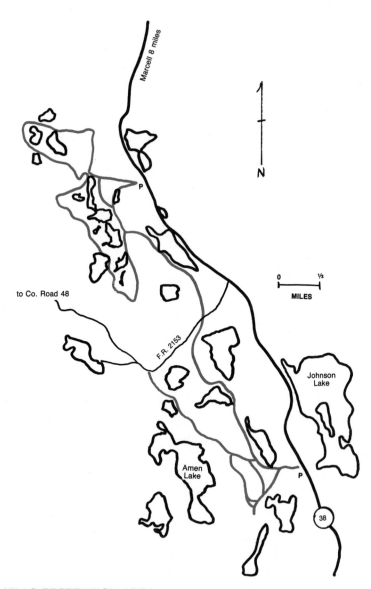

SUOMI HILLS RECREATION AREA

There are six primitive campsites (fire ring, pit toilet, tent pad) on site. Drinking water should be purified if obtained from the lakes. Handpumps are not available. Snowshoeing is welcome in the recreation area, but snowshoers must stay off the ski trails. Lodging and the rental of equipment is available in Grand Rapids.

For further information, contact

District Ranger, Marcell Ranger District, Chippewa National Forest, Marcell, MN 56657. 218-832-3161

Forest Supervisor, Chippewa National Forest, Cass Lake, MN 56633. 218-335-2226

See also Itasca County, Amen Lake Trails, page 127 and Blueberry Hills Ski Trail, page 84.

McCarthy Beach State Park
Hibbing, Minnesota

12.8 km (8 mi) of trails

intermediate

McCarthy Beach State Park is located in St. Louis County, near the city of Hibbing. Take Highway 169 north from Hibbing to County Road 5. Proceed north on this road for 15 miles to the park entrance. The park is situated between Sturgeon Lake and Side Lake.

First settlers to this area found giant red and white pines as far as the eye could see. Sturgeon Lake region was very attractive to early loggers. Two fellows named Hibbing and Trimble started the first sawmill at the site that is now Hibbing. This mill provided all the wood for the developing mining town. By 1895, a railroad owned by the Swan River Logging Company was moving lumber to the Swan River where the logs were floated to Minneapolis sawmills, via the Mississippi River.

The park's terrain is mainly rolling hills with many small valleys. This offers the visitor opportunities for observing wildlife, including black bear, timber wolves, and deer.

During the glacial period, ice gouged and tore at the region's volcanic bedrock. The glaciers moved south, retreated north, and flowed south again. The first glacier stopped where McCarthy Beach is now located, leaving moraines composed of boulders, stones, and other debris. The trails are situated along the ridgetops of these moraines.

The trailhead is at the park's information center. The trail moves the length of the narrow strip of land between Sturgeon and Side Lakes and proceeds around the northeast side of Sturgeon Lake. One of the three main loops skirts Pickerel Lake, with several spurs. The trail joins Taconite State Trail in the north end of the park. Snowmobiling is allowed in the park and the trails move parallel to and sometimes join with the ski trails.

Water, toilets, winter camping facilities, and a trail shelter are available. Food, lodging, and supplies may be obtained at Side Lake or Hibbing.

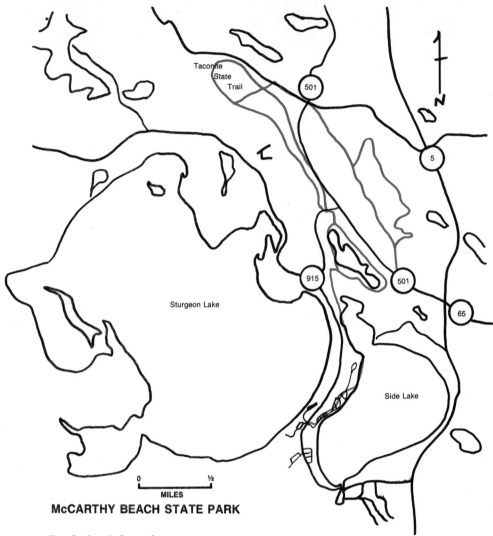

McCARTHY BEACH STATE PARK

For further information, contact

McCarthy Beach State Park, Park Manager, Star Route 2, Hibbing, MN 55746. 218-254-2411

Minnesota Department of Natural Resources, Division of Parks and Recreation, Box 39 Centennial Building, St. Paul, MN 55155. 612-296-4776

See also Scenic State Park, page 174; Virginia Ranger District/Superior National Forest, Sturgeon River Ski Trail, page 186; George Washington State Forest, Thistledew Ski Touring Trail, page 190.

Moose Lake Recreation Area
Moose Lake, Minnesota

6.4 km (4 mi) of trails

intermediate

Moose Lake Recreation Area is located in Carlton County, approximately 2 miles east of the town of Moose Lake. It is intersected by Interstate 35. To enter the park, take the Moose Lake exit on Interstate 35, and travel east on County Road 137 for 0.4 mile to the information center.

The trails are located in two spots in the park. One trail (2.9 km) begins at the information center and is set up in a three-loop system. A great part of the trail skirts the northeast side of Echo Lake. Camping is available on these trails. The other section of trail is located on the opposite side of Interstate 35, in the northwest corner of the park. It is a large loop (3.5 km) and approaches the shores of Moosehead Lake.

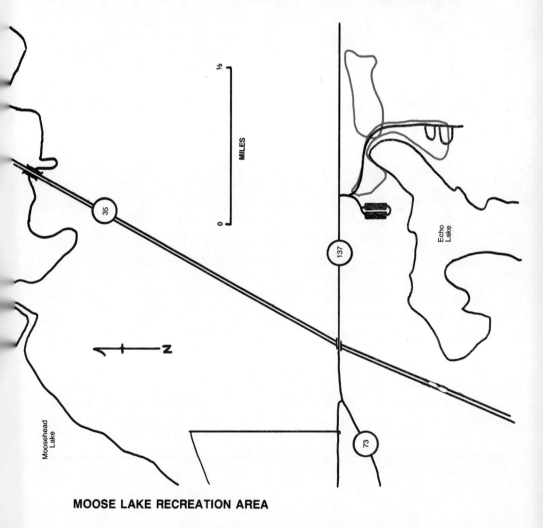

MOOSE LAKE RECREATION AREA

All trails are marked. Maps, outdoor privies, shelter, and parking are available at the park. Snowmobiling is allowed, but such trails are entirely separate from the ski trails, with the exception of a junction near the information center.

Food, lodging, and supplies may be obtained in Moose Lake.

For further information, contact

Moose Lake State Park, Park Manager, 1000 County Road 137, Moose Lake, MN 55767. 218-485-4059

Minnesota Department of Natural Resources, Division of Parks and Recreation, Box 39 Centennial Building, St. Paul, MN 55155. 612-296-4776

See also Fond Du Lac State Forest, page 99 and Jay Cooke State Park, page 87.

National Forest Lodge,
Isabella Minnesota

47 km (29.4 mi) of trails

beginner, intermediate, advanced

National Forest Lodge is located on Highway 1, approximately 35 miles southeast of Ely or 8 miles west of Isabella, which is 30 miles northwest of Highway 61 (Illgen City).

This facility is operated yearround and is immediately adjacent to the Flathorn-Gegoka Ski Trail of the Isabella Ranger District, Superior National Forest. All trails are marked, groomed, and track-set. The terrain is rolling to hilly. Instruction is available by reservation. Maps, toilets and ample parking are available at the lodge, as are ski and snowshoe rentals. There are condominiums, cabins, and a main lodge with a fireplace. Here, meals are served family style. No trail fee is charged.

For further information, contact

Bob Hunger, 3226 Highway 1, Isabella, MN 55607. 218-323-7676

See also Finland State Forest, Woodland Caribou Ski Trail, page 97 and Isabella Ranger District/Superior National Forest, Flathorn-Gegoka Ski Trail, page 123.

North Shore Mountains Ski Trail
Lutsen-Tofte Tourism Association
Little Marais to Grand Marais, Minnesota

203 km (126.9 mi) of trails

beginner, intermediate, advanced

North Shore Mountains Ski Trail system has been developed by the Lutsen-Tofte Tourism Association, in cooperation with the Superior National Forest, Cascade River State Park, Temperance River State Park, representatives of the Minnesota Department of Natural Resources, and private landowners. Ongoing assistance will be provided by volunteer groups, such as the North Star Ski Club.

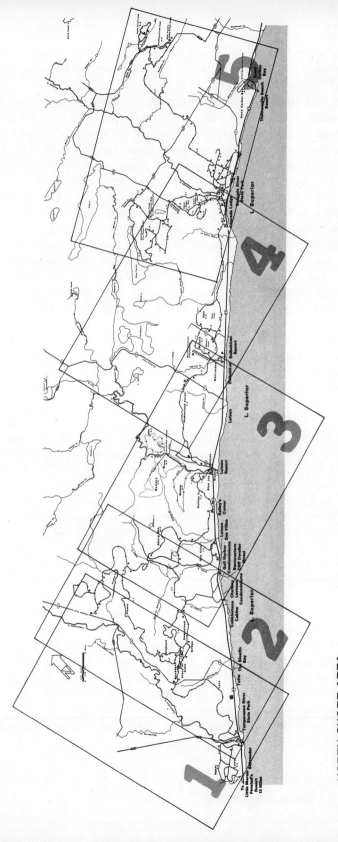

NORTH SHORE AREA

The Forest Service helped participants build the trails, with the efforts of a large group of North Stars. The state parks and private workers hired by the sponsoring resorts groom and track-set the trails.

The 203-km trail system is anchored on the southwest end by Temperance River State Park and on the northeast end by Bear Track Outfitting's Bally Creek Camp. The continuous network of trails runs roughly parallel with Highway 61 (the North Shore Drive) from just northeast of Schroeder to Grand Marais. Participating sponsors begin with Fenstad's Resort in Little Marais. Fenstad's Resort and Thomsonite Beach (in Grand Marais) are participating resorts that have their own separate trails.

The entire system is designed primarily for the beginner to intermediate skier; however, advanced areas will be encountered enroute. Skiers must keep in mind that certain weather and snow conditions produce very difficult conditions even on novice trails. Also, the considerable distances involved on some easier routes can make skiing quite a challenge for those who are not well-conditioned. Therefore, *ski within your ability* and *ski with caution*. The trails are well-marked, and there are caution indicators at many of the rough spots. The maps also designate the more difficult segments. NO DOGS, SNOWSHOES, OR MOTORIZED VEHICLES ARE ALLOWED ON THE TRAILS.

The area offers good skiing conditions both early and late in the season. You can tour usually into mid-April on the North Shore. Lake Superior exerts a tempering effect on the climate. Rarely is the weather bitterly cold near the shore. As visitors move inland a few miles or into the upper elevations of the Sawtooth Mountains, the snowfall becomes much heavier, assuring snow conditions of continuously high quality for ski touring.

At Lutsen Mountain Village, skiers can have the best of both worlds. For the price of a cross-country ticket at Lutsen Resort and Ski Touring Center, skiers may also use the chairlifts at the alpine area of the Village at Lutsen Mountain. The lifts take skiers to the tops of the Sawtooth Mountains where snow conditions are always top-notch and the views over the North Shore are most spectacular.

The use of the trails is free; however, the State of Minnesota does require the skier to possess the cross-country license on certain trail segments. Check with the participating resorts, the state parks, or the U.S. Forest Service for details.

There are four ski touring centers on the system that provide the convenience of rental equipment as well as the retail sale of equipment, relative supplies, and accessories. These centers will be noted in the following text.

Area lodging establishments offer a wide variety of accommodations from economically and moderately priced motels to cabins, lodges, condominiums, and townhouses. Participating resorts offer a lodge-to-lodge ski-through program that enables individuals or groups the opportunity of staying at one lodge and skiing on to another. Arrangements will be made for luggage to be transported point-to-point. Maximum distance between the resorts is 5–6 miles, with many much closer together. Their package costs $109.50 per person, double occupancy. It includes three nights of lodging; three breakfasts, three trail lunches, and three dinners; and luggage transport. Contact the establishments for further information.

In the past, the Tourism Association offered a Ski Challenge. For a modest fee, participants were given a North Shore Challenge patch and a passport that, when validated for sections skied, entitled the skier to a challenge pin. If three sections were skied, a bronze pin was awarded; for four sections, a silver pin; for five sections, a gold pin. Participants were also eligible for drawings, with equipment, dinners, and free lodging as prizes.

For further information, contact

Lutsen-Tofte Tourism Association, President, Char Erickson, Box 115, Lutsen, MN 55612. 218-663-7816, 800-652-9747 (toll free Minnesota), 800-328-1461 (toll free elsewhere)

Bill Blank, Trail Coordinator, Lutsen-Tofte Tourism Association, Solbakken Resort, ESR Box 170, Lutsen, MN 55612. 218-663-7566

North Shore Mountains Ski Trail
Fenstad's Resort
Little Marais, Minnesota

16 km (10 mi) of trails

Fenstad's Resort is the first participating establishment in the North Shore Mountains Ski Trail Ski-Through Program. It is located at Little Marais, 13 miles southwest of Temperance River State Park, on Highway 61. Fenstad's trail system is not interconnected with the North Shore Mountains Trail (neither is Thomsonite Beach by Grand Marais). Nevertheless, they are participants in the system, and all benefits and regulations apply. The 16 km of trails, which lead directly from the resort are entirely groomed.

The cabins hold two to six persons and have fireplaces, completely equipped kitchens, and shower baths.

For further information, contact

Fenstad's Resort, Star Route 25, Little Marais, MN 55661. 218-226-4724

North Shore Mountains Ski Trail
Temperance River State Park/Cross River Wayside
Schroeder, Minnesota

13 km (8.1 mi) of trails

intermediate

Temperance River State Park is located in Cook County, 1 mile northeast of the town of Schroeder, and 2 miles southwest of the town of Tofte on Highway 61. The park participates in the North Shore Mountains Ski Trail and is at the far southwestern terminus of the system. One participating establishment is further to the southwest, Fenstad's Resort; however, the 16 km of trails at the resort do not connect with the network. To the northwest of the park is the next participating resort, Bluefin Bay (formerly the Edgewater).

The trails in the park are basically set up in two systems: **Upper** and **Lower Cross River Loops** on one side of the Temperance River and **Temperance River Trail** on the other side of the river. Although interconnected, the sections are divided by the passage of the river through the area involved.

The trails to the west and southwest of the river are **Upper** and **Lower Cross River Loops**. There are two access points with parking lots: the main trailhead is at Temperance River State Park's parking lot on Highway 61; the other trailhead is on the Cross River Lower Loop at the end of a short gravel road that is located directly north of the gasoline station in Schroeder.

From the main trailhead, you follow a steady uphill grade for 1 km (0.6 mi) to an intersection with the Temperance River Road (Forest Road 343). The land is forested with white birch, aspen, and some spruce. The trail crosses the road and moves into an aspen regeneration area. Although the mature timber was cut in 1972, this section shows dramatically how under proper management a forest can quickly regenerate itself as a renewable resource. The trail then heads southwest to the Cross River where a covered shelter overlooks the river valley. There is a toilet here and a map that shows your location. You may ski southward into the Lower Loop (again, there is the Schroeder trailhead on this loop) or continue on the Upper Loop (follow the trail marked Sawbill back to the Temperance River Road. Traveling north on the road you may encounter snowmobiles for a distance of approximately 0.5 km (0.3 mi). You return to the harvested stand. Turn to the right (toward the Temperance), and follow the original route to the park's parking area.

Or, halfway through the original route, you may cross the Temperance River to **Temperance River Trail**, the second section of the park's trail system, the most attractive and difficult trail. Crossing the frozen river, which is very broad and shallow at this point, listen to the river as it falls through rock gorges just downstream. Continue straight ahead, and begin the loop in a counterclockwise direction.

The area is forested primarily in white birch, the same tree species used by the Ojibwe and French voyageurs for building canoes. The trail eventually crosses a steep ravine, the pre-historic riverbed of the Temperance. During the last glaciation, ice blocked the channel, and the river was diverted to its present course. The ravine is quite steep, and skiers may have to herringbone. The trail proceeds above the old riverbed— look down the smooth canyon walls and consider the ancient erosive forces. To the right, you pass an area cultivated to produce young tree sprouts for deer feeding. The trees are regularly cut so that the protein-rich shoots are within reach of deer. The trail begins a long descent to the river. The hills surrounding the river valley are open to view, and you pass above the cascades of the eighth pool of the Temperance. The final stretch of the trail parallels the river and returns to the original river crossing point.

On Temperance River Trail, you may also take **Lynx Trail** northeast toward Carlton Peak to Sugarbush Cross-Country Ski Trail, a system that is the next segment of the North Shore Mountains Ski Trail. It is an intermediate trail. Or, if visitors do not wish to ski up to Sugarbush, they may travel up Highway 61 to Tofte, and turn onto County Road 2 (Sawbill Trail) at Bluefin Bay. This road leads to a trailhead with the system. Parking is available.

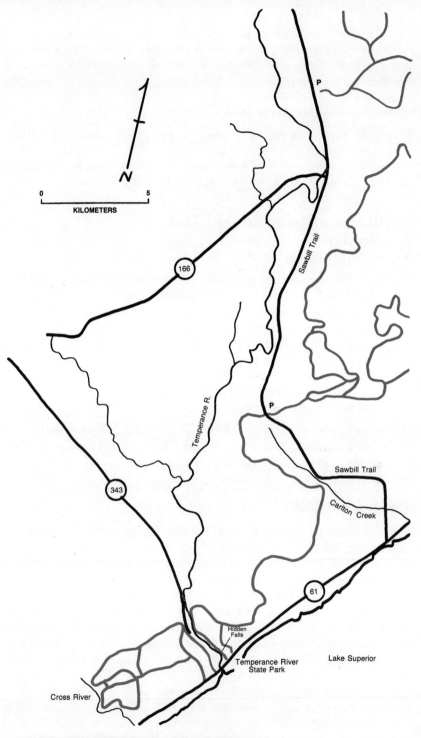

NORTH SHORE MOUNTAINS SKI TRAILS—1

In the state park, maps are available. Winter camping is allowed. Tourist accommodations and supplies may be obtained in Schroeder or Tofte. Check with Fenstad's Resort in Little Marais or Bluefin Bay in Tofte for the special accommodations and privileges for those staying at resorts participating in the North Shore Mountains Ski Trail.

For further information, contact

Temperance River State Park, Park Manager, Box 133, Schroeder, MN 55613. 218-663-7476

Minnesota Department of Natural Resources, Division of Parks and Recreation, Box 39 Centennial Building, St. Paul, MN 55155. 612-296-4776

North Shore Mountains Ski Trail
Bluefin Bay
Tofte, Minnesota

Bluefin Bay (formerly the Edgewater) is located at the intersection of Highway 61 and County Road 2 (Sawbill Trail). Guests may travel north and west on Sawbill Trail from Bluefin Bay to the junction with Lynx Trail, which connects the trails of Temperance River State Park to the southwest to the Sugarbush system of the Tofte Ranger District to the northeast. Britton Peak parking lot is 2 miles from Bluefin Bay. You may have immediate access to the Lynx Trail at this point.

Bluefin Bay offers comfortable accommodations, fine dining, cocktails, and entertainment. Banquet and conference facilities are available.

For further information, contact

Bluefin Bay, Tofte, MN 55615. 218-663-7227, 800-862-3656 (toll free)

North Shore Mountains Ski Trail
Tofte Ranger District/Superior National Forest
Tofte, Minnesota

SUGARBUSH CROSS-COUNTRY SKI TRAIL
beginner, intermediate, advanced
Superior National Forest's Sugarbush Cross-Country Ski Trail is a large portion of the North Shore Mountains Ski Trail network. It is accessible from Temperance River State Park to the southwest (via the Lynx Trail); Cobblestone Cabins, Chateau Leveaux, Gull Harbor Condominiums, all by Tofte; and the Best Western Cliff Dweller, the Lutsen Sea Villas, and Lutsen Resort, all by Lutsen. This segment not only involves trails maintained by the Forest Service, but also by the Minnesota DNR and participating private establishments. All trails are open to the public. No fee is charged.

The trails are entirely marked with blue degree-of-difficulty diamonds, directional arrows, caution signs, and you-are-here maps. Carefully follow the directional arrows to avoid unexpected caution hills and to protect the set track. At the beginning of each loop is a degree-of-difficulty diamond meant to protect skiers from overextending themselves and to challenge more skilled and experienced skiers.

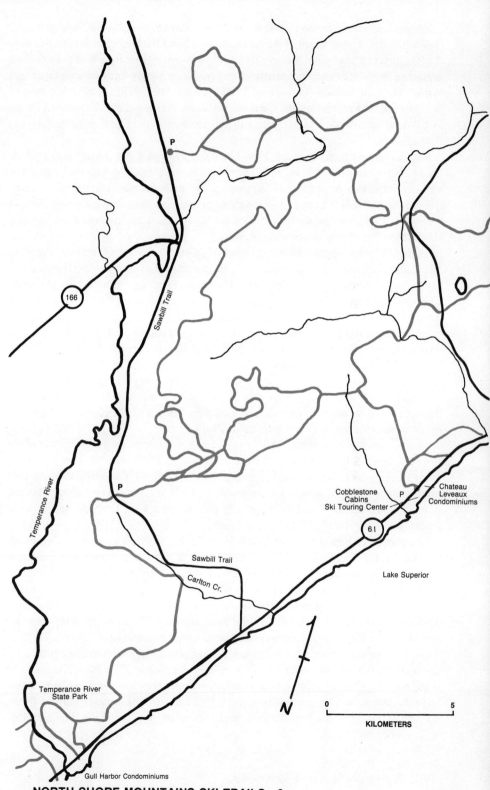

166

Temperance River

Sawbill Trail

P

P

Sawbill Trail

Carlton Cr.

Temperance River
State Park

Cobblestone
Cabins
Ski Touring Center

P

Chateau
Leveaux
Condominiums

61

Lake Superior

O

N

0   5
KILOMETERS

Gull Harbor Condominiums

NORTH SHORE MOUNTAINS SKI TRAILS—2

Immediate access to the trail is at the Britton Peak parking lot on County Road 2 (Sawbill Trail), 2 miles north of the intersection of 2 and Highway 61 near Bluefin Bay.

The first 0.8 km of the Sugarbush Trail is a two-way moderate access to the two beginning loops. The terrain consists of gently rolling slopes forested with large, old maple. The trail follows the base of Britton Peak. After skiing around the base of Britton Peak, Lake Superior and Carlton Peak come into view. As skiers travel on the loops of the Sugarbush, it is interesting to note their position in relation to the lake and Carlton Peak.

The first two beginning loops, **Woodduck** and **Piece of Cake**, are rolling, gradual, and easily negotiated by all skiers. Each loop is approximately 0.8 km in length. The trail is primarily in maple forests, although a few mixed conifer and aspen are interspersed throughout the maple. Traveling east on the beginning loops, the trail follows the base of a ridge and passes by a small pond. Again, there are vistas of Lake Superior and Carlton Peak through the large maples.

The first intermediate loop begins north of an incline from the Piece of Cake loop. The trail climbs through maple and birch, then levels off to overlook the Temperance River Valley and the many maple ridges. The terrain is rolling, with the hills becoming a bit more difficult. After a short, steep climb, the trail reaches the top of a hogback ridge. A caution hill and a test of skiing skills follows the hogback. If you are unable to negotiate the hill and the curve, feel free to use the runout provided. The trail then returns to novice level. You are now on the east side of Piece of Cake.

Other loops have been provided for advanced and long distance skiers who wish to spend the entire day touring. **Picnic** and **Homestead Loops**, longer and more difficulty, are well worth the expended time and effort. The trail is laid out to incorporate the overlooks and old road systems. There are overviews of the Temperance River Valley from the lookouts on the west side of Picnic.

Picnic Loop is the largest, 25.1 km (15.7 mi), and begins on the north side of the Hogback Loop of the Sugarbush Trail. It is strictly an advanced trail. It provides another access point to the Moose Fence Trail (see the following information) and connects with the Oberg Mountain Trail and with the trails to Cobblestone Cabins, Chateau Leveaux, Gull Harbor Condominiums, and Best Western Cliff Dweller, and with the Homestead Loop.

Homestead Loop is an intermediate loop, 7.5 km (4.7 mi) long. It connects with the loops of the Sugarbush Trail, the most adjacent loop being Bridge Run, and provides access to the same trails as the Picnic Loop.

Moose Fence Cross-Country Ski Trail is designed in a loop system. Both the beginning and end are at the White Pine Blister Rush Research sign, which is by the parking lot on County Road 2 (Sawbill Trail), approximately 7 miles north of the intersection of County Road 2 and Highway 61. The parking lot is regularly plowed. The trail is easily identified by blue marker diamonds. There are no facilities along the trail, such as a warming hut, toilets, water. No fee is charged for the use of the trail. The trailhead is located at a 10-acre research plot, where it is hoped that a strain of white pine can be produced that will be genetically resistant to the blister rust disease. This would allow the Forest Service to reforest the land with white pine, once the dominant tree species in this area. The trail gets its name from the fence around the research plot that was built to keep out the moose so that they would not eat the young trees. Moose Fence loops interconnect with Picnic Loop and, consequently, all trails relative to it.

Tourist accommodations are available in the Tofte area. Skiers are encouraged to check with the participating members in the North Shore Mountains Trail system for details concerning their special ski-through program.

For further information, contact

Tofte Ranger District, District Ranger, Leland Schaar, U.S. Forest Service, Tofte, MN 55615. 218-663-7280

Forest Supervisor, Superior National Forest, P.O. Box 338, Duluth, MN 55801. 218-727-6692

North Shore Mountains Ski Trail

The following four resorts are participants in the North Shore Mountains Ski Trail and are located on a trail system that winds past the Leveaux Mountain area to Sugarbush Cross-Country Ski Trail of the Tofte Ranger District of Superior National Forest. It is a difficult stretch in part and ultimately connects with the large Picnic Loop and the Homestead Loop of the Sugarbush Cross-Country Ski Trail. From the Picnic Loop, skiers may enter the Oberg Mountain Trail and travel into the trails of the Lutsen area.

Cobblestone Cabins and Ski Touring Center
Tofte, Minnesota

Cobblestone Cabins are located northeast of Tofte, between Bluefin Bay and Chateau Leveaux, on Highway 61. The winterized housekeeping cabins overlook Lake Superior. You choose modern or rustic lodging. They are heated with propane heaters or woodstoves and have modern bathrooms or outdoor biffies.

A complete line of ski rentals, lessons, and backwoods tours are available. There is ample parking at the resort.

For further information, contact

Cobblestone Cabins, Tofte, MN 55615. 218-663-7957

Chateau Leveaux, Condominium Motor Inn
Tofte, Minnesota

Chateau Leveaux is located northeast of the town of Tofte, between Cobblestone Cabins and Gull Harbor Condominiums, on Highway 61. Visitors vacation with every comfort possible—indoor pool, whirlpool and sauna, games arcade,and in-room movies. All units face Lake Superior and have complete kitchens, fireplaces, color TV, and sound system. VISA and Master Card are accepted.

For further information, contact

Chateau Leveaux, Tofte, MN 55615. 218-663-7223

Gull Harbor Condominiums
Tofte, Minnesota

Gull Harbor Condominiums is located on Lake Superior, northeast of the town of Tofte, between Chateau Leveaux and Best Western Cliff Dweller, on Highway 61. Luxury accommodations are available at Gull Harbor—all condominiums have two or three bedrooms, are fully equipped, and have fireplaces. A sauna and whirlpool are available for after-ski relaxation. VISA and Master Card are accepted.

For further information, contact

Gull Harbor Condominiums, Tofte, MN 55615. 218-663-7205

Best Western Cliff Dweller Motel
Lutsen, Minnesota

Best Western Cliff Dweller is located on a site overlooking Lake Superior. It is between Gull Harbor Condominiums and Lutsen Sea Villas, on Highway 61. This establishment has rooms with color TV, in-room movies, direct-dial telephones, and complimentary coffee and pizza. Plug-ins for cars are available. The motel is 3 miles from the Lutsen Ski Area. All major credit cards are accepted; ample parking is available.

For further information, contact

Best Western Cliff Dweller, Char Erickson, Lutsen, MN 55612. 218-663-7469

North Shore Mountains Ski Trail
Lutsen Sea Villas
Lutsen, Minnesota

intermediate, advanced

Lutsen Sea Villas are located on Highway 61, northeast of the Best Western Cliff Dweller Motel, and southwest of Lutsen Resort and the Village at Lutsen Mountain.

Trails from the Sea Villas run up to the Oberg Mountain Trail of the Sugarbush Cross-Country Ski Trail of the Tofte Ranger District, Superior National Forest. The trail is for intermediate skiers. However, one segment, where it joins the Picnic Loop, is advanced in difficulty. You may also ski a short distance up toward Oberg Mountain and turn to the right on the Rollins Creek Trail, which leads to Lutsen Resort and Ski Touring Center and the Village at Lutsen Mountain.

Sea Villas are yearround luxury condominiums, located on Lake Superior. All have electric heat, full kitchen facilities, fireplace, and lakeside deck. Units accommodate 2–12 persons. The Lutsen Resort pool and sauna are available to Villa guests. The condominiums are for rental or for sale.

For further information, contact

Lutsen Sea Villas, George Nelson, Jr., Lutsen, MN 55612. 218-663-7212, 800-232-0071 (toll free Minnesota), 800-346-1467 (toll free elsewhere)

North Shore Mountains Ski Trail
Lutsen Resort and Ski Touring Center
Village at Lutsen Mountain
Lutsen, Minnesota

Lutsen Resort and the Village at Lutsen Mountain are located on Highway 61, between Tofte and Lutsen. Lutsen Sea Villas are to the southwest, and Solbakken Resort is to the northeast.

At this point on the North Shore, the Sawtooth Mountains rise over 1,000 feet above Lake Superior. From the tops of these mountains, skiers can take in a panorama of the lake in contrast with the rocky, rugged North Shore terrain. In the valley between the mountains, the Poplar River roars through gorges and over falls and rapids.

Skiing opportunities in a modern resort setting are just tremendous at Lutsen. A $5.00 per person trail fee is charged. Children under 10 ski free. There are two systems located here. The first system is Lutsen Ski Touring Trails at Lutsen Resort. The second is Lutsen Mountains Norpine System at the Village at Lutsen Mountain.

LUTSEN SKI TOURING TRAILS
30 km (18.8 mi) of trails

beginner, intermediate, advanced

The trailhead is located just off Highway 61, at the Ski Touring Center. Here one can rent or buy equipment, wax skis, purchase refreshments, and obtain maps and information. The system's total length is 30 km, and all five trails begin at the Center. All trails are marked, groomed, and track-set.

RIVER TRAIL AND EASY CANYON RIDE — located on the east side of the Poplar River. This loop provides access to both the northeast segment of North Shore Mountains Ski Trail in the direction of Solbakken Resort and to the Norpine System at Lutsen Mountain.

WEST CANYON CIRCLE — a short loop offering many scenic views of the Poplar River; well-suited to skiers of all abilities.

ALDERWOOD ROUND AND TURNAGAIN TRAIL — a beginner to intermediate trail which moves through a woodsy section of land. Chances of seeing rabbits, fox, and deer are high.

UPPER AND LOWER BLUE JAY CIRCLES — an intermediate trail that winds through a deciduous hardwood forest. Immature growth and berries provide good forage for both blue and Canadian jays, ruffed grouse, squirrels, and deer.

LODGE RUN — this trail provides access to the southwest segment of North Shore Mountains Ski Trail in the direction of the Lutsen Sea Villas; to Oberg Mountain Trail, and to Best Western Cliff Dweller Motel.

At the Center, shuttle service is provided to the Sugarbush Trailhead, which is 4–6 hours away from the Center by skis, and to the Homestead Acres Trailhead, which is 2–4 hours away from the Center by skis.

Adjacent to the Lutsen Ski Touring Trails and the Touring Center is the resort's Main Lodge, where a dining room is located. Breakfast, lunch, and supper are served here; there is a beautiful view of the lake. Lutsen Resort offers a wide variety of food and lodging facilities, from luxury to economy. There are swimming pool, sauna, game room, and cocktail lounges.

LUTSEN MOUNTAINS NORPINE SYSTEM
intermediate, advanced

The second system in the area is Lutsen Mountains Norpine System. The main base for these trails is at the Village at Lutsen Mountain, the alpine ski area, which is on County Road 36, a short distance off Highway 61. This is northwest of the Lodge at Lutsen Resort. The trails of this system are located on the mountain tops above the downhill slopes. Skiers from Lutsen Resort need only show the trail tickets purchased at the Ski Touring Center to use the lifts to this area. The four main trails are all marked, groomed, and track-set.

MOOSE TRAIL — Moose Mountain Trail winds and rolls southwest along the ridge, with vistas on either side. The skier gradually descends and turns in a northwesterly direction. The trail continues to fall gently until it meets Moose Mountain Road where the skier can head toward the Mystery Loops, ski down toward the lake, or ski to the base of the Moose lift to repeat the adventure.

RIVER TRAILS — The skier leaving from the Village Chalet can ski downhill to the base of Moose Mountain for a lift to the summit of the Moose Trail, or can turn upriver from the base of Moose to ride the Poma lift out of the valley to the Mystery Loops. The skier leaving the Townhouse area skis along the Poplar River Ridge, past a spectacular view of the Moose alpine slopes, and down toward the lake. (From the Townhouse area, access to the North Shore Mountain Trail system can be made at two different points. See map.)

MYSTERY LOOPS — The most popular access to these loops is from the upper ski area parking lot. The skier heads out in a northwesterly direction, crosses the Poplar River, then gradually climbs past an old homestead to the top of Mystery Mountain. Here, you can stop for a breather at the Mystery Chalet before skiing slowly down and around the mountain into the valley between Mystery and Moose. At intersecting trail points, the skier may opt for a longer route by heading toward Moose or the River Trails or may continue to loop back toward the trailhead.

ULLR LOOP — The ULLR Loop has just the right pace for most skiers. Chairlift 3 takes the skier to the top of ULLR Mountain where the trail gradually descends to the Poplar River Valley and then follows the ridge along the valley to the parking lot.

At the Village at Lutsen Mountain are condominiums and townhouse units with fireplaces, fully equipped kitchens, ski storage, and decks with spectacular views.

For further information, contact

Lutsen Resort, Ivy Hocking, Box 128, Lutsen, MN 55612. 218-663-7281, 800-232-0071 (toll free Minnesota), 800-366-1467 (toll free elsewhere)
Village at Lutsen Mountain, Lutsen, MN 55612. 218-663-7241

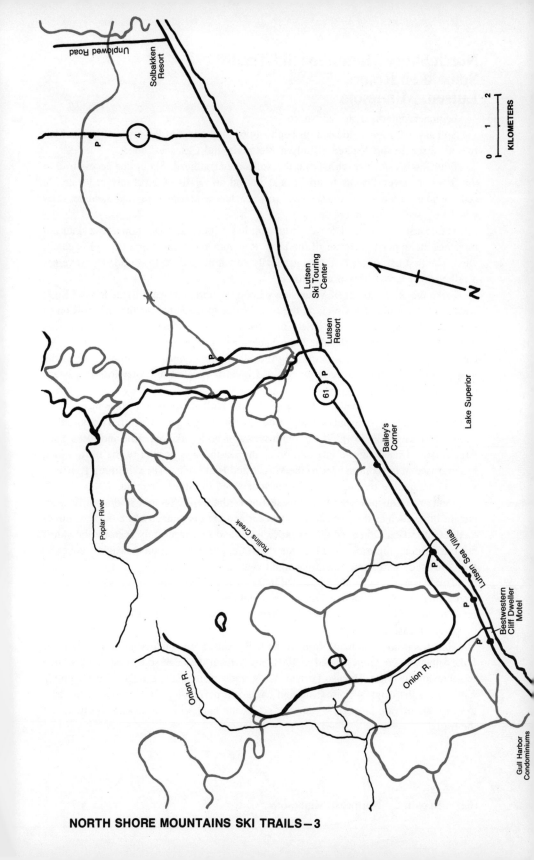

Unplowed Road

Solbakken Resort

4 P

Lutsen Ski Touring Center

Lutsen Resort

61 P

Bailey's Corner

Lake Superior

Poplar River

Rollins Creek

Lutsen Sea Villas

P

Bestwestern Cliff Dweller Motel

P

Onion R.

Onion R.

P

Gull Harbor Condominiums

2

1

0

KILOMETERS

N

NORTH SHORE MOUNTAINS SKI TRAILS–3

North Shore Mountains Ski Trail
Solbakken Resort
Lutsen, Minnesota

beginner, intermediate, advanced

Solbakken Resort is located on Highway 61, northeast of the town of Lutsen, between Lutsen Resort/Village at Lutsen Mountain and Cascade Lodge.

Four loops can be reached from the Solbakken trailhead. Ski up the access trail to the first one, **Deer Tracks Loop**. It is short and on relatively level terrain located in cedar woods with other mixed species. This is a deer wintering area, and the quiet skier will likely see several deer.

Whiteside's Loop is also a short loop. It has a short, steep section as the skier approaches the upper left corner of the loop. Recommended direction of travel is clockwise. The first part of the trail runs gradually downhill, and the lower portion traverses a rather level terrain that is easy to ski.

From the upper corner of Whiteside's Loop, a short spur leads to the Massie Road where you cross Jonvick Creek on the road bridge to reach the ski-through portion of the trail. **Massie Loop** has a variety of terrain, including open areas on the left side of the loop that offer spectacular Lake Superior vistas. After a steep climb, the skier enters birch woods before approaching the Massie homestead. The upper side of the loop passes through dense cedar woods and is fairly level. North Star Run is a steep, often fast downhill run.

Alternatively, you may ski the top portion of **Hall Loop**, with further increases in elevation, until you come out on a high ridge overlooking Lake Superior. The skier then begins a long, gentle downhill trek with views of both Lake Superior and Deer Yard Creek, before reaching the intersection of the ski-through portion of the trail, which is comprised of the bottom edge of the Massie and Hall Loops. The ski-through portion, with its undulating terrain, is a pleasant tour skied in either direction.

Deer are frequently seen from this section of the trail. You may also identify spectacular birds such as the pileated woodpecker and the uncommon black-backed, three-toed woodpecker. Other wildlife is more wary and less frequently seen by the skier, but tracks along the trail provide evidence of the presence of timber wolves, coyotes, fox, snowshoe hare, and numerous small rodents.

The Massie Farm was homesteaded in the early 1900s by Homer Massie, who operated a small farm that included dairy cows and an apple orchard. At one time, several more buildings occupied the site. The farm, abandoned since the 1950s, is on private property—please respect this.

Hall Loop takes its name from Hans K.P. Hall, a boatbuilder along the shore of Lake Superior. He homesteaded in 1901, away from the lake, so that he had a source of cedar for his boats. He also farmed. His grandson Jim Hall, a logger, lives with his family near the original homestead and has given permission for portions of the trail to cross his private property—your respect of the land will help ensure the future of the trail.

One particularly delightful ski trip, taking advantage of the change of elevation in this portion of the trail, begins at the Caribou Trail trailhead and travels generally downhill all the way to the Hall Road, where cars can also be parked. Passing Jonvick Creek, you may notice a trail paralleling the upper side of the Creek and heading back down to the shore. This is called Suicide Hill; it is a local-use unit, not maintained as part of the North Shore Mountains Ski Trail. It can be fast and dangerous—use it at your own risk!

Solbakken offers peace and solitude for the winter visitor. All units of the resort have kitchens—there are winterized waterfront cabins, a deluxe lake home with a fireplace, and an efficiency motel overlooking the lake.

On the premises is a book and gift shop that specializes in books about Minnesota, ski books, and nature guides. They also sell birchware, locally crafted products, and photographs. The resort has a lending library and hosts many after-ski gatherings. Snowshoe rental is available.

From the system by Solbakken, you may ski northeast to Cascade Lodge via the main artery trail that leads off the Hall Loop. Or you may ski to the Lutsen Resort/ Village at Lutsen Mountain area via the Homestead Acres Trail.

VISA, Master Card, and AAA are accepted.

For further information, contact

Solbakken Resort, Bill and Beth Blank, ESR Box 445, Lutsen, MN 55612. 218-663-7566

North Shore Mountains Ski Trail
Cascade Lodge, Restaurant, and Ski Touring Center
Lutsen, Minnesota

51 km (31.9 mi) of trails

beginner, intermediate, advanced

Cascade Lodge is located 9 miles southwest of Grand Marais, on Highway 61. It is situated northeast of Solbakken Resort and is immediately adjacent to Cascade River State Park. The trails of the Lodge and the state park are interconnected; the Cascade River is the geographic separation between them.

Cascade Lodge was an early leader in the development of cross-country skiing on the North Shore. The trails begin right at the Lodge and cabins of the facility. They are well-marked and groomed and will suit the abilities of all skiers, as well as give enough trailway to ski for several days. The park and the Lodge call their system the Cascade River and Deer Yard Lake Cross-Country Ski Trails and are the main trailheads of the network. Other access points can be reached by driving farther inland. A description of the park trails is included under its own heading, which follows this description of the Lodge.

The trails of the Deer Yard Lake area are fed by the Lodge and offer a landscape of astounding changes. Situated in the Sawtooth Mountains and environs, approximately 51 km (31.9 mi) of trails are included. There are nine loops of varying size,

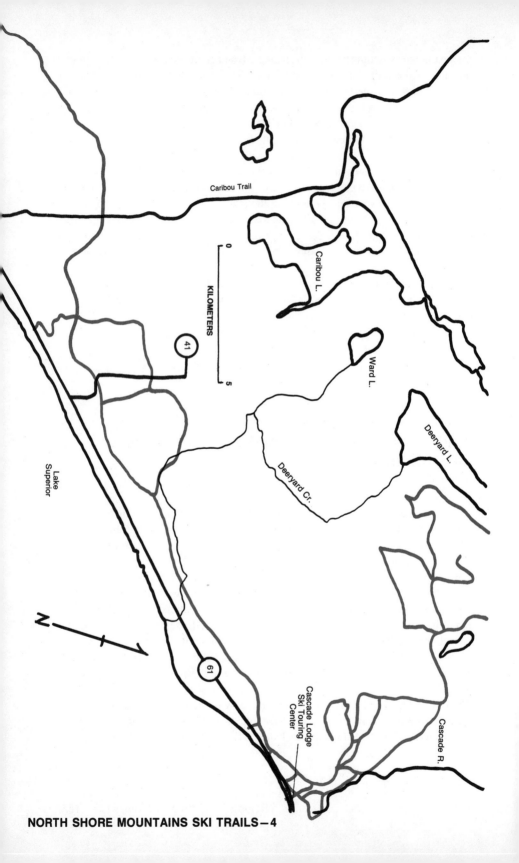

Caribou Trail

Caribou L.

Ward L.

Deeryard L.

Deeryard Cr.

0

KILOMETERS

5

41

Lake
Superior

N

61

Cascade Lodge
Ski Touring
Center

Cascade R.

NORTH SHORE MOUNTAINS SKI TRAILS—4

the largest being the loop at Deer Lake. The beginner and intermediate trail to Lookout Mountain is double-tracked and moves through a mixture of trees, especially moose maple. The summit is 617 feet above Lake Superior, and a nearby lookout provides a spectacular panorama of the lake and the forest. The shelter at the top is a good place to build a fire, lunch, and rest.

Upper and Lower Ridge Runs, both rated intermediate, are very popular because of the beautiful terrain. There is an 8.8-km (5.5-mi) loop called the Pioneer Trail, which takes the skier around ridge runs and gives the beginner some exciting opportunities.

The trails by Deer Yard Lake in the Jonvick Deer Yard will satisfy even the expert skier. The chance to see wildlife is high here—this is the largest winter deer yarding area in Minnesota. On the trail, a natural spring flows out of a bank and provides a cool, refreshing drink. Within this loop, you can ski up to the site of the Old Cascade Fire Tower and ride for almost a mile downhill to the start of the trail.

A loop within the Lodge system also skirts an area where there is a beaver pond. Many moose may be seen in the vicinity. Due to the greater snowfall inland from Lake Superior, Deer Yard Lake trails can be skied both earlier and later in the season.

The atmosphere at the Lodge is often described as warm, friendly, and wholesome. The main lodge has thirteen rental rooms, and other rooms provide games, TV, and fireplace. Other rental units include log cabins with fireplaces and a motel. Maximum lodging capacity at Cascade Lodge is 88 people. The restaurant has a reputation for fine food service and interesting decor. There is a gift shop at the restaurant. Group meeting facilities are available. Ski and snowshoe rentals, maps, and trail information are available in the Lodge. Master Card and VISA are accepted.

For further information, contact

Gene and Laurene Glader, Cascade Lodge, P.O. Box 93, Grand Marais, MN 55604. 218-387-1112

North Shore Mountains Ski Trail
Cascade River State Park
Lutsen, Minnesota

20.8 km (13 mi) of trails

beginner, intermediate, advanced

Cascade River State Park is located in Cook County southwest of Grand Marais, on Highway 61. Follow 61 northeast from Tofte for 21 miles to the park. The trails begin immediately northeast of Cascade Lodge.

The park is situated in a strip along the shores of Lake Superior. The setting offers diversity: the beautiful Cascade River with its many waterfalls, the rugged shoreline of Lake Superior, and the superb terrain produced by the Sawtooth Mountains. Of interest also is Minnesota's largest winter deer yarding area, the Jonvick Deer Yark, as well as the presence of other wildlife that make the park their yearround residence, such as moose, wolves, pine martins, and fishers.

The geological formations of the park began billions of years ago when ancient bedrock was covered with molten lava from volcanoes. The shallow seas, which covered the area at a later time, deposited sediment on the lava beds. This rock was affected by tremendous mountain-building forces. Later, glaciers covered the landscape several times, producing the geography we see today—a rugged, rocky expanse, thinly covered with soil, but densely covered with vegetation.

The marked and groomed trails of the park are of all levels of difficulty. They join with the trails at Cascade Lodge to the immediate southwest and Bally Creek Camp to the northeast, as part of the North Shore Mountains Ski Trail system. Trails are also accessible from inland roads, a favorite way for visitors to descend back into the park or to Cascade Lodge. The downhill runs are fast and exciting. There is a panoramic view of the lake from the summit of Moose Mountain. Shelters are available at several locations on the trails.

Indoor toilets, maps, and parking are at hand at the park headquarters. Winter camping is permitted. Food and lodging are available in Lutsen or Grand Marais. Visitors are encouraged to check with the adjacent resorts that participate in the North Shore Mountains Ski Trail Ski-Through Program for details on the special accommodations and privileges available at these facilities.

For further information, contact

Cascade River State Park, Park Manager, Lutsen, MN 55612. 218-387-1543
Minnesota Department of Natural Resources, Division of Parks and Recreation, Box
    39 Centennial Building, St. Paul, MN 55155. 612-296-4776

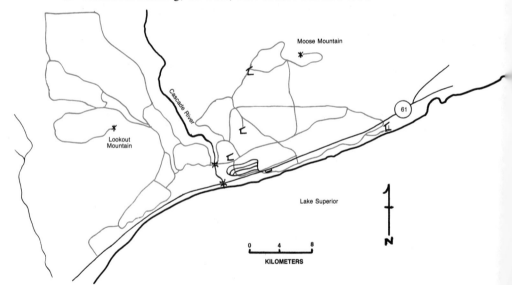

CASCADE RIVER STATE PARK

North Shore Mountains Ski Trail
Bear Track Outfitting and Ski Touring Center
Bally Creek Camp
Grand Marais, Minnesota

8 km (5 mi) of trails

beginner, intermediate, advanced

To get to Bear Track Outfitting's Bally Creek Camp, take County Road 7 west of Grand Marais to Forest Road 158; travel approximately 3 miles west-northwest on 158 to the Camp. A note of caution: drive carefully on Forest Roads due to the occasional presence of logging trucks. The trails of this facility form the northeast terminus of the North Shore Mountains Ski Trail system. There are two marked and groomed loops at Bally Creek. Sundling Loop is 4.5 km (2.8 mi) long and is rated beginner, intermediate, advanced. It begins at the camp trailhead. Bally Creek Loop, interconnected with Sundling Loop, is 3.5 km (2.1 mi) long and is a beginner trail. These wilderness trails wander through a variety of terrain and habitat, including gently rolling hills, deep forests, and secluded ice-covered ponds.

The easternmost trailhead to the North Shore Mountains Ski Trail system is located on Sundling Loop. This opens the door to the huge system of trails that wind through the Sawtooth Mountains. You may ski in deep forest and open clean-cut areas and behold breathtaking vistas of Lake Superior. The next facility on the system is Cascade River State Park, which is bordered by Cascade Lodge. The trail from Bally Creek to the park is 10.4 km (6.5 mi) long and is for advanced skiers, with some sections suited to those of intermediate ability. It crosses County Road 45 a little beyond the halfway mark; at this point parking is available.

Bally Creek Camp has some really wonderful options for the skier who endeavors to get away from it all. It is an ideal place for small parties, ski groups, and families who like to recreate in an isolated setting. Their cozy cabins are heated with wood and can accommodate from four adults (plus two children) to twelve adults. Light meals may be prepared on the woodstoves. There are NO phones, NO electricity, and NO televisions in the cabins. Guests provide their own sleeping bags.

Winter enthusiasts may also ski or snowshoe to the interior of the forest to their outpost tent cabins, which are wood-heated tents on wooden platforms. Or, skiers may plan three- to five-day trips, completely guided and accompanied by dogsleds.

Rental of ski equipment, snowshoes, mukluks, and winter camping equipment is available at the Camp. Please note: no dogs are allowed on the trails.

For further information, contact

David or Cathi Williams, c/o Bear Track Outfitting, Box 51, Grand Marais, MN 55604. 218-387-1162

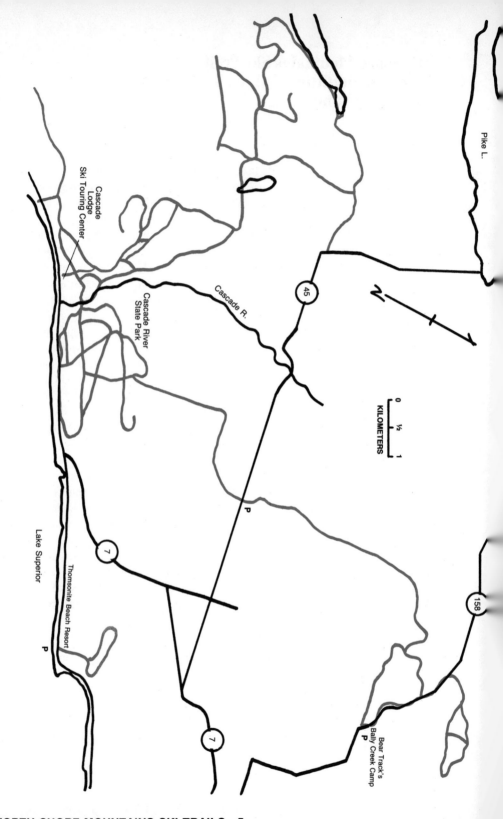

Pike L.

Cascade Lodge Ski Touring Center

Cascade R.

Cascade River State Park

45

N

0 ½ 1
KILOMETERS

P

Lake Superior

Thomsonite Beach Resort

7

P

7

158

Bear Track's Bally Creek Camp
P

NORTH SHORE MOUNTAINS SKI TRAILS—5

North Shore Mountains Ski Trail
Thomsonite Beach
Lutsen, Minnesota

beginner, intermediate, advanced

Thomsonite Beach is located on Highway 61, between Cascade River State Park and Grand Marais, on Good Harbor Bay.

The trails of the resort are not connected to the North Shore Mountains Ski Trail system, but the facility participates in the program. The large Good Harbor Loop begins right at the resort and has segments of every degree of difficulty. The loop bypasses Good Harbor Creek en route.

The resort offers both large and small luxury units, a guest house, and a motel. Some units have fireplaces and completely equipped kitchens. Color TV is included. The resort specializes in the sale of thomsonite jewelry and in the art of silversmithing.

VISA, Master Card, American Express,and AAA are accepted.

For further information, contact

Thomsonite Beach, ESR Box 470, Lutsen, MN 55612. 218-387-1532

Northwoods Ski Trail
Silver Bay, Minnesota

12.8 km (8 mi) of trails

beginner, intermediate

To reach the trailhead, travel 1 mile southwest, then 1 mile northwest on County Road 5 from Silver Bay. Or, on County Road 4, go 2 miles north from Beaver Bay to the junction with County Road 5.

The trail is marked, tracked, and groomed, and is situated on varied terrain that is entirely wooded. The initial stretch of trail runs along the bank of East Branch Beaver River and turns eastward along Cedar Creek. There are five rest stops on the trails, which are set up in a one-way loop system.

Parking is available, but there are no toilets or shelter on site. A snowmobile trail intersects the center of the system. A state user permit is required of visitors. Food and lodging are available in Silver Bay and Beaver Bay.

For further information, contact

Keith Johnson, Northwoods Ski Touring Club, 100 Hays Circle, Silver Bay, MN 55614. 218-226-4436

See also Tettegouche State Park, page 181.

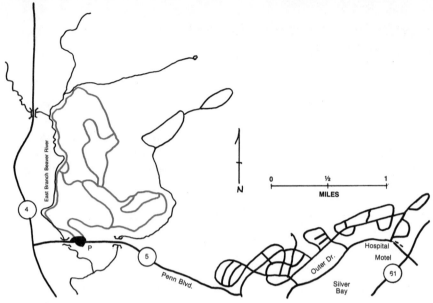

NORTHWOODS SKI TRAIL

Nor'Wester Lodge
Grand Marais, Minnesota

Carl and Luana Brandt's Nor'Wester Lodge is located 30 miles up the Gunflint Trail (Cook County Road 12), northwest of Grand Marais. The establishment faces south over Poplar Lake.

There is unlimited access to the trails of the Boundary Waters Canoe Area Wilderness (most of these trails are marked, but are not groomed). There is a 2 km (1.25 mi) stretch to the marked, groomed, and track-set arterial trail with 30 km (18.75 mi) available. One 14.4-km (9-mi) loop connects ultimately with the Banadad Artery Trail. Young's Dog Sledding Service, convenient to Nor' Wester, arranges dog team trips, with several day trip options available.

The main lodge is beautifully constructed of native logs and filled with an interesting collection of antiques from the area. The dining room has a view of the lake, and a full menu is available for breakfast, lunch, and dinner. Reservations are advised. The fireplace is always going, and the coffee is always on. Nor'Wester has modern lakefront villas and cabins, some with fireplaces.

For further information, contact

Carl and Luana Brandt, Nor'Wester Lodge, Box GT-S60, Grand Marais, MN 55604. 218-388-2252

See also Gunflint Area Cross-Country Ski-Thru Program, page 115; Golden Eagle Lodge, page 102; Gateway Hungry Jack Lodge, page 100; Heston's Country Store and Cabins, page 122.

Pine Valley Ski Area
Cloquet, Minnesota

7.5 km (4.7 mi) of trails

intermediate, advanced

Pine Valley Ski Area is located at the junction of Highway 33 and Armory Road. It is groomed by the city of Cloquet mainly for competition and training. Designed to specifications for Olympic and USSA practice, it is used for high school competition. The trails are used for training mainly during the week, so Sundays are best for recreation. There are two loops: the 5 km loop is for competition and the 2.5 km loop is for recreation. The terrain and course are quite demanding.

Restrooms and food service are available when the chalet is open. A map and parking are available on site.

For further information, contact

Michael Marciniak, 1505 Washington Avenue, Cloquet, MN 55720. 218-379-3347, 218-379-4606 (work number, if necessary)

Savanna Portage State Park
McGregor, Minnesota

25.6 km (16 mi) of trails

intermediate

Savanna Portage State Park is located 17 miles northeast of the town of McGregor, in Aitkin County. Take Highway 65 north from McGregor to County Roads 14 and 36. Proceed on 14 and 36 eastward for 10 miles to the park. The trailhead is located at the information center where visitors may park.

The park is situated on land that was a vital link in the fur trade in the eighteenth century, the land of the Savanna Portage. The main trade and travel route from Lake Superior to the Upper Mississippi River watershed was via the St. Louis River and its watershed. Even before whites began exploration, and the consequent fur trade with the Indians, this was a main route for Indian travel. Passage began at Fond Du Lac, Lake Superior. Four portages were encountered en route. The first was on the St. Louis River, near Fond Du Lac. The next portage, nearly nine miles, was near a point that is now Jay Cooke State Park. The third was by Knife Falls. The fourth, the East Savanna River route, was actually an alternate route, used mainly by whites because their canoes and cargo were so much heavier than the Indians' loads.

It was a 6-mile trip through high grass, reeds and wild rice. Following the river's course was very difficult, and the mud, blood-thirsty insects and weather problems made this segment of the passage extremely unpleasant and grueling. Eventually, the canoes couldn't be poled through the swampland or pushed or dragged, and the voyageurs carried their tremendously heavy packs over the gray quagmire. At long last, the ground became higher and more solid, and balancing the ponderous tote became easier. The portage moved through undulating terrain, forested with maple, birch, and basswood. Finally, the traders would reach West Savanna River, typically after at least five days on the portage. From the West Savanna, they could paddle their canoes to the Prairie River, thence to Big Sandy Lake and on to the Upper Mississippi River.

The trails for skiing traverse a portion of this portage and take in its best aspects. Rolling, wooded hills are dotted with lakes, ponds, and bogs, and all is intertwined by small rivers and creeks. The trail system is marked, groomed, and track-set (some trails are double-tracked). Numerous shelters are on the trails; a pit toilet is located at each shelter and at one trail intersection. The trail system is comprised of a series of loops. One loop borders Lake Shumway. A long spur takes a skier northward to Wolf Lake. Snowmobiling is allowed in the park and the systems are separate, except for two crossings on the Wolf Lake spur.

Winter camping is permitted. Maps may be obtained at the information center. Tourist accommodations and supplies are available in McGregor.

For further information, contact

Savanna Portage State Park, Park Manager, Route 3, McGregor, MN 55760. 218-426-3271

Minnesota Department of Natural Resources, Division of Parks and Recreation, Box 39 Centennial Building, St. Paul, MN 55155. 612-296-4776

See also Aitkin County, Long Lake Conservation Center, page 80 and Savanna State Forest, Remote Lake Solitude Area, page 173.

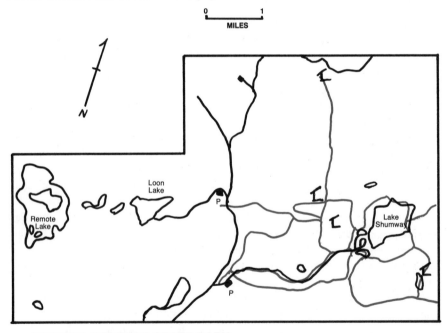

SAVANNA PORTAGE STATE PARK

Savanna State Forest
McGregor, Minnesota

REMOTE LAKE SOLITUDE AREA
19.8 km (12.4 mi) of trails

intermediate

Savanna State Forest is located in northeastern Aitkin County. To reach the Forest, take Highway 65 north from McGregor to County Road 14. Go northeast on 14 to County Road 36; proceed for 3 miles on 36 to the parking lot.

Savanna State Forest encompasses 218,450 acres of land. Its hilly terrain is covered with mixed hardwood types, primarily aspen, maple, basswood, and birch, as well as softwoods, such as black spruce, tamarack, and cedar. There are also large grass meadows. The Mississippi River skirts and cuts through the western part of the forest. Within the forest is Savanna Portage State Park, which contains Savanna Portage, the notoriously rough, swampy portage that linked the West Savanna River of the Mississippi River watershed and the East Savanna River, which empties into Lake Superior.

The ski trails are located within the Remote Lake Solitude Area, a multiple-use area managed by the Division of Forestry. To ensure the atmosphere of solitude, the only motorized vehicles allowed in this section of land are those used in logging. Harvesting of timber takes place in the summer and fall, leaving the snowy winter when trail use is highest, completely undisturbed. These trails are among the very earliest of Minnesota's marked, groomed, and tracked ski trails. They were designed by the North Star Ski Touring Club of the Twin Cities, in cooperation with the Division of Lands and Forestry. They remain fine trails today, serene and beautiful, designed to emphasize the finest points of the surroundings. The heron rookery, located at a trail junction, is quite fascinating. There are four rest areas en route, each with a shelter, picnic table, fire ring, and pit toilet. Information signs along the trails identify the different timber types and provide a better understanding of forest practices.

Maps are available at the Ranger Station. Tourist accommodations and supplies may be obtained in McGregor.

For further information, contact

Savanna State Forest, Sandy Lake District Forester, Sandy Lake, McGregor, MN 55760. 218-426-3407

Minnesota Department of Natural Resources, Division of Forestry, Box 44 Centennial Building, St. Paul, MN 55155. 612-296-4491

See also Savanna Portage State Park, page 171 and Aitkin County, Long Lake Conservation Center, page 80.

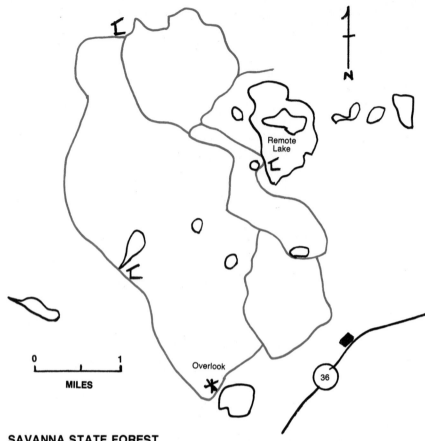

SAVANNA STATE FOREST

Scenic State Park
Bigfork, Minnesota

16 km (10 mi) of trails

beginner, intermediate

Scenic State Park is located in Itasca County, 7 miles east of the town of Bigfork on County Road 7. It protects the virgin pine shorelands of Coon and Sandwick Lakes, and three smaller lakes, Cedar, Tell, and Pine. Part of Lake of the Isles is included within the park. Several magnificent stands of old red and white pine make a beautiful setting for a ski tour.

The glacier that once covered this area dug deep depressions, pushed up high ridges, and, in its retreat, left deposits of soil. This prehistoric activity produced the land we see today: rolling hills that cradle lakes and ponds. Coon and Sandwick Lakes are water-filled depressions left from massive Glacial Lake Agassiz, which was produced by glacial meltdown. Running between the two lakes is a very narrow strip of land called an esker, a long ridge formed by a river tunnel within a glacier. One of the ski trails runs on this esker to its terminus, Chase Point, where there is a scenic overlook.

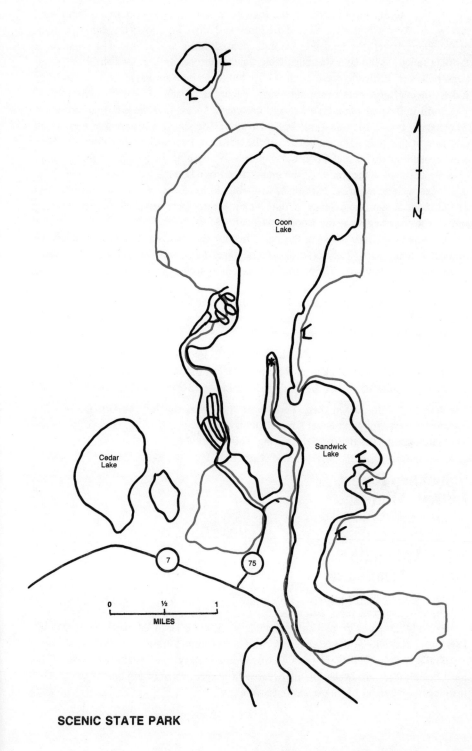

SCENIC STATE PARK

Coon
Lake

Cedar
Lake

Sandwick
Lake

7

75

0   ½   1
MILES

N

By the late nineteenth century, the logging industry was very active around what is now park land. Companies cleared the forest and drove logs down the Big Fork River to the Rainy River. As land was cleared, homesteaders moved in. Most attempts at farming failed, as the land was unsuitable for the cultivation of crops. These early settlers, however, battled to preserve the virgin birch and pine around Coon and Sandwick Lakes; their efforts were rewarded when Scenic State Park was established in 1921.

Trails in the park are all marked and groomed. Access is at the information center, where there is a 2.2-km (1.4-mi) beginner loop. The cutoff to Chase Point is on the east side of this loop. The remainder of the trails are intermediate in difficulty. They wind around Sandwick and Coon Lakes primarily. Several shelters and walk-in campsites are adjacent to the trails. At the main campground on the west side of Coon Lake is a lodge with a fireplace. Parking is available at this location. On the northern part of the trails, a short spur leads to Pine Lake, where there are shelters and camping spots. The spur begins at the Lookout Tower.

Snowmobiling is allowed in the park, but for the most part, such trails skirt the perimeter of the park. They do cross the beginner loop, and the skiers and snowmobilers share a common trail very briefly at three locations, and for 0.8 km (0.5 mi) on the northeast side of Coon Lake.

Maps are available at the park. Food, lodging, and supplies may be obtained in Big Fork.

For further information, contact

Scenic State Park, Park Manager, Big Fork, MN 56628. 218-743-3362

Minnesota Department of Natural Resources, Division of Parks and Recreation, Box 39 Centennial Building, St. Paul, MN 55155. 612-296-4776

See also McCarthy Beach State Park, page 145; Virginia Ranger District/Superior National Forest, Sturgeon River Cross-Country Ski Trail, page 186; George Washington State Forest, Thistledew Ski Touring Trail, page 190.

Solbakken Resort
Lutsen, Minnesota

See North Shore Mountains Ski Trail, page 162.

Spirit Mountain
Duluth, Minnesota

19.1 km (12 mi) of trails

beginner, intermediate, advanced

Spirit Mountain is located at the Boundary Avenue Exit of Interstate 35 in Duluth. Parking is available at the trailhead for the cross-country trails.

Trails at Spirit Mountain (also a large alpine facility) are situated in some of the most beautiful terrain in the Duluth area, with gorgeous vistas and one of the last remaining virgin stand of maple and basswood.

The system is entirely marked, groomed, and track-set. The four trails are arranged in nearly concentric circles. In the middle is **Eric Judeen Trail**, a 1-km (0.6-mi) beginner trail situated on a very gentle terrain. It is double-tracked and is a good place to learn and practice and to warm up for the longer trails. **Charlie Banks Trail** is considered to be one of Duluth's most enjoyable ski tracks. It is a 2.5-km (1.6-mi) intermediate trail. Another intermediate stretch is the 4.6-km (2.9-mi) **Larry Sorenson Trail**, which involves moderate hills and descents. The loop moves through a forested land, giving skiers a chance to see wildlife. **George Hovland Trail** is an 11-km (6.9-mi) advanced route, offering the seasoned skier a challenging and technically demanding experience because of its length and terrain. World-class competitors praise this trail.

There is a spacious, rustic warming hut at the trailhead. It is the place to get maps, snacks, pop, beer,and wine. A trail fee of $4.00 is charged of guests. After 2:00 p.m. you can ski for $2.00. There are lights for night skiing. Rentals are available on site.

Spirit Mountain has a cafeteria and a dining room. Two bars are at the facility, and, in the evening, live bands perform. Housekeeping villas are available. Spirit Mountain also participates with several motor inns in the Duluth area in arranging ski/lodging packages.

For further information, contact

Spirit Mountain, Bill Howard, 9500 Spirit Mountain Place, Duluth, MN 55810. 218-628-2891, 370-1271 (toll free Minneapolis/St. Paul)

See also Duluth (City of) Trails, Magney-Snively Trail, page 96 and Jay Cooke State Park, page 87.

Split Rock Lighthouse State Park
Two Harbors, Minnesota

9.4 km (5.9 mi) of trails

Split Rock Lighthouse State Park is located in Lake County, about 20 miles north of the town of Two Harbors, on Highway 61. The site of the Split Rock Lighthouse is operated by the Minnesota Historical Society and is, of course, the main feature of the park. It includes the lighthouse, fog signal building, oil storage house, and three stone residences. The information center at the historic site is closed in the winter, and you must contact Gooseberry Falls State Park for details about the facility. The lighthouse and adjunct buildings are a beautiful sight on the stark, rough North Shore coastline of Lake Superior.

The park boasts other historic sites. There is an old logging site at the mouth of the Split Rock River, where timber industry began in 1899 with the establishment of the Merrill and Ring Company. They logged mainly Norway and white pine, leaving today's vegetation of birch, spruce, fir, and ash. There is also a small abandoned quarry owned by the Minnesota Abrasives Company, now 3M.

The land of the park, the magnificent bluffs of the North Shore, are the result of many complex geological events. Eons ago, volcanic action was heavy in this area, spewing lava all along what is now the shoreline of Lake Superior. This lava bedrock was covered in time by sediment. Tremendous pressures within the earth compressed and deformed the bedrock, finally shaping the Sawtooth Mountains. A series of glaciers gouged and pulled at the land, shearing off the cliffs and scraping out the Lake Superior basin. After the meltdown and final retreat of the glaciers, Lake Superior and its rugged shoreline remained.

Tragic shipwrecks necessitated the construction of the lighthouse in 1909–1910. Through a series of transactions, the lighthouse and its environs have come under the jursidiction of the Minnesota Department of Natural Resources and the Minnesota Historical Society.

The ski trails are set up in a two-loop system, with two short crossovers and four spurs, two of which lead to overlooks on the cliffs at Corundum Point. One loop moves down to the mouth of the Split Rock River and returns parallel to Highway 61, along the highway's old road bed. It passes by a wayside rest along this stretch. Maps, toilets, and parking are available. Tourist accommodations are available in Beaver Bay or Two Harbors.

For further information, contact

Split Rock Lighthouse State Park, Park Manager, East Star Route, Two Harbors, MN 55616. 218-226-3065

Minnesota Department of Natural Resources, Division of Parks and Recreation, Box 39 Centennial Building, St. Paul, MN 55155. 612-296-4776

SPLIT-ROCK LIGHTHOUSE STATE PARK

Sugar Hills Winter Resort
Grand Rapids, Minnesota

70 km (43.75 mi) of trails

beginner, intermediate, advanced

Sugar Hills is located 14 miles southwest of Grand Rapids. Take Highway 169 south for 7 miles to the junction with County Road 17. Turn, and travel west on County Road 17 to the resort.

The trails are situated primarily to the south of Siseebakwet Lake and include a wide variety of hills, valleys, peaks, and ridges. They offer challenges to skiers of all abilities. The land is heavily wooded, full of wildlife, and has many spring-fed streams and lakes. The trails are entirely marked, groomed, and track-set. On weekends, a trail fee of $7.00 is charged. This is reduced on weekdays. Ski rentals are available.

This resort is also a large downhill facility. There is a main chalet where the Dining Room is open for breakfast and dinner. A cafeteria and lounge are also at the resort. No camping is allowed. Maps, parking, and restrooms are available at the chalet. The resort also has facilities for 300 at its convention center.

For further information, contact

Sugar Hills Winter Resort, Box 369, Grand Rapids, MN 55744. 218-326-0535

See also Camp Mishawaka, page 85 and Golden Anniversary Forest, Cowhorn Lake Ski Trail, page 101.

Superior National Forest
Forest Service, Department of Agriculture
Headquarters, Duluth, Minnesota

560 km (350 mi) of trails

beginner, intermediate, advanced

National Forests were originally established to protect watersheds and supply timber. In addition, these lands are also rich in wildlife, forage, and recreation opportunities. Superior National Forest encompasses three million acres of land, including the Boundary Waters Canoe Area Wilderness. It offers some of the finest, most spectacular recreational opportunities in the country. The northwoods winters are ideally suited to winter sports. Lake Superior exerts a moderating effect on extreme winter temperatures and increases snowfall (average annual snowfall is 60 inches).

Numerous trails in the Superior National Forest are designed especially for ski-touring, and many other hiking trails are also suitable. Primitive roads become excellent ski trails, offering a wider track and moderate grades for the skier to traverse easily. As with any winter activity, safety must be considered on cross-country ski trips, even short day trips. Windfallen trees and branches may be obstacles on some sections of the trails. Snowpack on unplowed roads may inhibit vehicle accessibility to some trailheads.

Ski touring may be combined with winter camping for a most rewarding experience. Most forest areas are open to camping; however, it is prohibited in day-use areas such as parking lots, boat landings, and picnic grounds. Many trails are within the BWCA Wilderness, and the normal rules also apply to winter visitors. Leave all cans and bottles at home. However, winter campers are not required to use developed campsites. You may camp at any suitable location. Although a visitor's permit is not required in the winter, it is recommended that all overnight campers make use of the Forest Service's voluntary registration form. Contact the nearest District Ranger office for help and advice in planning ski tours and camping, so that your excursion is suited to your needs and abilities and will be a pleasant memory.

Winter travel presents special hazards. Unexpected wind, snow, and cold can turn a happy outing into a tragedy. THIS AREA IS LARGELY WILDERNESS. Know your limitations and be prepared for the unexpected. Check weather forecasts before setting out on the trail. Ski with others and not alone. Select a group leader. Crossing lakes and rivers can be dangerous. Always travel with someone who knows local conditions when on ice. Test the ice carefully; be alert for water holes and weak ice. Layers of snow can insulate still water sufficiently to keep it from freezing solid. Running water and springs can weaken ice, if it forms at all. Weak ice occurs especially early and late in the skiing season. Familiarize yourself with the prevention, symptoms, and treatment of hypothermia, A REAL KILLER. Hypothermia, a dangerous loss of body heat, is caused by exposure to the cold. The onset of this condition is hastened by physical exhaustion, windy weather, and wearing wet clothing. Watch for frostbite. Party members should periodically observe their companions for signs, particularly on their noses and cheeks. Always carry extra clothing, warm drink, high-energy food, and a spare ski tip.

To avoid getting lost, stay on marked trails. Skiers should pay particular attention to trail markers indicating level of difficulty of the trail. All levels of difficulty are present in the Superior National Forest. Skiers should not take chances by attempting to exceed the limits of their ability. If you are not sure of your ability to safely negotiate a particular section of trail, remove your skis and walk along the edge of the trail until you reach a section that you know you can negotiate with skis.

ALWAYS have a COMPASS and GOOD MAP and KNOW HOW TO USE THEM. Leave your travel plans with a responsible person, and check in with that person when you return from your tour. Avoid excess tiring by not overestimating your abilities to travel long distances. Plan your trip so as to return well before darkness. Finally, respect private lands and cabins—KEEP OUT.

For further information and maps, contact the District Ranger in the region that has jurisdiction over the trail(s) in question. There are seven Ranger Districts in the Superior National Forest. The main headquarters and the office of the Forest Supervisor are in Duluth. All ski trails and the Ranger Districts are listed under separate headings in this region.

Forest Supervisor, Superior National Forest, P.O. Box 338, Duluth, MN 55801. 218-727-6692

Aurora Ranger District, P.O. Box 391, Aurora, MN 55705. 218-229-3371

Gunflint Ranger District, U.S. Forest Service, Grand Marais, MN 55604. 218-387-1750

Isabella Ranger District, U.S. Forest Service, Star Route Box 207, Isabella, MN 55607. 218-323-7722

Kawishiwi Ranger District, U.S. Forest Service, Box 149/118 South 4th Avenue East, Ely, MN 55731. 218-365-6185

La Croix Ranger District, U.S. Forest Service, P.O. Box 1085, Cook, MN 55723. 218-666-5251

Tofte Ranger District, U.S. Forest Service, Tofte, MN 55615. 218-663-7280

Virginia Ranger District, 505 12th Avenue West, Virginia, MN 55792. 218-741-5736

Temperance River State Park
Schroeder, Minnesota

See North Shore Mountains Ski Trail, page 151.

Tettegouche State Park
Silver Bay, Minnesota

15.8 km (9.9 mi) of trails

intermediate, advanced

Tettegouche State Park is located in Lake County, 4 miles northeast of Silver Bay, which is on Highway 61. The rugged, diverse topography of the park hides four lakes. Mic Mac, Nipisiquit, Tettegouche, and Nicado, and the beautiful Baptism River, which contains Minnesota's highest waterfalls. The forest once supported a large logging camp and two maple syrup camps. Deep in the river valley is Tettegouche Camp, a group of very old, rustic log buildings, built in 1910. The park's shoreline on Lake Superior is over a mile long and includes Shovel Point.

There is a two-loop system of marked and groomed trails in the park. They skirt the lakes and take in nine scenic overlooks, including the marvelous view at the summit of Mt. Baldy. **Tettegouche Camp Trail** is the access trail to the two interior loops, and its trailhead is at the park's parking lot. This trail is intermediate in difficulty and has one overlook on a short spur. It leads to the challenging first loop, **Mic Mac Lake Trail**, which is primarily for advanced skiers. Its northern portion is intermediate, however. It winds around both Nipisiquit and Mic Mac Lakes and involves three outstanding overlooks of the Palisades, Lake Superior, and Mic Mac Lake.

The second loop is **Tettegouche Lake Trail**, an expert trail with many scenic overlooks of the quiet river valley and lake. It involves many sharp turns and hills. The trail to **Mt. Baldy** is comprised of the northern and western sides of the MicMac Lake Trail and a portion of the eastern side of the Tettegouche Lake Trail. It is an intermediate route that travels to the highest point in the park where you stand 1,000 feet above Lake Superior and can see the lake, the Apostle Islands, and Wisconsin on a clear day.

An important warning has been issued from the park service: skiers are to use EXTREME CAUTION if they choose to ski on the lakes. It is strongly recommended that visitors stay on the trails, as the lakes have moving water at the inlets and outlets that may inhibit ice formation, or weaken the ice that does form. This danger may be hidden under snow. There is often a great deal of slush and water under the snow on the ice.

Today, the park is for day use only, and no camping is allowed, but the development plan calls for building a campground, picnic ground, and other visitor facilities within the next few years. Tourist accommodations are available in Silver Bay.

For further information, contact

Tettegouche State Park, Park Manager, Star Route 91 B, Silver Bay, MN 55614. 218-353-7386

Minnesota Department of Natural Resources, Division of Parks and Recreation, Box 39 Centennial Building, St. Paul, MN 55155. 612-296-4776

See also George H. Crosby-Manitou State Park, page 89 and Northwoods Ski Trail, page 169.

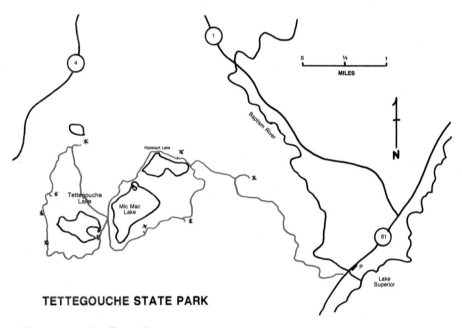

TETTEGOUCHE STATE PARK

Thomsonite Beach
Lutsen, Minnesota

See North Shore Mountains Ski Trail, page 169.

Tofte Ranger District, Superior National Forest
Tofte, Minnesota

See North Shore Mountains Ski Trail, page 154.

Two Harbors City Trail
Two Harbors, Minnesota

15 km (9.4 mi) of trails

beginner, intermediate

The trailhead is located on County Road 2, just north of Highway 61. Turn north at the Holiday Station (4th Street), and proceed on 2 to the 16th Avenue intersection. The trailhead and parking lot are opposite the police station at this intersection.

The trails are set up in a system of seven loops, all marked and groomed. A toilet is on the trail. The map may be obtained at City Hall in Two Harbors. Tourist accommodations are available in town also.

For further information, contact

Two Harbors City Trail, City Hall, Two Harbors, MN 55616. 218-834-4386

See also Gooseberry Falls State Park, page 103.

Virginia Ranger District, Superior National Forest
Virginia, Minnesota

There are four designated cross-country ski trails located in the Virginia Ranger District of the Superior National Forest. For further information on the Forest, see Superior National Forest, this region.

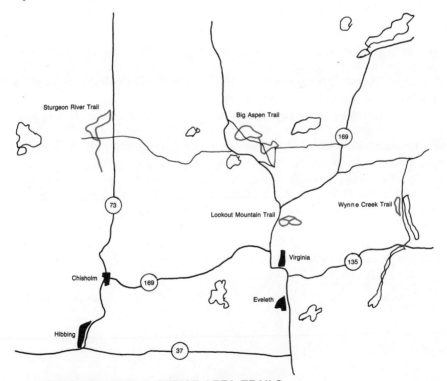

VIRGINIA RANGER DISTRICT AREA TRAILS

WYNNE CREEK CROSS-COUNTRY SKI TRAIL
GIANT'S RIDGE
6.4 km (4 mi) of trails

intermediate, advanced

Wynne Creek Trail is located just outside the town of Aurora. Take Highway 135 west to Pineville (approximately 2 miles). Turn north on County Road 416, and travel to Giant's Ridge facility. The trailhead is located at the chalet of the alpine ski area. Just past the trailhead, the Laurentian Snowmobile Trail crosses the ski trail, the only point where the trails intersect. Use extreme caution at the junction. For the remainder of the trail, motorized vehicles are prohibited.

As this is a demanding trail, offering some exciting slopes, do not attempt it if you are not confident of your ability. Passing through the forested land, the trail is two-way until it crosses Wynne Creek. It then changes to a one-way loop that moves in a counter-clockwise direction. Due to the difficulty of the trail, please observe the one-way signs. The trail is marked, groomed, and track-set. Although maintained by the U.S. Forest Service, the trail is groomed and track-set by the Iron Range Resources and Rehabilitation Board.

Maps, toilets, water, and ample parking are available at Giant's Ridge. Other tourist needs may be met in Aurora.

See also Giant's Ridge, page 100.

LOOKOUT MOUNTAIN CROSS-COUNTRY SKI TRAILS
24 km (15 mi) of trails

beginner, intermediate, advanced

The trailhead is located 3 miles north of Virginia on Highways 53 and 169, at the Laurentian Divide Picnic Area, a short distance south of the split in the two roads. Parking is available at the trailhead. Overflow parking, with a trail spur, is located at the highway junction.

At the trailhead is the large, color-coded trail map. The trails are primarily intermediate to advanced; a few are suited to the novice. They pass through forested land, with occasional scenic overlooks. A native log shelter is provided at one overlook. The trails are well-marked and indicate level of difficulty. They are groomed and track-set, except for a marked 10-km (6.25-mi) section reserved for bushwhacking. Grooming and maintenance is provided by the Lookout Mountain Ski Committee, Laurentian Nordic Ski Club. There are toilets and an adirondack shelter at the trailhead. No water is available. Dogs are not allowed on the trail. No license is required.

The cities of Virginia and Eveleth have many places where you can eat and stay overnight. Local ski shops rent equipment.

For further information, contact

Bob Peterson, Laurentian Nordic Ski Club, 326 Third Street, Parkville, MN. 218-741-9119

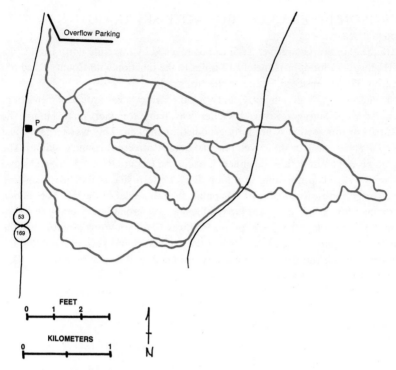

FEET

0   1   2

KILOMETERS

0   1

N

LOOKOUT MOUNTAIN CROSS-COUNTRY SKI TRAILS

BIG ASPEN CROSS-COUNTRY SKI TRAIL
22.4 km (14 mi) of trails
beginner, intermediate

Just north of Lookout Mountain Ski Trail is Big Aspen Trail. Take Highway 53 north from Virginia to County Road 302; turn northeast on 302; travel a short distance to the junction of County Roads 68 and 405. Go northwest on 405 to the first parking area, called Parking Area E. From this point, the road becomes Forest Road 257 (Old Angora Road), a narrow road that is not always plowed immediately after a snowfall. A short distance up 257 is the second trailhead with another parking area, called Parking Area W. Caution is advised in driving this distance if the road has not been plowed. Five hundred feet before Parking Area W, a road with a gate provides access to the trail.

A large map at the trailhead enables skiers to analyze the system beforehand and plan their trips according to their abilities. The trails move through young aspen and pine stands and primarily suit the beginner because most follow old logging roads with quite easy grades. A more challenging route can be selected. The trail network is set up in two sections. The west section, the largest, is a maze of several loops. There is a shelter on an outer stretch. The east section consists of two loops. Although the trail is maintained by the U.S. Forest Service, it is groomed and track-set by the Iron Range Resources and Rehabilitation Board.

Full tourist accommodations are available in Virginia and Eveleth.

STURGEON RIVER CROSS-COUNTRY SKI TRAIL
intermediate, advanced

The trailhead to Sturgeon River Trail can be reached by traveling north from Chisholm on Highway 73 for approximately 12 miles to the junction with County Road 65. Turn west on 65, and proceed 1 mile to the trailhead.

The northern loop, beginning at County Road 65, meanders around the twisting, turning course of the Sturgeon River. A shelter is available for skiers on this loop. The outermost part of this section is not fully groomed or tracked. This was formerly just a hiking trail and is still in the developmental stages for cross-country skiing. The southern loop is not entirely finished either. It begins on County Road 65 also and starts out as a two-way trail, proceeding to a loop. The western side is finished for skiing and runs down to Forest Road 279. At this point, the remainder of the trail is not completely groomed for skiing. It crosses the road and moves around the vicinity of Lakes Louise and Jean, ending at the gravel pit on Highway 73. Turn around, and return the same way that you came. When you arrive at the southern loop, keep in mind that the eastern portion (to the right) is not completely groomed, and it may be difficult. This section follows the East Branch of the Sturgeon River.

Maps are available from the Forest Service. All types of tourist accommodations are at hand in Chisholm and Hibbing.

For further information, contact

Virginia Ranger District, District Ranger, U.S. Forest Service, 505-12th Avenue West, Virginia, MN 55792. 218-741-5736

Forest Supervisor, Superior National Forest, P.O. Box 338, Duluth, MN 55801. 218-727-6692

Ray Svatos, IRRRB, Box 441, Eveleth, MN 55734

See also McCarthy Beach State Park, page 145 and George Washington State Forest, Thistledew Ski Touring Trail, page 190.

Voyageurs National Park
International Falls, Minnesota

The dominant feature of Voyageurs National Park is water. Over thirty lakes of varying size lie within its borders. These lakes extend to a vast system of bogs, marshes, and beaver ponds. The rock basins that cradle these waterways are made up of some of the oldest rock formations exposed anywhere in the world. If younger rock formations did exist here, they most likely were scraped away during the million-year period of glaciation. The glaciers were approximately two miles thick, and they pushed their way across the land four different times, removing its features, and leaving a fairly level landscape with depressions pockmarking the exposed rock. These basins now hold the complex waterways of the park. You can still see glacial scrape marks on some of the rock surfaces.

The system of lakes between the United States and Canada can be called the Voyageurs' Highway, and the park encompasses a 56-mile stretch of the route. The voyageurs were the famed French-Canadian canoemen who made so much of the area's future possible. They are the stuff of legends—adventuresome men who paddled up to sixteen hours a day, bringing beaver and other pelts out of the Canadian and American Northwest up to Montreal and taking back supplies and trade goods in exchange. The round-trip consumed four to five months. The voyageur's character has been described as daring, if not brave; knowledgeable, though uneducated. Above all, he was colorful. Daniel Harmon, a partner in the Northwest Company, wrote of them in 1819, "the Canadian voyageurs possess lively and fickle dispositions; and they are rarely subject to depression of spirits of long continuance, even when in circumstances the most adverse. Although what they consider good eating and drinking constitutes their chief good, yet when necessity compels them to it, they submit to great privation and hardship, not only without complaining, but even with cheerfulness and gaiety. . . . Trifling provocations will often throw them into a rage, but they are easily appeased when in anger, and they never harbour a revengeful purpose against those by whom they conceive that they have been injured."

Looking out across the landscape, one can see all the basic elements of the fur trade. The waters provided the highway, fur-bearing animals provided the goods, and the boundless forests provided the materials for the birch-bark canoe—that marvel of environmental adaptation. The canoes were constructed of birch-bark, cedar boughs, and cedar or spruce root bindings sealed with pitch. It was a skill developed by the Native Americans and readily exploited by early European explorers. The canoes were light, easily navigable, and quickly repaired with native materials. For several generations the fur trade was the continent's biggest industry, returning investments up to twenty-fold. One historian described the industry as a "vast empire held together by nothing stronger than birchbark."

Perhaps the most enduring aspect of the land's primitive character is the presence of wolves. The park is in the heart of the only region in the continental United States where the eastern timber wolf survives. Wolves are shy and secretive, and, contrary to folklore, they pose virtually no threat to humans. Their wariness and small numbers make it unlikely that you will see them during a visit, although you might see their tracks in the snow. Wolves usually live in packs of two to twelve and often kill large animals such as deer and moose for food. The timber wolf may cover as much as forty miles in a single night and can run several miles at 30–35 miles per hour. To hear the wolf's howl on a moonlit night is a rare pleasure.

From Christmas to late March, snow dominates the scene. Skiing at Voyageurs is possible on both land and lake. And with proper preparation, winter camping can make a ski tour a real treat. Two trails are designated as cross-country ski trails in the park. Both trails are open from the time the ice roads are plowed (usually around Christmas) until the snow is gone (usually in early March). Use of the trails is free—no ski license is required. No dogs are allowed on the trails or in the back country.

BLACK BAY SKI TRAIL
INTERNATIONAL FALLS, MINNESOTA
14 km (8.75 mi) of trails

beginner, intermediate, advanced

To reach Black Bay Ski Trail, drive east from International Falls on Highway 11 for 12 miles. Then travel on the ice road to Black Bay access (0.5 mile away) or to Dove Bay access (4 miles away). The trail is located on a point of land situated by the Black Bay Narrows between Black Bay and Rainy Lake.

The trail is composed of a series of one-way loops that are primarily beginner to intermediate in difficulty. A 3.8-km (2.4-mi) stretch on the northernmost loop is for advanced skiers. Deer, ruffed grouse, and chickadees are commonly seen on the trail. A toilet is provided at the Black Bay trailhead, and a toilet and picnic table are located at the trail's midpoint.

Parking is provided at each trailhead. Tourist accommodations (food, lodging, ski rentals) are available in International Falls. Winter camping is allowed in the park.

See also Grand Mound Center, page 105 and Kabetogama State Forest, Ash River Falls Ski Trail, page 128.

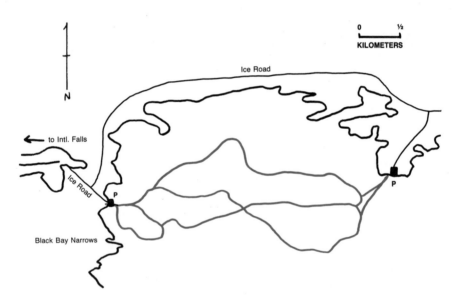

BLACK BAY SKI TRAIL

MUKOODA SKI TRAIL
CRANE LAKE, MINNESOTA
12 km (7.5 mi) of trails

intermediate

Mukooda Ski Trail can be reached by driving northeast from Orr on County Road 23 for 30 miles to Crane Lake. Then travel 3 miles on the ice road to the trailhead. It is located between Staege Bay of Sand Point Lake and Mukooda Lake.

The trail travels through beautiful woods, past huge boulders left by the glaciers, and offers outstanding vistas. Long downhill runs are an exciting feature of the trail. It is composed of two one-way loops. No grooming or tracking is done. No facilities are provided along the trail. Parking is available at the trailhead.

Lodging and food are available at Crane Lake Resorts, with advance reservations. A full range of services is provided in Orr. Winter camping is allowed in the park.

See also La Croix Ranger District/Superior National Forest, Herriman Lake Trail, page 140.

The park also offers off-trail skiing. Loop trips can be planned that combine skiing on a developed trail with skiing across beaver ponds, on old logging roads, and back onto the lakes. If visitors hit the right conditions, the park naturalist claims that this kind of touring is the best the park has to offer. In fact, the annual 30-km Voyageur

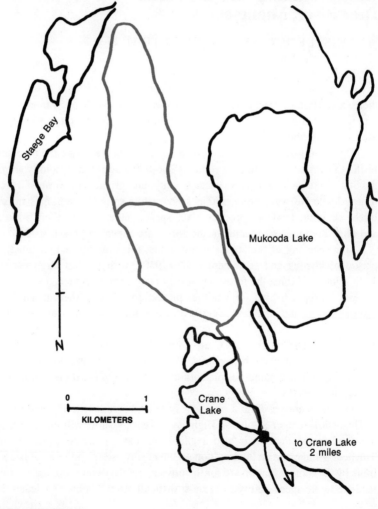

MUKOODA SKI TRAIL

Loppet travels over such a route. For this type of travel, proper equipment and preparation is a must. Winter is a force to be reckoned with here. *Take a compass and a good map*, KNOW HOW TO USE THEM. Dress in layers. Take extra clothing, hot drink, high-energy food, and an extra ski tip. Watch for the signs of hypothermia and frostbite, and NEVER TRAVEL ALONE. Leave your tour plans with a responsible person, and plan your trip according to your abilities, so that you will return well before dark. Talk to park staff, and let them know that you will be out on the trail. They can be of great assistance in setting up plans for a good trip.

For further information, contact

Ron Erickson, Rainy District Naturalist, Voyageurs National Park, P.O. Box 50, International Falls, MN 56649. 218-283-9821

George Washington State Forest
Deer River, Minnesota

THISTLEDEW SKI TOURING TRAILS
35.2 km (22 mi) of trails
beginner, intermediate, advanced

George Washington State Forest is situated in northeastern Itasca County. To get there, take Highway 169 northeast to Nashwauk, a distance of 21 miles. At Nashwauk, turn north on Highway 65, and travel to Highway 1. Proceed on 1 to Thistledew Ranger Station within the Forest.

This state forest was established in 1931 to commemorate the bicentennial of the birth of George Washington. It contains 306,000 acres of land, jointly administered by the State Division of Forestry, Itasca County, and private landowners. The uplands are forested with Norway, white, and jackpine, white spruce, aspen, balsam fir, and paper birch, while the lowlands produce black spruce, tamarack, northern white cedar, ash, and elm. Predominant species in the forest are aspen and black spruce.

Like so many of the state's forest lands, this area burned repeatedly during the period of logging and settlement (1880–1930), with the last large fire occurring in 1933. Since that time, the forest has slowly recovered, providing a site for outdoor recreation, a proper habitat for wildlife, protection for watershed, beautiful scenery for visitors and inhabitants, raw materials for the timber industry, and jobs for Minnesotans.

The Civilian Conservation Corps worked in the Forest 1933–41, and made possible a large part of today's attractiveness. They constructed campgrounds and many miles of road, established numerous plantations, and accomplished many soil and water conservation projects.

The trails are set up in a one-way system of five loops. The main access point is at Thistledew Ranger Station on Highway 1. Here, visitors will find ample parking, toilets, and maps. Parking is also available on the southeastern end of the system at Thistledew Lake and on the last loop on the northwestern end by Five Island Lake. The trails by the Ranger Station are for the novice, but the outer loops are for those of intermediate to advanced ability. The most difficult stretch is by Thistledew Lake. There are shelters at two points along the trails, with camping spots available at Buttonbox Lake and Thistledew Lake (the extreme outer limits of the system). Snowmobiling is allowed in the Forest, but the trail systems do not mix.

Full tourist accommodations are available in the area; the widest range will be found in Grand Rapids and in Cook.

For further information, contact

Area Forest Supervisor, George Washington State Forest, Box 157, Deer River, MN 56636. 218-246-8343

Minnesota Department of Natural Resources, Division of Forestry, Box 44 Centennial Building, St. Paul, MN 55155. 612-296-4491

See also McCarthy Beach State Park, page 145; Scenic State Park, page 174; Virginia Ranger District/Superior National Forest, Sturgeon River Cross-Country Ski Trail, page 186.

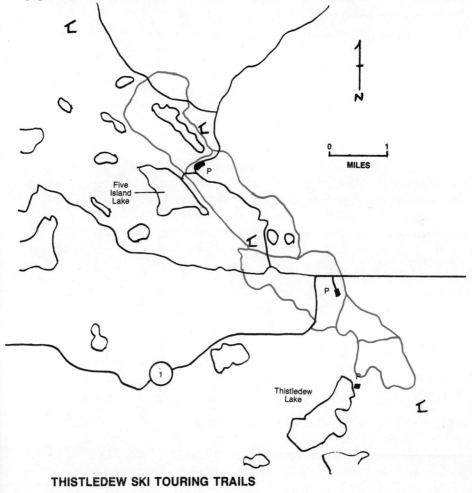

THISTLEDEW SKI TOURING TRAILS

REGION 3
CENTRAL MINNESOTA

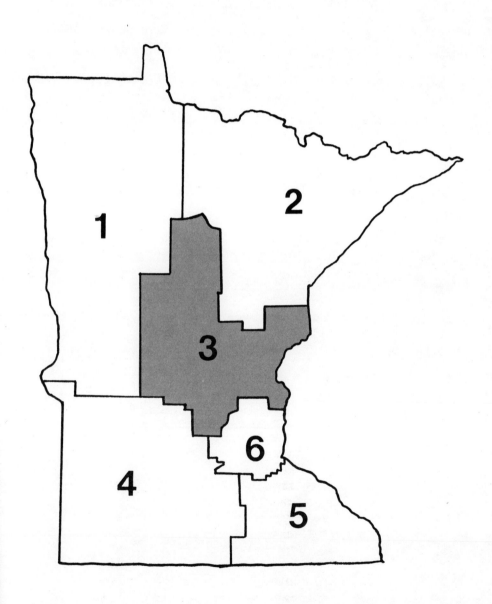

Banning State Park
Sandstone, Minnesota

9.6 km (6 mi) of trails
intermediate

Banning State Park is located in Pine County, four miles northeast of the city of Sandstone. Take the Sandstone exit from Interstate 35; then follow Highway 23 north to the park entrance. The near-6000 acres of parkland lie in a ten-mile strip on both sides of the Kettle River, a State Wild and Scenic River, the park's dominant feature. The famous Hell's Gates Rapids provide perhaps the most challenging river experience in the state for canoers and kayakers during the summer.

As the river has cut its course, it has exposed bedrock for much of the distance. In the northern part of the park, it has cut a relatively shallow and narrow valley through glacial debris. Within a few miles of this section the river valley becomes severely constricted; the Kettle roars through a gorge of sandstone 75–100 feet deep. At Hell's Gate, the sheer cliffs rise 20–40 feet above the river. Below this point, the river valley widens once again.

The land above the river basin is level to gently rolling. Originally, it was heavily forested with white and Norway pine. As a result of intense logging and forest fires, aspen and birch are now the dominant woodland species.

The site of the now nonexistent village of Banning and its companionate sandstone quarries are of historical interest. The quarries were developed on the river in the Hell's Gate region in the 1880s. The stone became such a popular building material that by 1882, the Quarrying Company employed 500 people engaged in stonecutting. But the Great Hinckley Fire of September 1, 1894, ravaged the area so severely that the company and the St. Paul and Duluth Railroad, which served the quarry, suffered extreme financial losses. Within two years, however, the town of Banning (named after the president of the St. Paul and Duluth Railroad) was platted above the quarry, and, by the turn of the century, it had grown to over 300 residents. But by this time, the advent of structural steel had taken place, and by 1905 the quarry ceased operation. The town began to fade and by 1912 ceased to exist.

The ski trails loop around the quarry area and skirt the Hell's Gate Region. They traverse the perimeter of the picnic grounds, where there is a spur down the Wolf Creek and Wolf Creek Falls. The trailhead is at the park's information center. All trails are marked and groomed. Parking, maps, water, and toilets are available at the park. Snowmobilers and skiers must move adjacent to another for a portion of the river region. Winter camping is allowed. Food, lodging, and other tourist accommodations are available in Sandstone.

For further information, contact

Banning State Park, Park Manager, P.O. Box V, Sandstone, MN 55072. 612-245-2668
Minnesota Department of Natural Resources, Division of Parks and Recreation, Box 39 Centennial Building, St. Paul, MN 55155. 612-296-4776

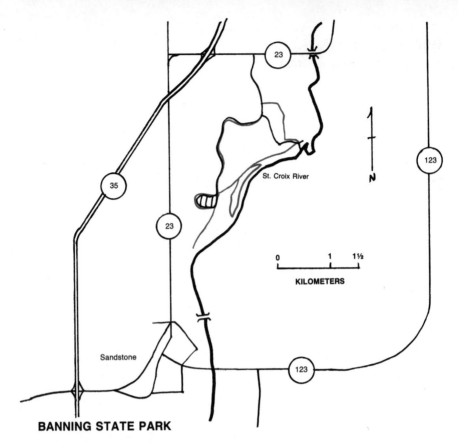

BANNING STATE PARK

Breezy Point Resort
Breezy Point, Minnesota

15 km (9.4 mi) of trails

beginner, intermediate, advanced

Breezy Point Resort is located in Crow Wing County on Big Pelican Lake, 20 miles north of the city of Brainerd. Take Highway 371 north to Pequot Lakes; turn east on County Road 11 to Breezy Point. It is a yearround facility with full accommodations.

The trails at the resort are marked and groomed fairly regularly. At the trailhead there is a clubhouse with bathrooms, water, and parking. On weekdays, you obtain maps at the clubhouse; on weekends, they are available at the front desk of the resort. There is no fee charged for trail use. In January and February the system expands from 15 km to 30 km, as a race trail is set up. Ski rentals are available.

For further information, contact

Breezy Point Resort, Front Desk, Breezy Point, MN 56472. 218-562-7811, 800-432-3777 (toll free Minnesota), 800-328-2284 (toll free elsewhere)

Paul Bunyan Arboretum
Brainerd, Minnesota

12 km (7.5 mi) of trails
beginner, intermediate

Paul Bunyan Arboretum is located just next to the city of Brainerd. Road signs on west 210 and 371 will direct visitors north on N.W. 7th for 3 blocks to the entrance gate.

Originally, there was only the 2-km **Acorn Trail** at the Arboretum. It has now expanded to over 12 km of trails that are groomed and maintained by the Brainerd Nordic Ski Club. The Acorn Trail is now illuminated for night skiing. There is an enormous variety of trails, set up in a network of one-way loops. Access to the trails is at five points on Prairie Road, the Arboretum's thoroughfare. Although the trails are for novices and intermediates, six slopes are more difficult.

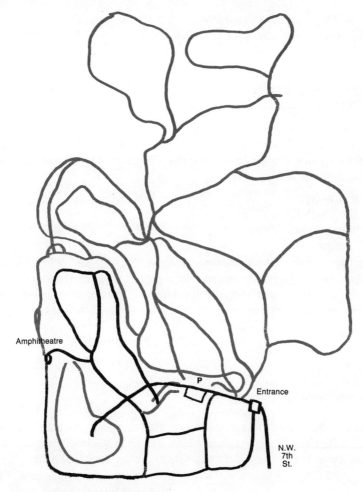

PAUL BUNYAN ARBORETUM

The Arboretum has a warming house, toilets, and a parking area. There are special snowshoeing trails (one parallels the Acorn Trail) and a skating rink. There are fees for using the trails: a day membership is $1.50 and is required of those over sixteen; annual membership is $7.50 for individuals and $15.00 for families. These annual memberships will enroll skiers in both the Arboretum and the Ski Club, whose efforts in trail development and maintenance are supported by fee collection.

On February 5, 1985, they will sponsor the Tenth Annual 16-km Lumberjack Jaunt and the 5-km Mini-Jaunt; the races will begin at 1:00 p.m. at the Brainerd Golf Course.

The Arboretum is open daily 8:00 a.m.–10:00 p.m. in the winter, from 8:00 a.m. to dusk in the summer. Maps are available at the Arboretum. Full tourist accommodations are available within a 0.75–1 mile radius of the Arboretum.

For further information, contact

Rudy Hillig, Director, Paul Bunyan Arboretum, Box 375, Brainerd, MN 56401. 218-829-8770

See also Crow Wing State Park, page 204; French Rapids Cross-Country Ski Area, page 211; Pillsbury State Forest, Rock Lake Solitude Area, page 221; Pine Beach Ski Touring Trail, page 223.

Cass County Ski Trails
Walker, Minnesota

Six trails in Cass County are designated as and groomed for ski touring. Some are interconnected. Skiers need a trail permit to use the trails. They basically are arranged in a very general line from Walker down to the Pine River area. The following list starts in Walker and proceeds to Pine River.

TOWER TRAIL
WALKER, MINNESOTA
9.6 km (6 mi) of trails
beginner, intermediate

The trail begins at the Walker Lookout Tower on the south end of Walker. It is marked and groomed, and is laid out in a one-way loop that winds around several small ponds. The south end of the loop skirts a golf course and, at its extreme southern end, becomes a two-way trail that crosses a primitive road and leads to Bakker Trail. A snowmobile trail runs adjacent to the loop at the golf course and crosses the ski trail at midsection. No toilets, shelter, or water are available on the trail.

BAKKER TRAIL
WALKER, MINNESOTA
7 km (4.4 mi) of trails
advanced

In addition to the two-way trail to the Tower Trail, access to the Bakker Trail is at two points on Highway 34, approximately 2 miles south of Walker. The trail is very rugged and challenging and is only for those who have very developed ability. It was originally designed as a training course. The trail is marked and groomed, and red flags indicate the trail's hazardous segments. It is a one-way trail set up in two loops. Due to the demanding terrain, skiers must strictly observe the one-way rule. Parking is available just off Highway 34 at the trailhead. No shelter, toilets, or water are at hand on the trail.

See also Walker Ranger District/Chippewa National Forest, all trails, page 229.

HOWARD LAKE SKI TRAIL
AKELEY, MINNESOTA
5 km (3.1 mi) of trails
beginner, intermediate

Access to the Howard Lake Trail is either from the far southwestern loop of the Shingobee Recreation Area (*See* Walker Ranger District, page 229) or from Earthome Resort, reached by taking Highway 34 south to County Road 83, turning south on 83, and traveling 1 mile to Forest Road 2314 (Howard Lake Road). The trail is a one-way, two-loop system and is periodically groomed by local ski enthusiasts. It is marked and contains two areas where skiers should exercise caution. Park at either Earthome or the Shingobee Recreation Area. No toilets, water, or shelters are available on the trail.

GOOSE LAKE RECREATION AREA
LONGVILLE, MINNESOTA
22.4 km (14 mi) of trails
beginner, intermediate

Goose Lake Recreation Area is reached by driving either 14 miles northeast of Hackensack or 5 miles west from Longville on County Road 5. The trailhead is just south of the intersection of County Road 5 and Forest Road 2107 (the Woodtick Trail).

This trail, well-marked, groomed, and double-tracked, exemplifies the cooperation of several agencies and organizations in developing a fine recreation facility. Although the trail is situated on land within the Chippewa National Forest, the trail is operated and maintained by Cass County. The grooming and tracking is done by a local ski touring club. The trail winds over gently rolling hills forested with pine, through clearings, and over wetlands—with Goose Lake in the middle of the center loop.

A license is required to ski the trail. Although a snowmobile trail crosses the system, snowmobilers are not permitted on the trail. Parking is available in a lot adjacent to County Road 5. There are no toilets, shelters, or water on site. Ski rentals are available in Walker at Walker Hardware. Food and lodging are at hand in Longville, Hackensack, or Walker.

This trail system is approximately 6 miles northeast of Deep-Portage Conservation Reserve. North Country Trail intersects the trail at spurs off the northern side of two of the loops.

See also Walker Ranger District/Chippewa National Forest, North Country Trail, page 230.

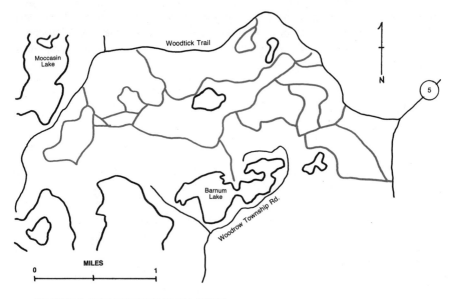

GOOSE LAKE RECREATION AREA

DEEP-PORTAGE CONSERVATION RESERVE
HACKENSACK, MINNESOTA
20 km (12.5 mi) of trails

intermediate, advanced

Deep-Portage Conservation Reserve is located in Cass County, southeast of the town of Hackensack. Go east from town on County Road 5 for 4.6 miles to County 46; travel 4.4 miles south and east on 46 to the entrance of the Reserve. This facility is approximately 6 miles southwest of the Goose Lake Recreation Area.

Deep-Portage is composed of 6,100 acres of glacial moraine set aside by Cass County in 1973 for the interpretation, preservation, and management of unique natural, cultural, and historic features of the area. This action was guided by the belief that the greater our appreciation of Minnesota's resources, the greater our incentive to maintain them. The Interpretive Center is open to the public during all seasons, and houses meeting space, displays, and research laboratories used in monitoring programs. In addition to staff, more than two hundred volunteers, many of them professionals in special fields, teach, do research, guide visitors, and help with other Reserve activities.

The 40 km of recreational trails are evenly divided between skiing and snowmobiling during the winter. Access to the ski trails is at the Interpretive Center, just to the south of Bass Pond. The groomed trails wind through rugged pine, birch, and aspen forests. Maps, water, toilets, and parking are available at the Interpretive Center. Food and lodging are at hand in Backus or Hackensack.

For further information, contact

Deep-Portage Conservation Reserve, Mike Naylon, Director, Route 1 Box 129, Hackensack, MN 56452. 218-682-2325

CUT LAKE CROSS-COUNTRY SKIING AREA
PINE RIVER, MINNESOTA

16.8 km (10.5 mi) of trails

beginner, intermediate, advanced

To reach the trailhead, take Highway 371 either southeast from Walker for 22 miles or northwest from Brainerd for 30 miles to Pine River. Turn west on County Road 2 at Pine River, and travel 10.5 miles to the trailhead.

This very beautiful trail winds around several lakes, the largest being Cut Lake and Deer Lake. It is well-marked, groomed, and track-set. There are seven loops. On the Deep Lake Loop is a shelter with a fireplace and an outdoor privy. On the Noname Lake Loop is another shelter with a fireplace. Benches for rest stops are located at sev-

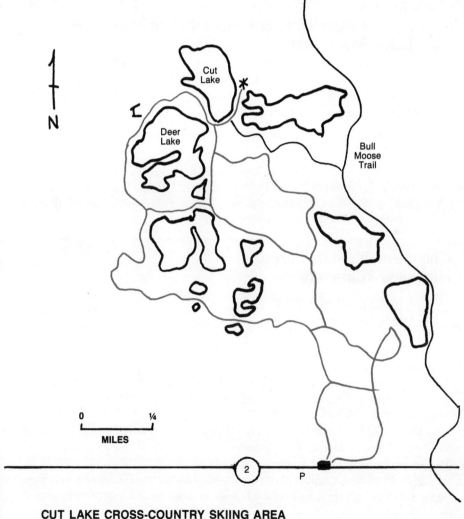

CUT LAKE CROSS-COUNTRY SKIING AREA

eral places along the trail. Parking is available at the trailhead. There is also a privy at this site. Although a snowmobile trail runs in the vicinity of the far northeastern side of the ski trail, the two trails do not intersect.

Food, water, and lodging are available in Pine River.

See also Foothills State Forest, Spider Lake Trail, page 209. This trail and the Cut Lake Trail have their trailheads approximately a quarter of a mile apart on County Road 2. For further information on the Cass County Trails and for maps, contact

Elso Ryks, Cass County Trail Coordinator, Deep-Portage Conservation Reserve, Route 1 Box 129, Hackensack, MN 56452. 218-682-2325, 218-587-4599 (evenings only)

Mr. Ryks can also provide more adventurous skiers with information on the Hunter/Walker Trails maintained by Cass County. These trails involve skiing on unbroken snow over routes that are meant to be used for hiking primarily.

Cass Lake Ranger District/Chippewa National Forest
Cass Lake, Minnesota

Cass Lake Ranger District does not groom its hiking trails, the Norway Beach Trail and the Star Island Trail, for cross-country skiing. The trails are located on extremely flat terrain and do *not* lend themselves to skiing.

For further information, contact

Cass Lake Ranger District, District Ranger, Chippewa National Forest, U.S. Forest Service, Cass Lake, MN 56633. 218-335-2283

See also Cass County Ski Trails, page 198; Walker Ranger District/Chippewa National Forest, page 229; Blackduck Ranger District/Chippewa National Forest, page 46; Deer River Ranger District/Chippewa National Forest, page 91; Marcell Ranger District/Chippewa National Forest, page 143.

Chengwatana State Forest
Hinckley, Minnesota

REDHORSE SKI TOURING TRAIL
16 km (10 mi) of trails
intermediate

Chengwatana State Forest is located on the St. Croix River in southeastern Pine and northeastern Chisago Counties. It can be reached by traveling either on County Roads 8 or 10 east from Pine City or on County Road 14 east from Beroun. The trailhead is on County Road 8. The Forest is immediately to the south of St. Croix State Park, which is in this region.

The landscape is composed of islands of forested uplands surrounded by marshland and brush. Three of Minnesota's main recreation rivers flow through Chengwatana. The Kettle River frames the northern and northeastern side of the Forest and empties into the St. Croix River, which runs on the southeastern border. The Snake River enters on the extreme southwestern side of the Forest, traverses its entire southern boundary, and meets the St. Croix. Millions of board feet of pine were logged in the vicinity in the late 1800s and were floated down the rivers to the St. Croix, where they proceeded on the journey to the large sawmills in Stillwater. Because of intensive logging and repeated fires, particularly the Great Hinckley Fire of September 1, 1894, the dominant woodland species are now aspen and birch.

State Forests exist to produce timber, provide a site for outdoor recreation, protect watersheds, and perpetuate and protect distinctive and often rare species of plant and animal life. The recreational sites are located primarily in the vicinity of the Forest's rivers.

The Redhorse Ski Touring Trail (named after the creek that intersects the route) begins at the County Road 8 entrance. Parking is available at this point. The Minnesota-Wisconsin Boundary State Trail also passes through at this point; for a distance of approximately 4 km (2.5 mi), the ski trail criscrosses the State Trail, following it across the Snake River. Grooming for skiing is not particularly good on this joint stretch, as the State Trail is used by snowmobiles. The ski trail then separates, crosses the Red-horse Creek, and runs in a large loop, skirting the St. Croix. It is very scenic in this part of the Forest, the rolling hills set off by the steep inclines to the river.

Full tourist accommodations are available in Pine City.

For further information, contact

Chengwatana State Forest, District Forester, DNR Forestry, Hinckley, MN 55037. 612-384-6146

Minnesota Department of Natural Resources, Division of Forestry, Box 44 Centennial Building, St. Paul, MN 55155. 612-296-4491

See also St. Croix State Park, page 224.

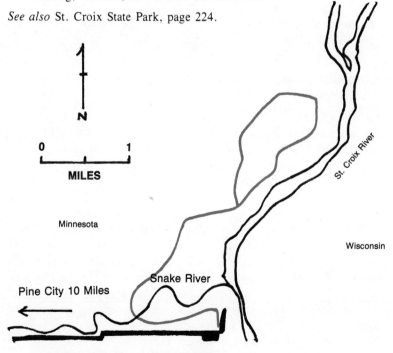

CHENGWATANA STATE FOREST

Chippewa National Forest
Forest Service, Department of Agriculture
Headquarters, Cass Lake, Minnesota

The Forest encompasses a total of 650,000 acres. Within this space the U.S. Forest Service works at achieving modern resource management, as well as meeting the requirements of our more primitive recreational activities. At the same time, efforts are made to protect the habitat and wildlife species such as the northern bald eagle. The Mississippi River has its source just to the west of the Forest, and it meanders through the area, contributing to an enormous network of lakes, smaller rivers, and streams. There are five Ranger Districts in the Chippewa National Forest. For information on the Blackduck Ranger District, please refer to Region 1; the Marcell and Deer River Ranger Districts may be reviewed in Region 2; and the Cass Lake and Walker Ranger Districts are located in this Region. In addition, the main headquarters and the office of the Forest Supervisor are located in Cass Lake.

Forest Supervisor, Chippewa National Forest, Cass Lake, MN 56633. 218-335-2226

Blackduck Ranger District, District Ranger, U.S. Forest Service, Blackduck, MN 56630. 218-835-4291

Cass Lake Ranger District, District Ranger, U.S. Forest Service, Cass Lake, MN 56633. 218-335-2283

Deer River Ranger District, District Ranger, U.S. Forest Service, Deer River, MN 56635. 218-246-2123

Marcell Ranger District, District Ranger, U.S. Forest Service, Marcell, MN 56657. 218-832-3161

Walker Ranger District, District Ranger, U.S. Forest Service, Walker, MN 56484. 218-547-1044

Crow Wing State Park
Brainerd, Minnesota

10.4 km (6.5 mi) of trails

beginner, intermediate, advanced

Crow Wing State Park is located at the juncture of central Minnesota counties Crow Wing, Cass, and Morrison. From the city of Brainerd, travel southwest on Highway 371 for 8 miles to County Road 27. Turn west on 27, and proceed 1 mile to park headquarters.

The park is situated at the confluence of the Mississippi and Crow Wing Rivers. Its name derives from the Ojibwe for the Crow Wing River, which translates as Raven's Wing River. The early French explorers called the waterway Rivière à l'Aile de Corbeau or River of the Wing of the Raven. English translation eventually became Crow Wing. Natural resources of every type were here for the support of early inhabitants. This was the site of a major battle between the Dakotah and Ojibwe in 1768 and, over the years, was home to many of the greatest Indians that have been documented, including the famous Ojibwe Chief Hole-in-the-Day who openly spoke against the exploitation of Indians by both fellow Indians and whites.

With the expansion of the fur trade, posts were soon established along the rivers. By the late 1820s there were three trading posts doing business with the Ojibwe.

This land was on a branch of the Red River Oxcart Trail between Pembina, North Dakota and St. Paul. Pembina was an important trading post of the Montreal-based North West Fur Company, where goods of trade, such as clothing, coffee, tea, tobacco, hardware, and alcoholic beverages, were exchanged for pemmican, Indian crafts, and furs.

By the late 1840s, commerce in the area had shifted from furs to timber. The vast white pine forests were logged off almost entirely, allowing for new multifarious growth to emerge. This regeneration brought in new wildlife, such as deer, beaver, grouse, and bear, which could not survive in a mature forest.

The Indian population was transferred to the White Earth Reservation in 1868, and the railroads chose Brainerd as their main terminal. This spelled the end for the Old Crow Wing settlement, which soon faded away.

The ski trails begin near the Historical Interpretive Center, south of the Old Crow Wing Town Site. They move to the south of the park, with a network of three loops to the southwest along the Mississippi, and another large loop with a crossover to the southeast. The river loops are situated on the most diverse terrain, while the southeast loop is quite level. All trails are marked and groomed. A map may be obtained at the

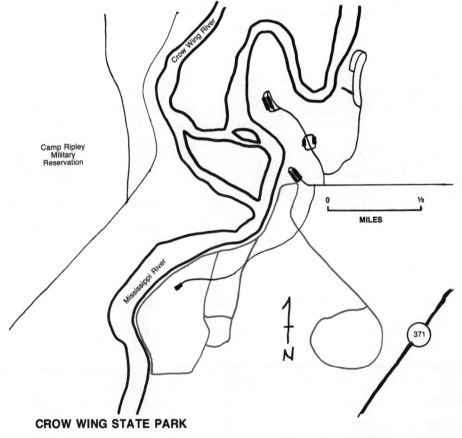

Camp Ripley
Military
Reservation

Crow Wing River

Mississippi River

0   ½

MILES

N

371

CROW WING STATE PARK

park headquarters. Parking is at the trailhead. Toilets and shelter are available. Snowmobiling is allowed at the park, but the trails do not intersect the ski trails and are located primarily in the northern part of the park.

Food, lodging, and other tourist needs may be obtained in Brainerd.

For further information, contact

Crow Wing State Park, Park Manager, Route 3 Box 342, Brainerd, MN 56401. 218-829-8022

Minnesota Department of Natural Resources, Division of Parks and Recreation, Box 39 Centennial Building, St. Paul, MN 55155. 612-296-4776

See also Paul Bunyan Arboretum, page 197; French Rapids Cross-Country Ski Area, page 211; Charles A. Lindbergh State Park, page 216; Pillsbury State Forest, Rock Lake Solitude Area, page 221; Pine Beach Ski Touring Trail, page 223.

Eagle Mountain Ski Area
Grey Eagle, Minnesota

10 km (6.25 mi) of trails

beginner, intermediate, advanced

Eagle Mountain Ski Area is located in Todd County, by the town of Grey Eagle, which is 35 miles northwest of St. Cloud. From Interstate 94, take the Freeport exit, and go north 13 miles to Eagle Mountain. Follow the signs to the entrance.

The trails at Eagle Mountain are marked, groomed, and double-tracked. There is a possibility that they may use quad-track by the 1984–85 season. The wooded terrain offers much variety. One of the scenic rest areas along the trail is at the highest point in Todd County. Wind shelters and firewood are supplied so this is a good spot for skiers to take a break and enjoy a trail picnic. On weekends, a cross-country ski instructor is on duty. A trail fee is charged: adults, $3.00; juniors, $2.00; and children, $1.25. There is a family rate also. Ski rentals may be arranged: Monday–Friday, $6.00; Saturday and Sunday, $6.50. Special group rates are available by reservation, with a minimum of 20 persons to qualify. Maps, toilets, water, and showers are available in the chalet for skiers.

The chalet features: the Pub, where domestic and imported beer and setups are sold and Country Western bands perform on Sundays 2–6 p.m.; the Grill, where light German and American foods and homemade doughnuts are served; the Ski Shop, where one can purchase ski equipment and accessories; and the Bunkhouse, for overnight accommodations ($7.50 per person, bring your own sleeping bag), where there is also a fireplace and gameroom. There are condominiums for rent with fully equipped kitchens, living room with hideabed, TV, fireplace, bedroom, and bath with shower and sauna.

This is also a downhill facility with eleven runs and snowtubing on three hills. Snowmobiling is allowed at Eagle Mountain; they have their own trails that at times cross ski trails.

For further information, contact

Eagle Mountain Ski Area, Grey Eagle, MN 56366. 612-573-2222, 612-285-4567

See also Charles A. Lindbergh State Park, page 216.

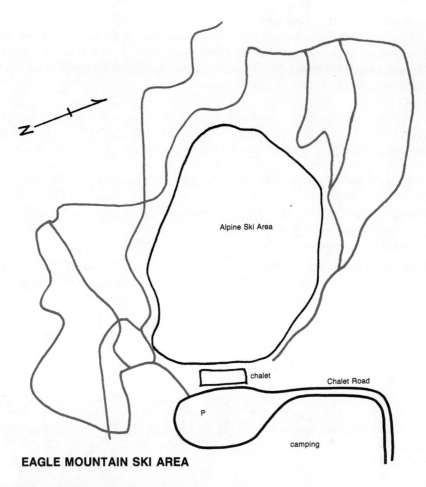

Alpine Ski Area

chalet

Chalet Road

P

camping

EAGLE MOUNTAIN SKI AREA

Father Hennepin State Park
Isle, Minnesota

4.8 km (3 mi) of trails

beginner, intermediate

Father Hennepin State Park is located on the southeast side of Mille Lacs Lake in Mille Lacs County, to the west of the town of Isle. The park entrance is on Highway 27, 12 miles east-northeast of Onamia.

The park is named for Father Louis Hennepin, a Belgian Jesuit missionary and explorer, the first-recorded European to have entered the area in North America that is now Minnesota. He entered the region around Mille Lacs Lake in 1680. He and two companions, from an expedition sent into the upper Mississippi River Valley by La-Salle, were captured by a band of Dakotah on Lake Pepin (*see* Frontenac State Park, Region 5). After the French were instrumental in settling a severe intertribal difficulty, the Europeans gained a new respect in the eyes of the Indians and continued to travel with them, more as guests than prisoners. Of course, this was a tremendous opportunity for the French to learn about the river valley from people who knew it well. They traveled with the Dakotah for about eight months and were in the region of Mille Lacs Lake, when they were met by an expedition under Sieur Duluht (whence the name Duluth). Duluht arranged for their transfer. The site of Hennepin's captivity is not at this state park, but at the area that is now Mille Lacs Kathio State Park, also in this region.

The park is situated on a natural headland on Mille Lacs Lake, the second largest fresh water lake entirely within Minnesota. The trails begin at the picnic area, to the northwest of the park headquarters. Parking is available at this location. The route moves westward through the campground and forms a loop at the second picnic area, which is situated on the lakeshore. There is a shelter on this loop. A snowmobile trail crosses the trail at this point. The trail continues to circle back eastward, winding through the wooded land of the southern region of the park. All trails are marked and groomed. Winter camping is allowed. Toilets are available.

For further information, contact

Father Hennepin State Park, Park Manager, Box 397, Isle, MN 56343. 612-676-8763
Minnesota Department of Natural Resources, Division of Parks and Recreation, Box
    39 Centennial Building, St. Paul, MN 55155. 612-296-4776

See also Izaty's Lodge, page 212 and Mille Lacs Kathio State Park, page 219.

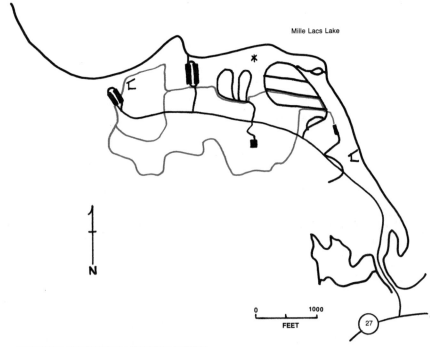

FATHER HENNEPIN STATE PARK

Fitzharris/Pirates Cove Touring Court
St. Cloud, Minnesota

28.8 km (18 mi) of trails
beginner, intermediate, advanced

To reach the trailhead, take Highway 10 north from St. Cloud for 6 miles; turn west on Watab Road for a short distance to the access point.

The trails are double-tracked and groomed. No fee is charged for trail use. Free instruction is available every Sunday at 2:00 p.m. Ski rentals are available for $3.00 per hour. Parking is at the trailhead. A full restaurant and lounge are on site.

For further information, contact

Fitzharris/Pirates Cove, Box 340, St. Cloud, MN 56301. 612-251-2344

See also Stearns County, Mississippi River County Park, page 228.

Foothills State Forest
Backus, Minnesota

SPIDER LAKE SKI TOURING AREA
27 km (16.25 mi) of trails
advanced

Foothills State Forest is located in central Cass County, beginning about 8 miles southeast of the city of Walker and ending about 40 miles northwest of Brainerd. Access to the Forest is from Pine River, Backus, or Hackensack (all are on Highway 371). Spider Lake Ski Touring Area is in the southern end of the Forest and may be reached by taking County Road 2 west from Pine River for approximately 10 miles to the trailhead.

Around the turn of the century, the timber industry was virtually the only business in the area. The land cleared by the loggers was homesteaded, but with little success, as the land is so ill-suited for agriculture. After the boom period of logging was over, the companies moved out of the area, and the railroads, dependent upon moving the timber, quickly followed suit. The few people that were left led an extremely isolated, self-sufficient existence. Evidence of this early period of activity may be seen all over the Forest.

In 1931, Foothills State Forest was established, and it has been developed to its present size of nearly 44,000 acres. The land is fairly level in the southwestern end of the Forest but is primarily rolling to steep in the remainder of the area. This wooded landscape includes hundreds of small lakes and potholes caused by ancient glacial activity.

State forests have been established all over Minnesota to produce timber and other forest crops, to provide a site for outdoor recreation, to protect watersheds, and to perpetuate rare and distinctive species of plant and animal life. Over 3,000 cords of wood are harvested annually at Foothills State Forest. An intense forest and wildlife habitat improvement program has also been undertaken, resulting in a strong resurgence of ruffed grouse and whitetail deer, in particular.

The trails at Spider Lake Ski Touring Area are only for a well-conditioned, experienced skier, as they involve traversing a fairly large distance over demanding, rugged landscape. There are four loops in the system. The trails wind around countless small lakes and potholes, pass by a lookout tower, and eventually lead to Spider Lake, the largest lake in the network. There is a picnic area at this point. One more loop extends beyond Spider Lake. The trail is marked and groomed. There are two shelters on the trail. A snowmobile trail crosses the ski trail at the first and third loops and runs adjacent to Spider Lake. The trailhead to Cut Lake is just across the road from Spider Lake trailhead.

Privies are available, and parking is at the trailhead. Maps may be obtained from the Forest Supervisor in Backus. Food and lodging are available in Pine River.

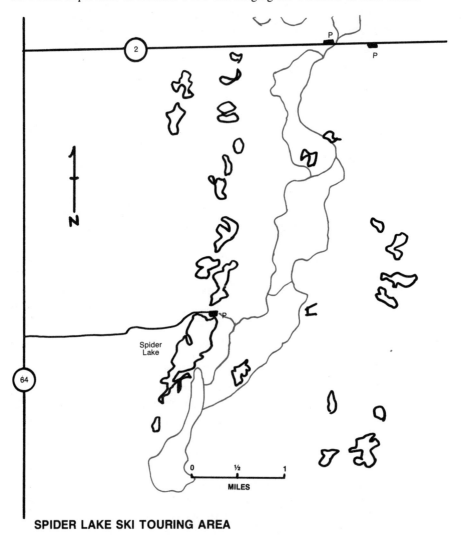

SPIDER LAKE SKI TOURING AREA

For further information, contact

Foothills State Forest, Backus Area Forest Supervisor, Box 34, Backus, MN 56435. 218-947-3232

Minnesota Department of Natural Resources, Division of Forestry, Box 44 Centennial Building, St. Paul, MN 55155. 612-296-4491

See also Cass County Trails, Cut Lake Cross-Country Ski Area, page 201.

French Rapids Cross-Country Ski Area
Brainerd, Minnesota

14 km (8.75 mi) of trails
advanced

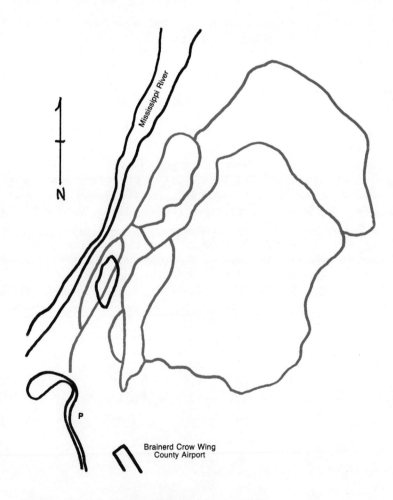

FRENCH RAPIDS CROSS-COUNTRY SKI AREA

French Rapids Ski Area is located in Crow Wing County, 5 miles northeast of the city of Brainerd. It is just off Highway 210, next to the Mississippi River and adjacent to the Brainerd airport entrance.

The trail system is groomed and maintained by the Brainerd Nordic Ski Club. It is well-marked. Although the initial part of the network is easy skiing, the trails become very demanding and should be attempted only by experienced skiers. The system is laid out in a series of loops; some are one-way, others are two-way. There are several hills involved in the ski area and the trails traverse two ponds. The tour is very scenic.

A map and parking are available at the trailhead. Full tourist accommodations are at hand in Brainerd.

For further information, contact

Brainerd Nordic Ski Club, P.O. Box 927, Brainerd, MN 56401
Crow Wing County Land Commissioner, County Courthouse, Brainerd, MN 56401.
   218-829-8770

See also Paul Bunyan Arboretum, page 197; Crow Wing State Park, page 204; Pillsbury State Forest, Rock Lake Solitude Area, page 221; Pine Beach Ski Touring Trail, page 223.

Izaty's Lodge
Onamia, Minnesota

43 km (26.9 mi) of trails, located in nearby Mille Lacs Kathio State Park
beginner, intermediate, advanced

Izaty's Lodge is located on the southern shores of Lake Mille Lacs. The only skiing that is immediately available at the lodge is on their golf course, which is good as a warm-up run or for beginners to hone their skills. However, 6 miles away is Mille Lacs Kathio State Park, which many authorities and seasoned skiers feel is the best skiing in Minnesota. At Kathio, the trails are marked, groomed, and tracked, with no snowmobiling allowed on the trails. For registered guests, Izaty's caters a special barbecue to the park every Saturday. They have said that at times they serve 60–70 people! They provide transportation to the park for guests who need it.

The lodge offers first-class accommodations, most with fireplace, color TV, stereo, and deck or patio overlooking the lake. They have an indoor swimming pool with whirlpool and sauna. They serve home-cooked meals, have wine and cheese parties, host hayrides, and maintain a skating rink.

For further information, contact

Izaty's Lodge, c/o Steve Dubbs, Onamia, MN 56359. 612-532-3101

See also Father Hennepin State Park, page 207 and Mille Lacs Kathio State Park, page 219.

Lake Maria State Park
Monticello, Minnesota

21 km (13.1 mi) of trails

beginner, intermediate

Lake Maria State Park is located in Wright County, about 23 miles southeast of St. Cloud. It is 6 miles southwest of Interstate 94. From the south take County Road 39 to County Road 111 to the park entrance. From the north take County Road 8 to County Road 111. The city of Monticello is 7 miles away.

The park lies within the St. Croix Moraine, which was formed during the last glaciation that pushed through the area. The region is characterized by a rough, wooded terrain and terminal moraines—accumulations of boulders, stones, and other debris left over 10,000 years ago when the last glacier retreated. The rough and rolling land is almost entirely wooded. Small lakes (the largest being Lake Maria), ponds, and marshes nestle in the depressions produced by the glaciers. This habitat is ideal for the growth and sanctuary of wildlife, which abounds in the park.

Lake Maria is situated on the northern end of the part of Minnesota that was called the Big Woods. About 3,030 square miles in area, it was approximately 100 miles from north to south and 40 miles wide at its southern end. It was a very densely forested area, covered with maple, basswood, white and red elm, red oak, tamarack (in swamps), and red cedar (on lake shores). In some areas, the woods were so dense that sunlight could not penetrate to the forest floor. For thousands of years, this area was a rich, abundant source of life for the Native Americans who inhabited the Big Woods. They produced maple syrup and gathered berries, wild fruit, nuts, and wild rice. Game animals existed in plentiful supply.

Today, this area is cleared and farmed. Numerous towns and suburbs with their accompanying industry are situated throughout the countryside. It is difficult to envision the land's former appearance. Lake Maria State Park encompasses a type of land that remains today as it was in the early settler period.

The ski trails at the park are laid out in a series of several one-way loops, which begin at the parking area just to the south of the information center. The loops to the south are for novices; those to the north are designed for intermediates. No snowmobiling is allowed in the park, enabling skiers to have a peaceful ski tour. There is a heated trail center with restrooms and drinking water available. Maps may be obtained at the park. Winter camping is permitted. Food, lodging, and other tourist needs are at hand in nearby Monticello.

For further information, contact

Lake Maria State Park, Park Manager, Route 1, Monticello, MN 55362. 612-878-2325

Minnesota Department of Natural Resources, Division of Parks and Recreation, Box 39 Centennial Building, St. Paul, MN 55155. 612-296-4776

See also Manitou Lakes (YMCA), page 218 and Wright County, Harry Larson Memorial County Forest, page 236.

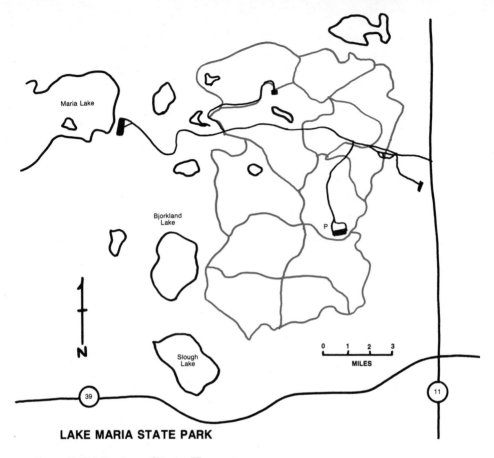

LAKE MARIA STATE PARK

Land O' Lakes State Forest
Outing, Minnesota

WASHBURN LAKE SOLITUDE AREA
23.9 km (14.9 mi) of trails

intermediate, advanced

Washburn Lake Solitude Area of the Land O' Lakes State Forest is located in Cass County, 3 miles northwest of the town of Outing. Outing is on Highway 6, between Crosby/Ironton and Remer. Travel north on Highway 6 for 2 miles from Outing, turn west on County Road 48, and proceed for 1 mile to the trailhead.

The 2,000-acre Washburn Lake Solitude Area is set aside for those who wish to ski (or hike) in an area reserved for non-motorized use. It is located in a beautiful region of Minnesota, heavily forested with old red pines and deeply etched with lakes, streams, and small swamps. Land O' Lakes State Forest provides pulpwood and saw-logs for Minnesota's timber industry and is managed with practices that enhance forest production, as well as emphasize recreation, outdoor aesthetic values, wildlife production, and watershed protection.

The trail system is composed of three loops to the north of County Road 48 and three loops to the south. They are entirely interconnected, with adirondack shelters on either section. The loops are various lengths and are situated on a level to gently rolling terrain. The northern system is situated to the east of Washburn Lake. The southern system skirts Grasshopper and Bear Lakes, as well as several other small lakes and ponds. Although a novice skier could get along quite easily on the level stretches, the entire system is rated as intermediate, with the exception of one advanced segment at the southwest end of the trails. The route is groomed regularly. Call the Washburn Lake Office (218-792-5383) for information on trail conditions.

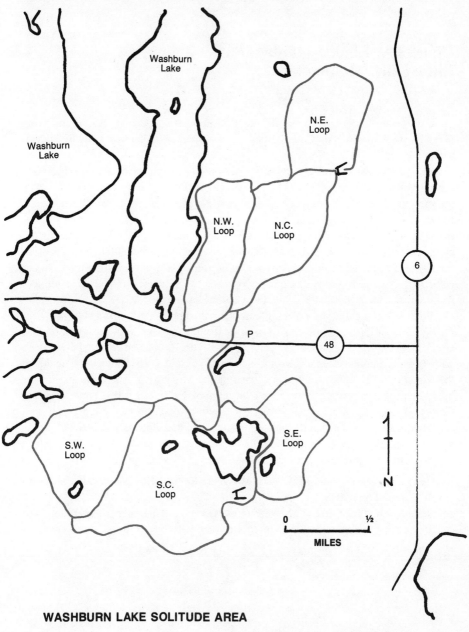

WASHBURN LAKE SOLITUDE AREA

A parking lot with a trail map is located at the trailhead. A pit toilet is on hand at this site. In the town of Outing, skiers will find restaurants, grocery stores, gas station, and resorts.

For further information, contact

Land O' Lakes State Forest, Washburn Lake Solitude Area, Forest Supervisor, Box 6, Backus, MN 56435. 218-792-5383, 218-947-3232

Minnesota Department of Natural Resources, Division of Forestry, Box 44 Centennial Building, St. Paul, MN 55155. 612-296-4491

Charles A. Lindbergh State Park
Little Falls, Minnesota

4.9 km (3 mi) of trails

beginner, intermediate

Charles A. Lindbergh State Park is located in Morrison County, 1 mile southwest of the city of Little Falls on County Road 52. It is situated on the west bank of the Mississippi River.

The park is named for the progressive Republican Congressman who represented central Minnesota from 1907 to 1917 and ran unsuccessfully for governor in 1918, with the support of the Nonpartisan League, one of the predecessors of the Farmer Labor Party. His son, Charles A. Lindbergh, Jr., made world history in 1927 with his solo transatlantic flight. The restored Lindbergh family home, run by the Minnesota Historical Society, is located on park land and contains family memorabilia. The Historical Society also administers an Interpretive Center at the park, documenting the lives and careers of three generations of Lindberghs—August, a pioneer settler who emigrated from Sweden in 1860, Charles Sr., and Charles Jr.

Both ski touring and snowshoeing are encouraged in the park. It is a non-motorized facility; these winter activities prove to be peaceful experiences for participants. Pike Creek flows through the park to the Mississippi River. It is named after Zebulon Montgomery Pike, a militaryman and explorer, who had a stockade encampment here during the winter of 1805–1806 while on a voyage up the Mississippi. The trails are laid out in a pattern that is relative to the creek, in large part. There are two large loops and two small loops, with many crossovers and spurs involved in the system.

Maps may be obtained at the park. Food, lodging and other tourist needs are available in Little Falls.

For further information, contact

Charles A. Lindbergh State Park, Park Manager, Route 3 Box 246, Little Falls, MN 56345. 612-632-9050

Minnesota Department of Natural Resources, Division of Parks and Recreation, Box 39 Centennial Building, St. Paul, MN 55155. 612-296-4776

See also Crow Wing State Park, page 204 and Eagle Mountain Ski Area, page 206.

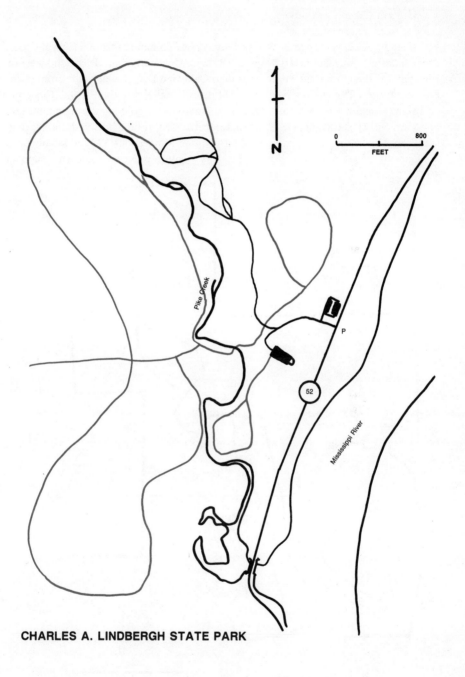

CHARLES A. LINDBERGH STATE PARK

Manitou Lakes (YMCA)
Monticello, Minnesota

35.2 km (22 mi) of trails

beginner, intermediate, advanced

Manitou Lakes is located in Wright County, just 35 minutes from the Twin Cities. From Interstate 94, take the Highway 25/Buffalo-Monticello exit. Turn southwest on Highway 25; then turn right (northwest) onto Oakwood Drive, which is in front of the Ford dealership. Travel 3.4 miles; turn right; travel 1 mile; turn right again. There will be a sign, Manitou Family Camp. Proceed 0.2 mile to the gold log cabin on the right.

Manitou Lakes encompasses 1,400 acres of wooded, rolling hills with four spring-fed lakes. The facility is owned by the Metropolitan Minneapolis YMCA and operated by their Northwest Branch in New Hope. It is a nature preserve, children's summer

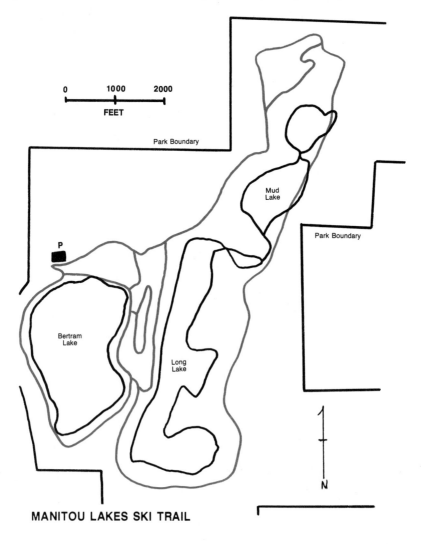

MANITOU LAKES SKI TRAIL

camp, and conference center. There are camping and picnic grounds, swimming beaches, boat landings, and hiking trails, which become cross-country trails in the winter. Maps are available at the entrance.

Skiing is excellent and diversified. It is an ideal place for families with children of all ages to tour. All trails are marked and groomed and will challenge skiers of every ability. The system meanders around the four lakes, with the novice trails located closer to the preserve's entrance and adjacent Bertram Lake. There are two picnic grounds in this area; there is another picnic area on the system's outermost loop. Snowshoeing and ice fishing are encouraged at Manitou Lakes.

Toilet facilities and ample parking are available—a parking donation is requested. The chalet is ideal for daytime groups of up to 36 people. It is furnished with two fireplaces (wood is provided), six sofabeds, two bedrooms, and a loft. There are bathrooms, kitchen and dining area, and gameroom. A large deck overlooks Bertram Lake. There are sleeping accommodations for 18 people. It has been used for workshops, retreats, sales meetings, celebrations, and reunions. Rental fees are very reasonable; the chalet can be rented for day use, overnight, weekend, or full week.

For further information, contact

Northwest Branch YMCA, 7601-42nd Avenue North, New Hope, MN 55427. 612-536-5700

See also Lake Maria State Park, page 213 and Wright County, Harry Larson Memorial County Forest, page 236.

Mille Lacs Kathio State Park
Onamia, Minnesota

43 km (26.9 mi) of trails

beginner, intermediate, advanced

Mille Lacs Kathio State Park is located in northern Mille Lacs County, approximately 7 miles northwest of the town of Onamia. The park is situated on the southern side of Lake Mille Lacs and may be reached by taking Highway 169 to County Road 26; from this point travel 1 mile to the entrance.

The word Kathio is an ill-derived form of the Dakotah word Izatys, and means "those who pitched tents at the Knife Lake." We now call the lake Mille Lacs Lake, from the French who referred to the general area as Mille Lacs, meaning "thousand lakes." The name eventually became synonymous with just the big lake. The park contains the source of the Rum River, which runs from Mille Lacs Lake through Lake Ogechie to Shakopee Lake and then continues its journey to Anoka, where it empties into the Mississippi River.

The length of time that humans have continuously lived in this area is tremendous, as is its history. Evidence of the presence of people from the Copper Culture (4,000 years ago) has been found in the area that is now the park's picnic ground. From the early 1600s to mid-1700s, the Dakotah established permanent villages in the area; they considered this to be the seat of their nation. The natural abundance of the land certainly was the prime reason for their continuous settlement. The lake, the vast rice beds that were once so heavy at Lake Ogechie, and the forest provided food. The forests furnished the people with countless other supplies, such as fuel and construction materials. It also offered sanctuary.

The Ojibwe, driven ever-westward by the pressures of the advancing settlement of the land by whites, fought a major battle with the Dakotah in 1745 over this area. The Ojibwe won decisively, as they were armed with gunpowder supplied by the French fur traders. Following their defeat, the Dakotah moved out onto the prairies.

By the 1850s, the timber industry became solidly established in the area and logged the vast forests of white and red pine intensively. The present forest is predominantly aspen, birch, maple, and oak.

The ski touring trails in the park are reputed by seasoned, devoted enthusiasts to be absolutely the finest in the state. They are all marked, groomed, and double-tracked and are laid out in a network of two-way loops. Novice trails are to the south of the system where the land is gentle. Intermediate and advanced trails are to the north on more rugged, demanding terrain. There are many access points to the trails via park roads; however, the primary trailhead is at the trail center just past the park entrance.

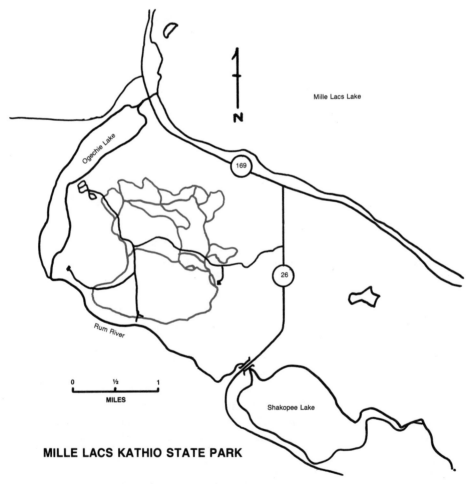

MILLE LACS KATHIO STATE PARK

Parking is ample. Maps, toilets, and water are available in the park. There is a heated shelter for skiers. Winter camping is allowed and firewood may be purchased at the park. Snowmobiling is permitted, but the trails do not conflict with the ski trails, and are generally situated at an opposite corner of the park. Food, lodging, and supplies are available in Onamia.

For further information, contact

Mille Lacs Kathio State Park, Park Manager, Star Route Box 85, Onamia, MN 56359. 218-532-3523

Minnesota Department of Natural Resources, Division of Parks and Recreation, Box 39 Centennial Building, St. Paul, MN 55155. 612-296-4776

Pillsbury State Forest
Brainerd, Minnesota

ROCK LAKE SOLITUDE AREA
12.8 km (8 mi) of trails
beginner, intermediate

Pillsbury State Forest, Minnesota's first state forest, is located in southern Cass County, about 10 miles northwest of Brainerd. To reach the Rock Lake Solitude Area, which is in the northwestern corner of the Forest, take Highway 210 west from Pillager for 0.5 mile to County Road 1. Turn north on 1, and travel 7 miles. Turn west on the Forest Road, and follow the signs.

In the late 1800s, millions of board feet of virgin pine were logged in this area. They were moved by sleigh or railroad to Gull Lake, rafted to the Gull River, and floated downstream to sawmills. At this time, settlers moved into the land to farm; but as the land was so ill-suited for agriculture, many farms were abandoned.

Pillsbury Forest Reserve was established in 1900, when former Governor John S. Pillsbury donated 990 acres of his own land to the State Forestry Board. It had been so intensively logged that it was totally devastated and barren. By 1903, the state's first forest tree nursery had been developed at Pillsbury Reserve. The forest was ultimately enlarged to its present size of 14,756 acres, which are administered jointly by the State Department of Forestry and Cass County.

The topography of the Forest is rolling to hilly, the result of past glacial activity. The many ponds and lakes within its boundaries are situated in the depressions of the glacial moraine. Northern hardwoods such as oak, maple, ash, elm, and basswood cover the land. Aspen and paper birch are common also.

The ski touring trail at the Rock Lake Solitude Area begins near the campground at Rock Lake. Parking is available at this point. The trail, marked and groomed, is arranged in a system of three loops. The first two are on a relatively flat terrain and are well-suited to the novice. The outermost loop is largest and intermediate in difficulty. There is a shelter on this loop. The variety of cover types in the area and the good chance of seeing wildlife while skiing make this an interesting tour. Snowmobiles are not permitted in the Solitude Area. Camping is allowed. An outdoor privy is situated on site. Maps are available in Brainerd at the Forest Supervisor's office.

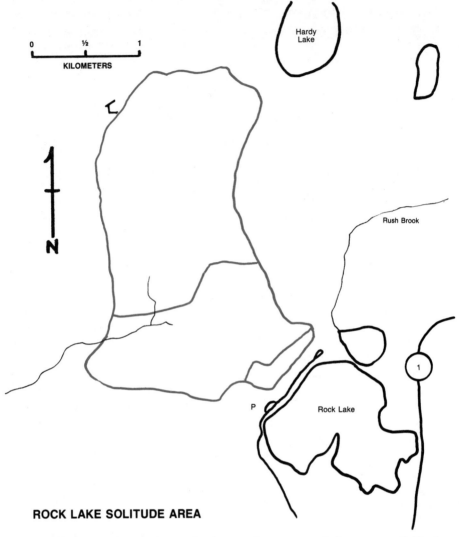

ROCK LAKE SOLITUDE AREA

Food, lodging, ski rentals, and other tourist accommodations are available in Brainerd.

For further information, contact

Pillsbury State Forest, Area Forest Supervisor, 203 W. Washington Street, Brainerd, MN 56401. 218-828-2565

Minnesota Department of Natural Resources, Division of Forestry, Box 44 Centennial Building, St. Paul, MN 55155. 612-296-4491

See also Paul Bunyan Arboretum, page 197; Crow Wing State Park, page 204; French Rapids Cross-Country Ski Area, page 211; Pine Beach Ski Touring Trail, page 223.

Pine Beach Ski Touring Trail
Brainerd, Minnesota

40 km (25 mi) of trails

beginner, intermediate

To reach the Pine Beach Ski Touring Trail, go northwest on Highway 371 for approximately 3 miles, then turn west on County Road 77 (Pine Beach Road), and proceed to the junction with Pine Beach Drive. Cragun's Lodge is to the north; Kavanaugh's is to the south.

The trail system, located in Cass County, is a joint effort between Kavanaugh's Sylvan Lodge and Cragun's Pine Beach Lodge. Together, they are known as the Pine Beach Ski Club. Their trails are marked, groomed, and double-tracked. Access is available at either Cragun's or Kavanaugh's. The trails skirt many lakes: Sylvan Lake (where Kavanaugh's is located), Dade Lake, Hardy Lake, and Steamboat Bay of Lower Gull Lake (Cragun's waterfront). They meander through a rolling landscape that is forested with pine and hardwoods and traverse an undulating open terrain. All trails are open to the public without fee. Parking and maps are available at either resort. No snowmobiling is permitted on the trails.

For food or lodging, contact either Cragun's or Kavanaugh's. Cragun's has full lodging (housekeeping or American Plan) and dining facilities, conference rooms, enclosed spa with swimming pool, whirlpool and sauna, ski rentals, and skating rink. Kavanaugh's offers full accommodations also; all are deluxe units with fireplaces. They offer both the American Plan and housekeeping plan, with special lodging packages available.

For further information, contact

Kavanaugh's Sylvan Lodge, RR 11 Box 204 M, Brainerd, MN 56401. 218-829-5226
Cragun's Pine Beach Lodge, RR 6 Box ST, Brainerd, MN 56401. 218-829-3591.

See also Paul Bunyan Arboretum, page 197; Crow Wing State Park, page 204; French Rapids Cross-Country Ski Area, page 211; Pillsbury State Forest, Rock Lake Solitude Area, page 221.

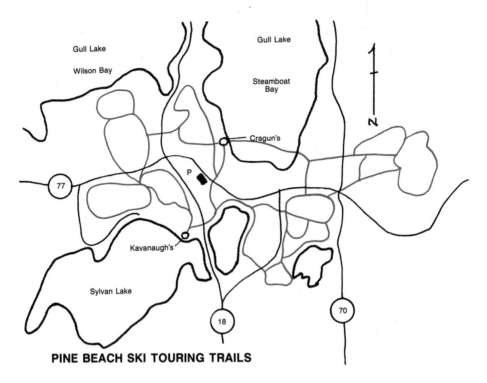

PINE BEACH SKI TOURING TRAILS

Map labels: Gull Lake, Wilson Bay, Gull Lake, Steamboat Bay, N, Cragun's, P, 77, Kavanaugh's, Sylvan Lake, 18, 70

St. Croix State Park
Hinckley, Minnesota

25.5 km (15.9 mi) of trails
beginner

St. Croix State Park is located in Pine County, 16 miles east of Hinckley on Highway 48. Park headquarters are on County Road 22, 5 miles south of the park entrance.

It is Minnesota's largest state park, encompassing 33,000 acres of mature forest, meadows, and marshes. The Kettle River and many creeks empty into the St. Croix River, which forms the entire eastern and southeastern boundary of the park. Designated a National Wild and Scenic River, it is easily the dominant feature of the park.

The geological history of this area is among the most complex in the world. The bedrock of the St. Croix River Valley is comprised of ancient lava rock. When the last glacier retreated approximately 10,000 years ago, it left debris consisting of boulders, stones, and granular, red sandy soil. The higher land forms are called moraines or glacier-made hills. Lowlands and marshes are due to slump brought about by the melting of buried chunks of glacial ice. The meltwater from ancient Glacial Lake Duluth created the St. Croix River and eroded its valley.

Although fur trapping was sparse in this area, the river served as a major highway in the fur trade between the Mississippi River and the Great Lakes. A French trading post was established here in 1800. It was also used as a main route for the Dakotah and later the Ojibwe to transport supplies. There were several Indian villages along its banks. By the late nineteenth century, the timber industry was thriving, and intensive logging almost eliminated the white pine. One of the park's campgrounds is named for

St. John, the operator of a logging camp. The Fleming Railroad, the transporter of the sawlogs from the area, followed the route of the park's entrance thoroughfare. The lumber industry came to an end, and settlers moved in to claim the land for farming. Most attempts failed, because the soil was so ill-suited for agriculture. The land was established as a state park in 1943.

This area is wonderfully suited for recreation, however. The ski trails begin at the heated trail center and run along the river. They suit the novice skier. At one point they cross Hay Creek, just north of Lake Clayton. There are outdoor privies available, as well as indoor restrooms with running water in the trail center. Winter camping is allowed. Snowmobile use may be heavy in the park at times, as the Minnesota-Wisconsin Boundary State Trail runs the entire length of the park. The park has its own snowmobile trails also. They do not mix with the ski trails, with the exception of two intersections that are at the cross-country trailhead.

Food, lodging, and other tourist needs may be obtained in Hinckley.

For further information, contact

St. Croix State Park, Park Manager, Route 3 Box 174, Hinckley, MN 55037. 612-384-6591

Minnesota Department of Natural Resources, Division of Parks and Recreation, Box 39 Centennial Building, St. Paul, MN 55155. 612-296-4776

See also Chengwatana State Forest, Redhorse Cross-Country Ski Trail, page 202.

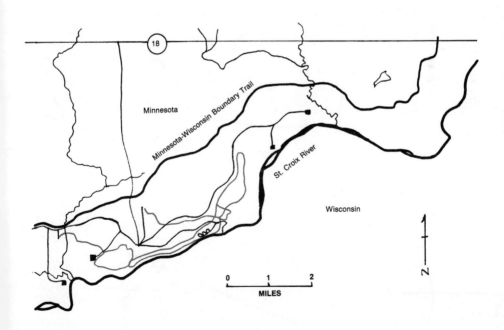

ST. CROIX STATE PARK

Sherburne National Wildlife Refuge
Zimmerman, Minnesota

Sherburne National Wildlife Refuge is located in Sherburne County, approximately 6 miles northwest of Zimmerman on County Road 9. It is situated in the middle of a triangle formed by St. Cloud to the northwest, Princeton to the northeast, and Elk River to the southeast. To reach the entrance to the Refuge, travel north from Zimmerman on Highway 169 to County Road 9, turn west on 9, and proceed to the Refuge. The headquarters is located about 1.25 miles from the entrance.

The primary function of the Refuge is to protect and perpetuate migratory waterfowl. The lush habitat provides sanctuary for a great number and variety of other wildlife also. In addition, the facility is an excellent resource in the field of environmental education.

Cross-country skiing and snowshoeing are allowed anywhere (not just roads and trails) in the Refuge. However, *only* ski touring is allowed on the trails. There are two trails for ski-touring, the Mahnomen Trail and the Blue Hill Trail. Neither trail is track-set, but they are well-marked and nearly always contain the tracks of previous skiers. No snowmobiling is allowed on Refuge land. No fees or trail license is required of visitors. Maps for both trails are available at Refuge Headquarters.

No camping is allowed because this is a day use facility. Small, open fires are allowed if the ground is completely snow-covered, if dead and down timber is used, and if the fire is located off roads and trails away from parking areas and buildings. Food, lodging and other tourist needs may be obtained in Princeton.

MAHNOMEN TRAIL
8.4 km (5.25 mi) of trails
beginner, intermediate

Rice Lake

Round Lake

9

MAHNOMEN TRAIL

The trailhead to the Mahnomen Trail is located on County Road 9, just to the east of the Refuge Headquarters. Park at the trailhead. The trail is aptly named, as it is situated to the north of Rice Lake, a shallow body of water that is fed by the St. Francis River. The marshland surrounding the lake supports huge wild rice beds, an important wildlife food source. The Ojibwe word for wild rice is mahnomen.

The trail is comprised of three loops, the smallest called Mounds Loop, named for the Indian burial mounds that are found there. It is estimated that they may be 7,000 years old. The trail winds through an area that is primarily forested with deciduous trees, with an occasional marshland or field en route. The trail is situated on rolling hills.

No water is available; there are outdoor privies at the trailhead.

BLUE HILL TRAIL
10.3 km (6.45 mi) of trails
beginner

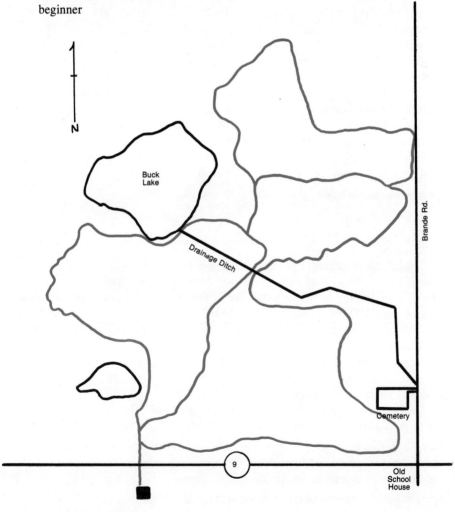

BLUE HILL TRAIL

The trailhead to the Blue Hill Trail is approximately 1 mile west of Refuge Headquarters on County Road 9. It is on the north side of the road. Park at the trailhead. The terrain is flat to gently rolling and the wide trail moves through deciduous and coniferous woods, along marshes, and across fields. The trail is set up in a system of four loops. No water or toilets are on site.

For further information, contact

Sherburne National Wildlife Refuge, Assistant Manager, Route 2, Zimmerman, MN 55398. 612-389-3323

Stearns County
St. Cloud, Minnesota

Two trails in the Stearn's County Park system are groomed for ski touring.

MISSISSIPPI RIVER COUNTY PARK
5.1 km (3.2 mi) of trails
beginner
To reach Mississippi River County Park, go north from St. Cloud on County Road 1 (Great River Road) 7 miles past Sartell to the park entrance, which is on the northeast side of the road. Drive into the park, bearing to the right until the parking area is reached. The trail begins at the parking lot.

The park is situated on the bank of the Mississippi River and contains some of the river's backwaters. Four loops are marked and groomed. Water, shelter, and toilets are available on site. No fee is charged. A snowmobile trail intersects the largest loop.

Tourist needs may be met in Sartell or in St. Cloud.

See also Fitzharris/Pirates Cove Touring Court, page 209.

TOKLE TRAIL
7.2 km (4.5 mi) of trails
advanced
Tokle Trail is located 3 miles south of the town of Avon, a short distance off County Road 9. About 1.25 miles southwest of Avon, a gravel road turns to the south from 9, at the curve just before Upper Spunk Lake County Park. Proceed southward approximately 1.75 miles, and turn east toward Big Watab Lake. The trailhead is on the north side of the road, just before the lake. A toilet and parking are available at the trailhead.

Some stretches may be regarded as intermediate on this trail, but it is primarily designed for the expert skier. Marked and groomed, it is a two-loop trail situated on a heavily wooded, challenging terrain.

Tourist needs may be met in Avon, St. Joseph, or St. Cloud.
For further information on either trail, contact

Park Headquarters, Stearns County Park Department, 425 South 72nd Avenue, St. Cloud, MN 56301. 612-253-6002
For additional information on the Tokle Trail, contact

Tokle Trail, Avon, MN 56310. 612-845-4314, 612-251-2253

Walker Ranger District, Chippewa National Forest
Walker, Minnesota

Three trails are designated as cross-country ski trails in the Walker Ranger District of the Chippewa National Forest. Two are National Forest Trails; the third is a non-motorized stretch of the National Scenic Trail, called the North Country Trail. Dispersed camping is available on National Forest Land.

COUNTY ROAD 50 TRAIL
14.4 km (9 mi) of trails
beginner, intermediate

To reach the trailhead, take Highway 34 south-southwest from Walker for approximately 2 miles to the junction with County Road 50. Turn south-southeast on 50, and travel for approximately 3 miles to the trailhead. At this point, there is a gated entrance. No fee is charged for trail use.

The trail is marked, but special grooming and tracking for skiing is not done. It winds around several small lakes and ponds and dead-ends at the Shingobee River. It consists of several loops and spurs. You will encounter dead ends at six locations, which are marked by barrier posts. This indicates that the skier is about to enter private property and should turn around. The North Country Trail (Walker Ranger District) passes through the northern section of this trail.

There are no toilets, shelter, or water on site. Food and lodging are available in Walker. Ski rentals may be obtained at Walker Hardware. Park on County Road 50.

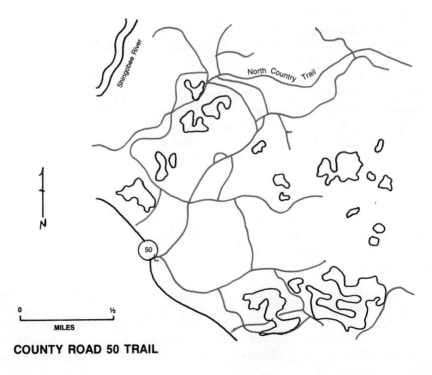

COUNTY ROAD 50 TRAIL

SHINGOBEE RECREATION AREA
9.6 km (6 mi) of trails

beginner, intermediate, advanced

Shingobee Recreation Area is located 6 miles southwest of Walker or 5 miles northeast of Akeley on Highway 34.

These trails have been designated as a National Recreation Trail System and may be the oldest maintained cross-country ski trails in Minnesota, with construction begun in 1933. Primary access to the trail is at the parking lot by the downhill area. The trails are well-marked and are tracked and groomed regularly. They are suited to the novice in many areas, but do have some very difficult, demanding stretches with steep hills— these are signed. The trails bypass the Shingobee River and Anoway and Recreation Lakes and run through forested land as well as cedar swampland. The scenery is outstanding. The North Country Trail passes through the Shingobee Recreation Area on the Recreation Lake Loop. No fee is required for trail use.

On weekends, the chalet is open at the old downhill site (now a sliding area), and warm shelter, water, and toilets are available at that time. There is a shelter on the southwest end of the trail. Park at the trailhead. There is a campsite on the loop which circles Recreation Lake.

Food, lodging, and supplies are available in Walker or in Akeley. Ski rentals may be obtained at Walker Hardware in Walker.

See also Cass County/Tower, Bakker, and Howard Lake Ski Trails, page 198.

NORTH COUNTRY TRAIL
NATIONAL SCENIC TRAIL
100.8 km (63'mi of trail)

beginner, intermediate, advanced

North Country Trail is part of the National Scenic Trail that, when completed, will run from New Hampshire to North Dakota. It is intended for non-motorized use and will emphasize hiking during warm weather and cross-country skiing during winter. The portion in the Chippewa National Forest runs from the Forest boundary 3 miles southwest of Walker east to the Forest boundary 6 miles east of Remer. Almost entirely finished, this area is scheduled to be completed by the winter of 1985.

The well-marked trail is groomed as a hiking trail. Track-set portions run from Shingobee Recreation Area to Goose Lake Recreation Area (*see* Cass County, page 199). The trail passes eastward through Shingobee Recreation Area, County Road 50 Trail, and Goose Lake Recreation Area. These are three of several access points. Although this is a non-motorized trail, an occasional errant snowmobiler may attempt to enter the trail. No water, shelter, or toilets are on the trails. Food and lodging are available in Akeley, Walker, Hackensack, Longville, and Remer. Ski rentals can be obtained in Walker at Walker Hardware.

For further information contact

Walker Ranger District, Dean Hickey, District Ranger, U.S. Forest Service, Walker, MN 56484. 218-547-1044

Forest Supervisor, Chippewa National Forest, Cass Lake, MN 56633. 218-335-2226

Elso Ryks, Cass County Trails Coordinator, Deep-Portage Conservation Reserve, Rt. 1 Box 129, Hackensack, MN 56452. 218-682-2325, 218-587-4599 (evenings only)

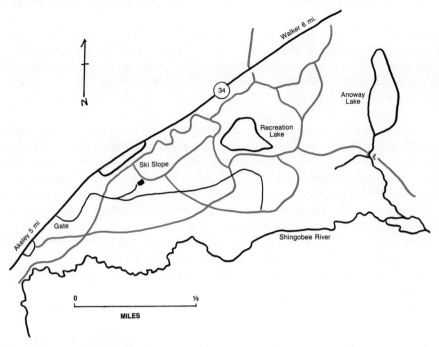

SHINGOBEE RECREATION AREA

Wild River State Park
Almelund, Minnesota

56–64 km (35–40 mi) of trails
beginner, intermediate, advanced

One of Minnesota's newest state parks, Wild River State Park, is located in Chisago County, 3 miles north of the town of Almelund. From Highway 95 at Almelund, turn north on County Road 12, and travel through town, continuing on 12 for 3 miles to the park entrance. The park's name is derived from the 1968 Congressional designation of the St. Croix River as a National Wild and Scenic River. The river forms a natural boundary along the entire length of the park between Minnesota and Wisconsin.

Approximately 600 million years ago, the region along the North Shore of Lake Superior down to Taylors Falls was in an extremely unstable state, fractured and shattered by earthquakes and volcanoes. Lava, disgorged from the earth, covered the area to a depth of 30,000 feet. This hardened volcanic rock forms the river bottom as well as the Dalles of the St. Croix in Taylors Falls. Following the volcanic period, glaciers bulldozed southward, pulling and tearing at the landscape and ultimately shaping it to its present appearance. As the last glacier retreated, ancient Glacial Lake Duluth and Glacial Lake Grantsburg were formed from the meltdown. This put the final touches on the St. Croix River Valley as we see it now. Today's uplands are old channel bars and stream terraces; the lowlands are the channels.

The river valley has been continuously occupied for at least 6,000 years. Its first inhabitants were a nomadic people. Then, for several thousand years, Dakotah lived in the area, followed by Ojibwe, Sauk and Fox. In relatively recent times, two British fur trading posts were established in what is now park land. In 1846, Maurice Samuels began a fur post; in 1847 Thomas Connor and his Indian wife started another at Goose Creek.

The logging industry began in earnest by the 1860s, after military roads were constructed in the region during Territorial times. The towns of Sunrise and Amador began when the timber business was flourishing, but never developed. A small railroad was briefly established in the area at this time also. In 1889–1890, the Nevers Dam was constructed on the river by the St. Croix Dam and Boom Company. It was considered to be the largest wooden, pile-driven dam in the world. In 1954–1955 it was dismantled. Only the ends of the dam are visible today.

The amount of ski touring possibilities available in the park is remarkable, as is the high quality of the trails. They are all clearly marked with degree-of-difficulty and directional signs, as well as you-are-here maps at major junctions. They are regularly

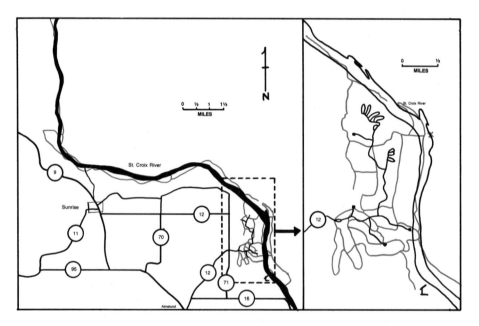

WILD RIVER STATE PARK

groomed and double-tracked. There is a ski-in picnic shelter en route, with pit toilets available. Skiers of all abilities and ambitions will be satisfied at this park. The scenery is just outstanding.

The park is also an excellent place for a first-time winter camping experience. Visitors use established campsites, each with table and fire ring. You can ski to four river campsites; water is available at some of these locations. There is a heated sanitation building with modern toilets, hot and cold water, and showers. Firewood is sold at the information station. There is also a beautiful, heated trail center (open all week during daylight hours) that has two fireplaces. Wood is always provided. This building also has hot and cold running water and modern toilets. On weekends, the park's impressive Interpretive Center is open 12:00–4:30, and the Naturalist is on duty. There are always special, family-oriented programs scheduled, which are free to the public. Maps may be obtained at the park. Food and lodging are available in Taylors Falls and North Branch. Supplies and food are available in Almelund.

For further information, contact

Wild River State Park, Park Manager, Rt. 1 Box 75, Center City, MN 55012. 612-583-2125

Minnesota Department of Natural Resources, Division of Parks and Recreation, Box 39 Centennial Building, St. Paul, MN 55155. 612-296-4776

Wright County
Buffalo, Minnesota

Four ski trails are administered by the Wright County Park Department.

COLLINWOOD COUNTY PARK
COKATO, MINNESOTA
8 km (5 mi) of trails
beginner, intermediate
Collinwood County Park is located 3 miles southwest of Cokato, off Highway 12. It is in the southwestern corner of Wright County and encompasses 308 acres.

The ski trail, marked and groomed, is situated on a wooded, hilly terrain between Collinwood and Little Lakes. There are several loops and spurs which wind around swamps surrounded by woods. There are scenic overlooks en route. Parking and toilets are available at the trailhead, just past the information station at the park's entrance. No fee is charged.

Food, lodging, and ski rentals are available in Cokato. For specific information on the park, call the park manager at 612-286-2801.

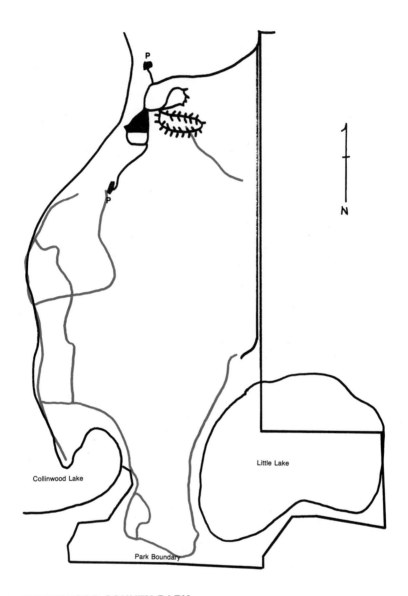

COLLINWOOD COUNTY PARK

STANLEY EDDY MEMORIAL COUNTY PARK RESERVE
SOUTHHAVEN, MINNESOTA

The Park Reserve is comprised of four separate units, totalling 620 acres. Ski touring is available at the northern and southwestern units. They are located south of Southhaven on County Road 2. No fees are charged at either unit. Food, lodging, and ski rentals are available in Annandale or Buffalo.

Northern Unit
6.4 km (4 mi) of trails
intermediate, advanced

Entrance to the 240-acre Northern Unit is 6 miles south of Southhaven, on a township road just off County Road 2. Parking, toilets, and a picnic site are located at the trailhead. The marked and groomed trails include many scenic overlooks. They are situated on very hilly, wooded terrain. A side trail runs past Widmark Lake and its companionate marsh and terminates in a loop. A pack-in campsite is available at this location. The main trail proceeds to a steep hill and the site of another campsite. It then moves on to its terminus at Pickerel Lake, where there is a third campsite. No fees or reservations are required for use of the campsites. Rest benches and picnic tables are located on the trail.

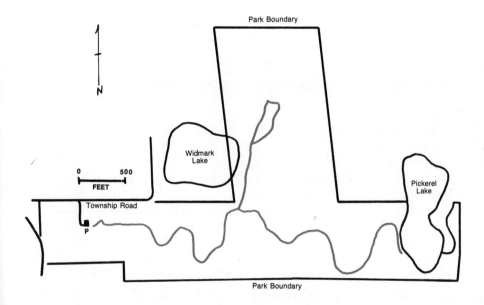

STANLEY EDDY PARK RESERVE – NORTHERN UNIT

Southern Unit
1.9 km (1.2 mi) of trails

beginner, intermediate

The 80-acre Southern Unit is located 8 miles south of Southhaven on County Road 2. Parking and toilets are located at the trailhead. The trails, marked and groomed, are arranged in two loops, Homestead Trail Loop and Pines Trail Loop. They are situated on a gently hilly terrain that is both wooded and open. The trails run through and bypass a few pine plantations. There are picnic sites en route.

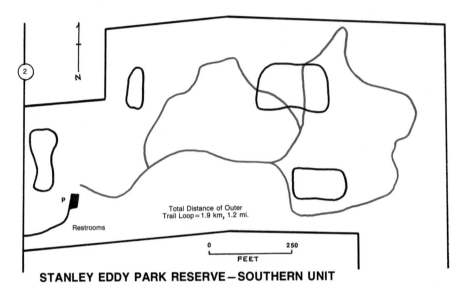

Total Distance of Outer
Trail Loop=1.9 km, 1.2 mi.

Restrooms

0   250

FEET

STANLEY EDDY PARK RESERVE — SOUTHERN UNIT

HARRY LARSON MEMORIAL COUNTY FOREST
MONTICELLO, MINNESOTA
3 km (1.9 mi) of trails

beginner, intermediate

The 170-acre Larson County Forest is located 4 miles west of Monticello on County Road 111. Park at the trailhead on the east side of the road; additional parking and toilets are available on the opposite side of the road by North Lake. The marked and groomed trails traverse wooded hills dotted with many pothole marshes. The Forest is mature oak and big tooth aspen. The trails are arranged in two one-way loops: Monticello Trail Loop, which bypasses a deer feeding area, and Enfield Loop. No fee is charged for trail use. Food, lodging, and ski rentals are available in Monticello.

See also Lake Maria State Park, page 213 and Manitou Lakes (YMCA), page 218.

For further information, contact

Wright County Park Department, John K. Vondelinde, Administrator, Rt. 1 Box 97-B, Buffalo, MN 55313. 612-682-3900, Ext. 182, 612-339-6881, Ext. 182 (Minneapolis/St. Paul)

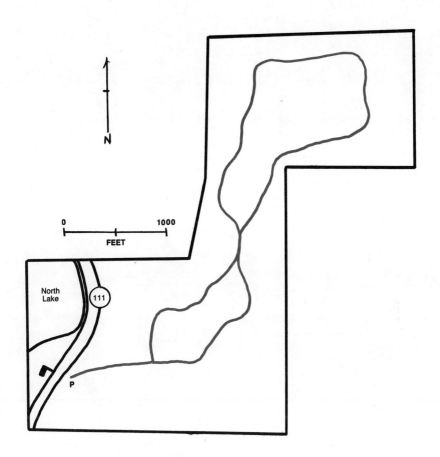

N

0   1000
FEET

North
Lake   (111)

P

HARRY LARSON MEMORIAL COUNTY FOREST

REGION 4
SOUTHWEST MINNESOTA

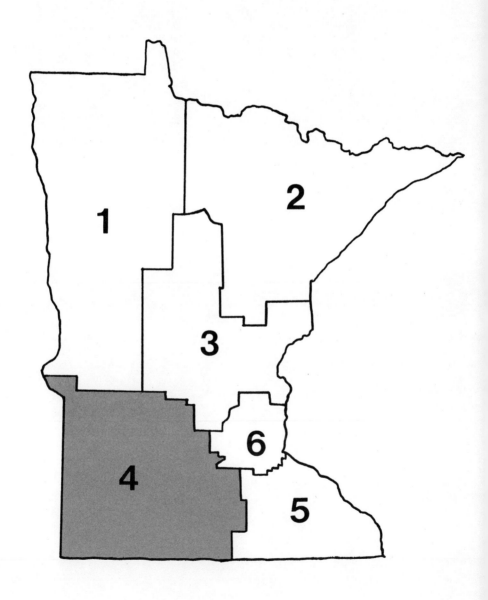

Blue Mounds State Park
Luverne, Minnesota

4.8 km (3 mi) of trails

beginner, intermediate

Blue Mounds State Park is located in Rock County in extreme southwest Minnesota, a short distance north of the city of Luverne. To reach the entrance, take Highway 75 either 4 miles north from Interstate 90 at Luverne, or 16 miles south from Pipestone.

The park is situated on the western (Missouri) slope of the Coteau des Prairie, or upland of the prairie, the continental divide that separates the Missouri and Mississippi River watersheds. The main efforts exerted at Blue Mounds are in the direction of re-establishing prairie habitat. Although this land has never been cultivated, repeated grassfires and heavy grazing by domestic livestock have introduced many plant species not native to the area. Prairie management eliminated all grazing except that of the park's small bison herd and introduced controlled burns in selected areas.

The Mound is an outcropping of hard red rock commonly called Sioux quartzite, or pipestone. It is estimated to be 1.5 billion years old. Formerly an ancient seabed, this rock is what has saved the area from the plow. It is a highly prized building stone and has been quarried in the vicinity of the park. The park's Interpretive Center and many buildings in Luverne are constructed of quartzite. This cliff appears to be blue when the sun sets behind it. The settlers who moved westward in the 1860s and 1870s named the landmark Blue Mounds.

Initial archaeological surveys reveal that this land contains living sites of very primitive people. Since sites dating back 17,000 years have been excavated in eastern North America, it is safe to say that these Asian game hunters migrated through southern Minnesota at an even earlier time. It is known that during the Hopewell Period (200 A.D.), primitive people from what is now Ohio maintained trade and relations with people in the Yellowstone area. And it is certain that they passed through the Pipestone quarries. On top of the Mound is a 1,250-foot wall that was presumably made by these prehistoric people. It is aligned precisely east and west. Perhaps it was used to mark the seasons. Today's visitors regularly hike to the wall on the first day of both spring and fall with this archaeological speculation in mind.

The native bison always were a life-source for the Native American of the plains. They called the animal Tahtonka—its presence meant food, shelter, clothing, and tools. They used the Mound to harvest this wealth. It is over a mile long and 100 feet high and provided a way to kill the bison. As novelist Fredrick Manfred wrote from his home on the Mound, "Buffalo always head into the wind, and when the wind was from the southeast, a herd would naturally head for the highest part of the cliff." One Indian would cover himself with a bison robe and lure the animals to the edge. Other men, who were hidden among the rocks, would surprise the animals, encircle them and stampede them over the edge. When settlers arrived in the area, they found enormous heaps of bones at the bottom of the cliff. These were harvested in the late nineteenth century for fertilizer production.

Today, the Manfred home serves as an Interpretive Center, to better clarify the aspects of native prairie habitat and the companionate culture of the Plains Indian.

The ski trails begin at the picnic grounds, to the north of the buffalo pasture. They are marked and groomed and arranged in one large loop that circles around both Upper and Lower Mound Lakes, which are formed by Mound Creek. Although snowmobiling is allowed in the park, such trails are located in the southern end of the park on top of the Mound.

Winter camping is allowed at the park's rustic sites at the south end of Upper Mound Lake. Privies are available. Water and maps may be obtained at park headquarters. Tourist accommodations and supplies are at hand in Luverne.

For further information, contact

Blue Mounds State Park, Park Manager, R.R. 1, Luverne, MN 56156. 507-283-4892
Minnesota Department of Natural Resources, Division of Parks and Recreation, Box
    39 Centennial Building, St. Paul, MN 55155. 612-296-4776

See also Split Rock Creek State Park, page 261.

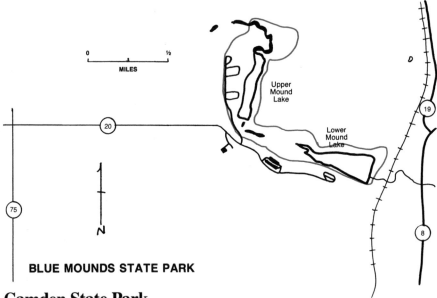

BLUE MOUNDS STATE PARK

Camden State Park
Lynd, Minnesota

9.6 km (6 mi) of trails
beginner, intermediate

Camden State Park is located in central Lyon County, off Highway 23, 9 miles southwest of the city of Marshall. Established in 1935, the park now includes nearly 1,600 acres.

The outstanding feature of the park is the deep, hardwood valley that descends from the surrounding prairie. It has been regarded as an oasis for as long as this part of Minnesota has been inhabited. The valley, for over 8,000 years, has supplied Native Americans and, more recently, white settlers with food, spring water, and shelter from the hot summer sun and wind and the powerful winter storms that move repeatedly through this part of the country. It is a hilly region of the Redwood River, which is a tributary of the Minnesota River. Redwood, in this instance, refers to a small native dogwood tree with red bark that the Indians mixed with tobacco to produce a better smoke. The river flows down the east side of Coteau des Prairies, or upland of the prairie, the continental divide that separates the Mississippi River/Missouri River watersheds. The valley was cut and shaped by the swift, powerful waters of meltwater during the last glacial retreat, which occurred about 10,000 years ago. In this erosive process, the former subterranean springs of the park were uncovered and, to this day, continuously release clean, free-flowing water.

People were not the only creatures to find haven in the valley; wildlife sought sanctuary here also. However, many species that were very common as recently as 100 years ago are now gone, including bison, elk, wolf, prairie chicken, and golden eagle. Still, a diverse wildlife population thrives in the valley to this day—it includes beaver, mink, racoon, many songbirds, red-tail hawks, and species not usually seen in this part of the country, such as mule deer.

In the 1840s a Frenchman named La Framboise set up a fur trading post in the valley but, upon request, joined the renowned American artist, George Catlin, to act as the guide and interpreter on an expedition to the Pipestone area. Other original settlers in the valley were also traders. One, named John Lynd, from whom the neighboring town takes its name, had the dubious distinction of being the first casualty of the 1862 Sioux Uprising.

But the area continued to develop, and eventually a thriving village took shape—it was called Camden after Camden, New Jersey, the old hometown of a resident. For more than twenty years, the town flourished and boasted a general store, hotel, blacksmith shop, and sawmill/gristmill. There was even a second gristmill, called the Jones Mill, a mile south of the village. But in 1888, the railroad line went to Marshall, which was also the Lyon County Seat. Camden faded but local people still called the valley Camden Woods and valued it as a special place, deserving recognition and protection. Thus, it came to be a state park.

The marked and groomed ski trails move up and down the forested valley, the novice loop situated on the more level land by the parking area at the trailhead. It circles around the area of two bends in the river, crossing it at two points. This loop joins the intermediate trails at a railroad underpass. The system then recrosses the river and passes the old Jones Mill site. The trails move along the river bed, up and down the beautiful, undulating terrain. There is a crossing on the railroad line that can be quite dangerous—please be alert. A primitive campsite is past the tracks by the river.

Maps, toilets, and warming house are available to visitors. Winter camping is allowed. Tourist accommodations and supplies are at hand in Marshall.

For further information, contact

Camden State Park, Park Manager, Lynd, MN 56157. 507-865-4530

Minnesota Department of Natural Resources, Division of Parks and Recreation, Box 39 Centennial Building, St. Paul, MN 55155. 612-296-4776

See also Lake Shetek State Park, page 253.

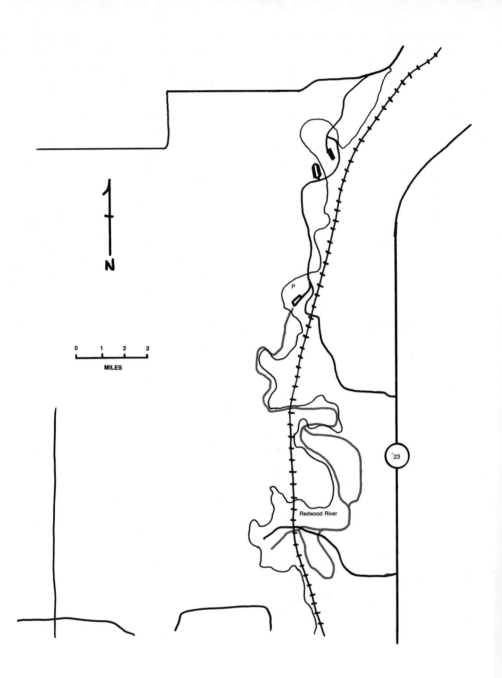

CAMDEN STATE PARK

Flandrau State Park
New Ulm, Minnesota

16 km (10 mi) of trails

beginner

Flandrau State Park is located in northeastern Brown County along the banks of the Cottonwood River, near its confluence with the Minnesota River. It lies partially within the limits of the city of New Ulm. The main entrance to the park is several blocks southwest of Highways 68 and 15 (Broadway) on Summit Avenue. An entrance is on the park's northwest side on County Road 13 (Center Street); another to the south is on Cottonwood Street. Both County Road 13 and Cottonwood Street intersect Highways 68 and 15.

The river meanders through the park, forming several oxbows and involving the attendant marshland of its floodplain. The valley is framed by steep walls, heavily forested and crowned with savanna oak. Sugar maple, basswood, and hackberry grow on the northern side, while oak, red cedar, and aspen favor the warmer southern slopes. Cottonwood trees of enormous dimension tower over the river bottomland. The valley is a favorite haunt of deer and other wildlife.

Archaeological evidence, including Native American artifacts, campsites, and petroglyphs, has been found in the area and gives us an idea of the region's earliest residents. They thrived in the valley's abundance, camping in the bottomland for shelter in winter and on the blufflands for the cooling breezes in summer that also provided good insect control.

By the mid-1600s explorers, fur traders, and adventurers began passing through the valley, and by the 1830s settlers were arriving, clearing and cultivating the land. Within 100 years, the state began to acquire the land for park development. It was originally called Cottonwood State Park. Many of the buildings, trails, and additional tree plantations were developed by the Civilian Conservation Corps and Work Projects Administration from 1935–1942. They also built three dams that were eventually damaged or destroyed by floodwaters, the most devastating flood occurring in 1969, when the decision was made to dismantle the dams completely, and let the river return to its natural state. Some time after its inception, the park's name was changed to Flandrau State Park, after Judge Charles E. Flandrau, a prominent lawyer and Indian agent who successfully led the defense of New Ulm during the Sioux Uprising of 1862.

Originally, the hiking trails of the park were jointly used for ski touring and snowmobiling, but recently the park has been enlarging its ski system, and snowmobiling should have stopped by now. However, visitors should consult with park staff as to the status of the situation. The trails are located primarily in the dense river bottom forest and are well-marked. They will be groomed for touring.

Water and modern toilets are available in the park. Tourist accommodations and supplies may be obtained in New Ulm.

For further information, contact

Flandrau State Park, Park Manager, 1300 Summit Avenue, New Ulm, MN 56073. 507-354-3519

See also Fort Ridgely State Park, page 247 and Minneopa State Park, page 255.

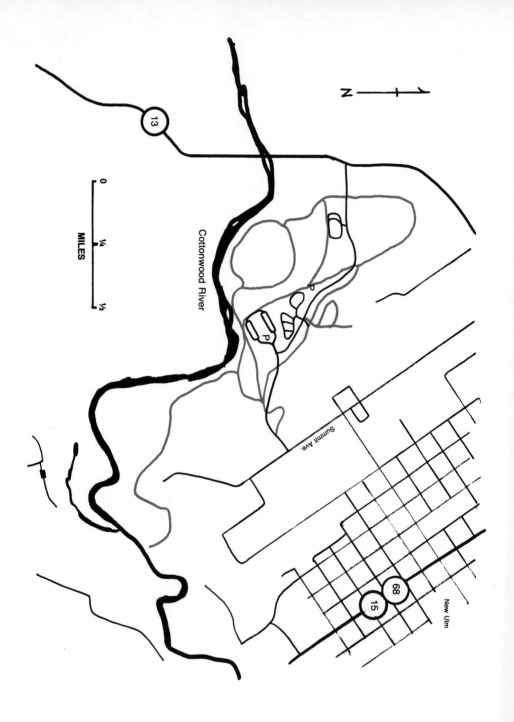

FLANDRAU STATE PARK

Fort Ridgely State Park
Fairfax, Minnesota

4.8 km (3 mi) of trails

intermediate

Fort Ridgely State Park is located in extreme northwest Nicollet County, and southeastern Renville County about 4 miles south of the town of Fairfax. It is northwest of New Ulm, on the north bank of the Minnesota River. Travel south from Fairfax on Highway 4, a short distance beyond the junction of 4 with County Road 5, to the park's entrance.

This historic park is located on a prairie highland that is surrounded on three sides by the heavily wooded valleys and ravines of the Minnesota River and Fort Ridgely Creek. The park acreage contains the remains of old Fort Ridgely, which are administered by the Minnesota Historical Society. The Fort was established in 1853 as an Army outpost to watch the Dakotah and to defend the southwest section of the Minnesota Territory. It was poorly located as the terrain and the cover that the woodland provided made it nearly indefensible against Indian attack. To make matters worse, it was not really a fort, but just a collection of unfortified buildings. There was not enough native stone available to build anything but the commissary and barracks. No walls or blockhouses were ever constructed. The remainder of the buildings were built of wood and scattered around the hilltop.

There was never a full garrison of troops stationed at the Fort, and, when the Civil War began, the situation was further aggravated by the regulars' being pulled out and sent to the South. They were replaced by the Minnesota Volunteer Infantry Regiments. Most men had no experience whatsoever in use of the cannons. One experienced artilleryman, John Jones, drilled the volunteers in their use, an effort which ultimately saved the Fort.

Over the years, the economy and culture of the Dakotah had been severely eroded by the white fur trade industry. Eventually, due to the settlers' demand for land, the Indians were moved to two small reservations on the Minnesota River, after they ceded rights to southwestern Minnesota to the U.S. government in the Treaties of Traverse de Sioux and Mendota in 1851. The Dakotah were humiliated and defrauded by the tragic experience, and their lives fell to desperate depths at the reservations. They were deprived of their life-source, the bison, and were forced to live on nearly nonexistent government dole. They were swindled by the agreements made by two of Minnesota's fathers, Henry Sibley and Alexander Ramsey. Extreme racism and bureaucratic indifference to their starvation and lack of shelter on the reservations pushed the Indians to desperate action. In August of 1862, rebellious bands of Indians attacked individual homesteads throughout western and southwestern Minnesota, massacring settlers and taking prisoners. Those who escaped or heard news of impending attack flocked to the Fort.

The Dakotah attacked the Fort on 20 August and were driven back by the three cannons that the Volunteers had wheeled into the earthworks. By the next day, the Indians were gone. They traveled to New Ulm and attacked the town, but again did not achieve a victory. The older tribal members were convinced that Fort Ridgely, the door to the frontier, must fall. On the 22 August, they returned to the Fort, with their numbers greatly increased. But they were poorly organized and could not surmount the power of the cannon fire. They did, however, hold the Fort in a state of siege for several days until General Sibley arrived to rescue the Fort and defeat the Dakotah. This crushed the uprising and broke the power of Indians in Minnesota for all time. Minnesota and the United States punished the Indians severely for their six weeks of war. Although nearly half of the Dakotah in Minnesota had not participated in the Sioux Uprising, all were hunted, killed, deported, imprisoned, or driven from the state. Only a handful ever returned to the streams and wooded bluffs of the homeland they had loved.

The park's beautiful setting offers visitors a picturesque view of the valleys, ravines, and waterways below. The excellent habitat provided by the heavy woods on the hillsides supports a diverse wildlife population. It is a perfect recreation site.

The marked and groomed trails are rated intermediate because of the downhill runs involved in the system. The segments on the plateau where the old fort site is located are flat and open, but the rest are hilly and heavily wooded. The skiing on the creek bottom is best, as it is in a sheltered area and the snow is always good. The ski trails are entirely separate from the snowmobile trails, although two bridges are shared. Winter camping is allowed in the area of the parking lot by the chalet, which serves as a heated warming house. Water, modern toilets, and electricity are located in this building.

Food, lodging, and supplies are located in Fairfax and Sleepy Eye.

For further information, contact

Fort Ridgely State Park, Rt. 1 Box 65, Park Manager, Fairfax, MN 55332. 507-426-7840

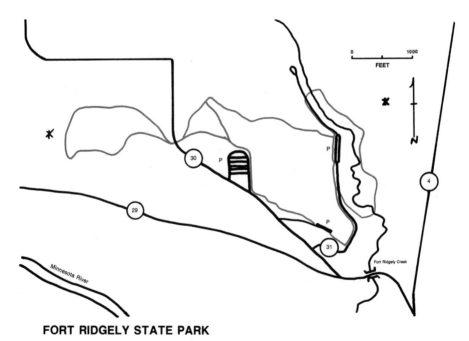

FORT RIDGELY STATE PARK

Golden Gate to Fun Campground
Sleepy Eye, Minnesota

beginner, intermediate, advanced

This facility is located 6 miles north of the junction of Highways 4 and 14, which is in Sleepy Eye. Travel north on 4 to Golden Gate Road. Turn east, and drive 1 mile, then north for 2 miles. Watch for signs.

Golden Gate Campground is on private land with no specific system of trails. It involves 150 acres of wooded hills which surround the campground. Ample parking, snack bar, and winter camping facilities are available. Supplies and accommodations are available in Sleepy Eye.

For further information, contact

Melvin Speckman, Golden Gate Campground, Sleepy Eye, MN 56085. 507-794-6586 (home), 507-794-7459 (office)

See also Fort Ridgely State Park, page 247 and Flandrau State Park, page 245.

Kilen Woods State Park
Lakefield, Minnesota

2.4 km (1.5 mi) of trails

beginner, intermediate

Kilen Woods State Park is located in Jackson County, 9 miles northeast of the town of Lakefield, which is about 2 miles north from Interstate 90. From Lakefield, take Highway 86 north to County 24, turn east and proceed to the park entrance. If you were to come from Windom (11 miles to the north), travel south on County Road 17 to the junction with 24.

The bulk of the park lies deep in the valley of the Des Moines River, which has its source in north central Murray County, at Lake Shetek. The river winds its way through southern Minnesota, flowing southeasterly into Iowa where it becomes that state's largest river. It ultimately joins the Mississippi. The valley is wide and deep, as it was created by the erosive power of a major drainage river from ancient Glacial Lake Minnesota, which covered several counties in southern Minnesota. The valley itself, with its river bottom meadows, flood plain forest, oak savanna uplands, and prairie, is the main feature of the park. Wildlife is abundant here, with the diverse habitat offering support and protection.

Over 6,000 years ago, a nomadic people hunted and lived in this area. Almost nothing is known of them; it is thought that they are the source of the Jeffers Petroglyphs, which are 30 miles north of the park. The Dakotah were the earliest known people to inhabit the valley. It was a place of shelter and abundance for them. For hundreds of years they hunted the bison, elk, and waterfowl that thrived here, and collected the rich edible produce of the prairie and forest. The bison and elk are now gone—and many of the small lakes and most of the wetlands that supported waterfowl have been drained for agricultural purposes.

By the mid-1700s, white adventurers, trappers, traders, and explorers began to penetrate the area. In the 1830s, the explorer and cartographer, Joseph Nicollet, led a major expedition that traversed the Des Moines River Valley. His maps and descriptions provide very accurate record of the nature of southwestern Minnesota. He described the area that rises several hundred feet above the prairies, which he called the Coteau des Prairies or upland of the prairie. This highland is the continental divide which separates the Mississippi River/Missouri River watersheds and offers spectacular vistas of the surrounding area.

In 1851, the Treaties of Traverse de Sioux and Mendota opened the land for white settlement. This involved the removal of the Dakotah to reservation land along the Minnesota River. Extreme racial cruelty, lack of shelter, and starvation caused some of the Indians to revolt in August of 1862. The tragedy produced by the inhumane treatment of the Indians was felt in this river valley, where twenty settlers lost their lives. Al-

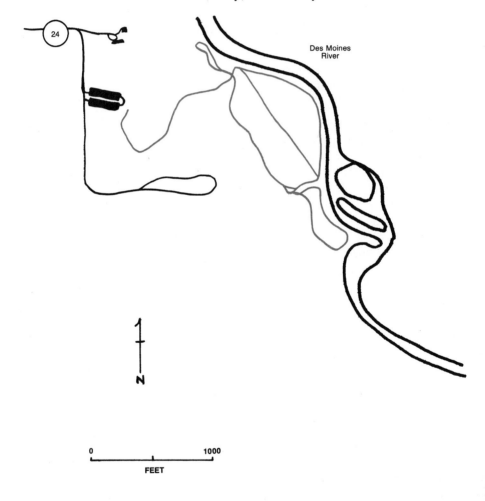

Des Moines River

24

N

0   1000

FEET

KILEN WOODS STATE PARK

though the Sioux Uprising was brutally crushed, the frightened white settlers moved out of the area for an extended period of time. When they returned, they changed the vast prairie wilderness into a land of farms and towns—which changed even more drastically with the arrival of railroads. The intensive, careless farming methods that were often employed destroyed the prairie and changed the face of the land for all times.

But the land of the valley was an oasis in the region. Most of what is now park land was purchased in the 1940s from a man named Agil Kilen—the acreage included twenty-one pioneer homesteads. It still is an area that contrasts beautifully with the enormous expanses of the plains.

The marked and groomed ski trails are located in the northern part of the park, and begin close to the Interpretive Center. Skiers must walk a short distance to the first bridge to reach the trailhead. This is a hilly area initially. The ravines are bridged in several places en route. The trails ultimately lead to the meadowland by the river. There are three fairly large loops on the bottomland, with two smaller loops also involved in the system. There is a warming house with toilets and water at the park. Winter Camping is allowed. Snowmobiling is permitted, but the trails are completely separate from the ski trails.

Tourist accommodations are available in Lakefield and in Windom.

For further information, contact

Kilen Woods State Park, Park Manager, Lakefield, MN 56150. 507-662-6258
Minnesota Department of Natural Resources, Division of Parks and Recreation, Box 39 Centennial Building, St. Paul, MN 55155. 612-296-4776

Lac Qui Parle State Park
Montevideo, Minnesota

10.4 km (6.5 mi) of trails
beginner

Lac Qui Parle State Recreation Area is located in Lac Qui Parle County, 10 miles northwest of Montevideo, on the Minnesota River. Take Highways 59 and 7 northwest from Montevideo to Chippewa County Road 13, turn west on 13, and cross the river. Chippewa County Road 13 changes to Lac Qui Parle County Road 33 at this point. Follow 33 across the Lac Qui Parle River, moving around the southwest side of the park to its entrance.

Lac Qui Parle Lake is actually a widening of the Minnesota River, caused by deltas of tributary streams that enter the river. The deltas serve as natural dams, most especially that delta formed at the confluence of the Lac Qui Parles River with the Minnesota River.

Lac Qui Parle is French for "Lake That Speaks." The early French explorers offered this name as their translation of the Dakotah name "Lake Speaks." It is unclear why the Indians referred to the lake in this way. People speculate that, during early winter and spring, sounds made by the wind and waves often echo eerily between the bluffs that frame the valley. Or, it may be that, under certain conditions, the waves on the rocks produce a special sound.

This region has been continuously inhabited for thousands of years, first by prehistoric nomadic hunters who may have seen Glacial River Warren occupying the entire valley width. This magnificent river flowed from Glacial Lake Agassiz through what we now call the Minnesota River Valley, first to the southeast, then to the northeast, plunging over a falls by St. Paul that was exceedingly more massive than Niagara Falls. The Dakotah followed the nomadic hunters and thrived in the great abundance of the valley for centuries. At a later time, following on the heels of the explorations by the French, many fur trading posts were established in the region. The last and best known was Fort Renville, built in 1826 by Joseph Renville, a colorful *coureur de bois* or independent fur trader. He was also instrumental, with Dr. Thomas Smith Williamson and Alexander Huggins, in founding the Lac Qui Parle Sioux Mission in 1835. This was the site of the first school in Minnesota Territory and was also the first Territorial enterprise to manufacture textiles that were used for clothing. The Minnesota Historical Society has done work on both the fort and mission sites to the east and the northeast of the park.

In recent times, the park's most successful accomplishment rests in the wildlife management program, including deer, geese, and prairie chickens. The most spectacular story is the geese program. In 1958 only 150 were counted in the park. Since then, with improved habitat and other wise management practices, up to 72,000 have been counted at one time. It has become a major resting place during migrations for not only geese, but many other types of waterfowl, including whistling swans and pelicans. The pelicans also nest on an island in the lake.

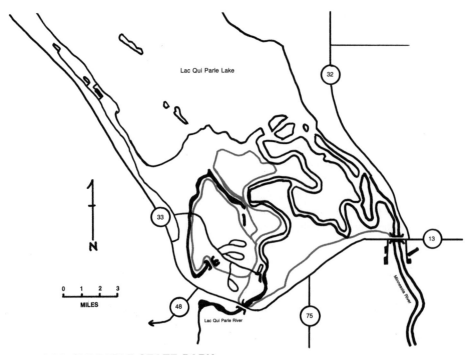

LAC QUI PARLE STATE PARK

The ski trails are primarily situated on the level land of the valley bottomland. For this reason, they are well-suited to the beginner. The land is forested with hardwood species and involves some open prairie land as well. In past years, snowmobilers and skiers have had to share the trails, but due to the popularity of the trails among skiers, snowmobiling has been banned in the park. All trails are marked and groomed. There is an enclosed shelter with a fireplace by the picnic grounds. The park provides firewood at all times. Pit toilets are available at the shelter; water and maps may be obtained at park headquarters. Winter camping is allowed. Tourist accommodations and supplies are available in Montevideo, Madison, Milan, and Appleton.

For further information, contact

Lac Qui Parle Park State Park, Park Manager, Rt. 5, Box 74 A, Montevideo, MN 56265. 612-952-4736

Minnesota Department of Natural Resources, Division of Parks and Recreation, Box 39 Centennial Building, St. Paul, MN 55155. 612-296-4776

See also Upper Sioux Agency State Park, page 263.

Lake Shetek State Park
Currie, Minnesota

2.4 km (1.5 mi) of trails
beginner

Lake Shetek State Park is located in Murray County, 14 miles north of Slayton and approximately 33 miles south of Marshall, near the town of Currie. From Highway 30, take County Road 38 north to the park entrance.

Shetek is an Ojibwe word which means "pelican." The voyageurs used it as a general description of a feature of the lakes in the area, referring to the fact that the region was a special nesting and rearing place for pelicans. The Dakotah named the group of lakes Rabechy "the place where pelicans nest." The largest lake, which is now called Shetek, is the headwaters of the Des Moines River. It lies trapped behind a natural dam that is part of a major glacial ridge, called the Altamont Moraine. This dam is made up of boulders, stones, and other debris that were bulldozed into place by a glacier that moved through the area over 10,000 years ago. The Altamont Moraine and the Bemis Moraine jointly make up the Coteau des Prairie or upland of the prairie, the continental divide which separates the Missouri and Mississippi River watersheds. The park sits on the east slope of the Coteau des Prairies.

Before white settlement, the region surrounding the lake was treeless prairie. So outstanding was the presence of single trees on these plains that they became major landmarks. It was a land of bison, elk, antelope, wolves, and prairie chickens. The first inhabitants who settled in the area were an ancient people called the Great Oasis Culture. They farmed with methods that had originated in the southeastern United States. When the horse was introduced to them, following Spanish settlement in the southwestern United States, they assumed a nomadic hunting lifestyle, following the enormous herds of bison upon which their existence depended. These rugged beasts especially favored Lake Shetek and the many adjacent lakes that dotted the prairie. The Plains

Culture developed and laid ground for the Dakotah to unfold and prosper. Until white adventurers, explorers, and fur traders entered the area, the Native Americans lived a balanced life, following the bison and gathering edible prairie produce. The whites saw the abundance and potential in the prairie and eventually drew up the Treaties of Traverse de Sioux and Mendota in 1851, by which the Dakotah tribes were forced to cede all their lands in southwestern Minnesota for white settlement. They were moved to two reservations on the Minnesota River, where their humiliation and loss was exacerbated by lack of shelter, starvation, and bureaucratic indifference. This led to the Sioux Uprising in August and September of 1862. Rebellious bands of Dakotah raided white settlements and homesteads throughout western and southwestern Minnesota. Lake Shetek was a major point of white settlement in this part of Minnesota, and twelve families were massacred. The Dakotah's efforts were poorly organized and severely fractured by dissension among both tribal members and leaders. The rebellion was quickly crushed, but further settlement of this part of the Minnesota Territory came to a standstill for nearly twenty years. Life became marginal, at best, for the white survivors. They were plagued by grasshoppers and drought for several seasons until, for many, their livelihood consisted of gathering bison bones to be used in fertilizer production.

When resettlement did begin to take place, farming over the next century eventually stripped nearly all native vegetation from southwestern Minnesota, transforming it to cropland. But in the Lake Shetek area, matured woodlots, planted by early settlers, now provide a sanctuary for wildlife and park visitors alike. They include stands of oak, hackberry, basswood, and ash.

The marked and groomed ski trails begin at the parking lot by the picnic grounds and the Prairie Campground. They move to the causeway or dike to Loon Island. The dike is an open, windswept area. In the early ski season, skis must be carried across the causeway until the ice has frozen on the lake and drifts have formed on the shoulders of the dike. Once on the island, the terrain is wooded and is quite level. One snowmobile trail crosses the ski trail on its initial segment to the causeway. Otherwise, the two systems do not mix. The picnic shelter at the picnic grounds has a woodstove, which is not constantly maintained by park staff. Visitors must either purchase wood or bring their own. This shelter is shared with snowmobilers. Winter camping is allowed. Park management have indicated that they would like advance notice (although this is not required) so that they can be sure that the road is plowed into the campgrounds. In the winter, water is available at a hydrant outside the park shop. There are pit toilets by the shelter near the parking lot.

Please note: Trails are closed each year when the muzzleloader firearms deer season is in progress. This is the last week in November until mid-December.

For further information, contact

Lake Shetek State Park, Park Manager, Currie, MN 56123. 507-763-3256
Minnesota Department of Natural Resources, Division of Parks and Recreation, Box 39 Centennial Building, St. Paul, MN 55155. 612-296-4776

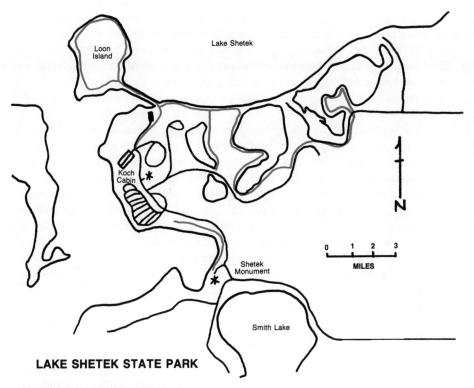

LAKE SHETEK STATE PARK

Minneopa State Park
Mankato, Minnesota

5.6 km (3.5 mi) of trails
beginner, advanced

Minneopa State Park is located west of the city of Mankato, in northern Blue Earth County. It is situated at the junction of Highways 68 and 169, overlooking the Minnesota River Valley. Highway 68 bisects the park's 1145 acres. One may enter the park's north side, which overlooks the river, directly from Highway 68. This is the section that contains the cross-country trails. The southern section is situated on Minneopa Creek and is accessible from either Highways 68 or 169 via County Road 117. This section contains the park headquarters.

Minneopa is a Dakotah word for "water falling twice," a reference to the two waterfalls that lie close together on Minneopa Creek near park headquarters. This two-step drop is the only major waterfall in southwestern Minnesota. It is geologically similar to Minnehaha Falls in Minneapolis and is equally popular with visitors to the area. The falling water has eroded a deep gorge in the soft limestone in the process, toppling rocks into the deep valley below. Above the valleys of the Minnesota River and the Minneopa Creek is a prairie area which the Dakotah called Tinta-inya-ota or "prairie with many rocks." More than likely they were speaking of the enormous granite boulders that lie strewn around the prairie. These are glacial erratics, that is, they are not of local origin and were deposited in the area by a glacier bulldozing through the state.

Over the ages, nature and the elements have transformed some of these boulders. In some cases, seasonal freezing and thawing have split the large stones.

The park staff has worked diligently to restore the native prairie. Before it was parkland, the prairie was used as a sheep pasture. The intensive grazing over the years destroyed the native grasses, allowing weedy European species to be introduced. Current management of the prairie includes periodic burning that rejuvenates the native prairie grasses and wildflowers.

The combination of upland prairie habitat and lush woodlands of the valleys and ravines provides a richly diverse habitat for wildlife. Winter visitors will see evidence of mink, fox, racoon, and deer. Just as this has always been an oasis for animals, it has also been a special haven for people throughout the ages. The Dakotah had a permanent village at the confluence of Minneopa Creek and the Minnesota River. This particular band of people were called the Tribe of Sixes, because they always built their lodges in groups or multiples of six. A half mile from the park, to the south, is a bed of blue clay the Dakotah called Mankato or "Blue Earth." This rare blue clay was revered by countless generations of Indians. It was used for decorating their bodies and tepees and to ward off misfortune and sickness. The explorer, Le Sueur, was drawn to the area by this clay. The French incorrectly thought that it contained commerical grade copper and dug boatloads of the sticky mud to take to France.

The first settler on Minneopa Creek was Isaac S. Lyons, who built a cabin in July, 1853. He set up a small water-powered sawmill the following year. Early settlers have chronicled living with the Dakotah, describing the white and Dakotah children playing lacrosse and other games. In 1858, a fellow named Miner Porter began to build a resort at Minneopa Falls. He planted trees, flowers, and arbors and built winding walkways, but his efforts were interrupted by the Civil War and further impeded by the Sioux Uprising. He finally abandoned it in 1870. The most enduring symbol of pioneer settlement is the stone Seppmann windmill, built in 1864 by a German settler named Louis Seppmann. With the help of his neighbor, Herman Hegley, Seppmann faithfully copied an old-world design and constructed one of Minnesota's first stone gristmills.

The area redeveloped into a popular tourist location for a short time after the initial fright of the Sioux Uprising had subsided. The little town of Minneopa enjoyed a brief but prosperous existence. It could boast of a grain elevator, hotel, store, blacksmith shop, lumberyard, and railway depot. Footbridges were built over the creek and the area became a site for picnic excursions. Crowds sometimes grew as large as 3,000–5,000 people. The town of Minneopa was destroyed in three summers in the 1870s by the great grasshopper plagues. But by 1905, the State had passed a law that protected the area and established the initial acreage of Minneopa State Park.

The marked and groomed trails begin at the picnic ground, with a 0.6-km advanced run down to the river. If skiers feel unsure of their ability to negotiate the hill, they should remove their skis and walk to the bottom, taking care to stay off the ski trail as walking on it will ruin the track. Once at the bottom, the terrain becomes level. It is heavily wooded on the valley floor and is more sheltered than the park's uplands. The trail proceeds along the river for a distance and eventually turns back up the hills to the blufftops. Skiers again encounter an advanced section, but once on the bluffs, the terrain is again level and easy to ski. The trail runs along the ridge to the Red Fox Campground, which is adjacent to the picnic area. This is the site of the Village of the Tribe of Sixes. The trail returns to the picnic ground.

Winter camping is allowed. There are pit toilets, but no shelter or water is provided. Food, lodging, and supplies are available in Mankato.

For further information, contact

Minneopa State Park, Park Manager, Rt 9 Box 143, Mankato, MN 56001. 507-625-4388

Minnesota Department of Natural Resources, Division of Parks and Recreation, Box 39 Centennial Building, St. Paul, MN 55155. 612-296-4776

See also Sakatah Lake State Park, page 257.

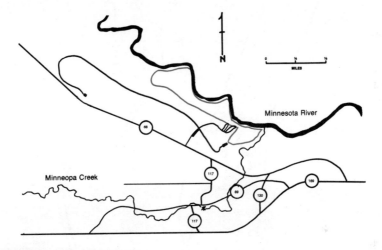

MINNEOPA STATE PARK

Sakatah Lake State Park
Waterville, Minnesota

4.8 km (3 mi) of trails

beginner, intermediate, advanced

Sakatah Lake State Park is 2 miles east of the town of Waterville or 15 miles southwest of Faribault on Highway 60. It is situated on the division line between southern Rice and LeSueur Counties.

This park preserves a remnant of the Big Woods that once covered east central Minnesota and the Mississippi River Valley. The forest species are hardwoods in the main, such as oak, maple, basswood, and walnut. It is situated in a hilly region of glacial moraine and offers visitors the opportunity to see what this part of Minnesota looked like when the first white settlers arrived. The trees are like an enormous canopy around the Sakatah Lakes, which are actually natural widenings of the Cannon River. The setting for Laura Ingalls Wilder's first book, *Little House in the Big Woods*, is near the area of the park.

The trails are marked hiking trails and are easy to follow. They are set up in a series of interconnected loops, skirting lake shore and circling around the campground and picnic area. The system involves many hills and the heavy woodlands of the region. A map may be obtained at the park. The Sakatah Singing Hills State Trail bisects the ski trail system.

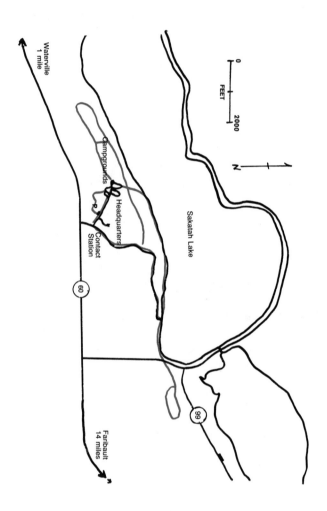

SAKATAH LAKE STATE PARK

Winter camping is allowed at the park. Pit toilets are available. Food and lodging are available in Waterville or Faribault.

For further information, contact

Sakatah Lake State Park, Park Manager, Route 2 Box 19, Waterville, MN 56096. 507-362-4438

Minnesota Department of Natural Resources, Division of Parks and Recreation, Box 39 Centennial Building, St. Paul, MN 55155. 612-296-4776

See also Minneopa State Park, page 255; City of Faribault, River Bend Nature Centure, page 275; Nerstrand Woods State Park, page 286; City of Owatonna, page 288; Rice County, Cannon River Wilderness Area, page 288; Rice Lake State Park, page 289.

Sibley State Park
New London, Minnesota

16 km (10 mi) of trails

beginner, intermediate, advanced

Sibley State Park is located in northern Kandiyohi County, 4 miles west of the picturesque town of New London. The main entrance is off Highway 71, on County Road 48. The park is 15 miles north of the city of Willmar.

The park is named after Henry Hastings Sibley, one of the fathers of the State of Minnesota. He was a general agent for the American Fur Company, a Territorial delegate to the Congress, and Minnesota's first governor. In the late summer of 1862 he led the military forces that crushed the Sioux Uprising. The following year, he continued his military exploits in Dakota Territory. The area that is now parkland is reputed to have been his favorite hunting ground.

Over 3,000 acres are included in Sibley State Park, a lovely area where the prairie meets the Big Woods. Sibley was surely correct about the abundance of wildlife in this region, for such diverse habitat provides the most ideal setting possible for the natural engendering, nurturing, and protection of animal life.

Sibley is located within the Alexandria Moraine Complex, a series of hills and lowlands produced by glacial action. The ice pushed and pulled at the land, leaving hills and ridges and hollowing out basins that often are steep-sided. Consequently, we now enjoy a most scenic landscape in this part of Minnesota, characterized by undulating hills that cradle countless lakes, ponds, and marshes. The highest hill in the moraine complex is Mt. Tom (el. 1352 feet). It has been a significant spot for centuries. The Indians used it both as a strategic lookout and as a place of spiritual importance. Stone pipes have been uncovered here and offer proof of the religious status of the hill.

In 1919, a man named Peter Broberg, the only member of the Broberg family to survive the Sioux Uprising, organized a group of local residents, who successfully lobbied in the State Legislature to obtain the funds used to purchase the park's initial acreage. They understood the special nature of the Mt. Tom/Lake Andrew area, and worked continuously with the county to preserve this acreage. Eventually, in 1934 it was made a state park. The following year, the Veterans Conservation Corps came to Sibley and built roads, trails, and the park's beautiful granite buildings.

Today, the park lends itself especially well to the sport of ski touring. The terrain offers a satisfying ski excursion. There are level places on the shores of Lake Andrew where the novice trails are located. The system continues back into the hills where the ambitions of the intermediate and advanced skiers will be satisfied. The land is heavily wooded throughout, dominated by species such as ironwood, basswood, hackberry, green ash, and aspen. Only on the occasional dry knolls will you find prairie.

Snowmobiling is allowed at the park, but the two trail systems are separate. The snowmobile trail intersects the ski trail at two points. The ski trails begin at the heated trail center. Next door is the Interpretive Center, open year around. Winter camping is allowed. Pit toilets and water are available. Tourist accommodations and supplies are at hand in New London, Spicer, and Willmar.

For further information, contact

Sibley State Park, Park Manager, Route 2 Box 700, New London, MN 56273. 612-354-2055

Minnesota Department of Natural Resources, Division of Parks and Recreation, Box 39 Centennial Building, St. Paul, MN 55155. 612-296-4776

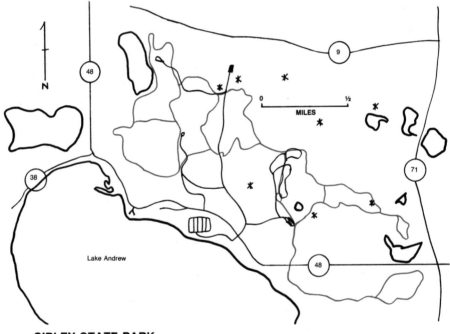

SIBLEY STATE PARK

Split Rock Creek State Park
Jasper, Minnesota

3.2 km (2 miles) of trails

Split Rock Creek Recreation Area is located in southwest Pipestone County at the town of Ihlen. It is approximately halfway between the towns of Jasper and Pipestone on Highway 23.

This is a popular summer recreation site because of the artificial lake, called Split Rock Lake, in the facility. It was created in 1938, when the decision was made to dam Split Rock Creek. Although this was formerly a treeless area, many elm and ash trees were planted during the construction of the dam. These trees have now matured and help to create an attractive recreation area. Sections of the park remain virgin prairie, never overturned by the plow—this hillside is located on the west side of the road leading to the campground.

The park is situated on the western slope of the Coteau des Prairies or upland of the prairie. This glacially produced highland is the continental divide that separates the Missouri and Mississippi watersheds. This is the only portion of Minnesota drained by the Missouri River.

Protruding from the prairie soil is a hard rusty pink bedrock known as Sioux quartzite, sometimes referred to as pipestone. Throughout the ages, it has been quarried by both prehistoric peoples and later by the Dakotah for ceremonial pipes. The quarry to the north of the park, by the town of Pipestone, was an especially favored spot; control of the area was an important symbol of strength and status among Native Americans. The last people to hold the quarries are the Yankton Band of the Dakotah. Through arrangement with the federal government, they have sole rights to work the quarries. Their handcrafts today are sold by the Pipestone Shrine Association to further research and interpretation of this significant area.

The ski trails begin at the heated trail center, immediately adjacent to the Interpretive Center. They are arranged in three interconnected loops on the west side of Split Rock Lake. The trails skirt the shore of the lake and lead to the campground on the northern extremity of the system and to the picnic ground, which is to the extreme south.

Maps, water, and toilets are available; winter camping is permitted. No snowmobiling is allowed within the park. Tourist accommodations and supplies are at hand in Jasper and Pipestone.

For further information, contact

Split Rock Creek State Park, Park Manager, Route 2, Jasper, MN 56144. 507-348-7908

Minnesota Department of Natural Resources, Division of Parks and Recreation, Box 39 Centennial Building, St. Paul, MN 55155. 612-296-4776

See also Blue Mounds State Park, page 241.

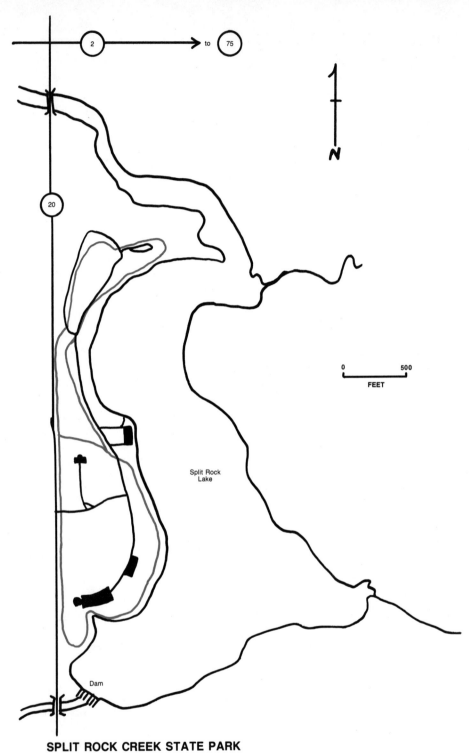

SPLIT ROCK CREEK STATE PARK

Upper Sioux Agency State Park
Granite Falls, Minnesota

4.8 km (3 mi) of trails

beginner, intermediate

Upper Sioux Agency State Park is located in eastern Yellow Medicine County, 8 miles southeast of Granite Falls on Highway 67. The parkland, encompassing nearly 1,300 acres, is situated on the southern bluffs of the Minnesota River, at its confluence with the Yellow Medicine River. The terrain is highly diverse, involving open prairie uplands and blufftops, deep, heavily wooded slopes of river valleys, meadows and wetlands of the river bottoms, and the rivers themselves.

As the last glacier to cover Minnesota retreated, Glacial Lake Agassiz was formed, filling the area now known as the Red River Valley. The meltwater flowed to the southeast in a powerful river known as Glacial River Warren. It eroded the present Minnesota River Valley, cutting to the bedrock in some places. But when Lake Agassiz declined, the water no longer drained into the river. A large valley, containing a comparatively small river, is all that remains. The bluffs of the valley are 200 feet above the valley floor. The Minnesota River now runs from its source, Big Stone Lake, for approximately 330 miles to its confluence with the Mississippi River at Minneapolis/St. Paul by Fort Snelling.

For centuries before white exploration, the Dakotah hunted, fished, and had villages in this area. They possessed an intimate knowledge of their surroundings and used their environment to its fullest. The main source of life for Native Americans was the bison—it provided food, shelter, clothing, and tools. In addition, they used many plants, including seeds, berries, roots, and nuts as they came into season. The plentiful wetlands provided muskrat, the main food source for many Dakotah in the winter months.

As soon as white settlers entered the region, it was the beginning of the end for the Native Americans. The first whites to enter the Minnesota River Valley were the *coureurs de bois* or independent fur traders. They began to arrive in the late 1600s. These traders deliberately distorted the truth concerning their travels and the native inhabitants encountered. In addition, they did not tell the truth about the abundance and natural wealth of the region. These lies were perpetuated in order to protect themselves and their interests, as the area was officially off-limits to traders and settlers. They guarded most fiercely from outsiders their lucrative trade with the Indians. Only a few people entered the region openly and tried to record accurately the customs and manners of the Indians. One such adventurer was George Catlin, a self-trained artist, who accurately, albeit naively, painted the Dakotah and their lifestyle.

Eventually, the population in the eastern United States demanded that the frontier of southern and western Minnesota be opened for settlement. Finally, after much clamor, the Treaties of Traverse de Sioux and Mendota were signed in July, 1851. In the treaties, Dakotah Chiefs signed away their tribal rights to over twenty-four million acres of southern Minnesota, and the Dakotah were removed from Iowa and Minnesota to a reservation, twenty miles wide, running along the Minnesota River Valley from Big Stone Lake to Fort Ridgely. Here their lives were reduced to those of stray animals.

They were defrauded of the bulk of the financial settlement due them, they were deprived of access to the bison and thus were without food and shelter, and they suffered the unbearable indignities of racism and extreme bureaucratuc indifference. This ultimately led to the Sioux Uprising of August and September, 1862, a desperate gamble on the part of the Indians to drive the whites from their land. In the process, the Upper Sioux Agency was destroyed, and many settlers were massacred. Within six weeks, the rebellion was brutally crushed by General Henry H. Sibley and the U.S. Army. As a consequence, the Dakotah moved, for the most part, to the plains of the Dakota Territory where their way of life and the heart of their existence was broken in November of 1890 at Wounded Knee.

The park's ski trail system is in an uncertain stage right now. The ski trails are not marked and groomed although the routes have been established. The park welcomes ski touring and snowshoeing and offers beautiful areas for skiing. This is not new country to skiers—the area in the west end of the park is especially favored. The valley of the Yellow Medicine River is one of the most scenic places in the southwestern part of the state. Winter camping is allowed. The Interpretive Center is open in the winter, is heated, and has running water and toilets. There are also primitive pit toilets and picnic areas in the park. Snowmobiling is allowed at Upper Sioux Agency, toward the center of the facility. Please check with the park staff as to the status of the ski trails. This delay, hopefully, will be resolved in the near future, as the park has great potential.

Food, lodging, and supplies are available in Granite Falls.

For further information, contact

Upper Sioux Agency State Park, Park Manager, Route 2 Box 92, Granite Falls, MN 56241. 612-564-4777

Minnesota Department of Natural Resources, Division of Parks and Recreation, Box 39 Centennial Building, St. Paul, MN 55155. 612-296-4776

See also Lac Qui Parle State Park, page 251.

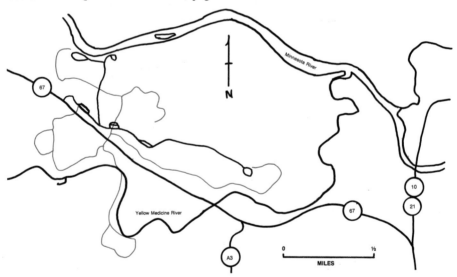

UPPER SIOUX AGENCY STATE PARK

REGION 5
SOUTHEAST MINNESOTA

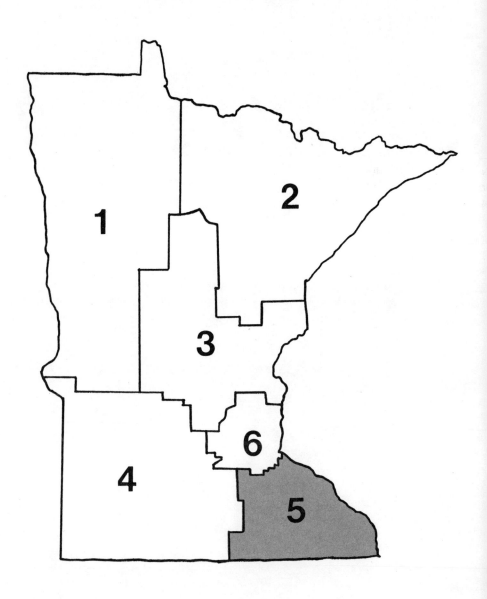

Beaver Creek Valley State Park
Caledonia, Minnesota

4.8 km (3 mi) of trails

beginner

Beaver Creek Valley State park is located in Houston County, 3 miles northwest of the town of Caledonia, on County Road 1. It involves over 1,200 acres of heavily forested land and is situated in an ancient post-glacial river valley. When the glacial meltdown was complete, the source of the river that once coursed through the area disappeared. The evidence of the river's existence and its pathway remains today in the park's valley, which is framed by deeply etched sandstone and limestone outcroppings and steep, forested hills. Nestled in the valley, spring-fed Beaver Creek winds its way through the deep ravine and empties into the Root River.

There are 12 km (7.5 mi) of hiking trails in the park; a word of caution is necessary relative to some of these trails. Switchback Trail and Quarry Trail are not suitable in the least for ski touring. They involve rugged, rocky pathways and, in some instances, rather high elevations and should not be attempted by anyone. However, there are beautiful marked and groomed trails beginning at the parking area and running throughout the campground and picnic area that will be a satisfying tour for many skiers. Visitors may also continue north from the picnic area up Beaver Creek. The groomed trail terminates at the bridge, but skiers may continue up to the Schechs Mill site on their own. This can be a fine addition to using the "official" ski trails. Or, rather than going to the Mill, skiers can turn to the northwest and ski the field edges by the park's boundary line.

The spacious picnic shelter is enclosed in the winter and is used as a warming area for skiers. There is a woodstove on the premises, but, because of the size of the shelter, it is never overly warm. Pit toilets are available, but there is no running water during the winter. Two springs in the park may be used for drinking water, however. Winter camping is permitted; unofficially, visitors are permitted to sleep in the picnic shelter. Tourist accommodations are available in Caledonia.

For further information, contact

Beaver Creek Valley State Park, Park Manager, Route 2 Box 57, Caledonia, MN 55921. 507-724-2107

Minnesota Department of Natural Resources, Division of Parks and Recreation, Box 39 Centennial Building, St. Paul, MN 55155. 612-296-4776

See also Richard J. Dorer Memorial Hardwood State Forest, page 270; Forestville State Park, page 276; O. L. Kipp State Park, page 280.

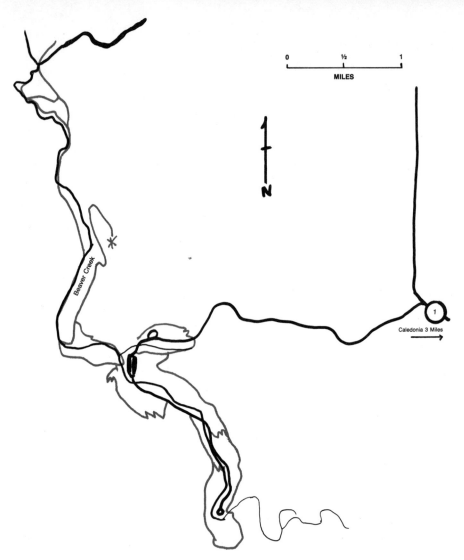

BEAVER CREEK VALLEY STATE PARK

James A. Carley State Park
Plainview, Minnesota

4.8 km (3 mi) of trails
beginner, intermediate

Carley State Park is located in southern Wabasha County, 4 miles south of the town of Plainview. The land for the park was donated by State Senator James A. Carley and the Bolt family to preserve a rare stand of white pine. The trees, unfortunately, were destroyed in an extremely severe hailstorm in 1957. The grove has since been replanted.

The steep, rugged valley walls enfold the North Branch/Whitewater River, which has an oxbow in the northern half of the park. The river's name is very old, a translation of the name given by the Indians who noted the strength and furosity of the river's waters after spring thaw and especially heavy rains. Typically, it is a small peaceful stream. The park is heavily forested with hardwoods and conifers.

You may begin skiing at the park's monument, near the park headquarters—however, this is not central to the trail system. It's better to begin at the picnic area, follow the inside of the river's oxbow in a counterclockwise fashion, cross the bridge, and continue along the park's periphery in a clockwise direction. Two more bridges will be encountered before returning to the picnic area.

There are pit toilets at the park. Winter camping is allowed. Tourist accommodations are available in Plainview.

For further information, contact

James A. Carley State Park, Rt. 1 Box 65, Plainview, MN 55964. 507-534-3400

See also Dorer Memorial Hardwood State Forest, page 270 and Whitewater State Park, page 291.

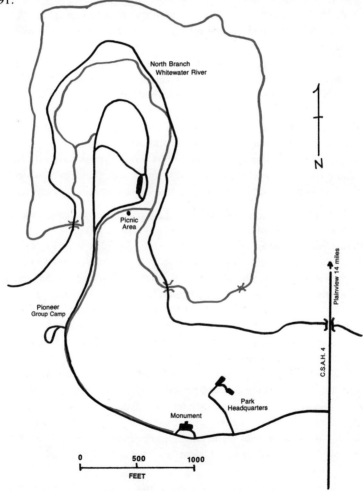

JAMES A. CARLEY STATE PARK

Richard J. Dorer Memorial Hardwood State Forest
Lake City and Lewiston, Minnesota

Dorer State Forest is the only state forest in this part of Minnesota, but it is an enormous facility, encompassing parts of eight southeastern counties and totalling 200,000 acres. It runs along the Mississippi River from Hastings to the southern border of the state. The Forest is named in honor of Richard J. Dorer, a former State Supervisor of Game, who, with other members of the Isaac Walton League, struggled for many years to make the State Forest a reality. It finally was established in 1961, as a tribute to Minnesota pioneers and veterans. Its main goals were and are, to this day, to control some of the severe erosion problems in southeastern Minnesota, provide sites for outdoor recreation, protect watersheds, improve fish and wildlife habitat, produce timber, and encourage the application of wise conservation practices on private lands within the Forest. This is, of course, the multiple-use philosophy of all state forest lands.

There are many state parks, recreation areas, and wildlife management areas within the Forest. This multitude of recreational opportunities is further enhanced by an abundance of county, local, and private efforts. Many feel that this is possibly the least known and underrated recreation area in the state.

Thousands of years ago in Minnesota, when the last glacier had begun to melt and retreat, huge volumes of water moved through this region, cutting deep channels through the bedrock. After the glacial meltdown was over, the powerfully erosive water disappeared and these countless river valleys and ravines remained. It is scenery of incredible beauty, unmatched for its drastic changes in elevation, heavy woodlands, abundance of wildlife, and numbers of streams and rivers.

There are six recreation areas in the Forest. Four of them have official ski touring trails. These trails are in all stages of development and adjustment, particularly in the dispatch of snowmobile and ski trails, so that there is minimal conflict.

HAY CREEK RECREATION AREA
6.4–8 km (4–5 mi) of trails

intermediate, advanced

The 1,500-acre Hay Creek Recreation Area is located in northern Goodhue County, approximately 3 miles south of Red Wing on County Road 58. The Hay Creek valley was among the first areas of forested land to be purchased in the county for development of Dorer Forest. The farmlands were badly eroded, of poor quality, and in desperate need of the initiation of conservation practices. On the other hand, its beautiful bluffs, heavy woods, and the presence of Hay Creek threading its way through the valley made it an outstanding recreation site.

The diversity of woodland species has strongly encouraged the wildlife population. The rugged upland areas are forested primarily with oak, intermixed with elm, birch, basswood, and cherry. Softwoods such as cottonwood, willow, soft maple, ash, and elm grow along the creek. There are plantations of pine and black walnut throughout the region. Efforts have been made on a continuous basis to improve the tree stands, control erosion, and develop new plantations on marginal croplands.

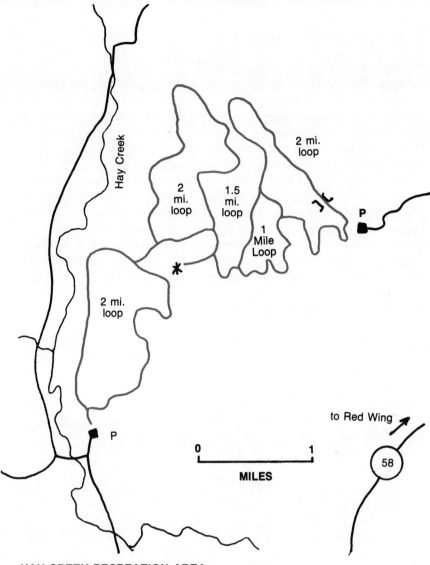

HAY CREEK RECREATION AREA

The original 12.8-km (8-mi) trail system, previously shared by snowmobilers and skiers, has been altered in 1984. The ski trails are basically in the same area, and the route has been shortened a bit, but snowmobiles will not be allowed on the system. The terrain is fairly challenging and should not be attempted by the novice. A shelter is being built on this trail; toilets are located to the southern end of the system at the picnic ground parking lot. The trailhead for skiers is located just off Highway 58, a few miles outside of Red Wing.

See also Frontenac State Park, page 278.

KRUGER RECREATION AREA
4.8 km (3 mi) of trails

beginner, intermediate, advanced

Kruger Management Unit is located in northeastern Wabasha County, approximately 5 miles west of Wabasha, just off Highway 60 on County Road 81. From Kellogg, the area may be reached by taking County Road 81 northwest for approximately 5 miles. This road into the unit is extremely scenic, as it is situated on a very rugged, steep terrain. The 1,000-acre unit is named for Willis Kruger, a retired game warden and longtime conservationist in Wabasha County.

Much of Kruger is located on the steep slopes overlooking the Zumbro River that winds through the area on the way to its confluence with the Mississippi River south of Wabasha. Forest species include immature pine and black walnut plantations, intermediate-sized stands of maple, basswood, and cherry, and mature stands of oak, ash, and maple. Aspen and birch are found along marginal areas at field periphery; softwoods such as willow, cottonwood, and silver maple grow along the creek and river. The Forest Service has done much to improve the vigor of the area. They have constructed fences to control woodland grazing, devised water control structures to reduce soil erosion, and implemented reforestation and timberstand improvement.

The initial part of the trail is used as an Easy Wheeling Nature Area during hiking seasons, suitable for wheelchairs and strollers. It is a 2.4-km (0.75-mile) segment, and is situated on a gently rolling, wooded terrain, following the creek bottom and returning to the picnic area. The creek crossings are well-bridged. This part of the system suits novice skiers. From the campground, an advanced trail moves to the southeast of the beginner loops. It is a large, comparatively undeveloped trail that would be very difficult for either beginners or intermediate skiers. But the scenery is outstanding and will be ample reward for the skier's efforts.

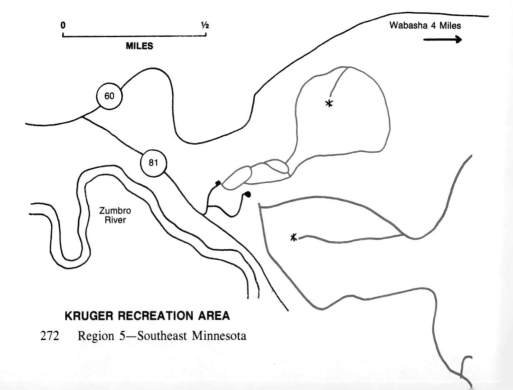

KRUGER RECREATION AREA

272   Region 5—Southeast Minnesota

Camping is allowed. A picnic shelter and a pit toilet are available at the picnic area. Tourist accommodations are at hand in Wabasha or Kellogg.

See also Frontenac State Park, page 278.

SNAKE CREEK RECREATION AREA
8 km (5 mi) of trails
beginner, intermediate, advanced

The 2,600-acre Snake Creek Management Unit is located in southeastern Wabasha County, south of Kellogg. The entrance is on Highway 61 although visitors may enter on the western side via County Road 42.

The topography is extremely rugged. The Snake Creek threads its way through the area, twisting through the deep valley, framed by steep slopes rising 300 feet above the valley floor. The predominant timber type is oak, but nearly every hardwood species native to Minnesota is found in this region. The Forest Service has developed pine and walnut plantations, improved established timber stands, and installed erosion control structures.

There are two trail systems at Snake Creek. On the valley's north side, there is a remote trail that is used for ski touring. The 2.4-km (1.5-mi) shorter loop is good for beginners, and the larger loop will satisfy the needs of the more experienced skiers. There is parking at the trailhead; no other facilities are available at this time. Tourist accommodations are available in both Wabasha and Kellogg.

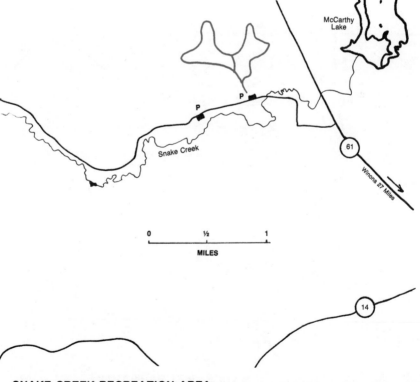

SNAKE CREEK RECREATION AREA

OAK RIDGE RECREATION AREA
WET BARK TRAIL
14.1 km (8.8 mi) of trails

beginner, intermediate, advanced

The 1,565-acre Oak Ridge Management Unit is located in northwestern Houston County, approximately 5 miles west of the town of Houston on County Road 13. The valley and ridge landscape of this area of Minnesota is extremely scenic. The steep hillsides and river bottoms are forested with oak, hickory, basswood, maple, and black walnut. A serious environmental problem in this part of the state is the extreme fragility of the soils. It is an area that was not covered by glaciers, and the earth is highly erosive.

The forest habitat has been enormously improved with the initiation of reforestation with black walnut, red oak, and white pine, the installation of three erosion control structures, and the establishment of wildlife food plots. The development of recreation sites includes the Wet Bark Trail, which is strictly for non-motorized use. It is marked and groomed and has several loops of varying difficulty; some rise and fall as much

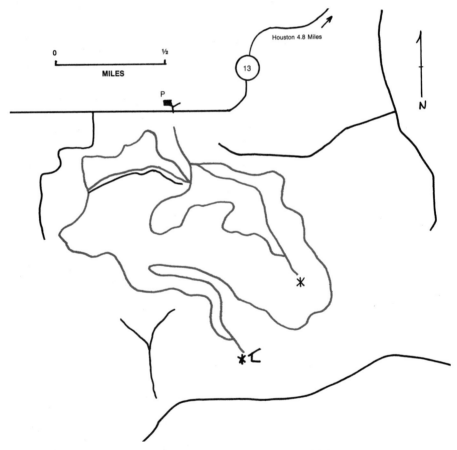

OAK RIDGE RECREATION AREA – WET BARK TRAIL

as 300 feet. Two scenic overlooks, one with a shelter, are located en route. The trail-head is 4.8 miles west of Houston on County Road 13. Parking and privies are available at this point, as is a small campground (four campsites). You must hike a short distance to the campground.

Tourist accommodations and supplies are located in Houston.

See also Beaver Creek Valley State Park, page 267 and O. L. Kipp State Park, page 280.

City of Faribault
Minnesota

RIVER BEND NATURE CENTER
10 km (6.25 mi) of trails

beginner, intermediate, advanced

River Bend Nature Center is located in Rice County, within the limits of the city of Faribault. From downtown, travel east on Highway 60 to its junction with Shumway Avenue. At Shumway, turn to the south and follow the brown Nature Center signs to the entrance on Rustad Road. Two parking lots are available at the Center. The trailside center is at the second lot that is most central to the trail system.

River Bend is a fine example of the effect that cooperation between private citizens and city government can have upon a region. It was a Bicentennial project for the city of Faribault. The Straight River follows a serpentine course through the area and is the Nature Center's focal point. The tongue-in-cheek humor of the Dakotah caused them to call the river Owatonna, which means "straight." Other diverse environmental experiences offered at River Bend include springs, maple-basswood forests, ponds, prairie remnants, marshes, a quarry, and agricultural lands.

The ski trails, marked, groomed, and track-set, are situated on a terrain that is varied but fairly level in the main. There are many interconnected loops; several run along the banks of the Straight River. The shelter is available upon request. It is entirely enclosed and has a wood stove, which may be used by groups. In the winter, outdoor privies are on hand for skiers.

On February 5, 1985, 10-km and 20-km ski races will be hosted at the Nature Center. There will be events all day, with the races in the morning and a triathalon and/or a relay in the afternoon. On Sunday, there will be noncompetitive events and a snow-shoe obstacle course race.

The center is open 6:00 a.m.–10:00 p.m. No alcoholic beverages are allowed. Hikers and snowshoers are to stay off the ski trails; skiers are not to bushwhack through the property. Pets are not allowed on the trails and must be leashed when out in the parking lots.

For further information, contact

Ron Osterbauer/Marilyn Renvers, River Bend Nature Center, P.O. Box 265, Faribault, MN 55021. 507-332-7151

See also Nerstrand Woods State Park, page 286; City of Owatonna, page 288; Rice County, Cannon River Wilderness Area, page 288; Rice Lake State Park, page 289; and Sakatah Lake State Park, page 257.

Forestville State Park
Preston, Minnesota

14.4 km (9 mi) of trails
beginner, intermediate

Forestville State Park is located within the Dorer State Forest, in central Fillmore County in southeastern Minnesota, about halfway between the towns of Preston and Spring Valley. Take Highway 16 to County Road 5, turn south on County Road 12. Turn east on 12, and proceed for 2 miles to the park entrance.

Forestville is located in the area of Minnesota thoroughly dissected by the ancient rivers that were fed by glacial meltwater thousands of years ago. These powerful streams profoundly eroded the sandstone, limestone, and shale that existed in the area, leaving deep, pronounced valleys that provide such a scenic setting for visitors today. The many springs, underground rivers, caves, and sinkholes within the boundaries of the park were produced by constant process of limestone dissolution, which is caused by weak acids in rainwater and decaying vegetation. Both of the park's creeks, the Canfield and the Forestville, emerge from caves several miles upstream. They enter the South Branch Root River within the park.

Devotees of Minnesota history will be in their element at Forestville. The old, now-defunct town of Forestville is within the park's boundaries. Two buildings remain—the store and a brick home built in 1867 by a man named Robert Foster. Originally, it was a good location for a town. The essential ingredients for settlement were there—water, wood, and good soil. The main characters involved in its origin were Foster, Forest Henry (for whom the town was named), and Felix and William Meighen. In 1853, the Foster-Meighen dry goods store was begun in a log cabin. It was very profitable, and, by 1857, the brick store was built. By the late 1850s, Forestville had become a prosperous town. It had two stores, two hotels, two sawmills, a gristmill, cooperage, chair factory, wagon shop, distillery, and tavern. Two stage lines passed through: the Burbank Line from Mankato to Brownsville and the St. Paul to Dubuque Line.

But Forestville's landscape brought about its demise. The valley was too deep for it to be practical to bring in rail lines. The town was bypassed. The final blow came when Preston was chosen as the County Seat, rather than Forestville. The town had no future, and people began to move away; commerce ceased. Finally in 1910, Thomas Meighen shut the doors to his store permanently. He left everything on the shelves—a marvelous time capsule for the Minnesota Historical Society, which has restored the store and opened it for tours. Robert Foster's home is also a public museum. As a major landowner in the area, Mr. Meighen provided the original idea for establishing a state park at Forestville in 1934, but due to political and financial complexities, this did not become a reality until 1963.

The park's enormous variety of terrain and vegetation and its constant water source provide an abundant habitat for wildlife and offer a beautiful recreational resource. The ski trails within the park enable visitors to explore and experience the park's impressive natural and historic features.

The trailhead for ski touring begins at the trail shelter at the picnic ground. Parking is available at this point. The first parking lot is for snowmobiles. Proceed a short distance into the old town site for the skiers' lot. The ski trails run on the east side of the Root River, first moving through the town (beginner skiing) and then veering southward, moving up the valley wall to the upper elevations (intermediate skiing). There is a heated warming house and a campground on this stretch of the trail. The end of the trail is terminated by a fairly large loop. All trails are marked and groomed. Winter camping is allowed. Snowmobile trails do not conflict with the ski trails and are located to the west of the river.

Tourist accommodations are available in Preston or Spring Valley.

For further information, contact

Forestville State Park, Park Manager, Route 2 Box 128, Preston, MN 55965. 507-352-5111

Minnesota Department of Natural Resources, Division of Parks and Recreation, Box 39 Centennial Building, St. Paul, MN 55155. 612-296-4776

See also Lake Louise State Park, page 282 and Richard J. Dorer Memorial Hardwood State Forest, page 270.

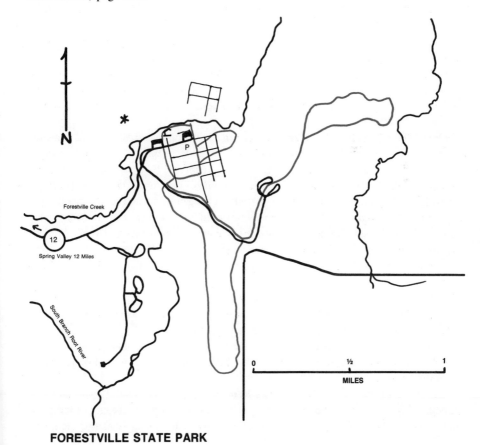

FORESTVILLE STATE PARK

Frontenac State Park
Lake City, Minnesota

8 km (5 mi) of trails

beginner, intermediate

Frontenac State Park is located in Goodhue County, on the shores of Lake Pepin, between Red Wing and Lake City. Lake Pepin is a portion of the Mississippi River that is widened by its confluence with the Chippewa River, which flows southward from Wisconsin. Take Highway 61 southeast from Red Wing for 10 miles or northwest from Lake City for 5 miles to County Road 2, which has its junction with 61 at Frontenac Station. Turn northeast on 2, and proceed into the park.

As the last glacier to cover most of Minnesota melted, Glacial Lake Agassiz was formed, a lake larger than the Great Lakes combined. From its southern end, a powerful river, called Glacial River Warren, cut a large valley through which the Minnesota River now flows. It picked up strength from the meltwaters that were coursing through the valleys that presently hold the Mississippi and St. Croix Rivers. This water power deeply eroded the limestone bedrock in southeastern Minnesota and shaped the Frontenac area as we see it today. The Frontenac limestone is of the highest quality and was chosen in 1883 by architects LaFarge and Heins for the construction of the Cathedral of St. John the Divine in New York City.

The area that is now Frontenac State Park has been inhabited by people for thousands of years. The hunting and fishing around the Lake Pepin region are particularly abundant. This land has always had tremendous spiritual significance to Native Americans. There is a piece of ground in the park which they consider to be hallowed, sacred to the spirit of In-Yan-Teopa, a giant rock which perches on the edge of the bluff overlooking Lake Pepin.

In 1680 the French explorer La Salle sent an expedition under Accault and Augelle to explore the upper Mississippi River. Father Louis Hennepin, a Jesuit missionary, accompanied the party. At Lake Pepin, they were captured by a band of Dakotah on its way to Lake Mille Lacs. Due to the efforts of one of the French in settling a severe intertribal difficulty, the status of these prisoners changed from captivity to friendship; the whites continued up the Mississippi with the Indians as their guests. After eight months of attachment with the Dakotah, the whites were returned to another French expedition under Sieur Duluht, at the place where Mille Lacs Kathio State Park is now located (*see* Region 3). It has been recorded that they left the Indians with great reluctance.

The French continued to dominate the area, both in exploration and commerce, as the fur industry was flourishing. Their control of the area ended in 1736; with the Treaty of Paris, the region came under British control.

The area was first settled by whites in the mid-1800s. The initial draw to the area was the fur trading, but this soon ended with the advent of the timber industry. Many sawmills eventually prospered in the region.

In 1854, two brothers from a wealthy Kentucky family, Israel and Lewis Garrard, came to hunt around Lake Pepin. They were so impressed with the beauty of the area and its easy accessibility by steamboat that they stayed and ultimately platted the town of Frontenac. By post-Civil War times, it had become a playground of the wealthy from New Orleans to St. Louis to St. Paul. It was in its heyday in the 1870s and 1880s. The plans for Frontenac specifically were designed to keep railroads out of the town. This eventually proved to be a disastrous flaw. The town faded when steamboat travel waned and rail travel gained popularity. Many years later, in 1957, the Frontenac area became a state park, to preserve its natural beauty and historical significance.

The trails begin at the trail center just beyond the park's entrance. The system, marked and groomed, encompasses landscape of tremendous variety. The two loops north of the trailhead move through a hilly terrain and eventually come to the area of the In-Yan-Teopa Rock. This stretch by the rock is intermediate in difficulty, whereas the first loop is suited to the beginner. There is a picnic area overlooking Lake Pepin on the outer loop. A beginner trail also moves southward from the trail center, skirting the Old Frontenac area. Its terminus is on Sand Point, the site of the old French stockade, Fort Beauharnois, and Minnesota's first church, the Jesuit Mission of St. Michael the Archangel. Evidence of the structure has vanished.

Snowmobiling is allowed at Frontenac. One trail crosses the northernmost ski loop. Otherwise the systems do not mix. Maps and pit toilets are available at the heated trail center. Winter camping is allowed. Tourist accommodations are available in either Red Wing or Lake City.

For further information, contact

Frontenac State Park, Park Manager, Route 2 Box 230, Lake City, MN 55041. 612-345-3401

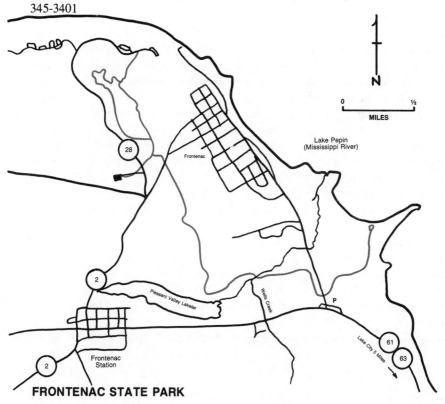

FRONTENAC STATE PARK

O. L. Kipp State Park
Winona, Minnesota

14 km (8.75 mi) of trails

beginner, intermediate, advanced

O. L. Kipp State Park is located in Winona County, about halfway between the cities of Winona and La Crescent. It is 1 mile northwest of the town of Dakota. To reach the park entrance, take Interstate 90 to the County Road 12 interchange, and follow 12 to the north side of 90. It will come to a "T" at this point and intersect with County Road 3 (Apple Blossom Drive). Turn onto 3, and proceed to the park entrance.

The park is named in honor of Orrin Lansing Kipp, a former Assistant Commissioner of the Minnesota Department of Highways, a man who was instrumental in the development of the State's Trunk Highway System. The park is part of the State's designated scenic Apple Blossom Drive. The facility grew from a need for better access to the scenic bluffland that overlooks the Mississippi River in southeast Minnesota. It lies within the Dorer State Forest (in this region) and is classified as a Natural State Park, which means that its emphasis is upon protection, perpetuation, and restoration of natural resources. Consequently, development is quite restricted and is undertaken only when it will enhance those features and values being preserved.

The park lies in Minnesota's driftless area, a small region in the upper midwest that was not covered by glaciers at any time during the last million years. Consequently, no glacial debris was deposited here—no boulders, rocks, gravel, or soil. This area runs through Winona and Houston Counties in Minnesota and includes parts of Wisconsin, Iowa, and Illinois. Although not covered by glaciers, the region was heavily affected by them. The powerful glacial meltwater deeply eroded the sandstone and limestone bedrock in the entire southeastern section of Minnesota, forming profound channels that are now this area's steep beautiful valleys. The largest, certainly, is the Mississippi River Valley. The land which constitutes O. L. Kipp State Park was created from this ancient geological activity and includes halfdome bluffs with sheer rock cliffs, steep valley walls, rolling uplands, and flat flood plains. The Jesuit missionary, Father Louis Hennepin, who accompanied both French explorers and Dakotah throughout the upper Mississippi, wrote that the Mississippi River "runs between the two chains of mountains that wind with the river."

After the last glacier retreated, the early inhabitants of the region built mounds on these bluffs. Some were burial mounds, others were not, and their specific purpose is not known. Most mounds are dome-shaped, but others are representational of objects, usually animals. One such effigy is of a bird, 44 feet long, 15 inches high, with a wing span of 76 feet. The mounds, constructed over thousands of years, are built with precision and symmetry. In some cases, the soil used was transported from the valley floor.

The soil in this area, although deep, is extremely fragile and highly erosive. Attempts at farming in the region have proven to be quite difficult, if not futile. Visitors to the park should stay STRICTLY on the trails to preserve the soil. The steep slopes are quite dangerous and should give people further incentive to remain on the paths.

The ski trails are situated on the bluff tops and take full advantage of the magnificent views of the Mississippi offered to those visiting the park. There are many scenic overlooks on the system. Take care when approaching these spots, especially if you are with children. Picnic tables, fire rings, and toilets, and camping facilities are en route. The trails, marked and groomed, primarily suit the novice. However, there are a few intermediate segments, as well as two rather brief advanced stretches. No snowmobiling is allowed in the park.

Tourist accommodations and supplies are available in La Crescent, Dakota, La Moille, or Winona.

For further information, contact

O. L. Kipp State Park, Park Manager, Route 4, Winona, MN 55987. 507-643-6849
Minnesota Department of Natural Resources, Division of Parks and Recreation, Box
    39 Centennial Building, St. Paul, MN 55155. 612-296-4776

See also Beaver Creek Valley State Park, page 267 and Richard J. Dorer Memorial Hardwood State Forest, page 270.

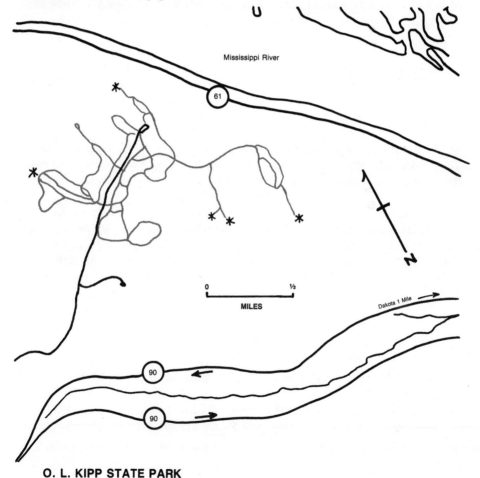

O. L. KIPP STATE PARK

Lake Louise State Park
Le Roy, Minnesota

4.8 km (3 mi) of trails

beginner

Lake Louise State Park is located in extreme southeastern Mower County, approximately 29 miles southeast of the city of Austin, near the town of Le Roy. To reach the park from Austin, take Highway 56 to its junction with County Road 14 at Le Roy. Turn north on 14, and proceed a short distance to the park entrance. Or, from Interstate 90, at the Dexter interchange or from Spring Valley, take Highway 16 to County Road 14, turn south on 14, and travel about 12 miles to the entrance.

Within what is now park property, two spring-fed creeks join to form the Upper Iowa River. It was an ideal area for settlement. The natural resources of the hardwood forests and prairie land as well as the water source began to draw people to the area in the 1850s. They soon dammed the river to run a gristmill. This formed a small lake, which was the focal point of the new community of Le Roy. But, as with many towns of the day, its future was dependent upon the development of the railroad. The new line was run through land approximately 3 miles to the south, and residents moved the entire town to this location.

The farsighted Hamrecht family purchased much of the old town land, which included property on the millpond and its surroundings. They called their acquisition Wildwood Park and determined that it was to be used as a nature preserve and recreational area. The small lake was named Lake Louise after a family member. The area's habitat is very diverse and consequently, can engender, support, and protect a wide range of wildlife, the most notable inhabitant being the wild turkey.

As in most of the state parks, the hiking trails are used for ski touring in the winter. The trailhead is located at the visitor parking lot by the campground. You will first pass the lot used by snowmobiles at the fork in the road. Keep to the right. This access point for ski touring is at the confluence of the two creeks. One loop is situated at the juncture. The trail then crosses the creek bed and proceeds to a system of loops on the eastern side of the creek to the north of Lake Louise. This is a beautiful, wooded area and includes a picnic ground and the park's museum. The trails run fairly close to the dam. They are all marked and groomed. Although snowmobiling is allowed in the park, such trails are completely separate from the ski trails and do not conflict with the ski touring facilities.

Winter camping is allowed at the park. Visitors must walk in to the campsites. There are sanitation buildings available. Tourist accommodations are at hand in Le Roy, Spring Valley, or Austin.

For further information, contact

Lake Louise State Park, Park Manager, Route 1 Box 184, Le Roy, MN 55951. 507-324-5249

Minnesota Department of Natural Resources, Division of Parks and Recreation, Box 39 Centennial Building, St. Paul, MN 55155. 612-296-4776

See also Forestville State Park, page 276 and Mower County, J.C. Hormel Nature Center, page 283.

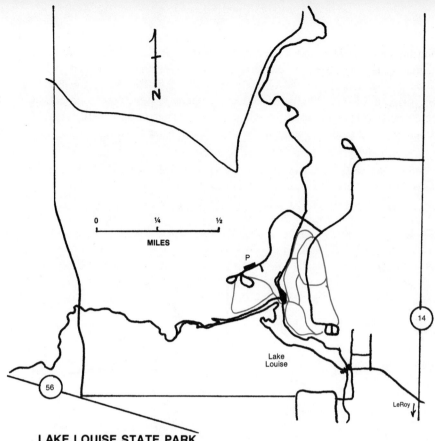

LAKE LOUISE STATE PARK

Mower County
Austin, Minnesota

J. C. HORMEL NATURE CENTER
12 km (7.5 mi) of trails
beginner

J. C. Hormel Nature Center is located in Mower County, in the northeast part of the city of Austin. Take the 21st Street N.E. (County Road 61) interchange from Interstate 90, and travel north for 0.25 mile to the Center.

The land of the Nature Center was once part of the estate of J.C. Hormel. Through federal funding, the city of Austin purchased the land to preserve and restore the estate's once-fabulous arboretum and its surrounding land. The Nature Center, with its Interpretive Building, was developed by Austin's Park and Recreation Board. It is an environmental education resource and offers programs for schools, as well as guided nature tours for the general public.

The trails are situated for the most part on the bottomland of the North and South branches of Dobbin Creek. They are marked, groomed, and track-set. The system is arranged in a series of loops that cross the arms of the creek at several points, moving into woodland and out into open areas. Marshlands, a pond, and part of a nearby country club are involved in the trails. The only access to the trails is at the Nature Center, where there is also a plowed, paved parking lot. Snowshoeing is permitted. No fees are charged. The trails are open daily 6:00 a.m.–10:00 p.m. The Interpretive Building is open Tuesday–Saturday, 9:00 a.m.–5:00 p.m.; Sunday, 1–5:00 p.m.; closed Monday. It is heated and has maps and rental equipment for skiers; restrooms are available. Food, lodging, and public camping are within 1 mile of the Center.

For further information, contact

J.C. Hormel Nature Center, Vincent Shay, P.O. Box 673, Austin, MN 55912. 507-437-7519

See also Lake Louise State Park, page 282 and Helmer Myre State Park, page 285.

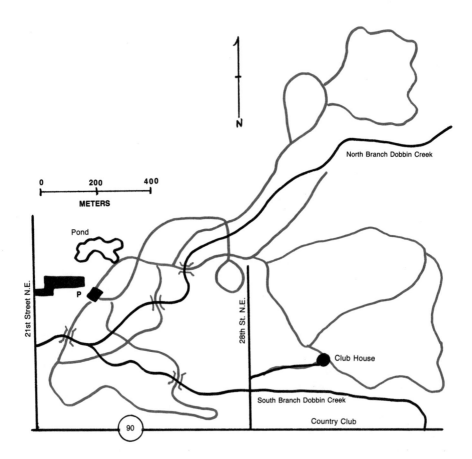

J. C. HORMEL NATURE CENTER

Helmer Myre State Park
Albert Lea, Minnesota

11.5 km (7.2 mi) of trails
beginner

Helmer Myre State Park is located in central Freeborn County, 3 miles south of the city of Albert Lea, on County Road 38. Interstates 35 and 90 have a junction to the north of Albert Lea; both have exits marked with large signs that direct visitors to the park. Exit 11 on Interstate 35 is the most convenient approach to the park.

The park's topography resulted from a series of glaciers that advanced and retreated across the area, the last glacial recession taking place about 10,000 years ago. The ice pushed and pulled at the region, producing hills called moraines. They consist of accumulations of boulders, stone, and other debris. A glacial peculiarity, called an esker, is also in the park. This is a long, narrow ridge of gravel that is deposited by a stream flowing in a tunnel under the ice of the glacier. The thrust of the ice also produced basins, that now contain marshlands, ponds, and lakes, the largest being Albert Lea Lake, which encompasses 26,000 acres and has over 70 miles of shoreline. Its average depth is three feet. In prehistoric times, it was clear with a sandy bottom. However, today it is eutrophic—there is an imbalance of mineral and organic nutrients in the lake, favoring the growth of plant life over animal life.

The lowlands of the park are a major part of our state's valuable wetland resources. The staunch farsightedness of various people throughout Minnesota, as well as the rest of the country, has protected such landscape and habitat by preventing initial drainage of an area or by restoring previously drained wetlands. A lifelong resident of the area, Owen Johnson, firmly and constantly defended the natural resources and enormous cultural heritage of the region. He had done much amateur archaeological study in the area and was instrumental in the park's establishment, which occurred in 1947. The facility was named after Helmer Myre, the senator from the district at the time of the park's conception. The Interpretive Center, named in Owen Johnson's honor, contains a large collection of Indian artifacts. It is open year-round and offers seasonal programs in environmental education to schools as well as to the general public. The naturalist also provides interpretation of the archaeological and historical data pertinent to this region.

The U.S. infantry, under Col. Stephen Kearny, entered the area in 1835. The staff included Lt. Albert Lea, who recorded the ongoing history of their expedition as well as the description of the physical features of the lands encountered in their travels. He produced many maps and provided names of his own choice for several landmarks. He named the lake White Fox Lake, but when an explorer named Joseph Nicollet remapped the area at a later time, he renamed the lake Albert Lea Lake.

The ski trails of the park are situated on the hiking trails. They are a system of marked and groomed one-way loops that encompass three different regions. The Big Island network begins at the Interpretive Center and winds around the campground and picnic area, traveling through the maple-basswood forest and skirting the lake shore. Parking and modern sanitation facilities are at the Center. Visitors may also park farther back on the Center thoroughfare and proceed on the trails to both the north and south of the road. The northern loops enter the White Fox Campground which contains an immature woodland. The trails to the south move into the park's marshland and down to Camp Moraine, a completely modern group camp. Although snowmobiling is allowed at Helmer Myre State Park, the trails remain separate from the ski trails, but for one intersection.

Winter camping is allowed at the park. Food, lodging, and supplies are available in Albert Lea.

For further information, contact

Helmer Myre State Park, Park Manager, Route 3 Box 33, Albert Lea, MN 56007. 507-373-5084

Minnesota Department of Natural Resources, Division of Parks and Recreation, Box 39 Centennial Building, St. Paul, MN 55155. 612-296-4776

See also Mower County, J.C. Hormel Nature Center, page 283.

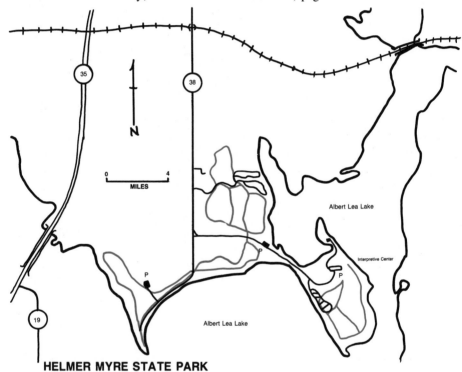

HELMER MYRE STATE PARK

Nerstrand Woods State Park
Northfield, Minnesota

11.2 km (7 mi) of trails

beginner, intermediate

Nerstrand Woods State park is located in east central Rice County, near the small town of Nerstrand. It is situated in the middle of a triangle formed by Northfield, Kenyon, and Faribault and is approximately 9 miles from any of these cities. Its entrance is on Highway 246.

The park takes its name from the nearby town of Nerstrand. This town was platted in 1855 by a Norwegian immigrant named Osmund Osmundson. He chose to call the village Nerstrand after his former seaport home in Norway. Deep nostalgia and loyalty were more important than the name's propriety; it means "near the sea."

The overwhelming bulk of the park is heavily forested with diverse woodland species. Nearly every tree native to Minnesota is found here, but hardwoods dominate. This area is one of the last remnants of the Big Woods that once covered south central Minnesota. Its terrain is very hilly as it is part of a system of moraines. The Prairie Creek threads through the park and has cut an extremely scenic valley that offers many picturesque views, some with waterfalls.

The ski touring area lies north of the main thoroughfare of the park. It begins at the picnic ground with a fairly short loop and proceeds across Hickory Bridge, which spans the creek. There is a waterfall here. There are four loops on the other side of the bridge, comprising Fawn Trail and Beaver Trail. A part of the ski trail system is an Easy Walker Trail that, during seasons without snow, accommodates wheelchairs and strollers. There are privies and an outdoor shelter at the picnic area. Winter camping is allowed. Although snowmobiling is permitted at Nerstrand Woods, such trails are located in the southern end of the park and do not intermingle with the ski trails.

Food, lodging, and supplies are available in Northfield, Faribault, and Kenyon.

For further information, contact

Nerstrand Woods State Park, Park Manager, Northfield, MN 55057. 507-334-8848

See also City of Faribault, River Bend Nature Center, page 275; City of Owatonna, page 288; Rice County, Cannon River Wilderness Area, page 288; Rice Lake State Park, page 289; Sakatah Lake State Park, page 257.

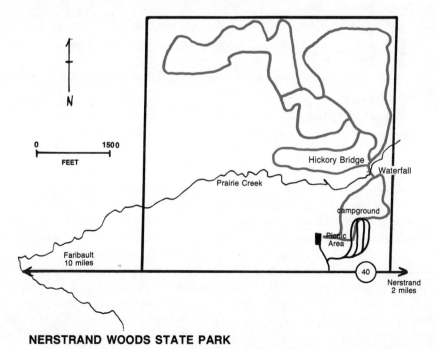

NERSTRAND WOODS STATE PARK

City of Owatonna
Minnesota

The Park and Recreation Department of the city of Owatonna administers two ski-touring trails within city limits. One is at Kaplan's Woods, the other at Mineral Springs Park. Both trails are marked and groomed twice weekly. Maps may be obtained through the Owatonna Chamber of Commerce or the Owatonna Park and Recreation Department.

KAPLAN'S WOODS
7.2 km (4.5 mi) of trails
beginner, intermediate

Kaplan's Woods and its trailhead are located at the corner of Mosher Avenue and 18th St. S.W., in southwest Owatonna. Parking is available at this point. The trails are arranged in a system of four interconnected loops nicely situated at a bend of the Straight River. No water, shelter, or toilets are available at Kaplan's Woods.

MINERAL SPRINGS PARK
6.2 km (3.9 mi) of trails
beginner, intermediate

Mineral Springs Park is located in northeast Owatonna, along Cherry Street. Parking is available within the park. The trail system involves two loops that encompass a stretch of Maple Creek, a tributary of the Straight River. Water and a shelter are available, but no toilets.

For further information, contact

Owatonna Park and Recreation Department, 500 Dunnell Drive, Owatonna, MN, 55060. 507-455-0800

See also City of Faribault, River Bend Nature Center, page 275; Nerstrand Woods State Park, page 286; Rice County, Cannon River Wilderness Area, page 288; Sakatah Lake State Park, page 257.

Rice County
Faribault, Minnesota

CANNON RIVER WILDERNESS AREA
6.4 km (4 mi) of trails
beginner, intermediate, advanced

One cross-country ski trail is administered by the Parks and Recreation Department of Rice County. It is located at the Cannon River Wilderness Area, approximately 4 miles northeast of the city of Faribault, off Highway 3. From Highway 3, turn east on County Road 75, then turn south on the first road encountered. You travel about 1 mile from Highway 3 to the parking area of the Cannon Wilderness Area.

The acreage of this facility runs along the Cannon River, from about 4 miles northeast of Faribault to a point about 5 miles southwest of Northfield. It is an extremely hilly area, and the river's presence makes it a very picturesque place for a ski tour. The trail system is marked but not groomed. The route is a hiking trail in warmer weather and, consequently, is easy to follow. It runs adjacent to the river, for the most part, with the exception of a spur that turns eastward for a short distance.

There are privies and a picnic shelter at the parking lot. No fee is charged for trail use. Tourist accommodations are at hand in Faribault or Northfield.

For further information, contact

Rice County Parks and Recreation Department, Glenn Cramer, Park Director, Rice County Highway Building, P.O. Box 40, Faribault, MN 55021. 507-334-2281 ext. 260

See also City of Faribault, River Bend Nature Center, page 275; Nerstrand Woods State Park, page 286; City of Owatonna, page 288; Rice Lake State Park, page 289; Sakatah Lake State Park, page 257.

Rice Lake State Park
Owatonna, Minnesota

6.4 km (4 mi) of trails
beginner

Rice Lake State Park is located in eastern Steele County and western Dodge County, 9 miles east of the city of Owatonna on County Road 19. The town of Claremont is a bit closer to the park than Owatonna and is located on Highway 14.

The bedrock of this area was produced over 500 million years ago when a shallow sea covered much of the continent. It is identical to the bedrock to the east in the blufflands of the Mississippi River Valley. However, none of the bedrock in Steele County is exposed, with the exception of one spot on the Straight River.

The park is situated in a transition zone, the broad area between the prairies to the west and the deciduous forests to the east. It is called the Southern Oak Barrens, which extends from the Twin Cities to beyond the Iowa border. The dominant vegetation was prairie, with occasional groves of burr oaks and scattered individual trees. The prairie produced topsoil of incredible richness and was highly prized by the white settlers who came to this area. It is one of the most fertile regions in Minnesota and has been farmed to such an extent that none of the prairie that produced it remains, except at various railroad grades or around old cemeteries such as the one in the northeast part of the park. This prairie habitat is now the rarest vegetative community type in Minnesota.

For ages before white settlement, early inhabitants came to the area around the lake to gather foods and to harvest the wild rice that grew in such abundance. None of these rice beds remains, due to the pressures of development and environmental change. From this region eastward to the bottomlands of the Zumbro River, Indians traveled with great regularity. The game hunting was especially good by the river where it was quiet and heavily wooded. Rice Lake is a headwater source for the Zumbro River, its outlet forming the South Branch of the Middle Fork. This outlet was dammed and diked to increase the energy of the water flow at a mill located to the east of the park at Wajiosa. It was not a success because the level of Rice Lake was undependable and the mill operation proved to be too costly. It was still an area of promise in the mid-1800s. A stagecoach line ran through the area, and the new town of Rice Lake showed great possibilities. But the development of the railroads through this part of Minnesota did not include the new settlement, and it faded from existence. The only building that remains of the town is the Rice Lake Church, built in 1857. It is located in the northeast corner of the park, adjacent to the cemetery.

One of the park's greatest assets is the birdlife that either lives here or uses the park as a migratory resting place. The land has a diverse habitat of marshlands, lake, meadows, and woods and is attractive to a great variety of birds. It is a major resting, feeding, and nesting place.

The marked and groomed trails move through deciduous forest, meadows, and along the shores of Rice Lake. They are arranged in three interconnected loops and involve the picnic area and the campground, as well as the area used as a beach and boat landing in the summer. Winter camping is allowed. Pit toilets are available. Snowmobiling is permitted within the park. One such trail crosses the ski trail at the campground. Otherwise, the systems are separate.

Tourist accommodations are available in Owatonna or Claremont.

For further information, contact

Rice Lake State Park, Park Manager, Route 3, Owatonna, MN, 55060. 507-451-7406
Minnesota Department of Natural Resources, Division of Parks and Recreation, Box
    39 Centennial Building, St. Paul, MN 55155. 612-296-4776

See also City of Faribault, River Bend Nature Center, page 275; Nerstrand Woods State Park, page 286; City of Owatonna, page 288; Rice County, Cannon River Wilderness Area, page 288; Sakatah Lake State Park, page 257.

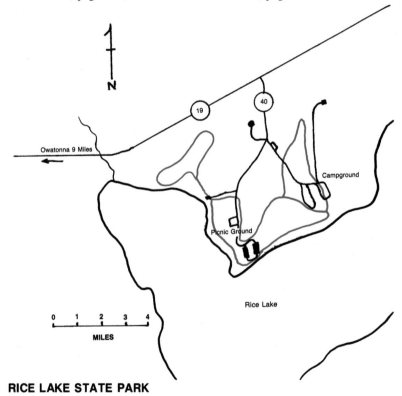

RICE LAKE STATE PARK

City of Rochester
Minnesota

QUARRY HILL PARK AND NATURE CENTER
SILVER CREEK TRAIL
7 km (4.4 mi) of trails
beginner, intermediate

Quarry Hill Nature center is located within Quarry Hill Park on Rochester's east side, north of the State Hospital on Silver Creek Road.

Years ago, this park held a limestone quarry. As the limestone was mined, the underlying sandstone was exposed. Because this bedrock is so soft, many caves were dug into the valley walls. The caves were used for food storage by the State Hospital before refrigeration was available. Now, all but a few of the caves are closed. Those still open are for public exploration.

The Park and Nature Center are a joint venture of the Rochester Parks and Recreation Board and the School District. The schools operate the Nature Center as an environmental education facility; consequently, it is open only on school days 8:00 a.m.–5:00 p.m.

The ski trails begin at the Nature Center and run through the valley, produced by the forces of Silver Creek. This stream winds around the park and offers beautiful scenery to the visitor. It is a heavily wooded area, a lovely encapsulation of fairly primitive landscape within a large city. The trails are not marked or groomed, but the pathways are wide, well-established and easy to follow. They climb the hills and traverse the flood plain of the creek bottom.

A large, paved parking lot is available at the trailhead, immediately adjacent to the Nature Center. Toilets and shelter are available only when the Nature Center is open. No fee is charged. A wide variety of tourist accommodations and cultural opportunities are available in Rochester.

For further information, contact

Quarry Hill Nature Center, 701 Silver Creek Road N.E., Rochester, MN 55901. 507-289-1687

Whitewater State Park
Altura, Minnesota

2.1 km (1.3 mi) of trails
beginner

Whitewater State Park is located in western Winona County on Highway 74, between the towns of Elba and St. Charles. It lies within the Richard J. Dorer Memorial Hardwood State Forest.

The park's name is taken from the name of the river that flows within its boundaries. Whitewater River is a translation of the Dakotah name that made reference to the appearance of the river during times of high water when it was white from both the clay eroded from the valley floor and the foam produced by swift current.

Whitewater River Valley, like all the others in southeastern Minnesota, was produced by the erosive meltwater from the last glacier, approximately 10,000 years ago. Its water cut through the sedimentary limestone and sandstone with relative ease, leaving many narrow river valleys that are spectacular to visit. The rich bottomlands are forested with oak, basswood, maple, and walnut while the uplands are oak savanna, that is, gently rolling prairie with scattered oak. The soil in this region is very fragile and highly erosive. Considerable effort has been made to restore the landscape, following the disastrous effect that settlement had on the area. Removal of trees and farming and attendant grazing nearly destroyed the habitat. This was further compounded by heavy flooding that began around 1900. This environmental horror continued for over four decades until state and federal agencies stepped in and instituted practices to restore and protect the land. They built dikes to control erosion and purchased farm land that was beyond its ability to support crops and livestock. State parks and the Dorer State Forest (in this region) were established over the years to further the cause of protection and conservation and to provide visitors with some of the loveliest recreation sites in the Midwest.

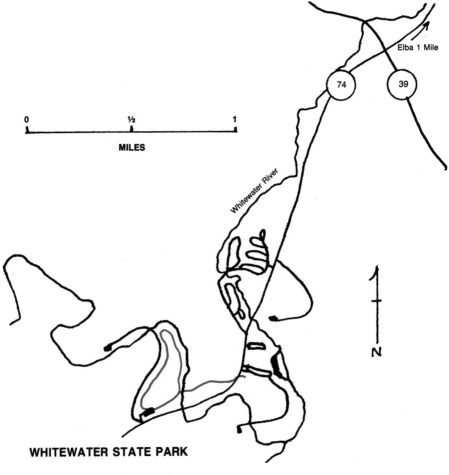

WHITEWATER STATE PARK

Many hiking trails in the park are not used for ski-touring, as they are situated on dangerously high ridges and would involve extraordinary skill, if not incredible luck, on the skier's part to be skied with success. The short trail that is used is located in the valley floor and provides easy skiing with a beautiful backdrop. It runs on both sides of the river, crossing it once on a bridge. Skiers are welcome to bushwhack in the park if they feel adventurous. No snowmobiling is allowed.

Winter camping is permitted. Privies, fire rings, and picnic tables are on site. Tourist accommodations are available in St. Charles, Elba, or Altura.

For further information, contact

Whitewater State Park, Park Manager, Altura, MN 55910. 507-932-3007

Minnesota Department of Natural Resources, Division of Parks and Recreation, Box 39 Centennial Building, St. Paul, MN 55155. 612-296-4776

See also James A. Carley State Park, page 268; Richard J. Dorer Memorial Hardwood State Forest, page 270; City of Rochester, Quarry Hill Park and Nature Center, page 291.

REGION 6
TWIN CITIES METRO AREA

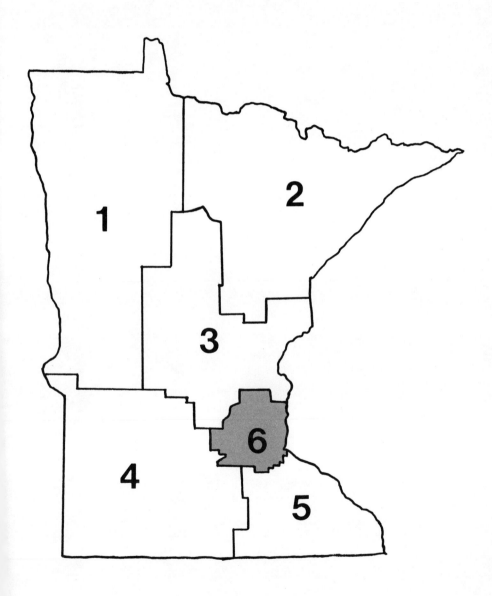

Afton State Park
Afton, Minnesota

28.8 km (18 mi) of trails

beginner, intermediate, advanced

Afton State Park is located in southeast Washington County, 40 miles southeast of St. Paul. It is situated on the St. Croix River, 4 miles south of the town of Afton and 6 miles north of Point Douglas. The park's entrance is at the junction of County Road 21 (St. Croix Trail) and County Road 20 (Military Road). The Afton Alps Downhill Ski Area is located in its western midsection.

The park is rather new, established in 1969 to preserve the unique natural characteristics of this area and to provide the opportunity for people to enjoy nature-oriented recreation. The setting is quiet and primitive. Great efforts have been made to preserve this natural setting, and development has been kept to a minimum. Campgrounds, the beach, and the park's interior are accessible only by trail. Afton lies on the bluffs overlooking the St. Croix River. The landscape is cut by deep ravines that fall 300 feet to the river below. Sandstone outcrops are common on the sides of the ravines. This terrain affords spectacular views of the river valley.

Oak, aspen, birch, and cherry trees grow in the ravines and in the river valley. This forestation and the rolling fields above the valley provide excellent habitat for a wide range of wildlife, including hawks, eagles, fox, deer, and badgers. Efforts have been made to restore the original prairie and savanna that once existed in the area.

The steep terrain offers rugged, demanding ski touring that will thoroughly invigorate park visitors. Many scenic overlooks occur on the trails. Although there are some novice loops by the Interpretive Center, the bulk of the trail system to the north of the Center is best suited to intermediate and advanced skiers. Do not attempt this area if your nordic downhill technique is not decently honed. Toilets, water, and shelters are located at various points out on the trail network. In addition, a Backpack Camping Area is out on the northern segment of the trails. Campers must register at the park office for a site. There is a Group Camp Area on the beginner trails. Snowmobiling is not permitted in the park.

The Interpretive Center is open year-round. It is heated with a woodstove for winter use. There are interpretive displays, modern toilets, maps, running water, and a pay telephone at this location.

For further information, contact

Afton State Park, Park Manager, 6959 Peller Avenue South, Hastings, MN 55033. 612-436-5391

Minnesota Department of Natural Resources, Division of Parks and Recreation, Box 39 Centennial Building, St. Paul, MN 55155. 612-296-4776

See also Washington County, South Washington Regional Park, page 345.

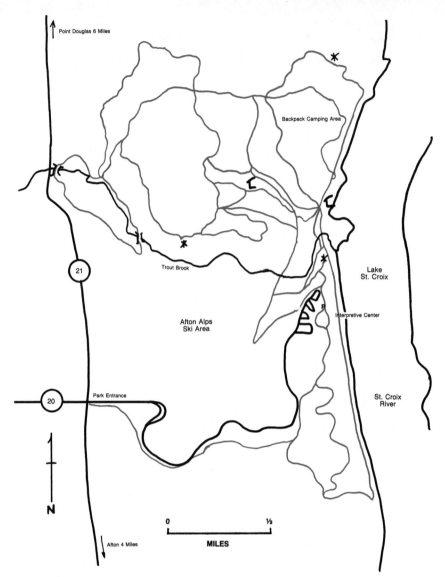

Point Douglas 6 Miles

Backpack Camping Area

Trout Brook

21

Lake
St. Croix

Afton Alps
Ski Area

Interpretive Center

St. Croix
River

Park Entrance

20

N

0   ½

MILES

Afton 4 Miles

AFTON STATE PARK

Anoka County
Anoka, Minnesota

BUNKER HILLS COUNTY PARK
29 km (18.1 mi) of trails
    beginner, intermediate, advanced

Bunker Hills County Park is located at the junction of Foley Boulevard and Highway 242 (Main Street), which is 3 miles east of Highway 10 and 2 miles west of Highway 65. Visitors may park at the golf course, the archery range, Bunker Lake, or the horse stables.

The trails are arranged in a system of entirely interconnected one-way loops, that wind through beautiful woodlands forested with deciduous and coniferous trees, and sand plain grasslands. The sand plain was left after the retreat of ancient Glacial Lake Grantsburg, over 10,000 years ago. The park is named for an early homesteader in Anoka County.

There are 17 km of advanced trails, 9 km of intermediate trails, and 3 km for beginners. The trails are thoroughly marked and color-coded, groomed, and tracked. Shelters and restrooms are scattered throughout the system. A map may be obtained at the clubhouse. Food, rentals, and instruction are available at Bunker Hills. The park is open 7:30 a.m.–9:30 p.m., all week.

For further information, contact

Anoka County Park Department, 550 Bunker Lake Boulevard N.W., Anoka, MN 55303. 612-757-3920

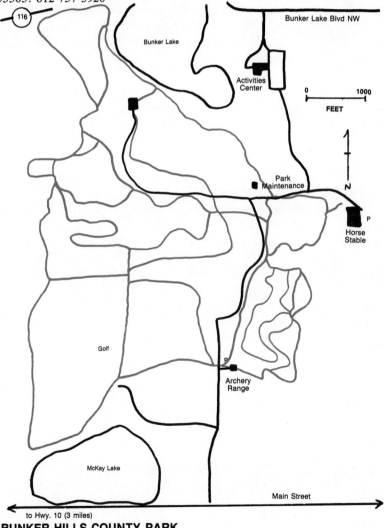

BUNKER HILLS COUNTY PARK

City of Bloomington
Minnesota

There are five trails in the park system of the city of Bloomington. No fee is charged for the use of the trails. Maps are available at the Park and Recreation Division Office. Ski rentals are available nearby at R.E.I. Co-op (Lyndale Avenue and West Shakopee Road) and Burger Brothers (9833 Lyndale Avenue South). Primitive winter camping is allowed by special permission only; contact the Park and Recreation Division.

CENTRAL PARK—NINE MILE CREEK TRAIL
18.3 km (11.4 mi) of trails
beginner, intermediate, advanced

The trailhead is located west of Interstate 35W, between West 106th Street and West Old Shakopee Road at the Moir Picnic Grounds/Park, which is at West 104th Street and Penn Avenue South. The trail follows Nine Mile Creek from Moir Park to the Minnesota River bottom and back to the park again. The creek derived its name in Minnesota's earliest days because its confluence with the Minnesota is nine miles from Fort Snelling.

The terrain involves mostly gradual hills forested with hardwoods. There are several steep, fast runs into the ravines of the river and creek bottoms. The trail is not groomed, but it is marked. Water, heated shelter, toilets, and ample parking are available during daylight hours at the Moir Picnic Grounds.

The trail interconnects with the Mound Springs Park Trail System at the river bottom.

GIRARD LAKE PARK TRAIL
1.7 km (1.1 mi) of trails
beginner

The trailhead is located on the south side of West 84th Street, between France Avenue South and Chowen Avenue South. This is approximately 1 mile south of Interstate 494. Parking is prohibited on West 84th Street; there is limited off-street parking at the trailhead.

The trail is a single loop around Girard lake. It is ideal for family use, as it runs on flat terrain, providing easy skiing for beginners. Although the trail is not groomed or track-set, it is well-marked and easy to follow. No water, shelter, or toilets are immediately available on site.

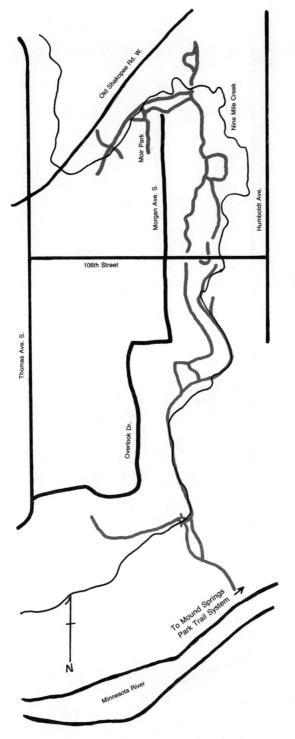

LEGEND

TA—TRAIL HEAD ACCESS

AC—TRAIL ACCESS

★—DISTANCE BETWEEN
INTERSECTIONS

TRAIL SURFACE

D—DIRT OR EARTH

S—SOD OR GRASS

Z—COMBINATION (D & S)

W—WOOD CHIPS

C—CONCRETE

G—GRAVEL

L—LIMESTONE

A—ASPHALT

O—OTHER

TOTAL TRAIL DISTANCE—

4210 FEET

0.80 MILES

1283 METERS

**CENTRAL PARK—
NINE MILE CREEK
TRAIL**

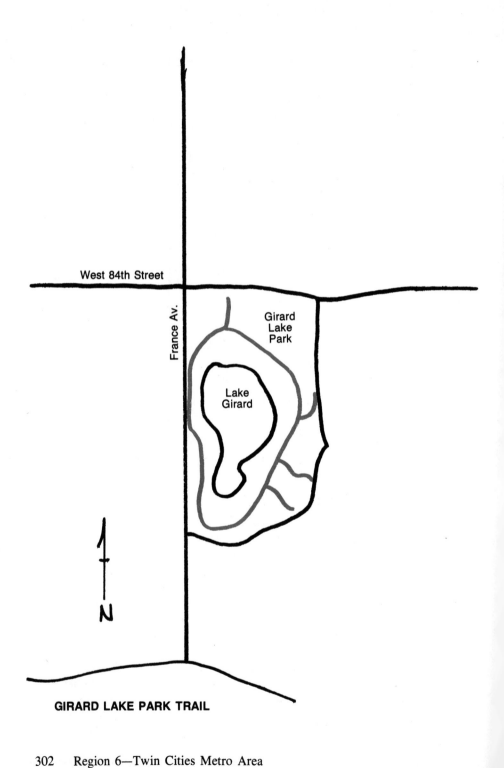

West 84th Street

France Av.

Girard
Lake
Park

Lake
Girard

N

GIRARD LAKE PARK TRAIL

MOUND SPRINGS PARK TRAIL

5.3 km (3.3 mi) of trails, measured point-to-point

beginner, intermediate, advanced

The main trailhead is located at the intersection of 11th Avenue South (the east side of the street) and East 100th Street. There are other access points at 10th Avenue Circle and 102d Street, near Columbus Road and Park Avenue South, at Hopkins Road and Hopkins Circle, and at the terminus of Lyndale Avenue South, where the Central Park-Nine Mile Creek Trail and the Mound Springs Park Trail interconnect. As this trail is not laid out in a loop, the full round-trip on the route is 10.6 km (6.6 mi).

The park is located on a steep headland overlooking the Minnesota River Valley, and is the site of Indian mounds that date back to a very early period of time. As this is a burial ground, the mound area should be treated with respect.

The first half-mile from the main trailhead descends to Minnesota River bottom, is very steep and narrow, and involves switchbacks. *All* skiers, even those with advanced skills must use *extreme* caution on this stretch and, in most cases, should remove skis and walk to the bottom. Once at the river bottom, the terrain is fairly flat with some gentle undulation. The trail is well-marked but not groomed or track-set. The entire trail passes through a deciduous forest that is primarily upland hardwoods; at the river bottom, the forest species are mainly elm and basswood.

Limited parking is available on streets at the trail access points. There are no toilets or water at the main trailhead. The nearest facility with such accommodations would be at Running Park at 12th Avenue South and Old Shakopee Road, about 0.75 mile north from the main trailhead.

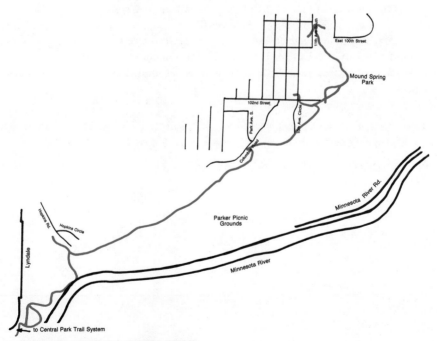

MOUND SPRINGS PARK TRAIL

MOUNT NORMANDALE LAKE PARK TRAIL

5.3 km (3.3 mi) of trails

beginner

There are two access points to the Mount Normandale Lake Park Trail: the first access is on West 84th Street, between Normandale Center and East Bush Lake Road; the second access is on Chalet Road, one block south of the intersection of West 84th Street and East Bush Lake Road. Parking is available at both points.

The trail is arranged in a loop around Mt. Normandale Lake on flat terrain, with one or two very gradual inclines. It moves through wooded meadowland, but mainly through open lakeshore meadowland that is intersected by Nine Mile Creek. The trail serves as a bike path during the warmer seasons of the year. It is marked, but not groomed. No toilets or water are available on site—find them at the Hyland Hills Ski Area on Chalet Road or at filling stations on Normandale Road.

This trail is located at the extreme northern end of the Hyland Lake Park Reserve.

See also Hennepin County Park Reserve District, Hyland Lake Park Reserve, page 321.

WEST BUSH LAKE PARK TRAIL

1.3 km (0.8 mi) of trails, measured point-to-point

beginner, intermediate, advanced

The main trailhead to the West Bush Lake Park Trail is at the park's entrance at the junction of West Bush Lake Road and 94th Street. There are two minor access points on West Bush Lake Road at the trail's ends—northwest and southeast of the main trailhead. Ample parking is available.

As this trail is not laid out in a loop, a round-trip is 2.6 km (1.6 mi). The terrain is gently rolling, with several downhill runs that are not steep. They can be easily skied by people exercising prudence and care not to overestimate their abilities. The trail is situated primarily in a hardwood forest and runs on the southwest side of Bush Lake, to the west of Hyland Lake Park Reserve. It is not marked or groomed but is easily followed.

For further information, contact

Terry Williams, City of Bloomington, Park and Recreation Division, 2215 W. Old Shakopee Rd., Bloomington, MN 55431. 612-887-9638

See also Hennepin County Park Reserve District, Hyland Lake Park Reserve, page 321.

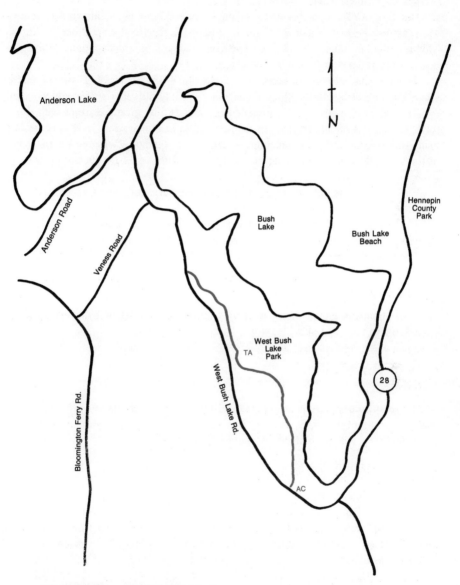

Anderson Lake

Anderson Road

Veness Road

Bush Lake

Bush Lake Beach

Hennepin County Park

West Bush Lake Park

TA

West Bush Lake Rd.

Bloomington Ferry Rd.

28

AC

N

WEST BUSH LAKE PARK TRAIL

Brackett's Crossing
Lakeville, Minnesota

25 km (15.6 miles) of trails

beginner, intermediate, advanced

Brackett's Crossing is located in Dakota County, 35 minutes south from downtown Minneapolis. Take Interstate 35W south to the Minnreg Road exit. Proceed west on Minnreg Road to Judicial Road. Turn north on Judicial Road, and continue a short distance to the Brackett's Crossing clubhouse.

This recreation center is named after Lakeville's first settler, J. J. Brackett. It is located in a beautiful rural setting; the terrain is rolling hills that are heavily wooded.

The trails begin at the clubhouse and are marked, fully groomed, some with single track, many with double tracks, and a few with up to four tracks. They wind around many small ponds and have something to offer every type of skier. Ten km (6.25 mi) of trails are illuminated for nighttime skiing. A trail fee of $1.00 per person per day is charged of guests; there is no parking fee.

The clubhouse is fully equipped with sauna, showers, complete restaurant, and ski shop for the rental and sale of equipment. Instruction is available.

Please note: the ski trails of the Murphy-Hanrehan Park Reserve in Savage interconnect with the trails of Brackett's Crossing.

For further information, contact

Brackett's Crossing, Baard Lovaas, Superintendent, 17976 Judicial Road, Lakeville, MN 55044. 612-435-7600

See also Hennepin County Park Reserve District, Murphy-Hanrehan Park Reserve, page 326 and City of Lakeville, Ritter Farm Park, page 327.

City of Burnsville
Minnesota

Three ski touring trails are maintained by the city of Burnsville. No trail fee is charged for use of the trails. The city is in the process of upgrading the maps of these trails, and they will be available in the late fall of 1984.

ALIMAGNET PARK
10 km (6.25 mi) of trails

beginner, intermediate

Alimagnet Park is located on County Road 11, between 138th Street and County Road 42. The trailhead is at the east side of the parking lot across from the baseball field. There are two groomed trails: 3 km long and 7 km long. No warming house or toilets are available.

CIVIC CENTER PARK
2.5 km (1.6 mi) of trails

beginner

Civic Center Park is located at 251 Civic Center Parkway. The parking lot is at the west end of the ice arena lot. The trail runs along 130th Street, east of Nicollet Avenue, and is marked and groomed. There are restrooms and hot and cold vending machines at the ice arena.

TERRACE OAKS PARK
12 km (7.5 mi) of trails
beginner, intermediate, advanced

The trailhead at Terrace Oaks Park is at the warming house below the 70-car parking lot east of County Road 11, between the Burnsville Parkway and 130th Street. The three major trails are 2, 4, and 6 km and require a variety of skills. They are marked and groomed. A heated shelter with restrooms is provided. Maps are available on site.

For further information, contact

City of Burnsville, Division of Parks and Recreation, 1313 East Highway 13, Burnsville, MN 55337. 612-431-7575

Carver County
Young America, Minnesota

BAYLOR PARK
6.4 km (4 mi) of trails

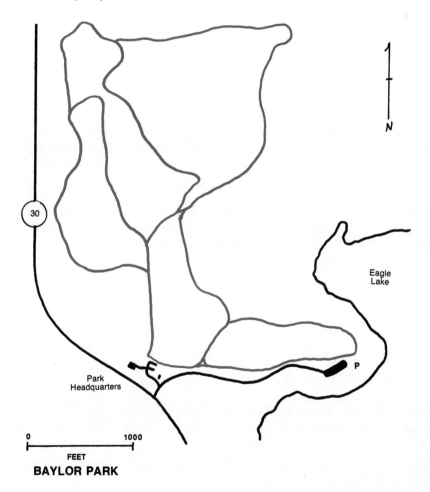

BAYLOR PARK

Carver County's Baylor Park is located on the northwest side of Eagle Lake near Young America. It is reached by traveling on County Road 33 for 2.5 miles north from Norwood or 6 miles south from New Germany.

It is a relatively new park, purchased in 1971 by Carver County, with much help from federal and state levels of government. It has a wide variety of physical features that include wooded lake shore, rolling open land, forest, and both large and small marshes and wetlands. Nearly 75 percent of the park area is being maintained in a natural state as a preserve.

The trails begin at the park headquarters, a barn that has the Carver County Historical Society's historical agricultural museum on its upper floor. Downstairs is an activity room that includes kitchen facilities, comfortable furniture, restrooms, and showers. The trails are laid out in several one-way loops to allow skiers a variety of routes from which to choose.

For further information, contact

Park Manager, Baylor County Park, Young America, MN 55397. 612-467-3145

Crabtree's Kitchen
Copas, Minnesota

Crabtree's Kitchen is a restaurant located by the old town of Copas, on Highway 95, a short distance north of Marine-on-St. Croix. The historic Swedish settlement of Scandia is northeast of Copas.

The ski trails of William O'Brien State Park are connected to groomed and tracked trails that run right to the front door of the restaurant.

Crabtree's Kitchen is a gastronomic institution in this area. They serve old-fashioned home-style meals and are famous for their homemade desserts, baked daily.

A new addition to the establishment is a bed-and-breakfast operation that includes four rooms furnished with antiques. The rooms are over the rear of the restaurant and have their own private entrance, a common living room, and a deck overlooking the St. Croix River Valley. Guests may choose whatever they like from the breakfast menu. The total price is $39.95 per night, double or single occupancy; no pets, no smoking, no children under the age of twelve. Reservations are required.

For further information, contact

Crabtree's Kitchen, Terry and Bev Bennett, 19173 Quinell Avenue North, Marine-on-
 St. Croix, MN 55047. 612-433-2455

See also William O'Brien State Park, page 337.

Dakota County
Hastings, Minnesota

Two cross-country ski trails are maintained by the Dakota County Parks Department. The first trail is in the east section of Lebanon Hills Regional Park in Eagan, and the second is in Spring Lake Park Reserve in Nininger Township, to the northeast of Hastings. Both parks are open 5:00 a.m.–11:00 p.m., every day of the week. There is no entrance fee. No pets are allowed on the trails.

LEBANON HILLS REGIONAL PARK

15.7 km (9.8 mi) of trails

beginner, intermediate

The east section of Lebanon Hills Regional Park is bordered by Pilot Knob Road (County Road 31) to the west, Cliff Road (County Road 32) to the north, Dodd Boulevard to the east, and 120th Street to the south. The main trailhead is on Cliff Road at a point that is 0.25 mile west of Dodd Boulevard. Parking, toilets, and maps are available at this location. A second access is also on Cliff Road, just to the west of the curve around Holland Lake. Parking is also available at this point.

Lebanon Hill Regional Park was formerly called the Holland-Jensen Park, and it encompasses approximately 1,600 acres of land that vary from gently rolling to challenging for the skier. There are wooded hills, marshland, lakes, and countless small lakes and ponds. It is reputed to be a fine place for winter birdwatchers, and you should

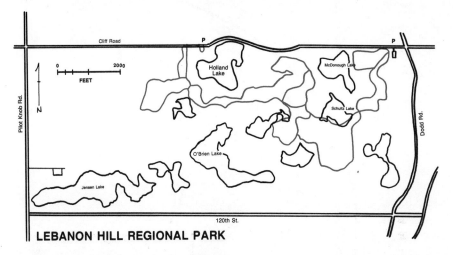

LEBANON HILL REGIONAL PARK

be sure to bring binoculars and an identification guide. The larger lakes that are involved in the ski touring system are Holland, McDonough, and Schultz. There is a small novice loop by the trailhead; otherwise, the system is intermediate in difficulty. It is set up in a complex network of one-way loops that wind around the lakes and potholes of the park. There is a trail shelter en route.

See also City of Eagan, Blackhawk Park and Patrick Eagan City Park, page 311; Fort Snelling State Park, page 312; Minnesota Zoological Garden, page 334.

SPRING LAKE PARK RESERVE

8 km (5 mi) of trails

beginner, intermediate

To reach the trailhead, take County Road 42 west and northwest for 2 miles from Highway 61 on the north end of Hastings, until it intersects Idell Avenue. Turn north on Idell, and proceed 0.25 mile to 127th Street. Turn west on 127th; this street splits. The road to the left leads to the Dakota County park office, and the road to the right leads to the parking lot at the trailhead. Maps and toilets are available at the parking lot.

The trails are arranged in a one-way loop system that basically follows the Mississippi River and the Spring Lake Bay of the River. They are marked and groomed. There are two rather small loops by the trailhead; the two outer loops are much larger, particularly the loop to the south. There is a trail shelter on this segment of the trail.

For further information, contact

Dakota County Parks Department, 8500-127th Street East, Hastings, MN 55033. 612-437-6608

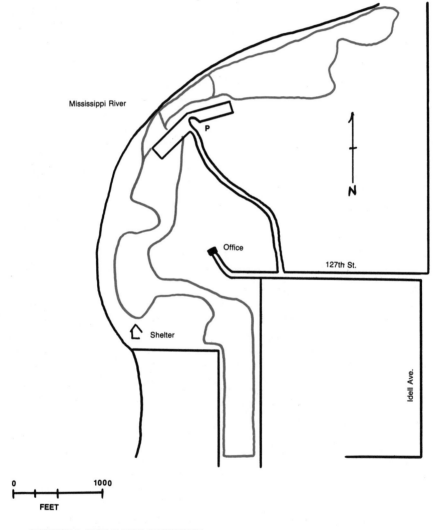

SPRING LAKE PARK RESERVE

City of Eagan
Minnesota

Two parks within the limits of Eagan offer ski touring and are administered by the city's Department of Parks and Recreation. Eagan is located in northwestern Dakota county, bordered on the northwest by the Minnesota River.

BLACKHAWK CITY PARK
1.6 km (1 mi) of trails
beginner, intermediate

This municipal park is located in a residential area of Eagan. The entrance is at the intersection of Palisade Way and Riverton Road, which is 0.9 mile north of the junction of Riverton Road and Diffley Road (County Road 30). The park's name is taken from Blackhawk Lake, the park's focal point, nestled among the park's hills. It is basically rolling prairie land; the lake's shoreline is bordered with trees.

The one-way trail starts at the park entrance. It is clearly marked and meanders around the hills, down to the lake, and back again.

PATRICK EAGAN CITY PARK
3.2 km (2 mi) of trails
beginner, intermediate

The entrance to Patrick Eagan is on Lexington Avenue (County Road 43), south of the intersection with Wescott Road, and is marked with a sign. Travel along the driveway to the parking area. Toilets are located at this point.

The park is situated in a heavily wooded valley that surrounds McCarthy Lake. The forest species are primarily hardwoods, with an occasional conifer grouping. The landscape is very scenic and has an isolated feeling about it; you could easily forget the immediate presence of the metropolitan milieu.

The trail is laid out in a loop around the lake. It was designed especially for ski touring and is well-signed and groomed accordingly. En route are rest stops with fireplaces and benches.

For further information, contact
City of Eagan, Department of Parks and Recreation, 3830 Pilot Knob Road, Eagan, MN 55122. 612-454-8100

See also Dakota County/Lebanon Hills Regional Park, page 309; Minnesota Zoological Garden, page 334; Fort Snelling State Park, page 312. There is a parking area with access to Fort Snelling State Park trails at the junction of Lone Oak Road (County Road 26) and Highway 13 in northwest Eagan. The Dakota County side of the park is its major wildlife sanctuary. The main trailhead to the Dakota County side of the park is its major wildlife sanctuary. The main trailhead to the Dakota County side of the park's trail system, however, is at the historic Henry Sibley home in Mendota Heights, just to the northeast of the junction of Highways 13 and 55.

Fort Snelling State Park
St. Paul, Minnesota

28.6 km (17.9 miles) of trails
beginner

The entrance to Fort Snelling State Park is situated at the junction of Highway 5 and Post Road at the southeastern side of Fort Snelling National Cemetery. The park is located at an enormously significant site in Minnesota's history: the confluence of the Minnesota and Mississippi Rivers occurs here.

The two rivers played an important role in the human culture of the region as well. That they always had been significant to countless generations of Native Americans there can be no doubt. They also made it possible for Minnesota to open to white settlement. The Minnesota River has its headwaters at Big Stone Lake on the western border between Minnesota and South Dakota. The Mississippi River has its source in north central Minnesota at Itasca State Park. In the years before good roads were constructed, both rivers were important avenues of transportation for industry, commerce and people. They are both used for such purposes today. Their confluence and attendant developments contributed greatly to the growth of St. Paul and Minneapolis.

Of couse, the history of Fort Snelling receives emphasis in the park. The land was initially purchased in 1805 by Lt. Zebulon M. Pike, a famous military man and explorer, while he was on an expedition to discover the source of the Mississippi River. This purchase and the consequent establishment of the Fort was made to give the United States control over the Upper Mississippi. By 1819, troops under Colonel Henry Leavenworth began construction of the Fort. In 1825, its name was changed from Fort St. Anthony to Fort Snelling, after its commander of the time, Colonel Josiah Snelling. The army at the Fort was used as peacekeeper in the conflicts that flared between the Dakotah and Ojibwe and the white traders and settlers. It served continuously as a military post until 1946. Scrupulous restoration of the Fort was undertaken in the 1960s by the Minnesota Historical Society, and their enthusiastic efforts continue to this day.

The ski trails of the park are situated on routes used for hiking in warmer seasons. They traverse land that is flat and smooth, which makes for easy skiing. A trail involving so few difficulties is perfect for skiing under a full moon! The trails are one-way and are basically set up in three systems.

Pike Island Trail begins at the Interpretive Center and is a single loop which skirts the island's perimeter. There are two crossovers. This trail interconnects with **Wood Duck Trail**, which is another large loop that passes by Snelling Lake, makes a circle on Picnic Island, continues around Snelling Lake, passing below the sandstone river bluffs. Airport and highway noise may be a problem on this trail. The third trail is located across the Minnesota River on the Dakota County side of Fort Snelling State Park. It is called the **Mendota Trail**, and it passes through the park's major wildlife sanctuary.

The main trailhead is near the historic Henry Sibley house in Mendota Heights, just northeast of the junction of Highways 13 and 55. A second access point is at the junction of Lone Oak Road (County Road 26) and Highway 13 in northwest Eagan. Parking is available at both points. **Mendota Trail** is situated on an old settler route through the river bottoms. It is yet another large single loop, with a two-way crossover parallel to Interstate 494. The long tour involves skiing nearly 16 km (10 mi). Skiers should carefully consider their endurance before attempting the entire route.

A special trail in the park is **Minnehaha Trail**, which joins the juncture between the Pike Island and Wood Duck Trails. It is situated on an old railroad grade that runs along and above the Mississippi River, providing a link between Fort Snelling, the Minneapolis trails system, and Minnehaha Park.

Ample parking, heated shelter, maps, water, and toilets are all available at the Park. For further information, contact

Fort Snelling State Park, Park Manager, Highway 5 and Post Road, St. Paul, MN 55111. 612-727-1961

See also Dakota County, page 308; City of Eagan, page 311; Minneapolis Park and Recreation Board, Minnehaha Park, page 329; Minnehaha Trail, page 332.

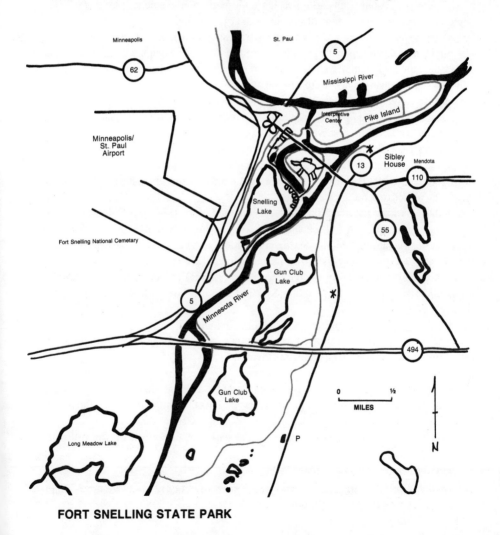

FORT SNELLING STATE PARK

Hennepin County Park Reserve District
Maple Plain, Minnesota

100 km (62.5 mi) of trails, combined

beginner, intermediate, advanced

Skiers of all abilities and ambitions can greatly enhance their winter season by making use of the Hennepin Park Reserve District. There are seven park reserves and three regional parks within the system. This involves a combined network of over 100 km (62.5 miles) of well-marked, groomed, and double-tracked trails that wind through forests and valleys, over meadows and creeks, and around secluded lakes and rivers. All trails are one-way. Skiers have the opportunity to recreate while immersing themselves in the winter beauty of improved and protected wildlife habitat that the District has achieved. Each park reserve or regional park has its own special qualities and facilities. There are heated trailhead buildings with modern conveniences at all facilities. Some have nature centers that offer educational programs.

Many special events are planned at the parks, such as winter picnics and barbeques, moonlight skiing, volksporting, exhibition of the latest ski equipment, talks and slide shows, and the 50 Kilometer Club. Rental of complete ski packages is available at certain parks. Ski touring schools are offered at various parks and include beginner, intermediate, and advanced lessons. You may choose private, semiprivate, or group instruction. Ski clinics on equipment preparation, waxing, fitness training, and racing are available at some of the reserves.

During peak skiing hours, volunteer patrol members are on duty to help insure safety and enjoyment on the trails. They are at least intermediate skiers and are certified in first aid and CPR. Park operating hours are 8 a.m. to sunset each day of the week. All parks are closed on 25 December.

A daily parking fee of $2.00 per car is charged at all Hennepin County Park Reserve District facilities. A $12.00 annual parking permit is available, with a permit for a second family car available for $6.00. In addition, all skiers ages 16–64 must display the Minnesota cross-country ski trail permit while at the reserves and parks. This license is available at all reserves: the annual fee is $5.00 for an individual, $7.50 for a husband and wife; a daily permit is $1.00. The parks have a few simple rules that they ask visitors to observe.

- Ski only during operating hours, 8 a.m. to sunset.
- Ski only on groomed trails. For everyone's safety and enjoyment, carefully observe the directional signs and trail markers.
- Do not take dogs on the trail system.
- The trails are maintained for ski touring only. Hiking, sledding, snowshoeing, and snowmobiling can ruin a good ski track. Check with the office for the availability of these activities.

The individual park reserves and regional parks are described on the following pages.

For further information, contact

Hennepin County Park Reserve District, Dave Schwartz, 3800 County Road 24, Maple Plain, MN 55359. 612-473-4693

MORRIS T. BAKER PARK RESERVE
MAPLE PLAIN, MINNESOTA
12.8 km (8 mi) of trails

beginner, intermediate, advanced

Baker Park Reserve is located near Maple Plain, approximately 18 miles west of the Twin Cities. Take Highway 12 west to County Road 19, travel north on 19 to County Road 24, turn east, and proceed to the park entrance.

This park reserve was the initial acreage developed by Hennepin County to begin the Park Reserve District. The core acreage was donated by the Baker Family Foundation in 1956 and was formerly farmland that supported crops, woodlots, and marshes and lakes. Four lakes are in the Reserve; involved in the trail system are Half Moon and Spurzem Lakes.

The trails bypass frozen wetlands and move through a great deal of wooded land, while climbing and descending the gentle hills of the Reserve. There is an occasional steep hill that should be attempted only by those with plenty of experience. These spots are well-signed and contain a bypass for those who don't feel up to the challenge. There are many scenic overlooks. The chances of seeing wildlife, early or late in the day, are high.

There are rest stops, toilets, and shelters scattered at various spots on the system. A 50 Kilometer Club stamper is located out on the Timber Trail. Rentals are available at this Reserve, as is instruction by reservation. Light snacks and beverages may be obtained at the park barn.

For further information, contact

Baker Park Reserve, Medina, MN 55359. 612-473-7418, 612-473-4693 (District Office)

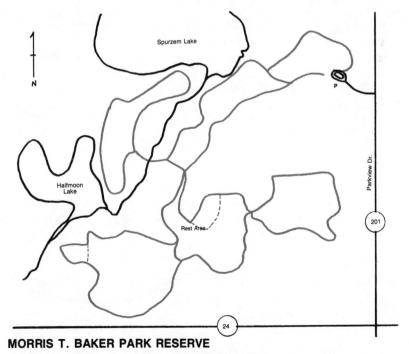

MORRIS T. BAKER PARK RESERVE

CARVER PARK RESERVE
EXCELSIOR, MINNESOTA
18 km (11.25 mi) of trails
beginner, intermediate, advanced

Carver Park Reserve is located west of Victoria between Highways 7 and 5 on County Road 11. The trailhead is to the west of County Road 11 (not at the Nature Center). A heated barn is situated at this site.

Two comparatively short loops by the trailhead may skied by novices; however, the remainder of the system is intermediate to advanced in difficulty. The trails wind through woods of basswood and maple and across marshlands. They skirt several lakes; one contains the Fred E. King Waterfowl Sanctuary. The land is quite hilly and makes for delightful touring. The Reserve contains a large deer population and many other animals active in winter. The bulk of the trails lies to the west of County Road 11. However, if you take the Nature Center Trail, you cross the road, traverse the narrows of Crosby Lake, and eventually arrive at the Lowry Nature Center. This is a year-round outdoor learning center where pertinent programs are conducted for groups and the general public. There are a variety of interesting displays at the center that also houses dining rooms, classrooms, laboratories, library, and bookstore. A visit to the Lowry Nature Center can greatly enhance a day of ski touring and provide a welcome rest stop. A 50 Kilometer Club stamper is located here also.

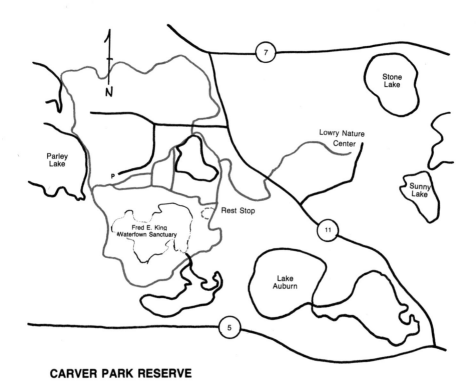

CARVER PARK RESERVE

Toilets, rest stops, and shelters are located at many points throughout the trail system. Rentals, maps, and toilets are available at the heated trail center at the trailhead. Instruction may be obtained by reservation.

For further information, contact

Carver Park Reserve, 7025 County Road 11, Excelsior, MN 55331. 612-472-4911, 612-473-4693 (District Office)

CLEARY LAKE REGIONAL PARK
PRIOR LAKE, MINNESOTA
7.2 km (4.5 mi) of trails
beginner, intermediate

Cleary Lake Regional Park is located in Scott County, to the south of Prior Lake. The entrance is on County Road 27, just north of its junction with County Road 68.

The park takes its name from its site on the south side of Cleary Lake. The trails traverse a gently rolling landscape, skirting the lake in part and winding through the woods. There are four loops in the system. The two loops at the trailhead are rated for beginners, but they are also a perfect place to work on form. Rest stops and shelters are located out on the trails, as is a 50 Kilometer Club stamper.

Rentals, toilets, light snacks, and maps are available at the heated trail center at the trailhead. Instruction is available by reservation.

For further information, contact

Cleary Lake Regional Park, Park Manager, Prior Lake, MN 55372. 612-477-2171, 612-473-4693 (District Office)

Hennepin County Park Reserve District, Greg Mack, 8737 E. Bush Lake Road, Bloomington, MN 55438. 612-941-7993

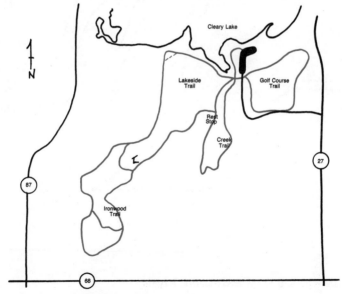

CLEARY LAKE REGIONAL PARK

COON RAPIDS DAM REGIONAL PARK
COON RAPIDS, MINNESOTA
5.8 km (3.6 mi) of trails

beginner

Coon Rapids Dam Regional Park is located on narrow strips of land on both sides of the Mississippi River by the dam in Coon Rapids. Consequently, part of the park is in Anoka County, and part is in Hennepin County. Likewise, there are two entrances. The Anoka County entrance is located at the junction of Hanson and Egret Boulevards, which both feed into County Road 1. The Hennepin County entrance is in Brooklyn Park on Highway 169, northwest of its junction with 97th Avenue North.

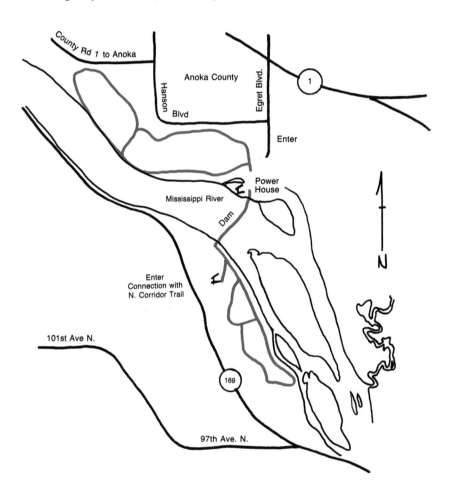

COON RAPIDS DAM REGIONAL PARK

The trails on both sides of the river are connected by a 1,000-foot walkway across the dam. They traverse flat terrain ideal for the novice. The Coon Rapids side is heavily wooded, while the Brooklyn Park side involves prairie-land with small wooded areas scattered throughout the trail. There is a heated visitor center on the Coon Rapids side. Maps and toilets are available at this point. Lessons are available by reservation.

An added feature of this park is the 10.4 km (6.5 mi) North Hennepin Corridor Trail that runs from the Brooklyn Park entrance of the Coon Rapids Dam Regional Park to Elm Creek Park Reserve in Osseo. The Corridor Trail is groomed and double-tracked.

For further information, contact

Coon Rapids Dam Regional Park, Park Manager, Coon Rapids, MN 55433. 612-757-4700, 612-473-4693 (District Office)

CROW-HASSAN PARK RESERVE
ROGERS, MINNESOTA
20 km (12.5 mi) of trails
beginner, intermediate, advanced

Crow-Hassan Park Reserve is located on County Road 203 at its junction with Ghostly Road and Hassan Parkway. It is across the Crow Wing River from Hanover.

The trailhead is located just inside the entrance to the Reserve. Here is a nice-sized loop for the novice. It moves through the woods and proceeds to the river, then turns back to the trail center. The remainder of the loops are designed for the skier with intermediate to advanced skill. Much of the outside portions of the loops run along the river bluffs. The vistas offered at several points are outstanding. A 50 Kilometer Club stamper is located along the river. The geography is mainly woodlands that border a restored prairie, the park's dominant feature. Rest stops, shelters, and toilets are located out on the trails. There is a heated trailhead building for resting and warmup. Maps are available at this point.

For further information, contact

Crow-Hassan Park Reserve, Park Manager, Rogers, MN 55374. 612-428-2765, 612-473-4693 (District Office)

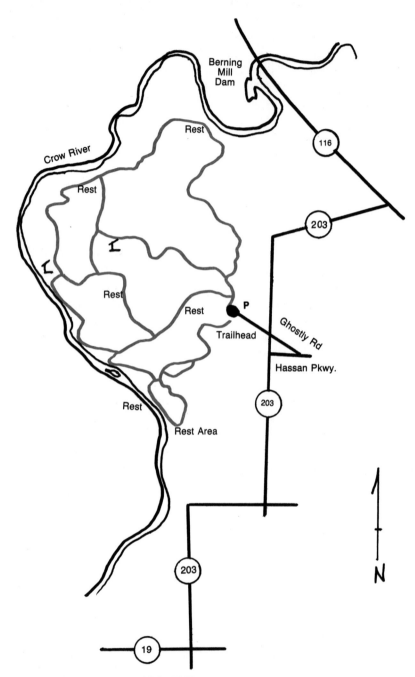

CROW-HASSAN PARK RESERVE

ELM CREEK PARK RESERVE
OSSEO, MINNESOTA
11.2 km (7mi) of trails

intermediate, advanced

Elm Creek Park Reserve is located by Osseo, in northern Hennepin County. There are two entrances for skiers. The main trailhead is on a Reserve road, which leads from Territorial Road, just northwest of the junction of Territorial Road and Highway 152. The second access point is at the Whitney H. Eastman Nature Center, which is on Elm Creek Road, east of the junction of Elm Creek Road and County Road 121.

The trails that start at the main trailhead involve two small beginner loops near the trailhead. Otherwise, trails are intermediate to advanced in difficulty. The landscape contains woodlands of aspen, oak, maple, basswood, and birch that shelter meadowlands, wetlands, lakes, and streams. A large intermediate loop circles Mud Lake. Like the other lakes at Elm Creek, it has a marshy shoreline that provides excellent habitat for waterfowl. It is a valuable resource for other wildlife, such as deer, beaver, and countless other animals. Many of the trails are quite challenging and suit the ambitions of the advanced skier.

Near the confluence of Elm and Rush Creeks is the Whitney H. Eastman Nature Center, a facility devoted to environmental education, offering continuous outdoor learning programs for both schools and the general public. In addition, it serves as a beautiful visitor center, a pleasant place to warm up with a hot drink and stamp your 50 Kilometer Club card, if you are a participant. At the heated trail center, which is located at the main trailhead, maps, ski rentals, light snacks, and toilets are available. One may also take ski lessons by advance reservation.

Skiers may tour the Coon Rapids Dam Regional Park via the North Hennepin Corridor Trail, which runs from the southeast side of Elm Creek Park Reserve to the Brooklyn Park entrance of the Coon Rapids Dam Regional Park. It is 10.4 km (6.5 mi) long, groomed, and double-tracked.

For further information, contact

Elm Creek Park Reserve, Park Manager, 13351 Elm Creek Road, Osseo, MN 55369.
   612-420-4300, 612-473-4693 (District Office)

HYLAND LAKE PARK RESERVE
BLOOMINGTON, MINNESOTA
11.2 km (7 mi) of trails

beginner, intermediate, advanced

The entrance to Hyland Lake Park Reserve is near the junction of Bush Lake Road and 96th Street, approximately 2 miles south of Interstate 494.

The trailhead is just to the south of 96th Street, within the Reserve. The acreage of the Reserve includes marshy lowlands, gently rolling meadows, lakes, and the highlands of the Mt. Gilboa area. The initial loop at the trailhead is for beginners. All other loops are for intermediate or advanced skiers. Rest stops and toilets are located out on the trail system. To the south, an intermediate loop circles Hyland Lake. Skiers are cautioned not to venture onto the ice, as it remains dangerously thin in places throughout

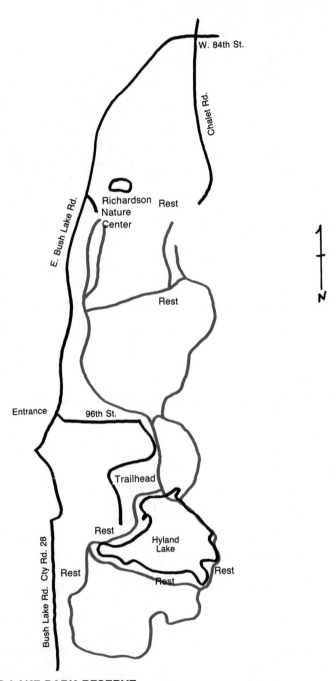

HYLAND LAKE PARK RESERVE

the winter. Beyond Hyland Lake, an advanced loop moves through the woods and involves very hilly terrain. North of the trail center is another advanced loop. A 50 Kilometer Club stamper is situated on its northern side. Beyond this loop, you enter the Hyland Hills downhill area, located on Mt. Gilboa, the highest hill in Hennepin County (el. 950 feet). Both downhill skiing and ski jumping are available at this area. Cross-country skiers may ride the chairlift to the top with a free ticket available at the ski chalet. The skiing in this area is situated in a heavily wooded part of the Reserve. To the west of the downhill area is the Nature Center spur, which leads to the Richardson Nature Center. The land around the Richardson Nature Center is comprised of forests, wetlands, and meadows. The staff is devoted to the task of environmental education for both schools and the general public and offers programs all year-round in outdoor learning. The facility is fully equipped with offices, laboratories, classrooms and exhibits; its entrance is on East Bush Lake Road, north of the Reserve's main entrance.

The trail center at the main trailhead is heated and has toilets, ski rentals, and maps. Ski instruction is available by registration.

For further information, contact

Hyland Park Reserve, Park Manager, 8737 East Bush Lake Road, Bloomington, MN 55438. 612-941-7993, 612-473-4693 (District Office)

See also City of Bloomington, Mt. Normandale Lake Trail and West Bush Lake Trail, page 304.

MEDICINE LAKE REGIONAL PARK
PLYMOUTH, MINNESOTA
5.8 km (3.6 mi) of trails
beginner, intermediate, advanced

The entrance to Medicine Lake Regional Park is on County Road 9 (Rockford Road), just to the east of its junction with County Road 154 (Medicine Lake Drive). This is a short distance from Interstate 494. Medicine Lake is the newest park in the system, opening in 1983–84. It is also the most centrally located facility in the county.

The park's acreage is located around the northwest arm of Medicine Lake, a complex network of bays, channels, narrows, and backwaters. The trail head is on the east central side of the park. Follow the entrance road to the trail center. The trails are arranged in three loops. The large southeastern loop for beginners passes through the park's most heavily wooded area, skirting the north side of Medicine Lake and passing over channels fed by the main bay of the lake. The central loop, northwest of the trail center, is for intermediate skiers. It leads to the Skyline Trail, which should not be attempted without advanced skills. This trail lies to the west of the arm of the lake.

As this is such a new facility, much is now in various stages of development. Skiers should be aware of the fact that many conveniences and services that are not presently at Medicine Lake certainly will be in the near future. At this time no shelter is available. Nor are there ski rentals, instruction, water, or snacks at the park. There are outdoor privies.

For further information, contact

Medicine Lake Regional Park, Park Manager, 12505 County Road 9, Plymouth, MN 55441. 612-559-4694 (weekends), 612-473-4693 (District Office), 612-472-4911 (weekdays)

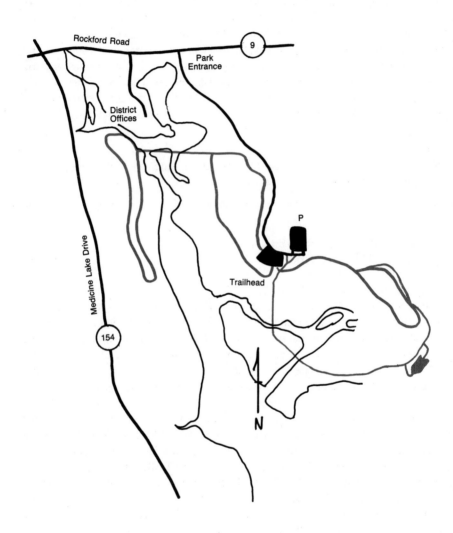

MEDICINE LAKE REGIONAL PARK

LAKE REBECCA PARK RESERVE
ROCKFORD, MINNESOTA
16 km (10 mi) of trails

beginner, intermediate, advanced

The entrance to Lake Rebecca Park Reserve is on County Road 50, north of the junction with County Road 11. It is situated between Delano and Rockford, 1 mile south of Highway 55 near Rockford or 3 miles north of Delano, which is on Highway 12.

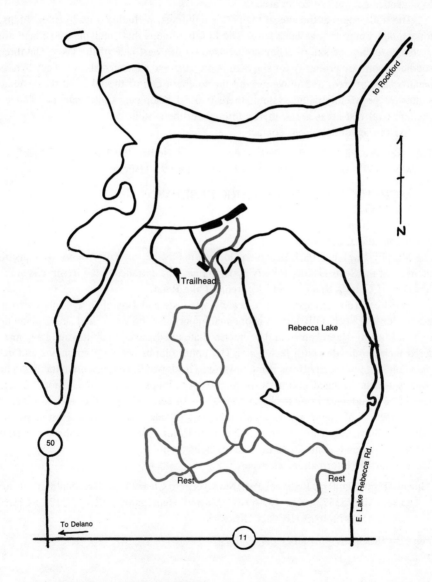

LAKE REBECCA PARK RESERVE

Nearly all of the acreage within this Reserve was once farm land and was drained for tillage. Part of the heavy forestland had been cleared. The primary program within Lake Rebecca Park Reserve has been restoration of the wetlands. The large population of waterfowl and, most especially, the winter holding area for trumpeter swans attest to the success of the program. The woodlands have also been greatly enlarged by relatively new plantations of both deciduous and coniferous species.

The obvious focal point of the Reserve is Lake Rebecca. The reclaimed marshland to the west of the lake gives visitors an idea of what restored and improved habitat does to engender natural life in an area.

The trails begin at the site of the park's buildings, including a trail center. Maps, toilets, and water are available here. The first two loops that enter the marshland are excellent for novice skiers. They are situated on the west side of the lake. The three southern loops are primarily for skiers of intermediate to advanced ability. They bypass small stands of trees and move around the southern end of the lake. At the extreme southwest perimeter of the system, there is a 50 Kilometer Club stamper. Toilets, shelters, and rest areas are scattered throughout the system.

For further information, contact

Lake Rebecca Park Reserve, Park Manager, Held House, Rt. 2 Box 418, Rockford, MN 55373. 612-477-4255, 612-473-4693 (District Office)

MURPHY-HANREHAN PARK RESERVE
SAVAGE, MINNESOTA
16 km (10 mi) of trails
intermediate, advanced

Murphy-Hanrehan Park Reserve is located in Savage, in Scott County. It is just to the west of the Scott/Dakota County division line. The entrance to the Reserve is at the junction of County Road 68 and Hanrehan Lake Road.

The Reserve's acreage is very heavily wooded, and Hanrehan Lake is its focal point. The extremely hilly terrain is of equal importance, however, and skiers planning to visit Murphy-Hanrehan should be intermediate to advanced in ability and have mastered their nordic downhill technique. The uphill climbs are very strenuous and demanding, but with such efforts come rewards. The downhill runs are breathtaking. The trail system is arranged in a network of five large loops and two small loops. Skiers should be scrupulous in their observance of the directional signs for safety's sake. A 50 Kilometer Cub stamper is located on the eastern side of the system. Rest stops and toilets are located out on the trails. The heated trail center at the trailhead has restrooms, maps, and a snack bar that serves light food.

For further information, contact

Murphy-Hanrehan Park Reserve, Park Manager, c/o Cleary Lake Regional Park, Prior Lake, MN 55372. 612-447-6913 (Murphy-Hanrehan), 612-477-2171 (Cleary Lake), 612-473-4693 (District Office)

See also Brackett's Crossing, page 306.

City of Lakeville
Minnesota

RITTER FARM PARK
18 km (11.25 mi) of trails
beginner, intermediate, advanced

This trail is administered by the Department of Parks and Recreation of the city of Lakeville in Dakota County. It is located west of Interstate 35W on 195th Street. An access road leads into the park from 195th Street.

The trails have been planned by international ski trail advisors and offer challenges to skiers of all abilities. They are marked, groomed, and track-set several times a week by the Lakeville Park Department. The rolling hills of Ritter Farm were once crop and grazing lands. Some old woodlots, groves, and orchards evidence this past. There are also heavily wooded areas, as well as open meadows. The terrain varies from flat, to gently rolling, to extremely hilly. Five one-way loops all begin at a common trailhead. Four of the loops move west and northwest of the trail center.

TRAIL 1 — MATTERHORN — 5.6 km, intermediate, advanced; involves difficult turns and hills. The more difficult stretch is in the woods, while the beginning and the end of the loop are easy skiing.

TRAIL 3 — TELEMARK — 3.5-5 km, depending upon the route chosen, beginner; medium hill climbs, exciting downhill runs.

TRAIL 4 — the quick return loop for those who are cold, have equipment problems, are out of shape, or have overestimated their abilities.

TRAIL 5 — BACK HOME — another return loop with a long downhill run most of the way back to the parking lot.

One trail moves to the southeast.

TRAIL 2 — KITZBUHEL — 2.5 km, intermediate, advanced; involves some difficult turns and hills; should be skied only by experienced skiers, as there are several demanding uphill climbs and steep downhill runs. The ski trail moves primarily through woodlands. A major snowmobile trail crosses this trail. Signs are posted but BEWARE. The snowmobile trail runs only on the park's boundary line, with the exception of its intersection with Trail 2.

The parking lot is located at the trail center. Maps and restrooms are available at this point. A $3.00 daily parking fee is charged; a seasonal parking ticket costs $15.00. Camping is not allowed. No liquor may be consumed in the park. No pets may be taken out on the trails, which are to be used strictly for ski touring.

For further information, contact

Lakeville Department of Parks and Recreation, c/o Steve Michaud, 8747-208th Street, Lakeville, MN 55044. 612-469-4431

See also Brackett's Crossing, page 306 and Hennepin County Park Reserve District, Murphy-Hanrehan Park Reserve, page 326.

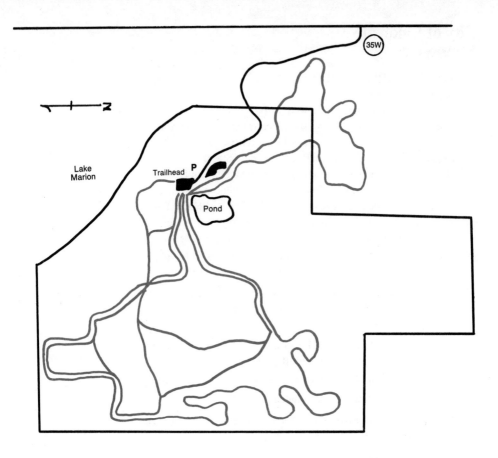

LUCE LINE STATE TRAIL

Luce Line State Trail
Plymouth to Clara City, Minnesota

9.6 km (6 mi) of trails

Luce Line is a state corridor trail. When completed, it will run from Vicksburg Lane in Plymouth to the town of Clara City, located in Chippewa County. It will encompass a distance of 97 miles. It makes use of an abandoned railroad right-of-way, like many of the other DNR corridor trails.

In 1902, a man named W. L. Luce began a 1,000-mile trail service, which was to involve commerce in a large area between Minneapolis and Brookings, South Dakota. In 1913, the Luce Electric Short Line Railway was begun, but due to financial difficulties, the line was terminated in Gluek, a small town northwest of Clara City. Later, the line was purchased by the Chicago Northwestern Railroad. It continued to be financially disastrous and was totally abandoned on 1971.

The Luce Line Trail Association brought forth the trail concept, and with their efforts, Luce Line Trail became one of Minnesota's corridor trails in 1973. For ages before the railroad era, this route was a well-established pathway used by the Dakotah. The trail involves rolling hills forested with hardwoods, prairie lands, and countless creeks, rivers, and lakes.

When the Luce Line Trail is completed, it will have a main corridor trail and a parallel treadway. In the summer, the main trail will be used for hiking and biking; and the treadway will be used by equestrians. In the winter, the main trail will be used by snowmobilers, and the treadway will be used by skiers.

However, the trail segment from Vicksburg Lane in Plymouth to Stubbs Bay Road in Orono is to be used strictly for ski touring in the winter. It is a 9.6-km (6-mi) stretch that is groomed and double-tracked. In Plymouth, the trailhead is located at the junction of Vicksburg Lane and Birch Briar Trail. This is between County Roads 6 and 15 (Waymouth Road). Parking and a rest area are available at this point. Another rest area is situated en route at the trail's intersection with Willow Drive in Orono/Long Lake. The terminus of the ski trail at Stubbs Bay Road in Orono is very close to the Morris T. Baker Park Reserve of the Hennepin County Park Reserve District.

Please note: Luce Line Trail is completed as far as the town of Winsted, in McLeod County. Skiers should know that from the Stubbs Bay Road, they will be using the parallel treadway and snowmobiles will be using the main corridor trail.

For further information, contact

Minnesota Department of Natural Resources, Trails and Waterways Unit, Box 52 Centennial Building, St. Paul, MN 55155. 612-296-6699

See also Hennepin County Park Preserve, Morris T. Baker Park Reserve, page 315.

Minneapolis
Park and Recreation Board

Within the Minneapolis parks, there are approximately 60.2 km (37.6 mi) of designated walking paths and 50.4 km (31.5 mi) of designated hiking/biking paths. The eight-foot wide bituminous paths were designated for two-way travel. Exceptions are at Lake of the Isles, Lake Calhoun, and Lake Harriet, where the paths are designed for one-way clockwise flow. The paths connecting Lake of the Isles with Lake Calhoun and Lake Calhoun with Lake Harriet are two-way. Cross-country skiing is possible all along the hike/bike trail system. It is especially popular along the lakes, creeks, the Mississippi River, and within the city's golf courses. These trails are excellent places for people within the metropolitan area to get winter exercise. Many people have their first ski touring experience on the city paths. There are no trailheads—simply enter the paths at a convenient point.

For example, you begin at Riverside Park on the West Bank of the Mississippi River, close to the Fairview Hospital/St. Mary's Hospital Complex, which is southeast of the Washington Avenue Bridge. The tour follows the river and West River Road to Minnehaha Park. You then either continue southward and ski the Minnehaha Trail to

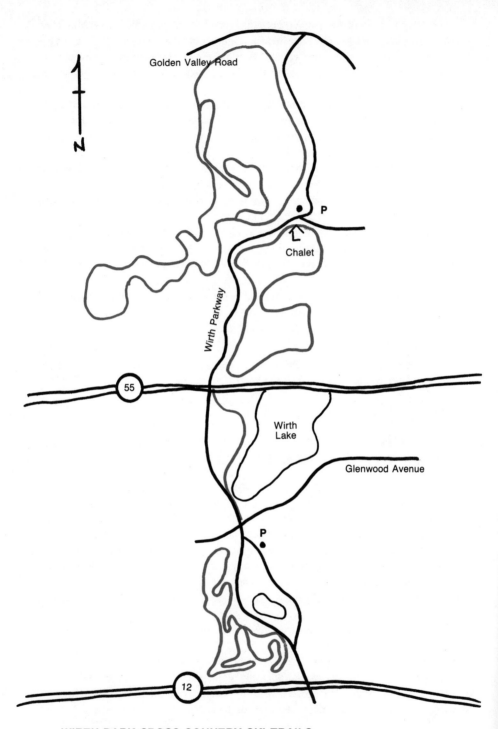

WIRTH PARK CROSS-COUNTRY SKI TRAILS

Fort Snelling State Park (*see* page 312) or turn westward and proceed along Minnehaha Creek to the paths that circle Lake Nokomis.

To the north of Lake Nokomis is the HIAWATHA GOLF COURSE. Trails at Hiawatha are for beginners and intermediates. They are marked, groomed, track-set, and 2.5 km (1.6 mi) of trails are illuminated for night skiing. Water, heated shelter, toilets, food concessions, and rental equipment are available when the facility is open: Monday and Wednesday, 6:00–10:00 p.m.; Saturday and Sunday, 9:00 a.m.–6:00 p.m.

From the Hiawatha/Nokomis area continue along Minnehaha Creek and Parkway. The trail begins to turn northward to Lake Harriet, where the path moves in a clockwise direction. After circling Lake Harriet, the two-way trail continues northward to Lake Calhoun; the pathway again becomes one-way, with a clockwise flow. Beyond Lake Calhoun, go to Lake of the Isles (again, a clockwise, one-way loop) where the path circles the lake. Or go westward to Cedar Lake. The trailway passes around the south and west side of Cedar Lake, moves northward, passes on the east side of Brownie Lake, crosses Wayzata Boulevard (Highway 12), and enters THEODORE WIRTH PARKWAY AND PARK. Ski past the west side of Birch Pond, and proceed to the Wirth Park Ski Trails.

This is an especially fine spot for metro ski touring. The Wirth Park system involves 20 km (12.5 mi) of trails for beginner, intermediate, and advanced skiers. They are marked, groomed, track-set, and 3.5 km (2.2 mi) of trails are illuminated for night skiing. The terrain, very hilly and heavily wooded is extremely scenic. You scarcely feel city pressures in this enjoyable setting. Wirth has a heated chalet where there are restrooms and food service. Rentals are also available at the chalet. Wirth Park is open Tuesday and Thursday, 6:00–10:00 p.m. and Saturday and Sunday, 9:00 a.m.–6:00 p.m.

You may cross Bassett Creek at the northeast end of Wirth Park and continue northward on Glenwood Parkway. After crossing Broadway (Highway 52), the path proceeds northward on Victory Memorial Drive, which turns eastward one block north of 44th Avenue North. The route veers southeast at its junction with Webber Parkway. At this point, you may follow Shingle Creek either northwest to Shingle Creek Park or southeast to North Mississippi Park. You can cross the river and do a bit of skiing on a designated pathway on the east bank. This is the end of the continuous Hike/Bike Trail System.

A very short distance to the east of the trail's terminus is COLUMBIA PARK AND GOLF COURSE, which has a developed ski touring area. There are 2.2 km (1.4 mi) of marked, groomed, and track-set trails with portions for skiers of all abilities. There is a heated chalet with restrooms, food service, and rentals. Columbia is open Wednesday, 6:00–10:00 p.m. and Saturday and Sunday 9:00 a.m.–6:00 p.m.

In addition, Park and Recreation ski touring is available at Meadowbrook Golf Course in St. Louis Park (Meadowbrook Road and Excelsior Avenue) and Francis A. Gross Golf Course, which is adjacent to Hillside Cemetery (Ridgeway Road and Broadway Road) near the Village of St. Anthony and Roseville.

Minneapolis Parks and Recreation also maintains a pathway on the East Bank of the Mississippi River with St. Paul Park and Recreation. It runs from the Washington Avenue Bridge, below the University of Minnesota, and follows East River Road to the boundary line between Minneapolis and St. Paul, just southeast of Shriners Hospital. It continues on Mississippi River Boulevard, maintained by St. Paul Parks and Recreation.

Beginner and intermediate lessons for people ages six and up are offered at Hiawatha, Wirth, and Columbia. They each have special schedules and should be contacted for further details. It should also be noted that all rental equipment at these locations is sold at the end of the season. Sales are held at each facility. Again, please check with the staff for further details.

For further information, contact

Minneapolis Park and Recreation Board, John Hanson, 310-4th Avenue South, Minneapolis, MN 55415. 612-348-2226

Columbia Park and Golf Course, 33rd Street and Central Avenue N.E., Minneapolis, MN 55418. 612-789-2627

Hiawatha Golf Course, 46th Street and Longfellow Avenue S., Minneapolis, MN 55406. 612-724-7715

Theodore Wirth Park, Chalet, Wirth Parkway and Plymouth Avenue N., Minneapolis, MN 55422. 612-522-4584

Minnehaha Trail
Minneapolis, Minnesota

8 km (5 mi) of trails

beginner, intermediate

This route connects Fort Snelling State Park with Minnehaha Park and the Hike/Bike Trail System of Minneapolis. It is a broad, well-marked, two-way trail beginning at Fort Snelling at the steamboat landing. It connects with the ski touring trails of the state park and takes off for Minnehaha Park at the juncture of Pike Island and Wood Duck Trails within the park.

It passes under the magnificent walls of the restored Fort and the nearby limestone cliffs. Most of the land is heavily forested, with few open areas. Skiers pass the wooden stairs that lead down to the river. This river bottom is the site where the U.S. Army, under Leavenworth, had a temporary encampment from 1819 until 1822, while the Fort was being constructed. They called it Camp Cold Water, after the great number of springs that flowed from the sides of the narrow valley into the river. The trail crosses the confluence of the Minnehaha Creek with the Mississippi River and continues into Minnehaha Park.

See also Fort Snelling State Park, page 312 and Minneapolis Park and Recreation Board, Minnehaha Park, page 329.

Minnesota Valley Trail
Jordan, Minnesota

Minnesota Valley Trail was established in 1969 to "provide a recreational travel route which provides access to or passage through areas which have significant scenic, historic, scientific, or recreational qualities." When the Trail is complete, it will follow the Minnesota River for nearly 75 miles, from Fort Snelling State Park to the city of LeSueur.

The Minnesota River Valley was shaped by Glacial River Warren nearly 10,000 years ago, producing a bottomland that is over 5 miles wide and 300 feet deep in places. The valley contains lowland features such as flood plain marshes, wet meadows, and lakes. The hills and bluffs that frame the valley support prairies as well as woodlands and provide countless vistas for the visitor. The variety of lush vegetation offers a rich wildlife habitat for feeding, breeding, nesting, growth, and wintering of many types of animal life.

American Indians called the Minnesota River Watapa Minnesota or the "river of cloud-tinted water." French fur traders named it Riviére St. Pierre when they arrived in the 1600s. It is an area full of the earliest documented history of Minnesota.

Because the Minnesota Valley Trail is a work-in-progress, at this time, 1984, you can ski only at the adjoining Carver Rapids and Lawrence State Waysides in Scott County.

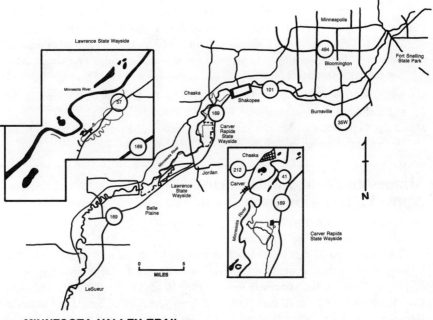

MINNESOTA VALLEY TRAIL

CARVER RAPIDS STATE WAYSIDE
MAZOMANI TRAIL
9.6 km (6 mi) of trails

intermediate

The trailhead is 6 miles south of the junction of Highways 41 and 169, near Chaska. A parking is located at this point, as well as a toilet and shelter. The Mazomani Trail is a single loop that passes through the Louisville Swamp Unit of the Minnesota Valley National Wildlife Refuge. It is located on the bluff above the river. Sand Creek passes through the area on its way to the river.

The main corridor trail for snowmobile use lies below the bluff in the bottomland and runs along the river bank. Food, lodging, and supplies are available in Chaska or Shakopee.

LAWRENCE STATE WAYSIDE
6.4 km (4 mi) of trails

beginner

The trailhead is 3 miles southwest of Jordan on County Road 57, which has its junction with Highway 169 between Jordan and Belle Plaine. Lawrence Wayside is situated on a flat flood plain that is forested with deciduous trees and interspersed with meadows.

The ski trails begin at the Ski Trail Center, just northeast of the Wayside office building. They wind through the woods and terminate at the river. There is also a short spur to the river which veers off the trail fairly close to the trailhead. A snowmobile trail runs along the river bank but does not conflict with the ski trails.

The Trail Center serves as a warming facility. Toilets, parking and maps are available here also. Food, lodging, and supplies are at hand in Jordan or Belle Plaine.

For further information, contact

Minnesota Valley Trail, Park Manager, 19825 Park Boulevard, Jordan, MN
612-492-6400

Minnesota Department of Natural Resources, Division of Parks and Recreation, Box 39 Centennial Building, St. Paul, MN 55155. 612-296-4776

Minnesota Zoological Gardens
Apple Valley, Minnesota
10 km (6.25 mi) of trails

beginner, intermediate, advanced

The Minnesota Zoo is located in Dakota County, 30 minutes south of the Twin Cities in Apple Valley. From Minneapolis, follow the new Cedar Avenue Expressway (Highway 77) across the Minnesota River to Cliff Road (County Road 32). Proceed on Cliff Road east for 2 miles, turn right on Johnny Cake Ridge Road, and follow the signs. From St. Paul, follow Highway 52 (Robert Street) south to Highway 3, continue south on 3 to Cliff Road. Proceed on Cliff Road for 4 miles, turn left on Johnny Cake Ridge Road, and follow the signs.

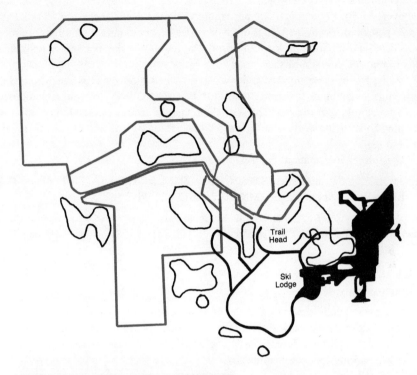

MINNESOTA ZOOLOGICAL GARDENS

The Minnesota Zoo's trails are well-marked, groomed, and track-set. They are always patrolled; first aid facilities are on site. They surely must be the state's most unusual system—you can see not just moose, but Bactrian camels, musk oxen, Siberian tigers, Asiatic wild horses, and red pandas out on the trails. The terrain is varied and involves beautiful hilly woodland, marshes, and gently rolling meadows. Trails for beginners are short and are situated on an easy terrain at the trailhead by the Ski Lodge. The system is mainly intermediate in difficulty, but there are two long, exciting trails for advanced skiers.

Ski rentals for people of all sizes are available at the Ski Lodge ($2.50 per hour, two hour minimum, last skis rented at 3 p.m.). They have accessories, such as waxes, for sale. Assistance is offered in waxing. Lessons are available for all ability levels, with free lessons given every Wednesday morning to those with rental equipment, half-price to those with their own. Register at least 48 hours in advance by calling 432-9010, Ski Lodge, extension 308.

The Lodge Cafe is open for food service on weekends and holidays and features pizza, hamburgers, snacks, and hot chocolate and cider.

The Zoo is open 9:30 a.m.–4:30 p.m. daily (closed Christmas). The North Country Ski Shop in the Ski Lodge is open 9:30 a.m.–4:30 p.m., weekends and holidays; 10:00 a.m.–4:30 p.m., weekdays. Skiers may not enter the trail system after 3:30 p.m., and all must be off the trails by 4:00 p.m. Admission is as follows: children under 6 are free; children 6–11, $1.00; youth 12–16, $1.50; adults 17 and over, $3.00; seniors 62 and over, $1.50. Parking is $1.00 per family vehicle. Buses are charged $5.00. There is a 20 percent discount for groups of 25 or more. Reservations are required for groups to receive their discount (at least 14 days). The fee to ride the monorail is additional. There is no fee charged to ski.

Skiing can be done any day of the week, provided snow cover is adequate and the wind chill temperature is warmer than -40° F. Call 432-9000 for trail conditions.

After skiing, tour the zoo. The staff claim that the facility has the largest apres-ski warming house in the world—the 1.5 acre Tropics Building—as well as five other major areas to visit.

For further information, contact

Minnesota Zoological Garden, Dave Carlson or Nancy Gibson, 12101 Johnny Cake Ridge Road, Apple Valley, MN 55124. 612-432-9010

See also Dakota County, Lebanon Hills Regional Park, page 309; City of Eagan, Blackhawk Park and Patrick Eagan City Park, page 311; Fort Snelling State Park, page 312.

City of Minnetonka
Minnesota

Five parks administered by the city of Minnetonka have maintained cross-country ski trails. All trails are marked, groomed, and track-set. They vary in length, terrain, difficulty, and facilities offered. The Minnesota State ski license is required at all parks. There are parking lots at all trailheads.

BIG WILLOW PARK
1.6 km (1 mi) of trails
beginner
Big Willow Park is located on Minnetonka Boulevard (County Road 5), 0.6 mile west of the intersection of Minnetonka Boulevard and County Road 73. The trail is set up in a one-way loop and encounters a small park bridge en route. There are no facilities for skiers at this park.

LONE LAKE PARK
4 km (2.5 mi) of trails
intermediate, advanced.
Lone Lake Park is located on Shady Oak Road (County Road 61), north of the intersection of Bren Road and Shady Oak Road, and south of Shady Oak Lake. There are two loops in the system; the 1.3-km (0.8-mi) loop is for intermediates, and the 2.7-km (1.7-mi) loop is for advanced skiers. This larger loop of the park is very hilly. The only facility offered is a picnic shelter. There are no toilets.

MEADOW PARK

2.9 km (1.8 mi) of trails

beginner

Meadow Park is located at the intersection of Oakland Avenue and Stone Road, southeast of the junction of Highway 12 and Interstate 494. The land is flat, wooded marshland. The trails are arranged in two interconnected one-way loops. There is a warming house and an outdoor privy at the park.

PURGATORY CREEK PARK

6.5 km (4 mi) of trails

beginner, intermediate, advanced

Purgatory Creek Park is located on the south side of Excelsior Boulevard (County Road 3), 0.2 mile east of the junction of Excelsior Boulevard and Highway 101. From the trailhead there is a large novice loop. Skiers will cross a small bridge almost immediately. A bit beyond this point, an intermediate trail veers off to the left. This trail leads ultimately to the advanced trails, at the south end of the system. All trails are one-way loops and entirely interconnected. The only facility at Purgatory Creek is a picnic shelter. There are no toilets.

VICTORIA-EVERGREEN PARK

1.3 km (0.8 mi) of trails

beginner

Victoria-Evergreen Park is located on Victoria Street, north of the intersection of Victoria Street and McKenzie Road. Accessibility to McKenzie Road is via Williston Road (County Road 145). The trail is arranged in one large loop. There are no facilities for skiers at this park.

For further information, contact

Minnetonka City Hall, Department of Parks and Recreation, 14600 Minnetonka Boulevard, Minnetonka, MN 55343. 612-933-2511, 612-938-1431 (Maintenance Department)

William O'Brien State Park
Marine-on-St. Croix, Minnesota

17.6 km (11 mi) of trails

beginner, intermediate, advanced

William O'Brien State park is located on the historic St. Croix River, in northeastern Washington County. Its entrance is on Highway 95, 2 miles north of Marine-on-St. Croix, Minnesota's oldest logging settlement—a small, picturesque town that is full of the past.

Ski touring and backpack camping are the park's winter specialties. The scenic bluffs on the river and the rolling, wooded terrain of the river valley make it a beautiful recreation area.

The predominant sandstone outcroppings in the park were developed millions of years ago by inland seas. The ancient glacial activity shaped the existing valley. Masses of glacial ice tore through the land, and in the meltdown and consequent retreat of the glaciers, the water that was released cut through the soft sandstone, forming the St. Croix River and its wide valley.

For centuries, the Dakotah and, after many bloody battles, the Ojibwe inhabited the valley. It was an area of great wealth for these people. By the 1600s, European trappers had entered the region; they both courted and competed with the Indians for furs. When the fur trade began to decline, the timber industry began to flourish, and people believed the virgin stands of white pine to be endless and the clearing of the land to represent progress. The aggressive, intensive logging virtually eliminated the white pine from most of Minnesota, certainly from this area. William O'Brien, a logger, bought much of the land from the Marine Lumber Company. In 1945, his daughter Alice O'Brien donated the initial acreage, which was to be enlarged by the State and developed into a state park in her father's memory. This gift to Minnesota was followed by another in 1958, when David Greenburg of St. Paul donated the 66-acre island in the St. Croix in his parents' memory. This isolated piece of land is a sanctuary for both wildlife and wildflowers.

The spring-fed artificial lake in the park is named in Alice O'Brien's honor. It is a pretty, idyllic recreation site and supports fish and wildlife. The diverse habitat and geography of the St. Croix River and its bottomland, the maple-basswood forest interspersed with conifers, the marshes and the lake, as well as the meadowland engender, support, and protect equally diverse wildlife.

The park is a wonderful place to ski tour. The winter scenery is beautiful, and the trails that meander through the forests over the rolling hills will surely satisfy the visitors' recreation needs. All trails are marked with a numbered marker system that is coordinated with the map of the park that is available to skiers. The trails are groomed and track-set. The route over to the Lake Alice area and river is for the novice. It is a gently rolling terrain with a pleasing mix of woods and open areas. The bulk of the trails are to the west and have something to offer every skier. The first half of the system is over a fairly easy landscape and is rated beginner and intermediate. From this point, the skiing becomes more difficult as the terrain grows more rugged. There are some demanding stretches on the outer limits of the trail network. Shelters are available at various places on the trails.

Winter camping is permitted at O'Brien. Visitors must backpack into the regular campsites where there are outdoor privies, fire rings, and picnic tables available. Campers must supply their own water. Snowmobiling is not allowed at the park.

Food, lodging, and supplies are available in Marine-on-St. Croix, Scandia, Taylors Falls, and Stillwater. Food and lodging are available in Copas.

For further information, contact

William O'Brien State Park, Park Manager, 16821 O'Brien Trail North, Marine-on-St. Croix, MN 55047. 612-433-2421

Minnesota Department of Natural Resources, Division of Parks and Recreation, Box 39 Centennial Building, St. Paul, MN 55155. 612-296-4776

See also Crabtree's Kitchen, page 308.

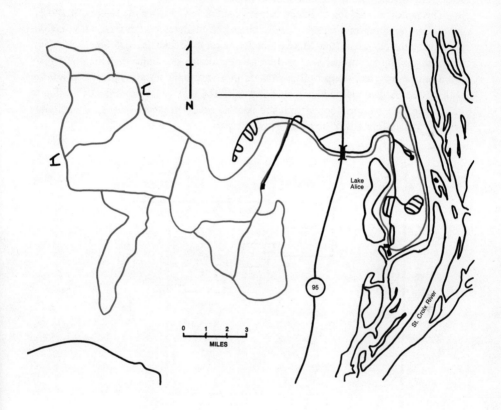

WILLIAM O'BRIEN STATE PARK

Ramsey County
St. Paul, Minnesota

BATTLE CREEK REGIONAL PARK
2.4 km (1.5 mi) of trails

advanced

Battle Regional Park is located in the southeast corner of St. Paul and the southern end of Maplewood. Entrance is on Winthrop Street, one block south of Upper Afton Road. A plowed parking lot is available at this point.

This park is named for an Indian battle waged in 1842, called the Battle of Kaposia. An Ojibwe band hid in the park's deep gullies before attacking the Dakotah village of Kaposia, situated across the Mississippi River on land that is now South St. Paul. Kaposia was the traditional seat of the line of Dakotah chieftains called Little Crow.

The one-way, two-loop trail is situated in a very hilly terrain, forested primarily with upland hardwoods such as maple and oak. The hills range from gently rolling to quite steep. The western loop affords the skier an excellent view of the St. Paul skyline and the Mississippi River flowing below the park.

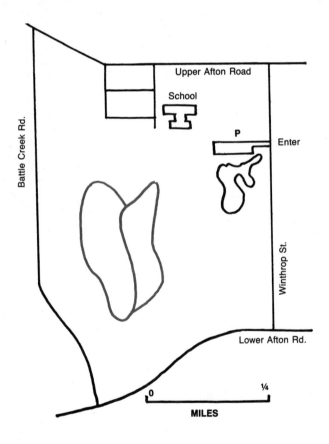

BATTLE CREEK REGIONAL PARK

A state ski license is required of trail users. The park is open from sunrise to one-half hour after sunset. No bushwhacking from the trails is allowed, nor is hiking, sledding, or snowshoeing on the trail. No snowmobiling is permitted in the park. No pets may run on the trails.

For further information, contact

Ramsey County Parks and Recreation Department, 1850 North White Bear Avenue, St. Paul, MN 55109. 612-777-1361

City of Richfield
Minnesota

Two cross-country ski trail systems are administered by the city of Richfield.

RICH ACRES
6.5 km (4.1 mi) of trails
beginner, intermediate

Rich Acres Ski Trails are at the Rich Acres Golf Course, located at 2201 East 66th Street. Take East 66th nearly to its eastern terminus at the intersection with Standish Avenue. This is a short distance east of Cedar Avenue.

There are three marked and groomed loops on the golf course, which begin at the clubhouse. **Cardinal Trail** runs 3 km (1.9 mi), is the longest and most difficult, and contains a variety of terrain. **Bluebird Trail** is 2.5 km (1.6 mi) long and winds over gently rolling hills. **Robin Trail** is 1 km long (0.6 mi) and traverses a level stretch of the course. It is a good route for beginners, seniors, or for those who wish to work on their form.

The clubhouse becomes a ski chalet in the winter. A variety of hot entrees appear on the menu. Full ski packages are available for rent: $3.00 for adults, $2.00 for youth or senior citizens (rates based on two hours of use). Lessons are available. Parking is at the clubhouse parking lot; water and toilets are in the clubhouse.

For further information, contact

City of Richfield, Rich Acres Golf Course, Rod Lidenberg, Manager, 6700 Portland Avenue, Richfield, MN 55423. 612-861-7144

WOOD LAKE NATURE INTERPRETIVE CENTER
4 km (2.5 mi) of trails
beginner

Wood Lake is a body of water located between Interstate 35W, West 66th Street, Lyndale Avenue, and West 73d Street. The main entrance to the Wood Lake Nature Interpretive Center, an environmental education facility, is at 735 Lake Shore Drive on the northeast side of the lake. A parking lot is at this location.

The terrain is flat, perfect for a beginner trail. There are two regularly groomed trails that begin at the entrance. One is quite short, running only 0.8 km (0.5 mi). The longer trail travels 3.2 km (2 mi). Both trails are located on a cattail marsh, winding in and out of the woods of the Nature Center. Restrooms are open Monday–Saturday, 8:30 a.m.–5:00 p.m.; Sunday, 12:00–5:00 p.m. Rentals are available Monday–Saturday, 8:30 a.m.–3:00 p.m.; Sunday, 12:00–3:00 p.m. Some instruction is offered.

For further information, contact

Wood Lake Nature Interpretive Center, 735 Lake Shore Drive, Richfield, MN 55423. 612-861-4507

City of Richfield, 6700 Portland Avenue, Richfield, MN 55423. 612-869-7521

Vinland National Center
Loretto, Minnesota

Vinland National Center is located on the north end of Lake Independence, 23 miles west of Minneapolis, near Loretto, Minnesota. On its 175-acre site, Vinland teaches health sports to people with disabilities. Cross-country skiing is a main activity during the winter months. Instruction of blind skiers, training of guides to ski with blind runners, and instruction in pulk skiing for mobility-impaired persons are offered at Vinland. In addition, Vinland sponsors the skiathon each year to raise funds, as Vinland is a nonprofit organization.

Trail development is currently underway.

For further information, contact

Vinland National Center, Lake Independence, Loretto, MN 55357. 612-479-3555 (Voice or TTY)

Washington County
Stillwater, Minnesota

Three parks administered by Washington County have trails that are marked and groomed especially for ski touring. They offer visitors the opportunity to increase their appreciation of the beauty of winters in Minnesota. The trails involve a great variety of landscape, including forests, meadows, and valleys. No fees are charged to use the trails, but skiers must display their Minnesota Ski Licenses. The hours at the park are 7:00 a.m. to a half hour after sunset. Moonlight skiing is available on certain nights throughout the winter. Parking is permitted only in designated lots. Fires are allowed in fireplaces and firegrates. Hiking, sledding, snowshoeing, and snowmobiling are not allowed on the trails, nor may pets run on the trails with skiers.

LAKE ELMO REGIONAL PARK RESERVE

19.2 km (12 mi) of trails

beginner, intermediate

The entrance to Lake Elmo Regional Park Reserve is on Keats Avenue, 1 mile north of the junction of Keats Avenue and 10th Street North (County Road 70). Its western boundary is Inwood Avenue North (County Road 13); the eastern boundary is Lake Elmo Avenue North (County Road 17). The park is 5 miles from St. Paul. Visitors may park in the designated lots on either side of the main thoroughfare within the park, which is a continuation of Keats Avenue.

The focal points in the park are Eagle Point Lake and Lake Elmo. The trail system is situated between the two lakes, and a new intermediate loop completely circles Eagle Lake. The land between the large lakes is dotted with several small lakes and ponds. The area is very scenic, with gently rolling hills and a mix of woods and open areas. The trails are arranged in several two-way loops that wind around all the lakes and ponds. Shelters are located in two areas out on the trails. Picnic tables, toilets, and trail maps are available at the park. A snowmobiling trail runs on the west and north boundary of the park but does not conflict with the ski trails.

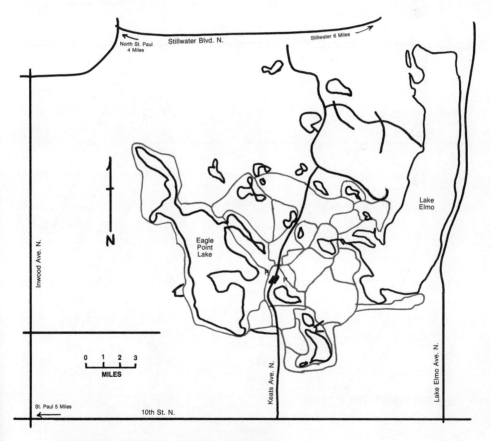

LAKE ELMO REGIONAL PARK RESERVE

PINE POINT SKI TRAILS

8 km (5 mi) of trails

beginner, intermediate, advanced

Pine Point Recreation Area is located at 11661 Myeron Road (County Road 61), across from the Washington County Public Works Department. It is a few miles east of the village of Withrow, between Lake Louise and Loon Lake. Myeron Road runs on the west side, 120th Street North on the north, and Norell Avenue (County Road 55) on the east. The park is to the northwest of Stillwater.

The park entrance is off Myeron Road, with a designated parking area a short distance up the park road. The trailhead is at this point. Much of the loop system is two-way. Most trails are rated beginner and intermediate. There are a couple of advanced stretches on the outer limites of the system. The trails move through heavily wooded areas between the two lakes and skirt portions of the shorelines. Some of the land is open meadowland, framed by the woods. The hills are gentle to fairly challenging. Picnic tables, barbeque grills, trail maps, and toilets are located in the area of the trailhead.

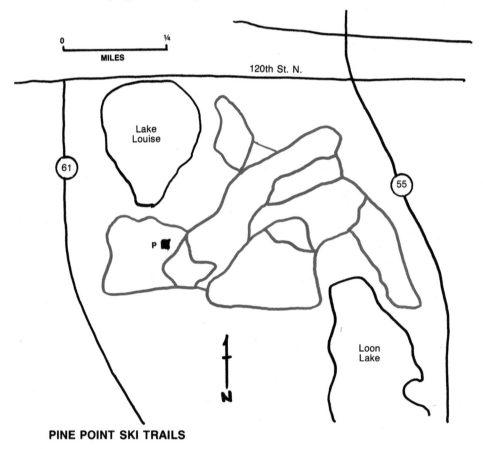

PINE POINT SKI TRAILS

SOUTH WASHINGTON REGIONAL PARK
8.5 km (5.3 mi) of trails
beginner, intermediate, advanced

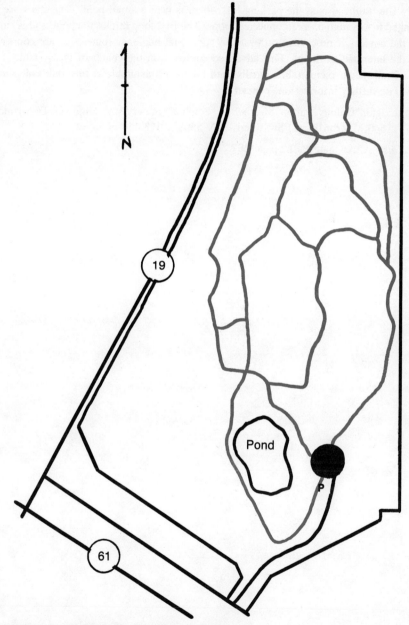

SOUTH WASHINGTON REGIONAL PARK

South Washington Regional Park is located at the northeast of the junction of Highway 61 with County Road 19A (Woodbury Drive) in Cottage Grove. The entrance is on 61, southeast of the junction. Drive a short distance into the park to the designated parking lot.

The trailhead is at the parking lot, which is near a small pond. The trails are arranged in a system of interconnected loops. The first loop circles the pond and is suited to the novice. It proceeds northward to additional beginner routes that are connected to the intermediate loops. One advanced stretch is in the center of the system.

Trail maps, picnic tables, grills, and toilets are available at the trailhead.

For further information, contact

Washington County Parks, Michael A. Polehna, Supervisor, Highway Department, 11660 Myeron Road, Stillwater, MN 55082. 612-439-6058

See also Afton State Park, page 297.

Wisconsin

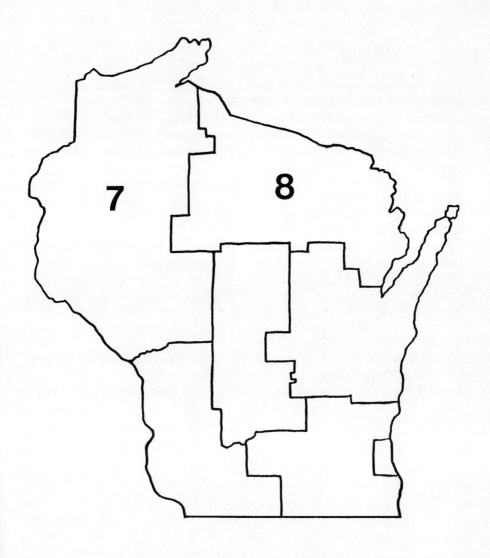

Introduction to Northern Wisconsin

We chose to describe the trails of Northern Wisconsin that are included in the Wisconsin Tourism Division's Indian Head Country and Northwoods regions.

Each trail listing has a map of Wisconsin in the upper right hand corner of the page. The Tourism region for that trail has been shaded on the map to provide a quick regional location reference, enabling readers to keep their bearings while reading through the information.

For an overall view of Wisconsin's regions, as well as Minnesota's and Michigan's, see the table of contents.

The addresses and telephone numbers for additional Wisconsin cross-country ski trail information are as follows:

State of Wisconsin, Department of Natural Resources, Box 7921, Madison, WI 53707

Tourism Regional Headquarters: Wisconsin Indian Head Country, Box 158, Altoona, WI 54720. 715-834-2781, 800-472-6654 (toll free Wisconsin), 800-826-6966 (toll free elsewhere)

Wisconsin Northwoods Council, Box 1167, Rhinelander, WI 54501. 715-369-2330

For a complete listing of the cross country ski trails in the entire State of Wisconsin, we highly recommend the following book:

Cross Country Skee, by John and Midge Schweitzer, Fall 1984 edition, $9.95 plus $1.50 for shipping and handling

Available from John Schweitzer, 638 South Mayflower Drive, Appleton, WI 54915,

REGION 7
INDIAN HEAD COUNTRY

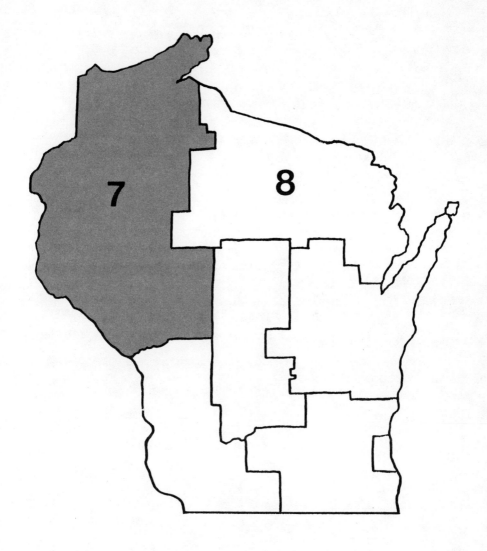

Arrowhead Lodge
Black River Falls, Wisconsin

5.6 km (3.5 mi) of trails

Arrowhead Lodge is located at the intersection of Interstate 94 and Highway 54, next to the city of Black River Falls.

The trails are marked and groomed and wind through flat, wooded terrain. No trail fee is charged. Black River State Forest Ski Trail is 12 miles east of Arrowhead Lodge and offers 38.4 km (12 mi) of trails.

The lodge has a restaurant, lounge, indoor pool, and 80 guest rooms.

For further information, contact

Arrowhead Lodge, c/o Steve Prigge, I-94 and Highway 54, Black River Falls, WI 54615. 715-284-9471

See also Black River State Forest, page 351.

Black River State Forest
Millston, Wisconsin

38.4 km (24 mi) of trails

beginner, intermediate, advanced

Black River State Forest is located 4 miles east of Millston on County Highway "O". Then drive north about 1 mile on Smrekar Road to Smrekar parking lot where there is a trail access. Or, drive 4 miles northeast of Millston on North Settlement Road to Wildcat parking lot, and enter the trails here. Millston in 12 miles southeast of Black River Falls on Interstate 94.

The trail has nine loops that are marked, groomed, and tracked through woodlands and rolling terrain. There are two rest areas along the trail with adirondack shelters, small fireplaces, and picnic tables. Scenic overlooks can be found on several trails. Overnight camping is recommended at these sites. Skiers are urged to follow the self-guided nature trail on the Central Trail. Narratives are available at the Smrekar parking lot. The entire cross-country area is closed to snowmobiling. Three trails, Ridge, Norway Pine, and Wildcat, are quite steep in places and are thus rated as advanced routes.

For further information, contact

Forest Superintendent, Black River State Forest, Route 4 Box 5, Black River Falls, WI 54615. 715-284-5301

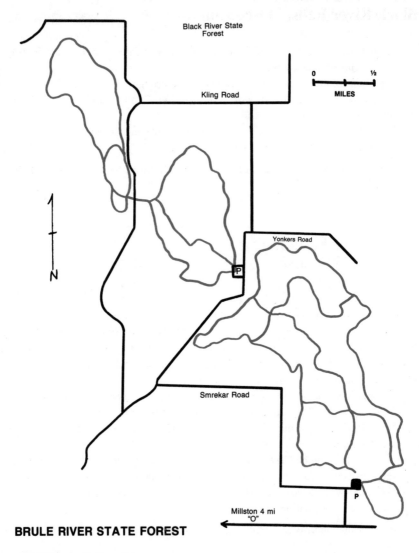

BRULE RIVER STATE FOREST

Brule River State Forest
Brule, Wisconsin

11.1 km (6.7 mi) of trails

beginner, intermediate

Brule River State Forest is located 0.5 mile west of Brule on Highway 2. Trails are marked and run through wooded terrain. Parking is available. You are likely to sight deer, eagles, snowy owls, osprey, and possibly bobcats while skiing along Brule River Trails.

For further information, contact

Brule River State Forest, Box 125, Brule, WI 54820. 715-372-4866

Brunet Island State Park
Cornell, Wisconsin

6.6 km (4 mi) of trails

Brunet Island State Forest is located 1 mile north of the town of Cornell, off Highway 64. The marked trail has two loops through wooded, gently rolling terrain. Parking is available at the headquarters building, which is adjacent to the beginning of the trail.

For further information, contact

Brunet Island State Park, Route 2, Cornell, WI 54732. 715-239-6888

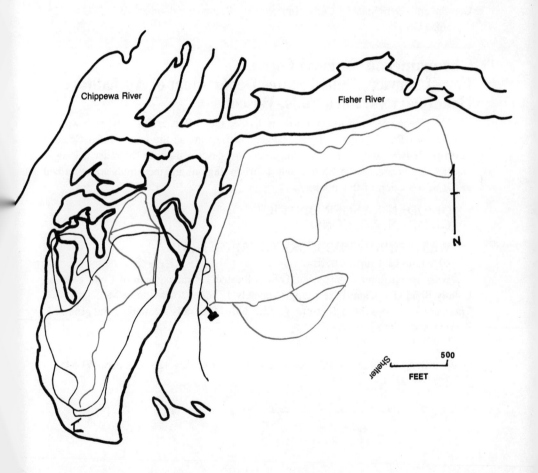

BRUNET ISLAND STATE PARK

Cedar Inn Resort
Bloomer, Wisconsin

22.4 km (14 mi) of trails

beginner, intermediate, advanced

Cedar Inn Resort is located 15 miles north of the city of Chippewa Falls. To reach the resort, go north on Highway 124, then west on Highway 64 to County Road AA. Turn north on AA, and travel to Hungry Run Road. Go east on Hungry Run Road to the Cedar Inn, following the signs.

The trails are mapped, marked and groomed. They are divided into three loops, one for each level of ability. A trail fee of $3.00 per day is charged; a season pass costs $15.00. Ski rentals, lunches, snacks, and a bar are available.

For further information, contact

Darwin and Deb Smack, Cedar Inn Resort, Route 1, Bloomer, WI 54724. 715-568-1174

Chequamegon National Forest
Forest Service, United States Department of Agriculture
Headquarters: Park Falls, Wisconsin

The Chequamegon National Forest is divided into 5 Ranger Districts, each with its own District Ranger Office. Three Ranger Districts are in the Indian Head Country Tourism Region, and their ski touring trails are described here. The other 2 Ranger Districts are located in the Northwoods Tourism Region, and their trails are described in the next section of this book.

GLIDDEN RANGER DISTRICT
GLIDDEN, WISCONSIN

WEST TORCH RIVER SKI TOURING TRAIL

20.1 km (12.4 mi) of trails

West Torch River Ski Touring Trail is located 1.5 miles south of Clam Lake on County Road GG. Clam Lake is approximately 17 miles southwest of Mellen on GG. There are four loops through gentle, wooded hills. The trails are marked and groomed. Parking and toilets are available.

For further information, contact

Glidden Ranger District, United States Forest Service, Box 126, Glidden, WI 54527. 715-246-2511

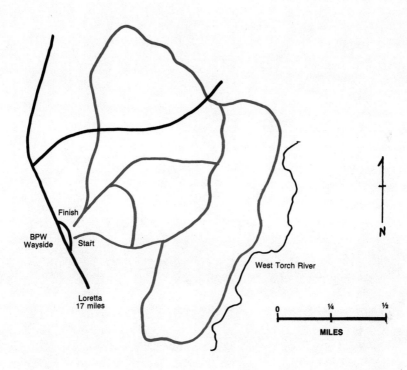

Finish

BPW
Wayside

Start

Loretta
17 miles

West Torch River

N

0   ¼   ½

MILES

Chequamegon National Forest

WEST TORCH RIVER SKI TOURING TRAILS

HAYWARD RANGER DISTRICT
HAYWARD, WISCONSIN

NAMEKAGON SKI TOURING TRAIL
9.7 km (6.2 mi) of trails

Namekagon Ski Touring Trail is located 17 miles northeast of Cable. Take County Road M to County Road D; take D to Forest Road 209; proceed on 209 to the trailhead, which is at the summer parking lot. Parking is available across the road. There are three loops through rolling and wooded hills. The trails are marked and groomed.

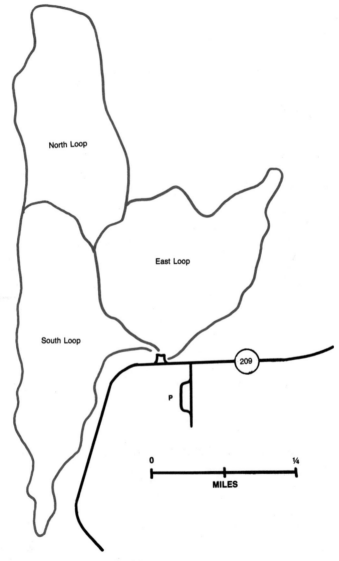

NAMEKAGON SKI TOURING TRAIL

ROCK LAKE SKI TOURING TRAIL
42.4 km (25.4 mi) of trails

beginner, intermediate, advanced

Rock Lake Ski Touring Trail is located 7.5 miles east of Cable on County Road M. Take M to the Lakewoods Resort. The terrain is rolling to hilly and wooded. The trails are marked and groomed. Parking is available.

For further information, contact

Hayward Ranger District, United States Forest Service, Box 232, Hayward, WI 54843. 715-634-4821

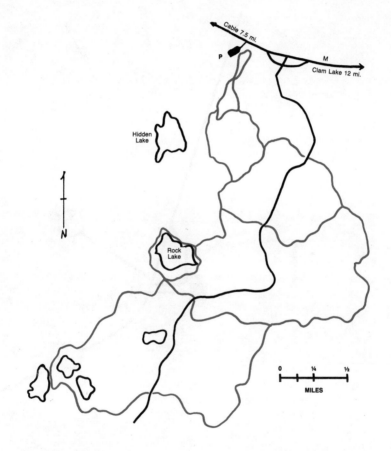

ROCK LAKE TRAIL

WASHBURN RANGER DISTRICT
WASHBURN, WISCONSIN

TEUTON SKI TOURING TRAIL
12.8 km (8 mi) of trails

Teuton Ski Touring Trail is located 8.5 miles northwest of Washburn on County Road C at Mt. Valhalla Winter Sports Area. Mt. Valhalla offers a scenic view of Lake Superior. The trails are marked, groomed, and track-set. There are three loops; loop C has a snowmobile trail running nearby. All trails begin and end at the chalet where toilets and water are available. Visitors should park at the chalet.

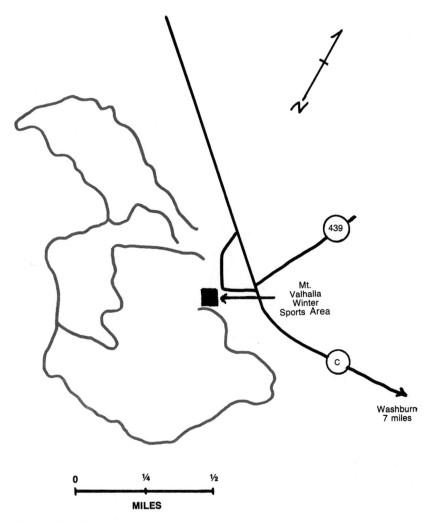

TEUTON SKI TRAIL

VALKYRIE SKI TOURING TRAIL
16.5 km (10.3 mi) of trails

Valkyrie Ski Touring Trail is also located at the Mt. Valhalla Winter Sports Area. This trail is marked, groomed, and track-set. It begins and ends at the chalet. There are three loops in the system. A snowmobile trail on the west side of the ski touring trails crosses the ski trails several times.

For further information or permission for group use of the chalet, contact

Washburn Ranger District, United States Forest Service, 103 East Bayfield, Washburn, WI 54891. 715-373-2667

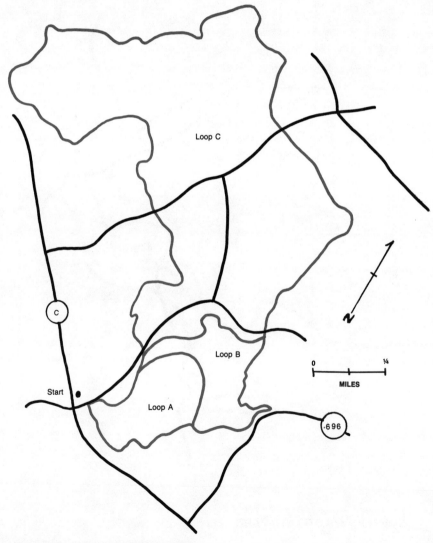

VALKYRIE SKI TOURING TRAIL

Copper Falls State Park
Mellen, Wisconsin

8.3 km (5 mi) of trails

Copper Falls State Park is located 3 miles northeast of Mellen. Take Highway 169 to County Road J at Loon Lake. Go north on J to the ski trails. The trails are marked, groomed, and track-set through wooded and rolling hills. Toilets and parking are available. A park sticker is required for entrance to the park.

For further information, contact

Copper Falls State Park, Box 438, Mellen, WI 54546. 715-274-5123

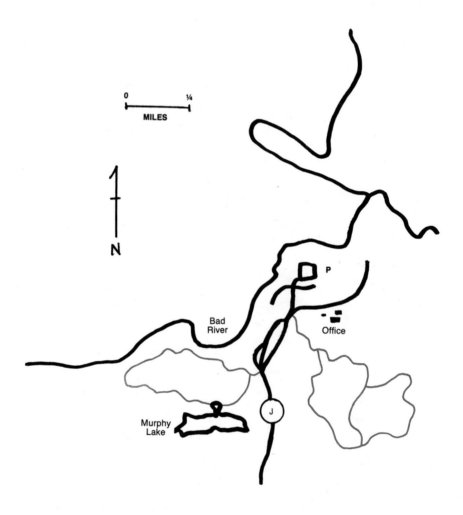

COPPER FALLS STATE PARK

Deepwood Ski Area
Wheeler, Wisconsin

2.9 km (1.8 mi) of trails

Deep Wood Ski Area is located 7 miles northeast of Wheeler on County Road N. Take Interstate 94 to Menomonie, and go north on Highway 25. Go through Wheeler, and travel 1 mile north to County Road N. Turn east, and travel 6 miles to Deep Wood.

The trails are groomed and tracked on Deep Wood's nine-hole golf course. A $3.50 trail fee is charged of visitors. A chalet at the facility offers food, water, and toilets. Park at the chalet. This is also an alpine facility.

For further information, contact

Deep Wood, Wheeler, WI 54772. 715-658-1394, 612-699-4540 (Twin Cities Office)

Dunn County
Menomonie, Wisconsin

There are two cross-country ski trails in Dunn County, both located in the Menomonie area.

HOFFMAN HILLS

13 km (8.1 mi) of trails

beginner, intermediate, advanced

Hoffman Hills State Recreation Area is located in Dunn County, near the town of Colfax. Take Interstate 94 east of Menomonie to the first interchange. Go north on County Road B for 3.5 miles, turn east, and travel 2 miles to Tainter Ch. Road. Go south 1.25 miles to Valley Road; then go east approximately 1.5 miles to the Hoffman Hills trailhead.

The trails are marked, groomed, and track-set. Water and toilets are available at the trailhead and at one location on the trail.

RED CEDAR STATE TRAIL

23.2 km (14.5 mi) of trails

The northern end of the Red Cedar State Trail is located in Menomonie, and the southern point is near the south side of the Chippewa River bridge crossing. The trail is an abandoned railroad right-of-way. The grades do not exceed 2 percent. As its name suggests, the trail follows the Red Cedar River through woodlands and unique rock formations. Snowmobiling is limited to the southern 2 miles of the trail from County Road Y, near the Dunnville Wildlife Area, to the south side of the Chippewa River. The trail is marked.

For further information on either trail, contact

Department of Natural Resources, Menomonie, WI 54751. 715-262-2631

Eau Claire County Parks Department
Eau Claire, Wisconsin

The three cross-country ski areas operated by Eau Claire County are Coon Fork Lake Ski Trail, Lowes Creek County Ski Trail, and Tower Ridge Ski Area. There are plans for expansion of the Lowes Creek Trail with the installation of a bridge that will span the creek and open up an additional 1.6–3.2 km (1–2 mi) of trails. Another planned expansion includes a 43.2-km (27-mi) loop trail in the heart of the Eau Claire County Forest.

COON FORK SKI TRAILS
5.3 km (3.3 mi) of trails
beginner, intermediate, advanced

Coon Fork Ski Trails are located 4 miles east of Augusta, which is 20 miles southeast of Eau Claire on Highway 12. Go east from Augusta on Highway 12 for 1 mile. Turn northeast on Coon Fork Road, and travel for 3 miles to the trail, south of Coon Fork Lake.

The trails are marked, groomed, and track-set regularly. Parking, trail maps, and a picnic shelter with grills are available.

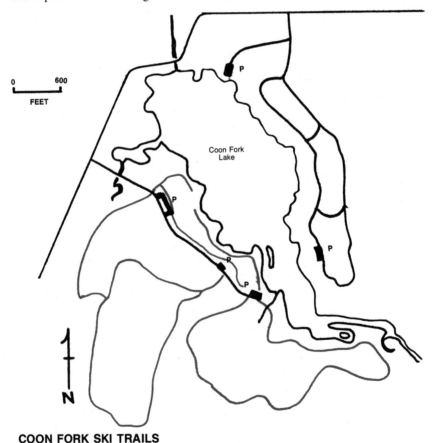

COON FORK SKI TRAILS

LOWES CREEK COUNTY PARK SKI TRAIL
3.7 km (2.3 mi) of trails

beginner, intermediate

Lowes Creek County Park Ski Trail is located on Lowes Creek Road, just to the south of Interstate 94, south of Eau Claire.

The trails are marked, groomed, and track-set regularly. Trails are one-way for skiing. Parking and a shelter are available for park visitors.

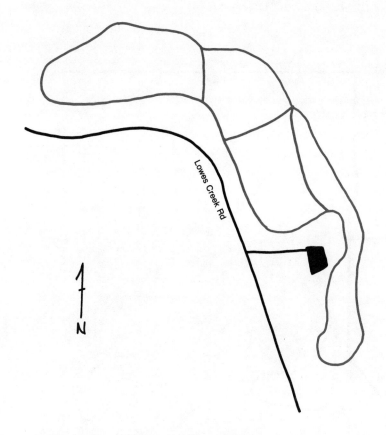

LOWES CREEK COUNTY PARK SKI TRAIL

TOWER RIDGE SKI AREA

17.9 km (11.2 mi) of trails

beginner, intermediate, advanced

Tower Ridge Ski Area is located 5 miles east of Eau Claire on County Road Q. Then turn south on 82nd Avenue, and go 0.75 mile to the ski area parking lot.

The trails are marked, groomed, and track-set regularly. Toilets are available at the trailhead.

For further information on any of these trails, contact

John Staszcuk, Forest and Parks Administrator, Eau Claire County, 721 Oxford Avenue, Eau Claire, WI 54701. 715-839-4738

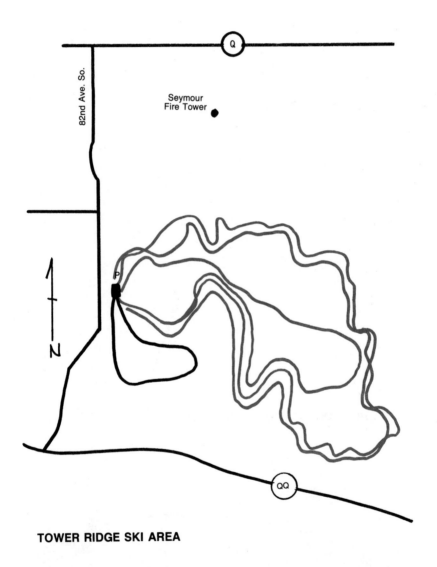

TOWER RIDGE SKI AREA

Flambeau River State Forest
Winter, Wisconsin

OXBO SKI TRAIL

12.8 km (8 mi) of trails

Oxbo Ski Trail of the Flambeau State Forest is located 16 miles west of Fifield (which is 4 miles south of Park Falls) on Highway 70.

The entire 87,000-acre Forest is open to cross-country skiing. The Oxbo Trail is marked, groomed, and tracked through the wooded hills of the Forest. There are five interconnected loops in the system. Parking is available at the trailhead.

For further information, contact

Superintendent, Flambeau River State Forest, Star Route, Winter, WI 54896. 715-332-5271

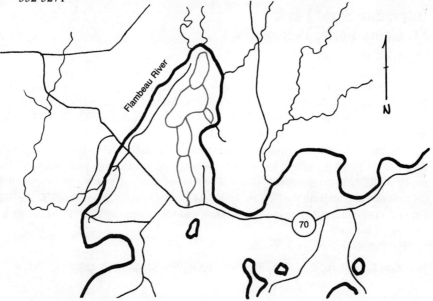

OXBO SKI TRAIL

Forest Point Resort
Gordon, Wisconsin

11.2 km (7 mi) of trails

Forest Point Resort is located 25 miles north of Hayward, off Highway 27 or 12 miles east of Gordon on County Road Y, off Highway 53. Follow the signs.

The trails are marked and traverse rolling hills and woods. Resort guests ski free; nonguests pay a $1.00 trail fee. Modern housekeeping cottages, food, and parking are available at the resort.

For further information, contact

Forest Point Resort, Dave and Andrea Babcock, Route 1 Box 156, Gordon, WI 54838. 715-376-2322

Game Unlimited Cross-Country Ski
Hudson, Wisconsin

25.6 km (16 mi) of trails

Game Unlimited Cross-Country Ski is located 5 miles northeast of Hudson on County Road E. Take County Road A east of Hudson through the town of Burkhardt to County Road E. Go east on E to the ski area parking lot.

The trail is marked, groomed, and tracked. A furnished lodge, snacks, ski equipment rentals ($4.00 per day), and overnight accommodations are available.

For further information, contact

Game Unlimited Cross-Country Ski, Route 2 Box 351, Hudson, WI 54016. 715-246-5475, 439-7282 (Twin Cities)

Interstate State Park
St. Croix Falls, Wisconsin

16 km (10 mi) of trails

beginner, advanced

Interstate State Park is located on the St. Croix River, just south of St. Croix Falls. This park is across the river from Taylors Falls, Minnesota. Take Highway 8 east of St. Croix Falls for 0.5 mile to Highway 35. Go 0.5 mile south on Highway 35 to the park entrance on the west side of the road.

The trails are marked, groomed, and track-set. A park sticker is required for entrance to the park. A parking lot, toilets, shelters, and the Ice Age Interpretive Center are all available to cross-country skiers. The view of the St. Croix River valley and its dalles is spectacular from the Skyline Trail—a 4.8-km (3-mi) loop on the bluff. The 3.5-km (2.2-m) Point Trail is on the river bottom and follows the bank of the St. Croix for one leg of the loop.

For further information, contact

Interstate State Park, Box 703, St. Croix Falls, WI 54024. 715-483-3747

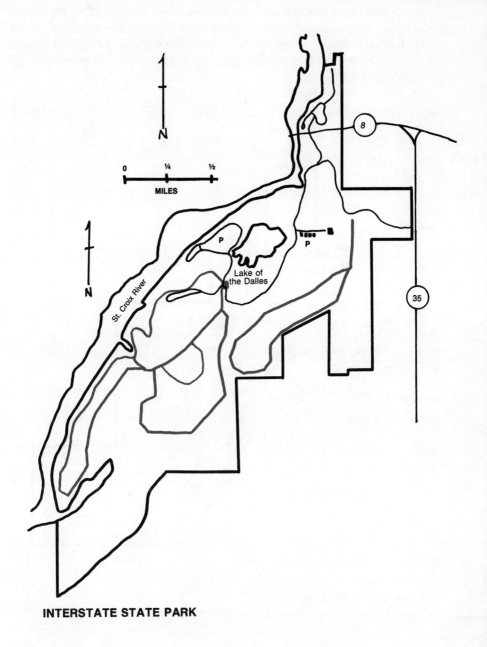

INTERSTATE STATE PARK

Lake Wissota State Park
Chippewa Falls, Wisconsin

18.4 km (11.5 mi) of trails

Lake Wissota State Park is located 5 miles northeast of Chippewa Falls on County Road "O".

The four ski trails, marked and groomed, travel through rolling and wooded hills. A park sticker is required for entrance to the park. Water, shelter, toilets, and parking are available at the park.

For further information, contact

Lake Wissota State Park, Route 8 Box 360, Chippewa Falls, WI 54729. 715-382-4574

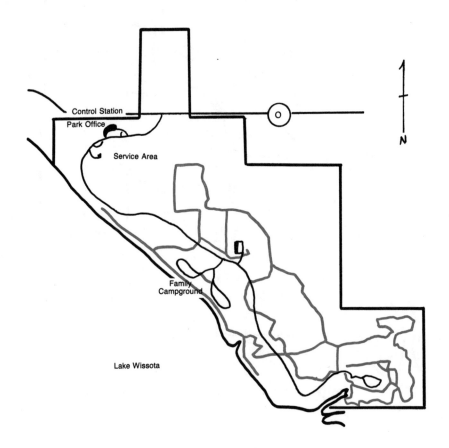

LAKE WISSOTA STATE PARK

Lost Land Lake Ski Trail
Hayward, Wisconsin

8.3 km (5.2 mi) of trails

Lost Land Lake Ski Trail is located 22 miles east of Hayward. Take Highway 77 east for 15 miles to Dow's Corner. Go north on Upper A for 5 miles to Empire Road. Take Empire Road straight ahead to Empire Lodge, or turn right after the mailboxes to Deer Path Lodge.

Lost Land Lake Trail leaves from both lodges and is marked, groomed, and tracked regularly. The trail is in the Chequamegon National Forest and traverses through hardwoods, pines, and swamps. There is no trail fee, but donations for grooming and tracking are appreciated.

Water, shelter, toilets, parking, food, and housekeeping cabins are available at both lodges.

For further information, contact

Patricia and Robert Kellogg, Deer Path Lodge, Route 7 T, Hayward, WI 54843. 715-462-3898

Empire Lodge, Route 7 T, Hayward, WI 54843. 715-462-3772

See also Chequamegon National Forest, page 354.

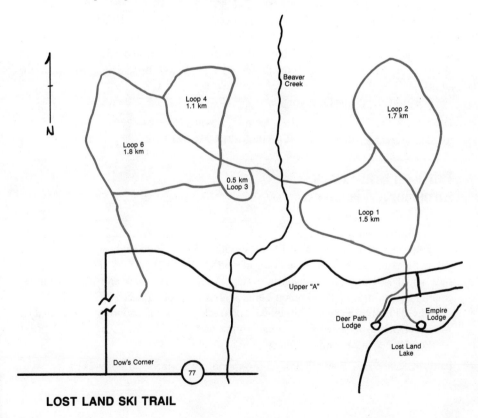

LOST LAND SKI TRAIL

Mt. Ashwabay
Bayfield, Wisconsin

30 km (18 mi) of trails

beginner, intermediate, advanced

Mt. Ashwabay is located 3 miles south of Bayfield on Highway 13.

The trails are marked, groomed, and double-tracked. Rentals, food, parking, water, and toilets are available at the chalet. Trail fees are as follows: those 11 and under, $2.00; 12–18, $3.00; and adults, $4.00. Rates are reduced on weekdays after Christmas vacation. Alpine skiing is also popular here.

For further information, contact

Gerald L. Carlson, Mt. Ashwabay, P.O. Box 928, Bayfield, WI 54814. 715-779-3227

Mount Hardscrabble
Rice Lake, Wisconsin

28.8 km (18 mi) of trails

beginner, intermediate, advanced

Mount Hardscrabble is located 7 miles east of Rice Lake on County Road C and 45 miles north of Eau Claire, off Highway 53.

The trails are marked, groomed, and double-tracked. The hills are gently rolling to very exciting. Rebuilding after last year's fire, Hardscrabble offers free parking, restaurant/bar, rental shop, waxing and warm-up building, and pro shop. The fees charged for trail use are: $2.00 for those under 12, $3.00 for students, and $4.00 for adults.

For further information, contact

Dann Kann, 516 West Allen, Rice Lake, WI 54868. 715-234-2707
Mt. Hardscrabble, Rice Lake, WI 54868. 715-234-3412

Pattison State Park
Superior, Wisconsin

8.8 km (5.5 mi) of trails

beginner, intermediate

Pattison State Park is located 12 miles south of Superior on Highway 35. The prime attraction of the park is Big Manitou Falls on the Black River. At 165 feet, it is the state's highest waterfall. Located upstream from the main falls and near the cross-country ski trails is Little Manitou Falls, with a drop of 31 feet.

The ski trails are marked, groomed, and tracked. Parking and toilets are available. A park sticker is required for entrance to the park.

For further information, contact

Pattison State Park, Route 2 Box 435, Superior, WI 54880. 715-399-2115

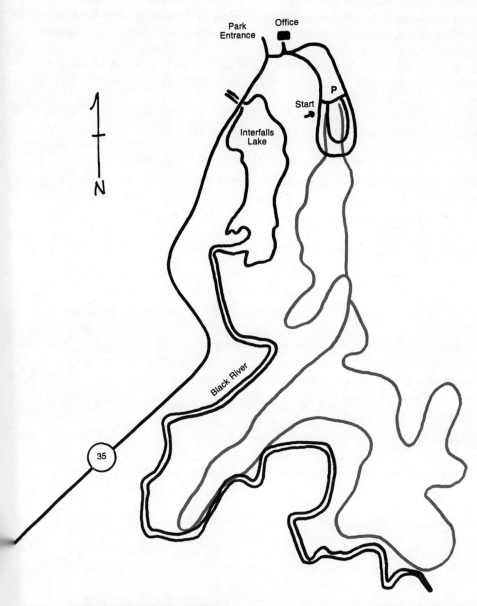

Park Entrance

Office

P

Start

Interfalls Lake

N

Black River

35

PATTISON STATE PARK

Perrot State Park
Trempealeau, Wisconsin

13.3 km (8 mi) of trails

Perrot State Park is located 2 miles northwest of Trempealeau, off Highway 93, at the confluence of the Mississippi and Trempealeau Rivers. The park is named after Nicolas Perrot, a seventeenth century French Canadian fur trader who wintered at this site in 1685.

The ski trails are marked. At the east end of the park, they run near a snowmobile trail. Parking and toilets are available. A park sticker is required for entrance to the facility.

For further information, contact

Perrot State Park, Trempealeau, WI 54661. 715-534-6409

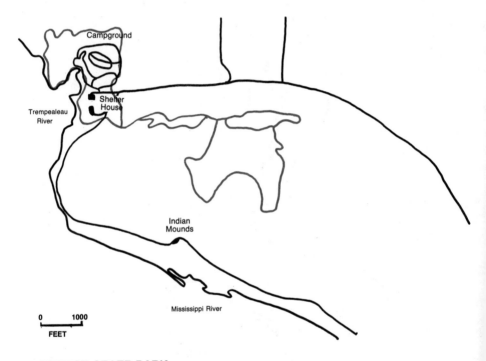

PERROT STATE PARK

St. Croix National Scenic Riverway/Trego Trail
National Park Service
Trego, Wisconsin

5.8 km (3.6 mi) of trails

beginner, intermediate, advanced

Trego Trail is located northwest of the town of Trego, on Trego Lake. Take Highway 53 north from Trego for 1 mile. Turn west on North Arm Road, and travel 2 miles to the parking lot.

This trail was designed by the National Park Service especially for beginner and intermediate skiers. The hills, except for the inner loop, are moderate and wipe-out areas are provided. The inner loop has steeper climbs and runs and is best-suited to the experienced skier. The trail system is groomed, tracked, and equipped with markers for ski touring. All trails are 1-way, except for the cut-across trail.

For further information, contact

St. Croix National Scenic Riverway, P.O. Box 63, Trego, WI 54888. 715-635-8346

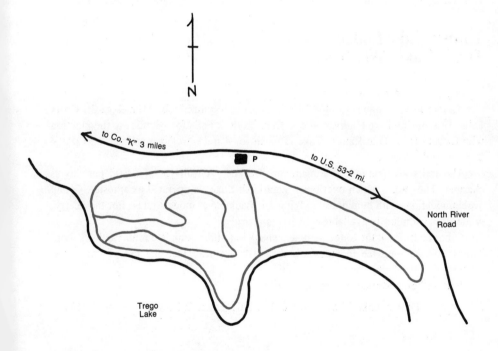

TREGO LAKE SKI TOURING TRAIL

Telemark Resort
Cable, Wisconsin

110 km (69.5 mi) of trails

beginner, intermediate, advanced

Telemark Resort is located 3 miles east of Cable on County Road M. Cable is on Highway 63, northeast of Hayward and Spooner.

The trails are marked, groomed, and track-set. There are warming cabins located throughout the system of trails. The American Birkebeiner, a 55-km World Loppet Race, is hosted by Telemark each February. Call the resort for dates and times. Fees to use the trails are as follows: on weekends, adults, $7.00; youth 13–17, $5.50; and children 12 and under, $3.50; on weekdays, adults, $5.50; youth, $4.00; and children, $2.50.

A 200-room lodge, complete with five restaurants, is available at the trailhead. Parking, alpine skiing, and over 200 pairs of rental skis are all available to visitors at Telemark.

For further information, contact

Tom La Blonde, Telemark Resort, Cable, WI 54821. 715-798-3811 (Ext. 7492)

Timber Lake Lodge
Turtle Lake, Wisconsin

24 km (15 mi) of trails

beginner, intermediate, advanced

Timber Lake Lodge is located 24 miles east of Taylors Falls, Minnesota/St. Croix Falls, Wisconsin. Take Highway 8 east from Taylors Falls for 18 miles to the junction with County Road D at Range. Take D north for 4 miles to County Road V. Take V 2 miles to the lodge.

The trails are marked, groomed, and tracked. A trail fee of $4.00 per day is charged. The lodge, which overlooks Sugarbush Lake, is operated as a hostel. Group accommodations with bunkhouse lodging are available at modest rates. For the hearty, wilderness camping is available—no fee is charged.

Other facilities at the lodge include a snack bar and a complete rental and ski shop. The $15.00 lodging fee includes a bed, a two day trail fee, and use of the sauna, kitchen, and the lounge with a fireplace.

For further information, contact

Jeff Byron, Timber Lake Lodge, Route 2, Turtle Lake, WI 54889. 715-986-2484

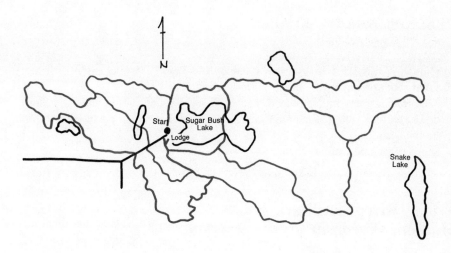

TIMBER LAKE LODGE

Trollhaugen
Dresser, Wisconsin

6.4 km (4 mi) of trails

Trollhaugen is located 1 mile east of Dresser, on County Road F. Dresser is 3 miles south of St. Croix Falls on Highway 35.

Nearly 6.4 km of trails exist at Trollhaugen, but, at the time of publication, the management had not decided if the trails would be groomed and tracked. Trollhaugen is primarily a downhill facility. At the chalet are a large restaurant and bar.

For further information, contact

Trollhaugen, Box 607, Dresser, WI 54009. 715-755-2955, 800-826-7166 (toll free)

Washburn County Trails
Spooner, Wisconsin

Two trail systems are maintained by Washburn County.

GULL LAKE
8 km (5 mi) of trails

Gull Lake Trail is located 1 mile northwest of Trego, which is 7 miles north of Spooner on Highways 53 and 63. Take Highway 53 north of Trego for 6 miles to County Road F. Travel on F for 1.5 miles east to the junction with Haynes Road. Go 2 miles north on Haynes Road to the trailhead.

Trails are marked and traverse wooded hills.

NORDIC WOODS SKI AREA

32 km (20 mi) of trails

beginner, intermediate, advanced

Nordic Woods Ski Area is located at Indian Hills Resort, 15 miles east of Spooner, 20 miles south of Hayward, and 25 miles north of Rice Lake.

The trails are marked, groomed, and track-set. Parking, water, toilets, shelter, food, and lodging with a sauna are available at Bobby Schmidt's Indian Hills Resort at the trailhead.

For further information, contact

Indian Hills Resort, Stone Lake, WI 54876. 715-865-2801

Willow River State Park
Hudson, Wisconsin

13.6 km (8.5 mi) of trails

beginner, intermediate, advanced

Willow River State park is located 5 miles northeast of Hudson on County Road A. There are seven trails through woods and hills. They are marked, groomed, and tracked. A park sticker is required for entrance to the park. Parking, water and toilets are available.

For further information, contact

Willow River State Park, Route 2, Hudson, WI 54016. 715-386-5931

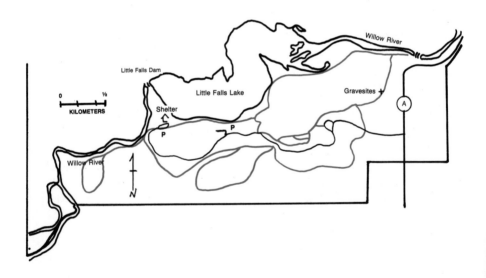

WILLOW RIVER STATE PARK

REGION 8
NORTHWOODS COUNCIL

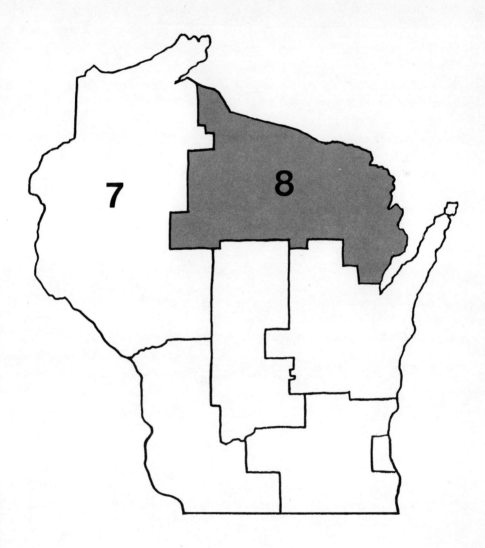

Afterglow Lake Resort
Phelps, Wisconsin

32 km (20 mi) of trails

Afterglow Lake Resort is located 2.5 miles northeast of the town of Phelps, which is 16 miles northeast of Eagle River on Highway 17. Take County Road E north of Phelps for 1 mile to Sugar Maple Road; turn east, and travel for 1 mile to the resort.

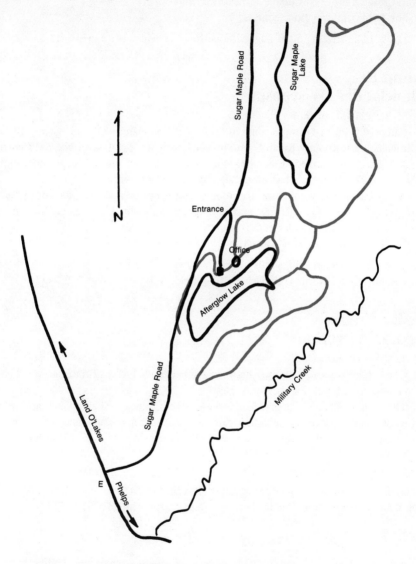

AFTERGLOW LAKE RESORT

The ski trails at Afterglow Resort are marked, groomed, and double-tracked through 240 acres of wooded land. For long-distance skiers, the Nicolet National Forest is adjacent to the property.

A whirlpool, sauna, ice skating rink, tobogganing and tubing hills, and snowmobiling trails are all available to the Afterglow guest. There are housekeeping cottages with fireplaces and gas or electric heat. Everything is provided except food and linens. Several restaurants are available in nearby Phelps.

For further information, contact

Afterglow Lake Resort, 5050 Sugar Maple Road, Phelps, WI 54554. 715-545-2560

Camp 10
Rhinelander, Wisconsin

35 km (21 mi) of trails

Camp 10 is located 6 miles south of the city of Rhinelander. Take Highway 17 out of Rhinelander to County Road A, and proceed on A for 2.5 miles to the Ski Center.

The trails are marked, groomed, and double track-set through gentle to rolling hills. A $3.50 trail fee is charged to support trail maintenance.

A day lodge with a cafeteria, bathrooms, and fireplace makes a pleasant place to start and finish a ski tour. Rentals and parking are available at the Center. Lodging is available at both Rhinelander and Tomahawk.

For further information, contact

Camp 10, Rhinelander, WI 54501. 715-362-6754
Gren Rudd, 19165 North Hills Drive, Brookfield, WI 53005. 414-782-0857

Cedar Trail
Saxon, Wisconsin

12.8 km (8 mi) of trails

Cedar Trail is located midway between Ashland and Hurley. Take Highway 2 east of Ashland for 21 miles to Highway 169.

The Frontier Bar and Campground is the western trailhead. The trail ends at Harbor Lights at Saxon Harbor on Lake Superior. It is a scenic and challenging trail, and is marked, groomed and tracked. Bars with food and parking are available at both ends of the trail.

For further information, contact

Frontier Bar and Campground, Star Route, Saxon, WI 54559.
Iron County Trails, Iron County Forestry Department, Hurley, WI 54532.

Chequamegon National Forest
Forest Service, United States Department of Agriculture
Headquarters: Park Falls, Wisconsin

Chequamegon National Forest is divided into five Ranger Districts, each with its own District Ranger Office. Two of the Ranger Districts are in the Northwoods Tourism Region, and their ski touring trails will be described here. The other 3 Ranger Districts are located in the Indian Head Country Tourism Region, and their trails are described in the previous section of this book.

PARK FALLS RANGER DISTRICT
PARK FALLS, WISCONSIN

NEWMAN SPRINGS SKI TOURING TRAIL
8.1 km (5.1 mi) of trails

beginner, intermediate

Newman Springs Ski Touring Trail is located 12 miles east of Park Falls on Highway 182.

The trails are marked, groomed, and track-set. Four loops travel through glaciated terrain, varying from upland ridges to lowland marshes. White birch, red pine, and northern hardwoods are in abundance. Many scenic vistas overlook the spring-fed ponds. A large parking area and toilets are at the trailhead. Winter camping is permitted.

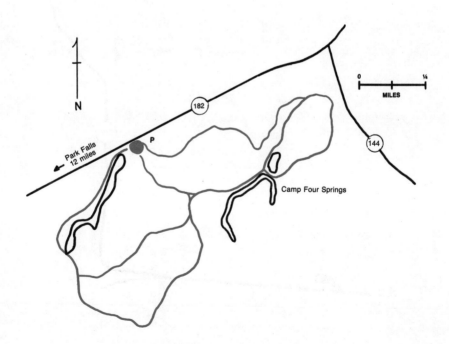

NEWMAN SPRINGS SKI TOURING TRAIL

WINTERGREEN SKI TRAIL
10.5 km (6.3 mi) of trails

beginner, intermediate

Wintergreen Ski Trial is located 5 miles east of Fifield on Highway 70. Fifield is 4 miles south of Park Falls.

The trail consists of three marked, groomed, and tracked loops that meander through rolling terrain. Forest types include red pine, lowland conifers, hardwoods, and aspen. Parking and toilets are available at the trailhead.

For further information, contact

Park Falls Ranger District, United States Forest Service, P.O. Box 280, Park Falls, WI 54552. 715-762-2461

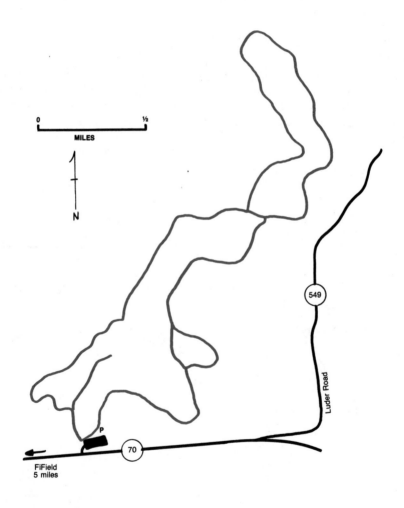

WINTERGREEN SKI TRAIL

MEDFORD RANGER DISTRICT
MEDFORD, WISCONSIN

SITZMARK SKI TRAIL
19.3 km (12 mi) of trails

Sitzmark Ski Trail is located 21 miles northeast of Medford. Take Highway 64 east of Medford for 18 miles to Forest Road 119. Go north on 119 for 4 miles to the Sitzmark trailhead.

There are four trails; the longest, Trail 321 measures 12.9 km and includes the Chequamegon Waters Flowage for a portion of the trail. The trails are marked, groomed, and tracked. Parking, water, and toilets are available at the trailhead.

For further information, contact

Medford Ranger District, United States Forest Service, Box 150, Medford, WI 54451.
715-748-4875

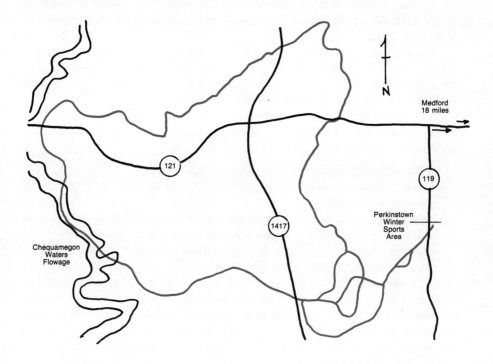

SITZMARK SKI TRAIL

Consolidated Papers' Cross Country Ski Trails Wisconsin

Recreational use of Consolidated Papers' forestland has been a popular activity in Wisconsin for many years. Cross-country skiing in the forests is a favorite recreation. Two trails are maintained in the Northwoods Tourism Region. Monico Trail is in southern Oneida County near Rhinelander, and Winchester Trail is in northwest Vilas County near the Michigan border.

The presence of wildlife is a special pleasure that these trails offer. It is not uncommon to see and encounter deer, ruffed grouse, snowshoe hares, and an occasional weasel, mink, or porcupine while skiing.

MONICO CROSS-COUNTRY SKI TRAIL

8 km (5 mi) of trails

beginner, intermediate

The trail is about 10 miles east of Rhinelander on Highway 8-47. Look for signs on the south side of the highway. Turn south on Leith Road, going just over a mile to the parking lot.

The trail basically follows old logging roads, providing varying degrees of length and difficulty. The western loop of the trail is 3.5 km of gently sloping terrain that challenges the beginning skier. The eastern loop is 2.4 km of considerably more difficult surface that qualifies as an intermediate trail.

Some of this area has been recently logged and presents visual evidence of a forest's ability to renew itself. Red pine plantations, mixed hardwoods, white pine, and aspen combine for a picturesque tour.

WINCHESTER CROSS-COUNTRY SKI TRAIL

12 km (7.5 mi) of trails

beginner, intermediate

The trail is about 4 miles north of Manitowish Waters on Highway W. Turn east at the junction of Highway J, going only a short distance to the parking lot.

Although much of the trail can be handled by a beginning skier, this tour also offers a variety of challenges and enjoyment for more accomplished skiers. The outside perimeter is approximately 6.4 km of gently rolling forestland that offers a few good hills. Trail spurs within the system are also on moderate terrain, although the extreme western area contains steeper slopes. Several muskeg swamps and small lakes are scattered throughout the system. The trails pass and cross a number of beaver ponds. A birch and maple forest dominates the area, with pine and oak intermixed.

For further information, contact

Consolidated Papers, Inc., c/o James Suski, Public Affairs Department, P.O. Box 50, Wisconsin Rapids, WI 54494. 715-422-3789

Eagle River Nordic Center
Eagle River, Wisconsin

55 km (33 mi) of trails

Eagle River Nordic Center is located 8 miles east of Eagle River. Take Highway 70 from Eagle River to Fire Road 2178; travel on 2178 to Fire Road 2181. Proceed on 2181 to the Center.

The trails are marked, groomed, and double-tracked. A ski shop, rentals, instruction, lodging, pool and sauna, toilets, and parking are all available at the Center. Eagle River has a new earth-sheltered warming hut.

This facility is considered to be one of northern Wisconsin's premier cross-country centers.

For further information, contact

Eagle River Nordic Center, Box 936, Eagle River, WI 54521. 715-479-7285

Fay Lake Resort
Long Lake, Wisconsin

16 km (10 mi) of trails

beginner, intermediate, advanced

Fay Lake Resort is located 35 miles east of Eagle River. Take Highway 70 east of Eagle River for 30 miles to Highway 139. Travel south on 139 for 10 miles to the resort.

The trails are marked, groomed, and tracked weekly. Beginner trails are on relatively flat land. Water, toilets, food, and parking are available at the resort as are complete lodging facilities.

For further information, contact

Fay Lake Resort, Box 102, Long Lake, WI 54542. 715-674-3829

Gateway Lodge and Recreation Area
Land O'Lakes, Wisconsin

15.6 km (9.4 mi) of trails

beginner, intermediate, advanced

Gateway Lodge and Recreation Center is located at the intersection of Highway 45 and County Road B at Land O'Lakes.

The trails are marked, groomed, and tracked. The bulk of the system is intermediate in difficulty (9.4 km), with 4.9 km for beginners, and 1.3 km for advanced skiers. A trail fee is charged for non-guests.

Lodging, restaurant, rentals, pool and sauna, and parking are all available at the lodge.

For further information, contact

United Resorts, Inc., Gateway Lodge, Box 147, Land O'Lakes, WI 54540. 715-547-3321

Hintz's North Star Lodge
Star Lake, Wisconsin

22 km (13.2 mi) of trails

Hintz's North Star Lodge is located 14 miles northwest of Eagle River. Take County Road G northwest of Eagle River to County Road N; travel north on N to County Road K; proceed west on K to the lodge.

Fifteen km of the trails are groomed and tracked. A lodge with fireplace, toilets, water, rentals, and food are all available to skiers. There is no trail fee for lodge guests.

For further information, contact

Hintz's North Star Lodge, P.O. Box 2, Star Lake, WI 54561. 715-542-3600

Indian Shores Camping Resort
Woodruff, Wisconsin

5 km (3 mi) of trails

Indian Shores Camping Resort is located approximately 22 miles northeast of Rhinelander. From Woodruff, take Highway 47 for 4 miles to the resort.

The trails, marked, groomed, and tracked, are situated on a terrain that is quite hilly. Parking is available at the bar. Cottages, camping, and a restaurant with fireplace are available to guests. There are toilets at the restaurant.

For further information, contact

Dick or Janet Giebel, Indian Shores Camping Resort, Box 12, Woodruff, WI 54568. 715-356-5552

Lakewood Cross-Country Ski Club Trail System
Lakewood, Wisconsin

30 km (18 mi) of trails

beginner, intermediate, advanced

Lakewood Trail System is located 1 mile south of Lakewood on Highway 32. Lakewood is 80 miles northeast of Green Bay in the Nicolet National Forest.

The trail system was developed and is maintained by the Lakewood Cross-Country Ski Club. The trails are marked, groomed, double-tracked, and color-coded. The terrain is wooded with varying elevations. Ski rentals are available at Prospect Lodge. There are parking lots at eight locations along the trail.

For further information, contact

Lee Spletter, Box 222, Lakewood, WI 54138. 715-276-7222
Prospect Lodge, Star Route, Lakewood, WI 54138. 715-276-6479

Minocqua Winter Park and Nordic Center
Minocqua, Wisconsin

35 km (21 mi) of trails

beginner, intermediate, advanced

Mincoqua Winter Park and Nordic Center is located 6.5 miles west of Minocqua. Take Highway 70 west of Minocqua to Squirrel Lake Road. Go south for 4.5 miles on Squirrel Lake Road to Scotchman's Road. Continue on Scotchman's Road to Winter Park.

The marked trails are groomed and tracked daily by the Lakeland Touring Federation. This facility is one of the region's finest. In addition to the superb trail system, there are inner tube runs, tube rentals, ski instruction (including Telemark clinics), a heated chalet, with snack bar and ample parking. A daily trail fee of $3.00 is charged of skiers.

For further information, contact

Minocqua Winter Park and Nordic Center, Box 558, Minocqua, WI 54548. 715-356-3309

Moraine Springs Nordic Center
Presque Isle, Wisconsin

20 km (12 mi) of trails

beginner, intermediate, advanced

Moraine Springs Nordic Center is located on the Wisconsin/Michigan border, in northwest Vilas County. Take County Road W for 4 miles west of Presque Isle, and turn at the large yellow sign.

The five-looped trail is marked, groomed, and machine-tracked. It runs through a hilly, heavily wooded terrain. A trail fee is charged: $4.00 for adults, $2.00 for children 12 and under. Beginning instruction can be arranged.

There is a heated chalet on the premises with a fireplace, restrooms, and snack bar. Ski rentals are available. There is ample parking at the chalet. Accommodations may be found at several nearby resorts.

For further information, contact

Moraine Springs Nordic Center, Route 2 Box 167, Presque Isle, WI 54557. 715-686-2461

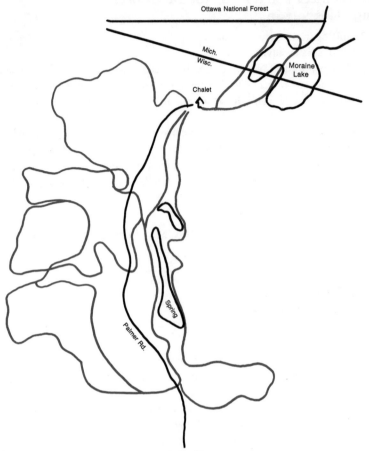

MORAINE SPRINGS NORDIC CENTER

Ottawa National Forest

Mich.
Wisc.

Moraine
Lake

Chalet

Spring

Palmer Rd.

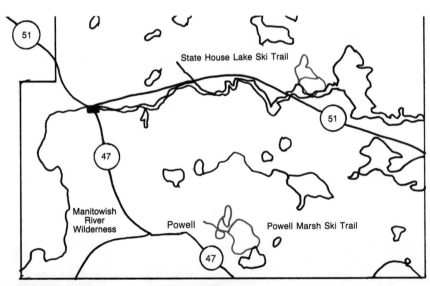

NORTHERN HIGHLAND STATE FOREST

51

State House Lake Ski Trail

51

47

Manitowish
River
Wilderness

Powell

Powell Marsh Ski Trail

47

Northern Highland State Forest
Woodruff, Wisconsin

There are nine trails in the Northern Highland State Forest that are designated as cross-country ski trails. The Forest is located in northern Wisconsin in Vilas County, near the Wisconsin/Michigan border. The trails are all marked and groomed. A park sticker is required for entrance. The following is a list of the trails. Map coordinates that facilitate trail location are given in brackets.

ESCANABA — 12 km (7.5 mi), toilets available, [H½, 4½]; SCHLECHT — 3.5 km (2.2 mi), [E½, 2½]; MCNAUGHTON — 11.4 km (7 mi), [G, 4]; MADELINE — 15.2 km (9.5 mi), [H, 7½]; RAVEN — 6.4 km (4 mi), toilets available, [F, 3½]; SHANNON — 11.2 km (7 mi) [K, 6½]; LUMBERJACK — 2.4 km (1.5 mi), [I½, 2½]; STATEHOUSE LAKE — 6.2 km (3.9 mi) [D½, 3]; POWELL MARSH — 11.2 km (7 mi), [D, 4].

For further information, contact

DNR Area Headquarters, Box 440, Woodruff, WI 54568. 715-356-5211

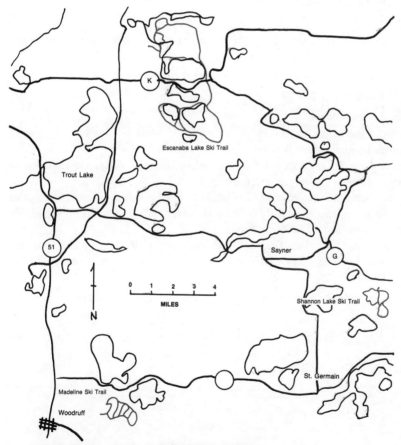

NORTHERN HIGHLAND STATE FOREST

Nicolet National Forest
Forest Service, United States Department of Agriculture
Headquarters: Rhinelander, Wisconson

In huge Nicolet National Forest are four designated ski touring trails. The following list is a brief sketch of these trails. For further details and trail conditions, contact the Forest Service at the address below.

ANVIL LAKE TRAIL — located 8 miles east of Eagle River on Highway 70. There are 18.2 km (11.4 mi) of marked and groomed trails.

ED'S LAKE TRAIL — located 10 miles southeast of Crandon, on County Road W. There are 8 km (5 mi) of marked, groomed, and track-set trails.

GIANT PINE TRAIL — located 11 miles southeast of Three Lakes. Take Highway 32 to Fire Road 2183; travel on 2183 to Fire Road 2414; proceed to the trailhead. There are 9.3 km (5.8 mi) of marked trails.

LAUTERMAN TRAIL — located 13 miles west of Florence. Take Highway 70 to Fire Road 2154, and proceed to the trailhead. There are 12.5 km (7.8 mi) of marked, groomed, and tracked trails.

For further information, contact

Nicolet National Forest, United States Forest Service, 68 South Stevens, Rhinelander, WI 54501. 715-362-3415

Olympia Sport Village
Upson, Wisconsin

45 km (27 mi) of trails

beginner, intermediate, advanced

Olympia Sport Village is located 5 miles south of Upson, which is midway between Mellen and Ironwood, Michigan on Highway 77.

The trails are marked, groomed, and tracked. The system is arranged in a series of loops, 3–5 km in length. A daily trail fee is charged of visitors: $3.00 for adults, $2.00 for children, and $7.00 for a family.

The main lodge has a bar, fireplace, and food service. Rentals are also available at this location. Lodging/skiing/meals packages are available, as are group packages.

For further information, contact

Olympia Sport Village, Lake O'Brien, Upson, WI 54565. 715-561-4427

Outdoor Expeditions
Crivitz, Wisconsin

10.4 km (6.5 mi) of trails

beginner, intermediate

Outdoor Expeditions is located 1 mile north of Crivitz, which is 50 miles north of Green Bay on Highway 141.

The trails are marked, groomed, and tracked. A trail fee of $1.00 is charged. The terrain is hilly to gently rolling. There is a restaurant at the trailhead, and lodging is available across the highway. Parking, toilets, and water are also available at the trailhead. Rental of a ski package costs $7.00 per day on weekends and $5.00 per day on weekdays.

For further information, contact

Paul Matty or Norm Lentz, Route 4 Box 357, Crivitz, WI 54114.

Palmquist's "The Farm"
Brantwood, Wisconsin

35 km (21 mi) of trails

"The Farm" is located 2.5 miles east of Brantwood, which is between Prentice and Tomahawk on Highway 8. Travel north from Highway 8 for 1 mile on River Road.

The trails are marked, groomed, and track-set regularly. The trail fee is $3.00 per day. Lodging, food, rentals, and a sauna are available for guests. Make a reservation for a sleigh ride! Weekend packages are available.

For further information, contact

Jim Palmquist, "The Farm," River Road, Brantwood, WI 54513. 715-564-2558

Paust's Woods Lake Resort
Crivitz, Wisconsin

50 km (30 mi) of trails

beginner, intermediate, advanced

Paust's Woods Lake Resort is located 17 miles northwest of Crivitz by way of County Road A and County Road X.

The trails are marked, groomed, and tracked. A trail fee of $1.50 is charged. Meals, parking, and toilets are available at the resort. The resort offers both the Housekeeping and modified American Plans on their accommodation schedule. Lodging packages are available.

For further information, contact

Paust's Woods Lake Resort, Crivitz, WI 54114. 715-757-3722

Pine-Aire Resort
Eagle River, Wisconsin

2 km (1.2 mi) of trails

beginner

Pine-Aire Resort is located north of Eagle River. Go north from town on Highway 45 for 2.5 miles. Turn east on Chain O'Lakes Road, and travel a short distance to the resort.

The trail is marked and tracked. There is no trail fee charged of visitors. Winter camping, cottages, store, lounge with fireplace, and ample parking are among the amenities at the resort.

For further information, contact

Pine-Aire Resort, 4443 Chain O'Lakes Road, Eagle River, WI 54521. 715-479-9208

Whitecap Mountain Nordics, Rossignol Touring Center Montreal, Wisconsin

50 km (30 mi) of trails

beginner, intermediate, advanced

Whitecap Mountain is located 3 miles north of Iron Belt on County Road E. Iron Belt is 4 miles southwest of Montreal on Highway 77.

The trails are marked, groomed, and double-tracked. The fee for trail use is $5.00 per day. The ski rental package is $10.00 per day. An alpine facility, lodging, sauna and whirlpool, ski instruction, and ample parking are all available for guests.

For further information, contact

Whitecap Mountain Nordics, Rossignol Touring Center, Montreal, WI 54550. 715-561-2227, 800-272-7000 (toll free)

Wild Wolf Inn
White Lake, Wisconsin

17.6 km (11 mi) of trails

beginner, intermediate, advanced

Wild Wolf Inn is located 25 miles east of Antigo. Go east from Antigo on Highway 64 to White Lake, then south on Highway 55 for 6.5 miles to the inn.

The trails in the Nicolet National Forest are marked, groomed, and track-set. No trail fee is charged. Meals are served daily at the Inn. Cottages, motel lodging, ski rentals, lessons by reservation, and ample parking are available to visitors.

For further information, contact

Wild Wolf Inn, Herb and Genie Buettner, Highway 55, White Lake, WI 54491. 715-882-8611

Michigan

9

INTRODUCTION TO MICHIGAN'S UPPER PENINSULA

We include 25 cross-country ski trails in the western half of the Upper Peninsula of Michigan because of their close proximity to Minnesota. Escanaba—on Lake Michigan and our farthest point east in the Upper Peninsula—is approximately 350 miles from St. Paul. Ironwood, at the western end of the Upper Peninsula, is only 225 miles from St. Paul.

- The Upper Peninsula offers some excellent skiing and breathtaking vistas on two of the Great Lakes.
- The Upper Peninsula boasts 1,100 miles of Great Lakes shoreline.
- There are almost four million acres of state and federal land in the Upper Peninsula.
- The Upper Peninsula has 4,300 inland lakes and 150 waterfalls.
- The western portion of the Upper Peninsula averages 165 inches of snowfall annually.

The cross-country ski trails in Michigan's State Forests are called Pathways. We have included trail information and maps for Pathways in the Upper Peninsula. In 1983 the Michigan Department of Natural Resources stated: "Funding for Michigan's State Forest Pathway Program has been cut from the state's budget. As a result, all maintenance on the Pathways listed here has been eliminated. You are advised to use extreme caution in the use of any of these state forest facilities."

In talking with the Department of Natural Resources District Managers in the summer of 1984, the prognosis seemed to be that funds for grooming and track-setting trails would be reinstated for the 1984–1985 ski season. They suggest that skiers call the appropriate DNR District office to check on the grooming and conditions before planning a trip to a Pathway. The offices, the areas served, and phone numbers are listed below.
Baraga for the Ironwood, Houghton, Copper Harbor area: 906-353-6651
Crystal Falls for the Iron River, Iron Mountain area: 906-875-6622
Escanaba for the Gladstone, Marquette area: 906-786-2351

There is also a toll free number for the Michigan Travel Bureau: 800-248-5700. For the latest seasonal information on skiing and snow conditions, call toll free: 800-248-5708.

We include only the trails west of a line from Marquette to Escanaba. The trails east of this region are fewer and farther between and farther from Minnesota. If you wish to receive information on trails in this eastern Upper Peninsula area, contact the DNR District Office in Newberry at 906-293-5131 or the Michigan Travel Bureau at 800-248-5700, toll free.

REGION 9
UPPER PENINSULA

Anderson Lake Pathway
Gwinn, Michigan

16.6 km (10.3 mi) of trails

beginner, intermediate, advanced

Anderson Lake Pathway is located south of Marquette, near the town of Gwinn. Take Highway 35 east of Gwinn to County Road 557. Turn south on 557 and travel to the Pathway parking lot.

The trail consists of three loops, one for each level of difficulty. Please refer to the introductory comments on the Michigan Region that describe the grooming of State Pathways.

For further information, contact

DNR District Office, Escanaba, MI 49829. 906-786-2351

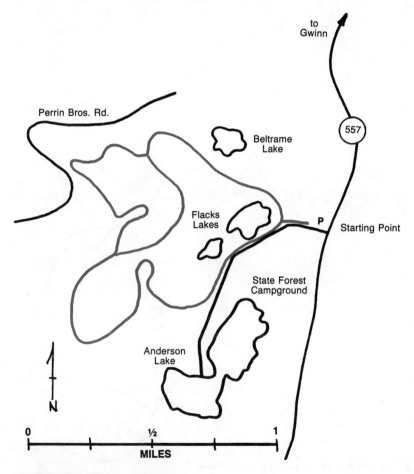

ANDERSON LAKE PATHWAY

Black River Pathway
Ishpeming, Michigan

24.8 km (15.5 mi) of trails

Black River Pathway is located 8 miles southwest of Ishpeming, near Marquette. Take County Road 581 for 8 miles to County Road CS. Turn west on CS and take the first right to the Pathway parking lot.

The trail consists of three loops through rolling terrain. Please refer to the introductory comments on the Michigan Region that describe the grooming of State Pathways.

For further information, contact

DNR District Office, Escanaba, MI 49829. 906-786-2351

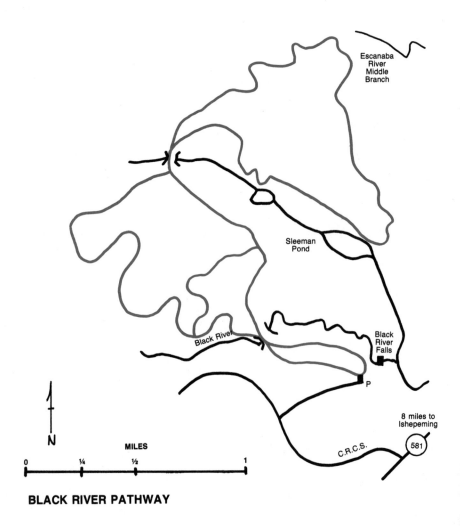

BLACK RIVER PATHWAY

Blueberry Ridge Pathway
Marquette, Michigan

15.3 km (10.2 mi) of trails

beginner, intermediate, advanced

Blueberry Ridge Pathway is located 6 miles south of Marquette on County Road 553. The Pathway parking lot is located at the southwest quadrant of the intersection of County Road 553 and County Road 480.

The trail consists of three loops, with snowmobile trails intertwined throughout the system. Please refer to the introductory comments on the Michigan Region that describe the grooming of State Pathways.

For further information, contact

DNR District Office, Escanaba, MI 49829. 906-786-2351

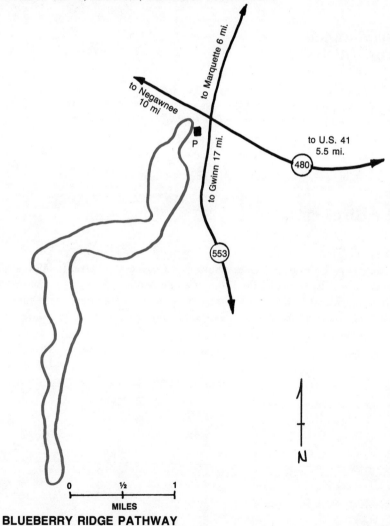

BLUEBERRY RIDGE PATHWAY

Bond Falls Outpost
Bruce Crossing, Michigan

22.4 km (14 mi) of trails

beginner, intermediate, advanced

Bond Falls Outpost is located 4 miles east of Paulding on Bond Falls Road. Paulding is 13 miles north of Watersmeet on Highway 45.

The marked, groomed, and track-set trails go around beautiful Bond Falls. Ski rentals ($6.00 per day), light lunches, and primitive campsites are available. There are two motels nearby, the Sunset Motel in Watersmeet (13 miles south) and the Tulppos is 13 miles north of the Outpost.

For further information, contact

Bond Falls Outpost, P.O. Box 37, Bruce Crossing, MI 49912. 906-827-3708

Briar Mountain
Vulcan, Michigan

8 km (5 mi) of trails

Briar Mountain is located 10 miles east of Iron Mountain, just off Highway 2 in Dickinson County.

There are two trails: 3 km long and 5 km long. This is also an alpine facility. A rental shop, lodge, cafeteria, chalet, and motel are on site.

For further information, contact

Briar Mountain, Box 503, Vulcan, MI 49892. 906-563-9293

Cedar River Pathway
Cedar River, Michigan

28 km (17.5 mi) of trails

Cedar River Pathway is located southwest of Escanaba. Travel 6 miles north of Cedar River on River Road to the Pathway parking lot.

The trail consists of four loops along the Cedar River. See the introductory comments on the Michigan Region that describe the grooming of State Pathways.

For further information, contact

DNR District Office, Escanaba, MI 49829. 906-786-2351

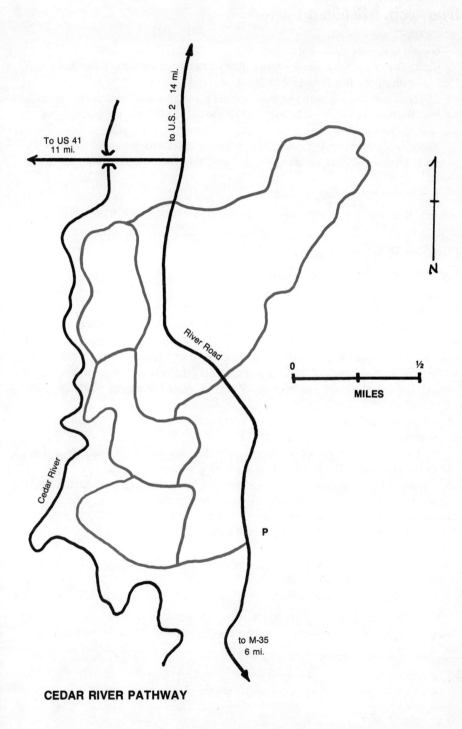

to U.S. 2   14 mi.

To US 41
11 mi.

N

River Road

Cedar River

0   ½

MILES

P

to M-35
6 mi.

CEDAR RIVER PATHWAY

Circle Hills Resort
Ironwood, Michigan

11 km (7 mi) of trails

beginner, intermediate

Circle Hills Resort is located 8 miles north of Bessemer on Black River Road, just 2 miles north of the Big Powderhorn Ski Area.

The trails are laid out with one base trail loop and five additional loops radiating out from the base trail. The $3.50 trail fee helps to cover the costs of marking, grooming, and track-setting the trail.

There is a complete ski rental shop. A motel, condominiums, and facilities for groups (with reservations) are also available at Circle Hills. Meals are served at the resort.

For further information, contact

Dorothy Nelmark, Circle Hills Resort, Ironwood, MI 49938. 906-932-3857

Copper Harbor Pathway
Copper Harbor, Michigan

25 km (15 mi) of trails

beginner, intermediate, advanced

The trailhead to the Copper Harbor Pathway is at the Fanny Hooe Resort in Keweenay County at the north end of Highway 41. The trails are arranged in a system of loops, with distances ranging from 1–8 km. The trail fee is by donation only. This fee helps support the costs of marking and grooming the network. A snowmobile trail parallels 3.4 km of the ski touring trails. Points of interest along the trail include the following:

- Fort Wilkins Historic Complex—a restored fort of the 1840s situated on Lake Superior.
- Clark Mine — an abandoned copper mine that was one of the first mines in the Upper Peninsula. The ruins include a smelting chimney.
- Estivant Pines Sanctuary — a nature preserve known for its gigantic pines. Some are over 500 years old, 100 feet tall, and 5 feet in diameter.

The trails are marked but not groomed. This area is owned by the Michigan Nature Association, and they intend a trip through the sanctuary on its 2.4-km trail to be a true wilderness experience.

Lodging and full accommodations are available at the Fanny Hooe Resort, located at the west end of Lake Fanny Hooe.

For further information, contact

DNR District Office, Baraga, MI 49908. 906-353-6651

Fanny Hooe Resort, Jeff Meilahn, Box 116, Copper Harbor, MI 49918. 906-289-4451

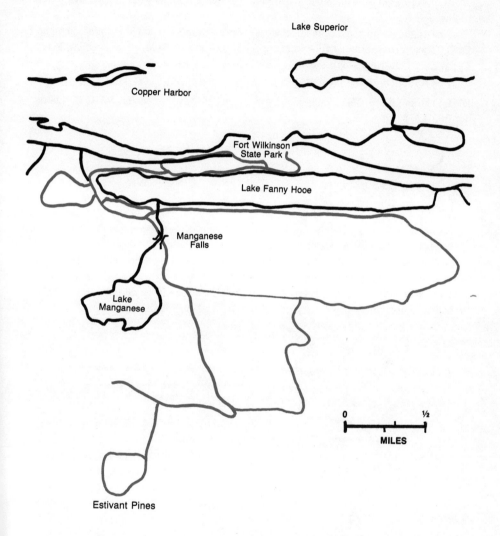

Lake Superior

Copper Harbor

Fort Wilkinson
State Park

Lake Fanny Hooe

Manganese
Falls

Lake
Manganese

Estivant Pines

0   ½
MILES

COPPER HARBOR PATHWAY

Days River Pathway
Gladstone, Michigan

35 km (21.9 mi) of trails

Days River Pathway is located in Delta County north of Escanaba and Gladstone on Highway 2. Go to Days River Road, and proceed 1.5 miles west to the Days River trailhead.

The trails are in the Escanaba State Forest and are maintained by the Michigan DNR. There are a series of four loops: 3.5 km, 6.4 km, 10.4 km, and 14.8 km long. The trail system runs along the west side of the Days River.

For further information, contact

DNR District Office, Mike Zuidema, Days River Pathway, Escanaba, MI 49829. 906-786-2351

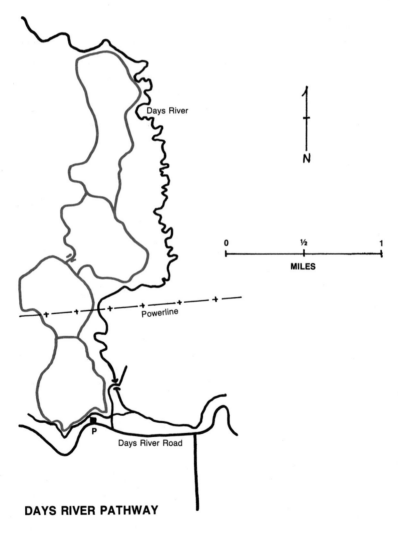

DAYS RIVER PATHWAY

Gladstone Ski Park
Gladstone, Michigan

4.8 km (3 mi) of trails

beginner

Gladstone Ski Park is located within the city limits of the town of Gladstone, which is north of Escanaba. This winter facility is at the Gladstone Sports Park.

Trails are marked and groomed and set with double tracks. The Sports Park chalet is the beginning and end of the single loop. The terrain is mostly flat. Restrooms and snacks are available. No fee is charged for trail use.

For further information, contact

Joe Dehlin, P.O. Box 32, Gladstone, MI 49837. 906-428-2311

GLADSTONE SKI PARK

Harlow Lake Pathway
Marquette, Michigan

9.6 km (6 mi) of trails

beginner, intermediate, advanced

Harlow Lake Pathway is located 8 miles northwest of Marquette on County Road 550. It is situated on the shore of Lake Superior.

The trail consists of three loops. Please refer to the introductory comments on the Michigan Region that describe the grooming of State Pathways.

For further information, contact

DNR District Office, Escanaba, MI 49829. 906-786-2351

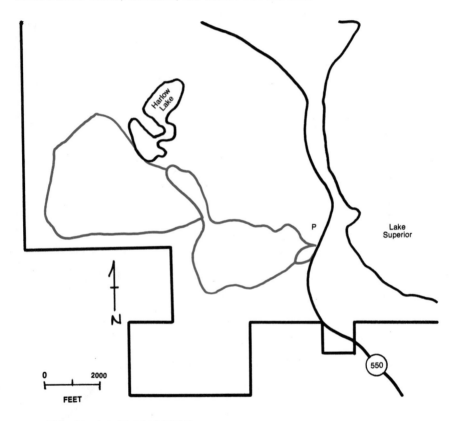

HARLOW LAKE PATHWAY

Indianhead Mountain Resort
Wakefield, Michigan

10 km (6.25 mi) of trails

beginner, intermediate, advanced

Indianhead Mountain Resort is located between Bessemer and Wakefield, 1.5 miles north of Highway 2, on Indianhead Road.

There are two marked, groomed and track-set trails: the West Trail for beginner and intermediate skiing, and the East Trail for intermediate and advanced skiing. No trail fee is charged. Services are available and include equipment rental, instruction, lodging, food service, sauna, pool, and alpine skiing.

For further information, contact

Indianhead Mountain Resort, Indianhead Road, Wakefield, MI 49968. 906-229-5181

Johnson's Nordic Ski Trails

21.6 km (13 mi) of trails

beginner, intermediate, advanced

Johnson's Nordic Ski Trails is located 1.5 miles east of Wakefield on Old Highway 2 (see map).

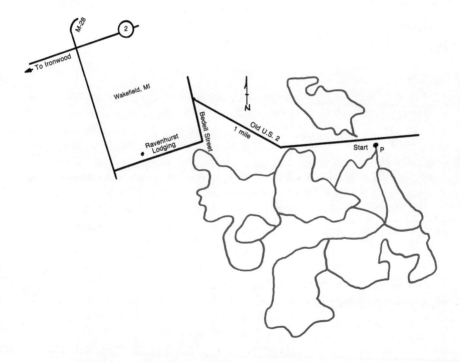

JOHNSON'S NORDIC SKI TRAILS

All trails are marked, groomed, and track-set. There are 3.2 km for beginners, 12.8 km for intermediates, and 5.6 km for advanced skiers. A trail fee is charged $3.00 for adults and $1.50 for children (under 13 years of age). Two parking lots and outdoor toilets are located at the trailhead. A warming cabin with snacks for skiers and ski equipment rental are available. These trails are widely regarded as the best-maintained system in the region.

For further information, contact

Johnson's Nordic Ski Trails, Route 1 Box 161, Wakefield, MI 49968. 906-224-4711

Lake Mary Plains Pathway
Crystal Falls, Michigan

15.5 km (9.6 mi) of trails

Lake Mary Plains Pathway is located between Crystal Falls and Sagota, 1 mile south of Highway 69. The trail consists of two loops; loop 1 is 5.5 km long and Loop 2 is 10 km long. Please refer to the introductory comments on the Michigan Region that describe the grooming of State Pathways.

For further information, contact

DNR District Office, Crystal Falls, MI 49920. 906-875-6622

Maple Lane Touring Farm
Skandia, Michigan

12 km (7.2 mi) of trails

beginner, intermediate

Maple Lane Touring Farm is located 15 miles south of Marquette, just off Highway 41. The trails are marked, groomed, and track-set three times weekly, weather permitting. The terrain is rolling, and the presence of a winding creek threading its way through the land necessitates two bridges for trail crossings. A trail fee of $1.00 per day is charged.

Rentals are available on a daily, weekly, or weekend basis. The warmup and rest area has picnic tables, fireplace, and snack bar.

For further information, contact

Ron Stenfors, Maple Lane Sports, 124 Kreiger Drive, Skandia, MI 49885. 906-942-7662

Mont Ripley
Houghton, Michigan

7.5 km (4.5 mi) of trails

Mont Ripley is located 0.5 mile east of the bridge on Highway 26 in Houghton-Hancock. The trails are groomed and maintained by Michigan Technological University. An alpine ski area with lodging is nearby.

For further information, contact

Michigan Technological University, Houghton, MI 49931. 906-487-2340

Mt. Zion
Ironwood, Michigan

3 km (1.8 mi) of trails

beginner

Mt. Zion is located on the campus of Gogebic Community College in Ironwood. The access road is Greenbush Street North.

Trails are marked, groomed daily, and set with a dual track. No trail fee is charged. There is a shelter at the Mt. Zion Ski Area at the trailhead. Rental equipment, parking, and snack bar are available.

For further information, contact

Randy Mezzano, Gogebic Community College, Ironwood, MI 49938. 906-932-3718

Pine Mountain
Iron Mountain, Michigan

10 km (6 mi) of trails

intermediate, advanced

Pine Mountain is located 2 miles from downtown Iron Mountain, on the Wisconsin-Michigan border.

Each of the two trails is 5 km; both are groomed and double track-set as needed. The intermediate trail is on open, gently rolling terrain. The advanced trail is on hilly and heavily wooded land. Both trails originate and terminate at Pine Mountain Lodge. No trail fee is charged. Services include: lodge, pool, rentals, alpine skiing, meals, and lounge. There is also a facility for hockey and ice skating.

For further information, contact

Pine Mountain Lodge, N3332 Pine Mountain Road, Iron Mountain, MI 49801. 906-774-2747

Porcupine Mountains Wilderness State Park
Ontonagon, Michigan

40 km (25 mi) of trails

beginner, intermediate, advanced

Porcupine Mountains Wilderness State Park is located 17 miles west of Ontonagon on Highway 107 on Lake Superior.

All trails are groomed and double track-set. They traverse mountain terrain and pass through stands of virgin timber. One trail leads to Union Spring, the largest above-ground spring in the Upper Peninsula. The East and West Vistas offer spectacular over-looks of Lake Superior from the tip of the Porkies.

No user fee is charged, but a vehicle permit of $2.00 per day is required. A snow-mobile trail runs along the north and east sides of the cross-country ski trail region. This is also an alpine ski area. A fully equipped chalet with a cafeteria is on site. Lodging is available 1–17 miles away.

For further information, contact

Porcupine Mountains Wilderness State Park, Route 2 Box 314, Ontonagon, MI 49953.
906-885-5798

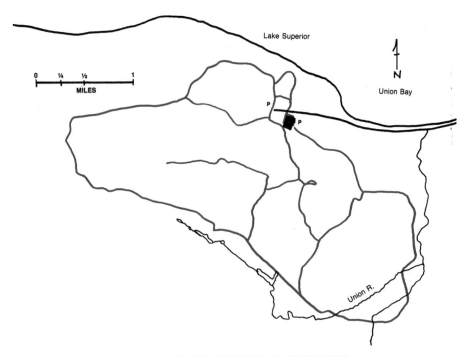

PORCUPINE MOUNTAINS WILDERNESS STATE PARK

Al Quaal Ski Area
Ishpeming, Michigan

24.5 km (14.7 mi) of trails

The Al Quaal Ski Area is located at Al Quaal Recreation Area in Marquette County, near Ishpeming, Michigan. There are four trails, ranging in length from 2.5 km, 5 km, and 7 km to 10 km. Rental equipment and instruction are available. These trails are sponsored and maintained by the Ishpeming Ski Club. Alpine skiing and lodging are nearby.

For further information, contact

Al Quaal Ski Area, City Building, Ishpeming, MI 49849. 906-486-6181, 906-486-6581

Ski Brule Ski Homestead
Iron River, Michigan

40 km (24 mi) of trails

beginner, intermediate

Ski Brule Ski Homestead is located 5 miles southwest of Iron River, between Highway 189 and Highway 73 along the Brule River.

Ski Brule and Ski Homestead are adjacent alpine ski areas, their ski trails run between the two facilities, around the mountain, and along the Brule River. The trails are marked, groomed, and track-set. Trail fees are $5.00 for a full day and $3.00 for a half day.

Restaurant, cafe, ski shop, restrooms, lodging (650 beds), and rentals are available. Parking is available at both facilities.

For further information, contact

Larry J. Hutchinson, 397 Brule Mountain Road, Iron River, MI 49935. 906-265-4957

Snowcrest
Bessemer, Michigan

28 km (16.8 mi) of trails

beginner, intermediate, advanced

Snowcrest is located 1.5 miles east of Bessemer (7 miles east of Ironwood) on Highway 2, and then north 1.5 miles on Prospect Road.

There are six looped trails with distances 1–10 km; they are marked, groomed, and track-set. There is no trail fee for Snowcrest Lodge guests. Others will be charged $4.00 for trail use. Rentals, parking, rest areas with toilets, snacks, and a ski shop are all available at Snowcrest.

Blackjack Ski Area, next door, offers additional lodging and alpine skiing.

For further information, contact

Paul Semmerling, Snowcrest, 609 East Longyear, Bessemer, MI 49911. 906-667-0719

Swedetown Trails
Calumet, Michigan

22.5 km (15 mi) of trails

beginner, intermediate, advanced

Swedetown Trails are located north of Houghton, by Calumet, off Osceola Road. There are five loops with several steep hills. Please refer to the introductory comments on the Michigan Region that describe the grooming of State Pathways.

For further information, contact

DNR District Office, Baraga, MI 49908. 906-353-6651

Copper Island Cross-Country Ski Club, P.O. Box 214, Calumet, MI 49913. 906-337-4520 (Daytime), 906-337-1965 (Evening)

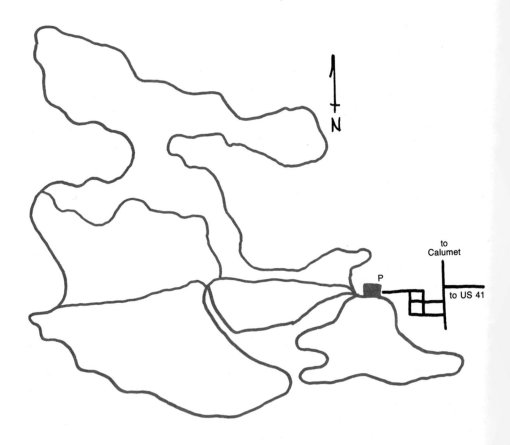

SWEDETOWN TRAILS

Sylvania Recreation Area
Watersmeet, Michigan

64 km (40 mi) of trails

beginner, intermediate

Sylvania Recreation Area is located on Highway 2, 1 mile west of Watersmeet, in Gogebic County. The trailhead is at the Sylvania Outfitters Ski Touring Center.

There are 32 km of marked and groomed trails and another 32 km of ungroomed trails in the 21,000 acre Sylvania Tract. These trails that are not machine-groomed because no motorized vehicles are allowed in this area. This will enable visitors to have a quiet and peaceful ski touring experience.

The terrain varies greatly—from gentle hills in the southern pine country near Land O'Lakes to the intermediate hills and turns of the northern part of the system near the Sylvania Outfitters.

Rentals, a ski shop, lounge, and ski instructions are available at Sylvania Outfitters. For further information, contact

Bob Zelinski, Sylvania Outfitters, West U.S. Highway 2, Watersmeet, MI 49969. 906-358-4766

Chamber of Commerce, Watersmeet, MI 49969.

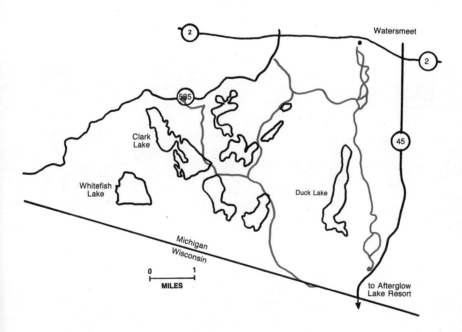

SYLVANIA RECREATION AREA

Wolverine Trail
Bessemer, Michigan

13.5 km (8.1 mi) of trails

beginner, intermediate, advanced

Wolverine Trail is located between Ironwood and Bessemer on Highway 2. Easy access points are at Trek and Trail (906-663-4791) where rentals, instruction, sales, and tour guides are available; and at Big Powderhorn (906-932-3100), a nearby alpine facility.

The trails are marked, groomed, and track-set by the Wolverine Nordic Ski Club.

For further information, contact

John C. Kusz, 919 Washington Street, Ironwood, MI 49938. 906-932-0150

SKI TRAIL REFERRALS

We invite you, our readers, to add to or amend the information on ski trails in Minnesota, Northern Wisconsin, and Michigan's Upper Peninsula. We shall include new entries and make corrections in a future edition. Mail all trail information to

Gary and Elizabeth Noren, Route One Box 94A, Taylors Falls, MN 55084. 612-583-2843

Include as much as possible of the following information:

- Trail name and address, directions to the trailhead
- A contact for trail information
- Administering agencies and their addresses
- Trail distances, number of loops and size of each loop
- Maps of the layout of the trail and geographical reference points, such as landmarks and towns as well as adjacent roads
- Trail descriptions: Are they marked, groomed, track-set (single, double)? With what regularity are the trails maintained? How are the trails rated for degree of difficulty (beginner, intermediate, advanced)? Is a fee charged for use of the trail? Are parking, toilets, shelter, water, and sites for camping available?
- Availability of accommodations: lodging, food, supplies, rental of ski equipment
- Other practical or intriguing points

INDEX

Afterglow Lake Resort, 379

Afton State Park, 297

Aitkin County, 79; Brown Lake Ski Touring Trail, 79; Long Lake Conservation Center, 80; No Achen Bicentennial Ski Trail, 80

Alimagnet Park. *See* City of Burnsville

Amen Lake Trails. *See* Itasca County

Anderson Lake Pathway, 397

Andes Tower Trails, 43

Angleworm Lake-Spring Creek Trail. *See* Kawishiwi Ranger District

Anoka County, 298; Bunker Hills County Park, 298

Anvil Lake Trail. *See* Nicolet National Forest

Arrowhead Lodge, 351

Ash River Falls Ski Trail. *See* Kabetogama State Forest

Arrowwood Inn and Resort, 43

Astrid Lake Trail. *See* La Croix Ranger District

Aurora Ranger District, 81; Bird Lake Ski Trail, 81

Baker Park Reserve (Morris T.). *See* Hennepin County Park Reserve District

Bakker Trail. *See* Cass County

Bally Creek Camp. *See* North Shore Mountains Ski Trail/Bear Track Outfitting

Banning State Park, 195

Battle Creek Regional Park. *See* Ramsey County

Baylor Park. *See* Carver County

Bearhead Lake State Park, 83

Bearskin Lodge Ski Touring Center. *See* Gunflint Ski-Thru Program

Bear Track Outfitting/Bally Creek Camp. *See* North Shore Mountains Ski Trail

Beaver Creek Valley State Park, 267

Becker County, 44; Detroit Lakes Community Ski Touring Trails, 44; Dunton Locks Ski Trails, 44; East Frazee Ski Trails, 45

Bemidji City Trail, 46

Best Western Cliff Dweller. *See* North Shore Mountains Ski Trail

Big Aspen Cross-Country Ski Trail. *See* Virginia Ranger District

Big Moose Trail. *See* La Croix Ranger District

Big Ridge Cross-Country Ski and Hiking Trail. *See* Itasca County

Big Willow Park. *See* City of Minnetonka

Birch Lake Plantation Trail. *See* Kawishiwi Ranger District

Bird Lake Ski Trail. *See* Aurora Ranger District

Black Bay Ski Trail. *See* Voyageurs National Park

Blackduck Ranger District, 46; Carter Lake Trail, 47; Meadow Lake Trail, 48; Webster Lake Trail, 49

Blackhawk City Park. *See* City of Eagan

Black River Pathway, 398

Black River State Forest, 351

Bloomington (City of), 300; Central Park-Nine Mile Creek Trail, 301; Girard Lake Park Trail, 300; Mound Springs Park Trail, 303; Mount Normandale Lake Park Trail, 304; West Bush Lake Park Trail, 304

Blueberry Hills Ski Trail, 84

Blueberry Ridge Pathway, 399

Bluefin Bay. *See* North Shore Mountains Ski Trail

Blue Hill Trail. *See* Sherburne National Wildlife Refuge

Blue Mounds State Park, 241

Bond Falls Outpost, 400

Borderland Land Lodge. *See* Gunflint Ski-Thru Program

Brackett's Crossing, 306

Breezy Point Resort, 196

Briar Mountain, 400

Brown Lake Ski Touring Trail. *See* Aitkin County

Brule River State Forest, 352

Brunet Island State Park, 353

Buffalo River State Park, 50

Bunker Hills County Park. *See* Anoka County

Bunyan Arboretum (Paul), 197

Burnsville (City of), 306; Alimagnet Park, 306; Civic Center Park, 306; Terrace Oaks Park, 307
BWCA, rules of use for winter travel, 35

Camden State Park, 242
Camp Mishawaka, 85
Camp Northland (YMCA), 86
Camp 10, 380
Cannon River Wilderness Area. See Rice County
Carley State Park (James A.), 268
Carter Lake Trail. See Blackduck Ranger District
Carver County, 307; Baylor Park, 307
Carver Park Reserve. See Hennepin County Park Reserve District
Carver Rapids/Mazomani Trail. See Minnesota Valley Trail
Cascade Lodge. See North Shore Mountains Ski Trail
Cascade River State Park. See North Shore Mountains Ski Trail
Cass County, 198; Bakker Trail, 198; Cut Lake Cross-Country Skiing Area, 201; Deep-Portage Conservation Reserve, 200; Goose Lake Recreation Area, 199; Howard Lake Trail, 199; Tower Trail, 198
Cass Lake Ranger District, 202
Cedar Inn Resort, 354
Cedar River Pathway, 400
Cedar Trail, 380
Central Park-Nine Mile Creek Trail. See City of Bloomington
Chateau Leveaux. See North Shore Mountains Ski Trail
Chequamegon National Forest/Indian Head Country, 354; Glidden Ranger District, 354; Hayward Ranger District, 356; Washburn Ranger District, 358
Chequamegon National Forest/Northwoods Council, 381; Medford Ranger District, 383; Park Falls Ranger District, 381
Chester Bowl. See City of Duluth
Chengwatana State Forest, 202; Redhorse Ski Touring Trail, 202
Chippewa National Forest/Region 1, 52; Blackduck Ranger District, 46
Chippewa National Forest/Region 2, 87; Deer River Ranger District, 91; Marcell Ranger District, 143
Chippewa National Forest/Region 3, 204; Cass Lake Ranger District, 202; Walker Ranger District, 229
Circle Hills Resort, 402

Civic Center Park. See City of Burnsville
Cleary Lake Regional Park. See Hennepin County Park Reserve District
Cobblestone Cabins. See North Shore Mountains Ski Trail
Collinwood County Park. See Wright County
Columbia Golf Course. See City of Minneapolis
Consolidated Papers' Ski Trails, 384; Monico Cross-Country Ski Trail, 384; Winchester Cross-Country Ski Trail, 384
Cooke State Park (Jay), 87
Coon Fork Ski Trail. See Eau Claire County
Coon Rapids Dam Regional Park. See Hennepin County Park Reserve District
Copper Falls State Park, 360
Copper Harbor Pathway, 402
County Road 50 Trail. See Walker Ranger District
Cowhorn Lake Trail. See Golden Anniversary State Forest
Coxey Pond Trails. See Kawishiwi Ranger District
Crabtree's Kitchen, 308
Cragun's Pine Beach Lodge, 223
Crosby-Manitou State Park (George H.), 89
Crow-Hassan Park Reserve. See Hennepin County Park Reserve District
Crow Wing State Park, 204
Cut Foot Sioux Trail. See Deer River Ranger District
Cut Lake Cross-Country Skiing Area. See Cass County

Dakota County, 308; Lebanon Hills Regional Park, 309; Spring Lake Park Reserve, 309
Days River Pathway, 404
Deep-Portage Conservation Reserve. See Cass County
Deepwood Ski Area, 361
Deer River Ranger District, 91; Cut Foot Sioux Trail, 91; Simpson Creek Trail, 92
Detroit Lakes Community Ski Touring Trails. See Becker County
Devil's Cascade. See La Croix Ranger District/Sioux-Hustler Trail
Dorer Memorial Hardwood State Forest (Richard J.), 270; Hay Creek Recreation Area, 270; Kruger Recreation Area, 272; Oak Ridge Recreation Area/Wet Bark Trail, 274; Snake Creek Recreation Area, 273
Douglas County Kensington Runestone County Park/Trollskøgen Ski Area, 52; Douglas State Trail, 37

Duluth (City of), 93; Chester Bowl, 93; Hartley, 93; Lester-Amity, 95; Lester Park Golf Course, 96; Magney-Snively, 96; Piedmont, 96

Dunn County, 361; Hoffman Hills, 361; Red Cedar State Trail, 361

Dunton Locks Ski Trail. *See* Becker County

Eagan (City of), 311; Blackhawk City Park, 311; Patrick Eagan City Park, 311

Eagle Mountain Ski Area, 206

Eagle River Nordic Center, 385

East Frazee Ski Trails. *See* Becker County

Eau Claire County, 362; Coon Fork Ski Trails, 362; Lowes Creek County Park Ski Trail, 363; Tower Ridge Ski Area, 364

Stanley Eddy Memorial Park Reserve. *See* Wright County

Ed's Lake Trail. *See* Nicolet National Forest

Elm Creek Park Reserve. *See* Hennepin County Park Reserve District

Ely (City of), 97; Hidden Valley Ski Area, 97

Escanaba Trail. *See* Northern Highland State Forest

Faribault (City of), 275; River Bend Nature Center, 275

Father Hennepin State Park, 207

Fay Lake Resort, 385

Fenstad's Resort. *See* North Shore Mountains Ski Trail

Fernberg Tower Area Trail. *See* Kawishiwi Ranger District

Finland State Forest, 97; Woodland Caribou Ski Trail, 97

Fitzharris/Pirates Cove Touring Court, 209

Five Dog Trail. *See* Grand Portage Lodge

Flambeau River State Forest, 365; Oxbo Ski Trail, 365

Flandrau State Park, 245

Flash Lake Trail. *See* Kawishiwi Ranger District

Flathorn-Gegoka Cross-Country Ski Trail. *See* Isabella Ranger District

Fond Du Lac State Forest, 99

Foothills State Forest, 209; Spider Lake Ski Touring Area, 209

Forest Point Resort, 365

Forestville State Park, 277

Fort Ridgely State Park, 247

Fort Snelling State Park, 312

French Rapids Cross-Country Ski Area, 211

Frontenac State Park, 278

Frontier Bar and Campground. *See* Cedar Trail

Game Unlimited Cross-Country Ski Trail, 366

Gateway Hungry Jack Lodge, 100

Gateway Lodge and Recreation Area, 385

Giant Pine Trail. *See* Nicolet National Forest

Giant's Ridge, 100

Girard Lake Park Trail. *See* City of Bloomington

Glacial Lake State Park, 53

Gladstone Ski Park, 405

Glidden Ranger District, 354; West Torch River Ski Touring Trail, 354

Golden Anniversary State Forest, 101; Cowhorn Lake Trail, 102; River Road Trail, 102

Golden Eagle Lodge, 102

Golden Gate to Fun Campground, 249

Gooseberry Falls State Park, 103

Goose Lake Recreation Area. *See* Cass County

Grand Mound Center, 105

Grand Portage Lodge, 107; Five Dog Trail, 110; Grand Portage Trail, 114; Loon Lake Ski Trail, 110; Moose Ridge Trail, 111; Mount Sophie Ski Trail, 112; North Lake Ski Trail, 113; Old Homestead Ski Trail, 113; Partridge Falls Ski Trail, 114; Portage Valley Ski Trail, 108; Sawmill Trail, 110; Section 11 Ski Trail, 111; Skyline Trail, 108; Sugar Bush Ski Trail, 109; Three Dog Trail, 110

Grand Portage Trail. *See* Grand Portage Lodge

Gull Harbor Condominiums. *See* North Shore Mountains Ski Trail

Gull Lake. *See* Washburn County

Gunflint Area Cross-Country Ski-Thru Program, 115; Bearskin Lodge Ski Touring Center, 116; Borderland Lodge, 119; Gunflint Lodge, 118; Young's Dog Sledding, 117

Gunflint Lodge. *See* Gunflint Ski-Thru Program

Gunflint Ranger District, 120; Pincushion Mountain Ski Trail, 120; Washington Memorial Pine Plantation Ski Trail (George), 121

Hanson Lake Area Trail. *See* Kawishiwi Ranger District

Harlow Lake Pathway, 406

Hartley. *See* City of Duluth

Hay Creek Recreation Area. *See* Dorer State Forest

Hayes Lake State Park, 55

Hayward Ranger District, 356; Namekagen Ski Touring Trail, 356; Rock Lake Ski Touring Trail, 357

Heartland State Trail, 37

Hennepin County Park Reserve District, 314; Baker Park Reserve (Morris T.), 315; Carver Park Reserve, 316; Cleary Lake Regional Park, 317; Coon Rapids Dam Regional Park,

318; Crow-Hassan Park Reserve, 319; Elm Creek Park Reserve, 321; Hyland Lake Park Reserve, 321; Lake Rebecca Park Reserve, 325; Medicine Lake Regional Park, 323; Murphy-Hanrehan Park Reserve, 326. North Hennepin Corridor Trail—*See* Coon Rapids Dam or Elm Creek

Hegman Lakes Trails. *See* Kawishiwi Ranger District

Herriman Lake Trail. *See* La Croix Ranger District

Heston's Country Store and Cabins, 122

Hiawatha Golf Course. *See* City of Minneapolis

Hidden Valley Ski Area. *See* City of Ely

Hintz's North Star Lodge, 386

Hoffman Hills. *See* Dunn County

Hogback Trail. *See* Isabella Ranger District

Hormel Nature Center (J. C.). *See* Mower County

Howard Lake Ski Trail. *See* Cass County

Hubbard County, 56; Itascatur Trail, 56; Itascatur Family Trail, 56; Long Pine Trail, 57

Hyland Lake Park Reserve. *See* Hennepin County Park Reserve District

Indianhead Mountain Resort, 407

Indian Hills Resort. *See* Washburn County

Indian Shores Camping Resort, 386

Interstate State Park, 366

Iron County Trails. *See* Cedar Trail

Isabella Ranger District, 123; Flathorn-Gegoka Cross-Country Ski Trail, 123; Hogback Trail, 125; Pow Wow Trail, 126

Itasca County, 127; Amen Lake Trails, 127; Big Ridge Cross-Country Ski Trail, 127; Wabana Trails and Wildflower Sanctuary, 127

Itasca State Park, 58

Itasca Trails, 128

Itascatur Family Trail. *See* Hubbard County

Itascatur Ski Trail. *See* Hubbard County

Izaty's Lodge, 212

Johnson's Nordic Ski Trails, 407

Kabetogama State Forest, 128; Ash River Falls Ski Trail, 128

Kaplan's Woods. *See* City of Owatonna

Kavanaugh's Sylvan Lodge, 223

Kawishiwi Ranger District, 130; Angleworm Lake-Spring Creek Trail, 130; Birch Lake Plantation Trail, 132; Coxey Pond Trails, 132; Fernberg Tower Area Trail, 133; Flash Lake Trail, 134; Hanson Lake Area Trail, 134; Hegman Lakes Trails, 134; North Junc-

tion Trails, 135; South Farm Lake Trails, 136; Stuart River-Baldpate Trails, 136

Kensington Runestone County Park/Trollskøgen Ski Area. *See* Douglas County

Kilen Woods State Park, 249

O. L. Kipp State Park, 280

Kruger Recreation Area. *See* Dorer State Forest

Lac Qui Parle State Park, 251

La Croix Ranger District, 137; Astrid Lake Trail, 137; Big Moose Trail, 139; Herriman Lake Trail, 140; Norway Trail, 140; Sioux-Hustler Trail/Devil's Cascade, 141; Stuart Lake Trail, 142

Lake Bemidji State Park, 60

Lake Bronson State Park, 61

Lake Carlos State Park, 62

Lake Elmo Regional Park Reserve. *See* Washington County

Lake Louise State Park, 282

Lake Maria State Park, 213

Lake Mary Plains Pathway, 408

Lake Rebecca Park Reserve. *See* Hennepin County Park Reserve District

Lake Shetek State Park, 253

Lakeville (City of), 327; Ritter Farm Park, 327

Lake Wissota State Park, 368

Lakewood Cross-Country Ski Club Trail System, 386

Land O'Lakes State Forest, 214; Washburn Lake Solitude Area, 214

Larson Memorial County Forest (Harry). *See* Wright County

Lauterman Trail. *See* Nicolet National Forest

Lawrence State Wayside. *See* Minnesota Valley Trail

Lebanon Hills Regional Park. *See* Dakota County

Lester-Amity. *See* City of Duluth

Lester Park Golf Course. *See* City of Duluth

Licensing, Minnesota cross-country ski permit, 34

Lindbergh State Park (Charles A.), 216

Lone Lake Park. *See* City of Minnetonka

Long Lake Conservation Center. *See* Aitkin County

Long Pine Trail. *See* Hubbard County

Lookout Mountain Ski Trail. *See* Virginia Ranger District

Loon Lake Ski Trail. *See* Grand Portage Lodge

Lost Land Lake Ski Trail, 369

Lowes Creek County Park Ski Trail. *See* Eau Claire County

Luce Line State Trail, 38, 328

Lumberjack Trail. *See* Northern Highland State Forest

Lutsen Resort and Ski Touring Center. *See* North Shore Mountains Ski Trail

Lutsen Sea Villas. *See* North Shore Mountains Ski Trail

Madeline Trail. *See* Northern Highland State Forest

Magney-Snively. *See* City of Duluth

Mahnomen Trail. *See* Sherburne National Wildlife Refuge

Manitou Lakes (YMCA), 218

Maplelag, 63

Maple Lane Touring Farm, 408

Maplewood State Park, 64

Marcell Ranger District, 143; Suomi Hills Recreation Area, 143

Mazomani Trail. *See* Minnesota Valley Trail/Carver Rapids

McCarthy Beach State Park, 145

McNaughton Trail. *See* Northern Highlands State Forest

Meadow Park. *See* City of Minnetonka

Meadow Lake Trail. *See* Blackduck Ranger District

Medford Ranger District, 383; Sitzmark Trail, 383

Medicine Lake Regional Park. *See* Hennepin County Park Reserve District

Mille Lacs Kathio State Park, 219

Mineral Springs Park. *See* City of Owatonna

Minneapolis Hike/Bike Path. *See* City of Minneapolis

Minneapolis (City of), 329; Columbia Golf Course, 331; Hiawatha Golf Course, 331; Hike/Bike Path, 329; Minnehaha Trail, 329, 332; Wirth Park Ski Trails, 331

Minnehaha Trail, 332. *See* City of Minneapolis, *See* Fort Snelling State Park

Minneopa State Park, 255

Minnesota Valley Trail, 333; Carver Rapids/Mazomani Trail, 334; Lawrence State Wayside, 334

Minnesota-Wisconsin Boundary State Trail, 38

Minnesota Zoological Gardens, 334

Minnetonka (City of), 336; Big Willow Park, 336; Lone Lake Park, 336; Meadow Park, 337; Purgatory Creek Park, 337; Victoria-Evergreen Park, 337

Minocqua Winter Park and Nordic Center, 387

Mississippi River County Park. *See* Stearns County

Monico Cross-Country Ski Trail. *See* Consolidated Papers' Cross-Country Ski Trails

Mont Ripley, 408

Moose Lake Recreation Area, 147

Moose Ridge Trail. *See* Grand Portage Lodge

Moraine Springs Nordic Center, 387

Mound Springs Park Trail. *See* City of Bloomington

Mt. Ashwabay, 370

Mount Hardscrabble, 370

Mount Normandale Lake Park Trail. *See* City of Bloomington

Mount Sophie Ski Trail. *See* Grand Portage Lodge

Mt. Zion, 409

Movil Maze Trail, 65

Mower County, 283; Hormel Nature Center (J. C.), 283

Mukooda Ski Trail. *See* Voyageurs National Park

Murphy-Hanrehan Park Reserve. *See* Hennepin County Park Reserve District

Myre State Park (Helmer), 285

Namekagen Ski Touring Trail. *See* Hayward Ranger District

National Forest Lodge, 148

Nerstrand Woods State Park, 286

Newman Springs Ski Touring Trail. *See* Park Falls Ranger District

Nicolet National Forest, 390; Anvil Lake Trail, 390; Ed's Lake Trail, 390; Giant Pine Trail, 390; Lauterman Trail, 390

No Achen Bicentennial Ski Trail. *See* Aitkin County

Nordic Woods Ski Area. *See* Washburn County

North Country Trail. *See* Walker Ranger District

Northern Highland State Forest, 389; Escanaba Trail, 389; Lumberjack Trail, 389; Madeline Trail, 389; McNaughton Trail, 389; Powell Marsh Trail, 389; Raven Trail, 389; Schlect Trail, 389; Shannon Trail, 389; Statehouse Trail, 389

North Hennepin Corridor Trail. *See* Coon Rapids Dam, Elm Creek, Hennepin County Park Reserve District

North Junction Trails. *See* Kawishiwi Ranger District

North Lake Ski Trail. *See* Grand Portage Lodge

North Shore Mountains Ski Trail, 148; Bear Track Outfitting/Bally Creek Camp, 167; Best Western Cliff Dweller, 158; Bluefin Bay, 154; Cascade Lodge, 163; Cascade River State Park, 165; Cobblestone Cabins, 157; Chateau Leveaux, 157; Fenstad's Resort, 151; Gull Harbor Condominiums, 158;

Lutsen Sea Villas, 158; Lutsen Resort, 159; Solbakken Resort, 162; Sugarbush Ski Trail, 154; Temperance River State Park, 151; Thomsonite Beach, 169; Tofte Ranger District, 154; Village at Lutsen Mountain, 159
North Shore State Trail, 38
Northwoods Ski Trail, 169
Norway Trail. See La Croix Ranger District
Nor'Wester Lodge, 170

Oak Ridge Recreation Area/Wet Bark Trail. See Dorer State Forest
O'Brien State Park (William), 337
Old Homestead Ski Trail. See Grand Portage Lodge
Old Mill State Park, 67
Olympia Sport Village, 390
Outdoor Expeditions, 391
Owatonna (City of), 288; Kaplan's Woods, 288; Mineral Springs Park, 288
Oxbo Ski Trail. See Flambeau River State Forest

Palmquist's "The Farm", 391
Park Falls Ranger District, 381; Newman Springs Ski Touring Trail, 381; Wintergreen Ski Trail, 382
Partridge Falls Ski Trail. See Grand Portage Lodge
Patrick Eagan City Park. See City of Eagan
Pattison State Park, 370
Paust's Woods Lake Resort, 391
Perrot State Park, 372
Piedmont. See City of Duluth
Pillsbury State Forest, 221; Rock Lake Solitude Area, 221
Pincushion Mountain Ski Trail. See Gunflint Ranger District
Pine-Aire Resort, 392
Pine Beach Ski Touring Trail, 223
Pine Lake Ski Trail. See Tamarac National Wildlife Refuge
Pine Mountain, 409
Pine Point Ski Trails. See Washington County
Pine Valley Ski Area, 171
Pomme De Terre Trails, 68
Porcupine Mountains Wilderness State Park, 409
Portage Valley Ski Trail. See Grand Portage Lodge
Powell Marsh Trail. See Northern Highland State Forest
Pow Wow Trail. See Isabella Ranger District
Purgatory Creek Park. See City of Minnetonka

Quaal Ski Area (Al), 411

Quarry Hill Park and Nature Center/Silver Creek Trail. See City of Rochester

Radisson Arrowwood Inn and Resort. See Arrowwood Inn and Resort (Radisson)
Ramsey County, 340; Battle Creek Regional Park, 340
Raven Trail. See Northern Highland State Forest
Red Cedar State Trail. See Dunn County
Redhorse Ski Touring Trail. See Chengwatana State Forest
Red Lake Falls Club Ski Touring Trails, 69
Remote Lake Solitude Area. See Savanna State Forest
Rice County, 288; Cannon River Wilderness Area, 288
Rice Lake State Park, 289
Richfield, (City of), 341; Rich Acres, 341; Wood Lake Nature Center, 341
Ritter Farm Park. See City of Lakeville
River Bend Nature Center. See City of Faribault
River Road Trail. See Golden Anniversary State Forest
Rochester (City of), 291; Quarry Hill Park and Nature Center/Silver Creek Trail, 291
Rock Lake Ski Touring Trail. See Hayward Ranger District
Rock Lake Solitude Area. See Pillsbury State Forest

St. Croix National Scenic Riverway/Trego Trail, 373
St. Croix State Park, 225
Sakatah Singing Hills State Trail, 39
Sakatah State Park, 257
Savanna Portage State Park, 171
Savanna State Forest, 173; Remote Lake Solitude Area, 173
Sawmill Trail. See Grand Portage Lodge
Scenic State Park, 174
Schlect Trail. See Northern Highlands State Forest
Section 11 Ski Trail. See Grand Portage Lodge
Shannon Trail. See Northern Highlands State Forest
Sherburne National Wildlife Refuge, 226; Blue Hill Trail, 227; Mahnomen Trail, 226
Shingobee Recreation Area. See Walker Ranger District
Sibley State Park, 259
Silver Creek Trail. See City of Rochester/Quarry Hill Park and Nature Center
Simpson Creek Trail. See Deer River Ranger District

Sioux-Hustler Trail. *See* La Croix Ranger District

Sitzmark Trail. *See* Medford Ranger District

Ski Brule-Ski Homestead, 411

Skyline Trail. *See* Grand Portage Lodge

Snake Creek Recreation Area. *See* Dorer State Forest

Snowcrest, 411

Solbakken Resort. *See* North Shore Mountains Ski Trail

South Farm Lake Trails. *See* Kawishiwi Ranger District

South Washington County Regional Park. *See* Washington County

Spidahl's Ski Gård, 69

Spider Lake Ski Touring Area. *See* Foothills State Forest

Spirit Mountain, 176

Split Rock Creek State Park, 261

Split Rock Lighthouse State Park, 177

Spring Lake Park Reserve. *See* Dakota County

Statehouse Lake Trail. *See* Northern Highland State Forest

Stearns County, 228; Mississippi River County Park, 228; Torger Tokle Trail, 228

Stuart Lake Trail. *See* La Croix Ranger District

Stuart River-Baldpate Trails. *See* Kawishiwi Ranger District

Sturgeon River Ski Trail. *See* Virginia Ranger District

Sugarbush Cross-Country Ski Trail. *See* Tofte Ranger District

Sugarbush Ski Trail. *See* Grand Portage Lodge

Sugar Hills Winter Resort, 179

Suomi Hills Recreation Area. *See* Marcell Ranger District

Superior National Forest, 179; Aurora Ranger District, 81; Gunflint Ranger District, 120; Isabella Ranger District, 123; Kawishiwi Ranger District, 130; La Croix Ranger District, 137; Tofte Ranger District, 154; Virginia Ranger District, 183

Swedetown Trails, 412

Sylvania Recreation Area, 413

Taconite State Trail, 39

Tamarac National Wildlife Refuge, 70; Pine Lake Ski Trail, 70

Telemark Resort, 374

Temperance River State Park/Cross River Wayside, 151

Terrace Oaks Park. *See* City of Burnsville

Tettegouche State Park, 181

Teuton Ski Touring Trail. *See* Washburn Ranger District

Thistledew Ski Touring Trails. *See* Washington State Forest (George)

Thomsonite Beach. *See* North Shore Mountains Ski Trail

Three Dog Trail. *See* Grand Portage Lodge

Timber Lake Lodge, 374

Tofte Ranger District, 154; Sugarbush Cross-Country Ski Trail, 154

Tokle Trail. *See* Stearns County

Tower Ridge Ski Area. *See* Eau Claire County

Tower Trail. *See* Cass County

Trego Trail. *See* St. Croix National Scenic Riverway

Trollhaugen, 375

Trollskøgen Ski Area. *See* Douglas County

Two Harbors City Trail, 183

Ulen Park Trail, 72

Upper Sioux Agency State Park, 263

Valkyrie Ski Touring Trail. *See* Washburn Ranger District

Victoria-Evergreen Park. *See* City of Minnetonka

Village at Lutsen Mountain. *See* North Shore Mountains Ski Trail

Vinland National Center, 342

Virginia Ranger District, 183; Big Aspen Ski Trail, 185; Lookout Mountain Ski Trail, 184; Sturgeon River Ski Trail, 186; Wynne Creek Ski Trail, 184

Voyageurs National Park, 186; Black Bay Ski Trail, 188; Mukooda Ski Trail, 188

Wabana Trails and Wildflower Sanctuary. *See* Itasca County

Walker Ranger District, 229; County Road 50 Trail, 229; Shingobee Recreation Area, 230; North Country Trail, 230

Washburn County, 375; Gull Lake, 375; Nordic Woods Ski Area, 376

Washburn Lake Solitude Area. *See* Land O'Lakes State Forest

Washburn Ranger District, 358; Teuton Ski Touring Trail, 358; Valkyrie Ski Touring Trail, 359

Washington County, 342; Lake Elmo Regional Park Reserve, 343; Pine Point Ski Trails, 344; South Washington Regional Park, 345

Washington Memorial Pine Plantation Ski Trail (George). *See* Gunflint Ranger District

Washington State Forest (George), 190; Thistle-
   dew Ski Touring Trails, 190
Webster Lake Trails. *See* Blackduck Ranger Dis-
   trict
West Bush Lake Park Trail. *See* City of Bloom-
   ington
West Torch River Ski Touring Trail. *See* Glidden
   Ranger District
Wet Bark Trail. *See* Dorer State Forest/Oak
   Ridge Recreation Area
White Cap Mountain Nordics, Rossignol Tour-
   ing Center, 392
Whitewater State Park, 291
Wilderness Bay Resort and Campground, 72
Wild River State Park, 231
Wild Wolf Inn, 392
Willow River State Park, 376
Winchester Cross-Country Ski Trail. *See* Con-
   solidated Papers' Ski Trails

Wintergreen Ski Trail. *See* Park Falls Ranger
   District
Wirth Park Ski Trails. *See* City of Minneapolis
Wolf Lake Resort, 73
Wolverine Trail, 414
Wood Lake Nature Center. *See* City of Richfield
Woodland Caribou Ski Trail. *See* Finland State
   Forest
Wright County, 233; Collinwood County Park,
   233; Eddy Memorial County Park Reserve
   (Stanley), 235; Larson Memorial County
   Forest (Harry), 236
Wynne Creek Trails. *See* Virginia Ranger Dis-
   trict

Young's Dog Sledding. *See* Gunflint Ski-Thru
   Program

Zippel Bay State Park, 75